Travel Discount Coupon

This coupon entitles you to special discounts
when you book your trip through the

⬤ TRAVEL NETWORK ®
RESERVATION SERVICE

Hotels ◆ Airlines ◆ Car Rentals ◆ Cruises
All Your Travel Needs

Here's what you get: *

A discount of $50 on a booking of $1,000** or more
for two or more people!

A discount of $25 on a booking of $500** or more
for one person!

Free membership for three years, and 1,000 free miles
on enrollment in the unique Miles-to-Go™ frequent-
traveler program. Earn one mile for every dollar spent
through the program. Earn free hotel stays starting at
5,000 miles. Earn free roundtrip airline tickets starting
at 25,000 miles.

Personal help in planning your own, customized trip.

Fast, confirmed reservations at any property
recommended in this guide, subject to availability.***

Special discounts on bookings in the U.S. and around
the world.

Low-cost visa and passport service.

Reduced-rate cruise packages.

Call us toll-free in the U.S. at 1-888-940-5000, or fax
us at 201-567-1832. In Canada, call us toll-free at
1-800-883-9959, or fax us at 416-922-6053.

* To qualify for these travel discounts, at least a portion of your trip must
include destinations covered in this guide. No more than one coupon discount
may be used in any 12-month period, for destinations covered in this guide.
Cannot be combined with any other discount or program.
**These are U.S. dollars spent on commissionable bookings.
***A $10 fee, plus fax and/or phone charges, will be added to the cost of
bookings at each hotel not linked to the reservation service. Customers
must approve these fees in advance.

Valid until December 31, 1997. Terms and conditions of the Miles-to-
Go™ program are available on request by calling 201-567-8500, ext 55.

S0-ARM-845

Frommer's 97

Walt Disney World & Orlando

by Rena Bulkin

Macmillan • USA

ABOUT THE AUTHOR

Rena Bulkin began her travel writing career in 1964 when she set out for Europe in search of adventure. She found it writing about hotels and restaurants for the *New York Times International Edition*. She has since authored dozens of magazine articles (including a roundup of the nation's best theme parks) and travel guides to far-flung destinations. She contributes to *Frommer's Florida* and has been covering the Sunshine State for years.

MACMILLAN TRAVEL

A Simon & Schuster Macmillan Company
1633 Broadway
New York, NY 10019

Find us online at **http://www.mcp.com/mgr/travel**
or on America Online at **Keyword: Frommer's.**

Copyright © 1996 by Simon & Schuster, Inc.

ISBN 0-02-860910-7
ISSN 1082-2615

Editors: Lisa Renaud, Ian Wilker
Production Editor: Phil Kitchel
Design by Michele Laseau
Digital Cartography by Ortelius Design and John Decamillis
Page Creation by Hilary Smith, Lissa Auciello, Linda Quigley, Vic Peterson, Sean Decker, Kathleen Caulfield, Heather Pope, CJ East, Jerry Cole, and Toi Davis
All maps copyright © by Simon & Schuster, Inc.

SPECIAL SALES

Bulk purchases (10+ copies) of Frommer's travel guides are available to corporations at special discounts. The Special Sales Department can produce custom editions to be used as premiums and/or for sales promotion to suit individual needs. Existing editions can be produced with custom cover imprints such as corporate logos. For more information write to: Special Sales, Simon & Schuster, 1633 Broadway, New York, NY 10019.

Manufactured in the United States of America

Contents

List of Maps

AN INVITATION TO THE READER

In researching this book, I discovered many wonderful places—hotels, restaurants, shops, and more. I'm sure you'll find others. Please tell me about them, so I can share the information with your fellow travelers in upcoming editions. If you were disappointed with a recommendation, I'd love to know that, too. Please write to

Rena Bulkin
Frommer's Walt Disney World & Orlando '97
Macmillan Travel
1633 Broadway
New York, NY 10019

AN ADDITIONAL NOTE

Please be advised that travel information is subject to change at any time—and this is especially true of prices. We therefore suggest that you write or call ahead for confirmation when making your travel plans. The authors, editors, and publisher cannot be held responsible for the experiences of readers while traveling. Your safety is important to us, however, so we encourage you to stay alert and be aware of your surroundings. Keep a close eye on cameras, purses, and wallets, all favorite targets of thieves and pickpockets.

WHAT THE SYMBOLS MEAN

✪ Frommer's Favorites

Hotels, restaurants, attractions, and entertainment you should not miss.

⑤ Super-Special Values

Hotels and restaurants that offer great value for your money.

The following abbreviations are used for credit cards:

AE	American Express	EU	Eurocard
CB	Carte Blanche	JCB	Japan Credit Bank
DC	Diners Club	MC	MasterCard
DISC	Discover	V	Visa
ER	enRoute		

Introducing Walt Disney World & Orlando

Orlando was a sleepy southern town ringed with sparkling lakes, pine forests, and citrus groves until Walt Disney turned 43 square miles of swampland into a Magic Kingdom. He sparked an unprecedented building boom, as hotels, restaurants, and scores of additional attractions arose to take advantage of the tourist traffic he had generated.

The world's most famous mouse changed central Florida forever. Though the citrus industry still exists here, orange groves have largely given way to high-rise apartment complexes, vast hotels and resorts, and shopping malls. Many national firms have relocated their headquarters to this thriving Sunbelt region, and it has also become one of the fastest-growing high-tech centers in the country.

For travelers, Orlando represents a vacation from stressful reality to a world of make-believe—one where there are parades every day and fireworks every night. Forget all your problems but one: How are you possibly going to cram so many attractions into one short vacation?

And that's a tough one. But never fear. I've checked out every square inch of all the parks, ridden every ride, and inspected every hotel and restaurant. In the pages that follow, I'll share my discoveries and tips with you and help your own itinerary—one that helps you get the most out of your trip and minimizes the time you spend standing on line.

Though in recent years Disney has been aggressively marketing itself as a vacation spot for adults traveling alone (personally, without the kids, I'd rather go to Paris), Orlando is obviously America's number-one destination for families . . . the vacation your kids clamor for. Everything here is geared for kids, and I'm not just talking about the parks. Hotels, most of them whimsically themed, all have video-game arcades and other child-pleaser features, and just about every restaurant in town has a low-priced children's menu.

In this city, visitors are the real VIPs. The major players are vying for your business, as they engage in an ongoing high-stakes game of one-upmanship. Disney's innovative movie-magic-motif MGM Studios theme park was countered a year after it opened by Universal Studios Florida, which brought in Steven Spielberg as a creative consultant. When Church Street Station, a single-price-admission

Florida

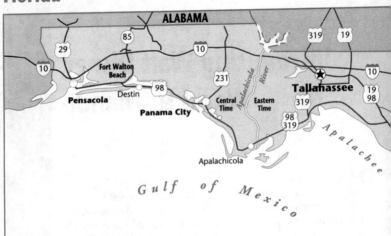

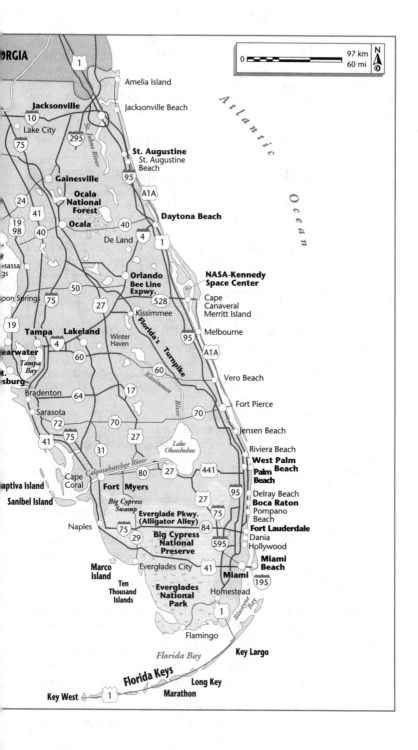

entertainment complex, opened in downtown Orlando, Disney stole its thunder with Pleasure Island (see chapter 9). And now Universal is getting into the act with a slick nightlife park of its own called the E-Zone ("E" for entertainment, that is) and plush themed resorts that will rival Disney's. Wet 'N' Wild in town? Disney has three water parks of its own and provides free transportation to them for its vast numbers of on-premises resort guests. It's rather fascinating, this battle of the titans. And make no mistake, we are the spoils. Now that Universal is building a Jurassic Park attraction, will Disney have to create real dinosaurs from DNA found in amber?

1 Frommer's Favorite Orlando Experiences

- **Splash Mountain:** This Magic Kingdom attraction combines gorgeous scenery with Disney magic and a theme park thrill—a five-story splashdown! Don't chicken out. It's great.
- **The Daily Parade and SpectroMagic:** The daily 3pm parade at the Magic Kingdom is enchanting. And SpectroMagic, which takes place after dark, adds high-tech dazzle to Disney's genius for spectacle. The Toy Story Parade at Disney-MGM Studios is also a delight.
- **The Making of Me:** Martin Short teaches the facts of life in this very charming 15-minute film at Epcot's Wonders of Life pavilion.
- **Cranium Command:** Another Wonders of Life feature, this hilarious multi-media attraction is one of Epcot's best. It stars a handful of *Saturday Night Live* actors and other comedians.
- **Wonders of China:** This 360-degree Circle-Vision film at Epcot's China pavilion explores 6,000 years of Chinese history and ranges the country's landscape in stunning cinematography.
- **Sports Activities:** Though most people come for the rides and attractions, Walt Disney World and the surrounding area offer numerous sporting options for the whole family . . . great golfing, tennis, boating, fishing, waterskiing, cycling; you name it.
- **Jim Henson's Muppet Vision 3D:** High-tech 3-D Muppets, with lots of special-effects wizardry. At Disney-MGM Studios.
- **Universal Studios:** Universal combines cutting-edge high-tech effects with great creativity. Not-to-be-missed attractions here: Back to the Future, Jaws, Kongfrontation, and Earthquake: The Big One.
- **Mermaids, Myths & Monsters:** A thrilling nighttime multimedia spectacular at Sea World that features fireworks and hologram-like imagery against a towering 60-foot screen of illuminated water.
- **Cypress Gardens:** Two hundred acres of gorgeous botanical gardens punctuated by lakes and lagoons, waterfalls, and sculpture.
- **The Adventurers Club at Pleasure Island:** This unique improvisational comedy club features a cast of zany characters who interact with guests. You might encounter Otis T. Wren, the curmudgeonly ichthyologist, oft seen racing up the stairs muttering about being forced to mix with riffraff; mix it up with Graves, the club's lugubrious butler; or have a fling with Mandora, a leopard-skin-clad adventuress.
- **Harry P. Leu Gardens:** A delightful, 56-acre botanical garden in Orlando on the shores of Lake Rowena.
- **Water Parks:** Spend a day tubing, swimming, and careening down water slides at the water parks in Walt Disney World or Kissimmee—a relaxing contrast to traipsing around attractions in the hot sun.

2 Orlando Today & Tomorrow

In the 1990s, Orlando enjoys the best overall business climate in the state. In addition to tourism, its dynamic economy thrives on diverse industry, thousands of technology-related companies, and agriculture. The only remnant of Orlando's slow-paced pre-Disney southern image is its down-home friendliness. This burgeoning Sunbelt metropolis looks forward to the future with unbounded optimism.

For the observant visitor, this part of Florida is very different from the rest of the state. Indeed, it's unlike any other place on the planet. Mile after mile of perfectly manicured landscape (courtesy of Disney and other major players here), in an area consisting largely of strip malls and spotless theme parks, creates a kind of sterile *Twilight Zone* quality. And this plastic presence is only going to increase, as Walt Disney World and other parks continue to expand. They're even building a whole Disney town (see below)! Those who like a bit of gritty reality in their environment had best look elsewhere.

Major developments coming up in the next few years include

- **Disney's Wild Animal Kingdom,** an exotic "live animal adventure park" five times the size of the Magic Kingdom. Centering on a 14-story "tree," it will combine thrill rides, exotic landscapes, and close encounters with great herds of wild animals. In addition to real animals, guests will meet up with unicorns and dragons, storybook animals, and dinosaurs. It's scheduled to open in 1998.
- **Disney Cruise Lines,** which will offer park vacations in conjunction with Caribbean cruises. Aboard ships reminiscent of classic luxury liners, guests will enjoy a choice of theme restaurants, nightclubs, family entertainment, supervised children's activities, and much, much more. Projected opening date is January 1998.
- **Celebration, Florida,** a 4,900-acre planned community (surrounded by a protected greenbelt of almost equal size), with 8,000 residences, a prototype public school, a downtown retail area with many buildings on a promenade girding a lake, a Michael Graves–designed post office, a vast adjoining office complex, comprehensive health-care facilities, and extensive recreational facilities including an 18-hole championship golf course. The preview center is already open.
- **Universal Studios** also has multibillion-dollar expansion plans. Utilizing 600 presently undeveloped acres, the company will be creating some competition for Disney with five movie- and television-theme resorts comprising more than 4,300 rooms; a golf-villa community centered on an 18-hole championship course; a top-of-the-line tennis complex; a series of lakes, winding rivers, canals, and other waterways that will be traversed by water taxis and ferries; a streamlined people-mover system; and a 12-acre entertainment park (details on the latter in chapter 9). But perhaps the biggest news is Universal's Islands of Adventure . . . billed as a "21st-century theme park set among the exotic coastlines of the oceans." Among numerous rides, shows, and attractions, it will include a Jurassic Park.

3 History 101, or How a Sleepy Southern Town Met a Mighty Mouse

It would almost seem that the history of Orlando could be condensed into two terse sentences: (1) There were orange groves. (2) Walt Disney came. There is, however, considerably more juice to be squeezed from the story. The modern metropolis of

Dateline

- 1513 Spanish explorer Ponce de León, in search of the

continues

fabled "fountain of youth," discovers and names Florida.

- **1817–18** The First Seminole War. Aligned with refugee Creeks from Georgia, native Appalachees, and runaway slaves, the Seminoles battle Andrew Jackson's troops while Florida is still a Spanish territory.
- **1821** After centuries of European struggle for supremacy in the New World, Spain cedes the territory of Florida to the United States.
- **1835–42** Resistance to white settlement results in the Second Seminole War. Many Native Americans migrate south to central Florida.
- **1843** Mosquito County is renamed Orange County.
- **1845** Florida becomes the 27th state in the Union.
- **1856** Orlando becomes the official seat of Orange County.
- **1861** Florida secedes from the Union. The demise of slavery sounds the death knell for the area's burgeoning cotton industry.
- **1870** Cattle ranching and citrus growing replace cotton as the bulwark of Orlando's economy.
- **1875** Orlando is officially incorporated as a municipality under state law.
- **1880** The South Florida Railroad facilitates the expansion of Orlando's agricultural markets.
- **1884** Fire rages out of control, destroying much of Orlando's fledgling business district.
- **1894–95** Freezing temperatures destroy 2 years of citrus crops and wreck orchards. Many growers lose everything.

continues

Orlando began as a rough-and-tumble Florida frontier town.

SETTLERS VS. SEMINOLES: THE ROAD TO STATEHOOD

Florida history dates back to 1513—more than a century before the Pilgrims landed at Plymouth Rock—when Ponce de León, in search of the fabled "fountain of youth," spied the beaches and lush greenery of Florida's Atlantic coast. He named it La Florida—"the Flowery Land." After years of alternating Spanish, French, and British rule, the territory was ceded (by Spain) to the United States in 1821. Lost in the international shuffle were the Seminoles, who, after migrating from Georgia and the Carolinas in the late 18th century to settle on some of Florida's richest farmlands, were viewed by the Americans as an obstacle to white settlement. After a series of compromise treaties that left both sides dissatisfied, the federal government threw down the final gauntlet with the Indian Removal Act of 1830, stipulating that all eastern tribes be removed to reservations west of the Mississippi. This cruel edict sparked the Second Seminole War (1835–42). At a treaty conference at Payne's Landing in 1832, a young warrior named Osceola strode up to the bargaining table, slammed his knife into the papers on it, and, pointing to the quivering blade, proclaimed, "The only treaty I will ever make is this!"

Guerrilla warfare thwarted the U.S. army's attempt to remove the Seminoles for almost 8 years, during which time many of the resisters drifted south into the interior of central Florida. In what is today the Orlando area—on a small triangular parcel of land formed by Lake Gatlin, Lake Gem Mary, and Lake Jennie Jewell—the Americans built Fort Gatlin in 1838 to offer protection to pioneer homesteaders. The fort, sited near an ancient oak tree where followers of Osceola frequently met to discuss strategies, was the scene of many skirmishes. The Seminoles kept up a fierce rebellion until 1842, when, undefeated, they accepted a treaty whereby their remaining numbers (about 300) were given land and left in peace. The same year, the Armed Occupation Act offered 160 acres to any pioneers willing to settle here for a minimum of 5 years. The land was fertile, wild turkeys and deer abounded in the woods, grazing for cattle was equally plentiful, and dozens of lakes provided fish and watering for livestock. In 1843, what had been Mosquito County was more invitingly renamed Orange County. And with the Seminoles more or less out of the way (though sporadic cattle rustling and bloody uprisings still occurred), the Territorial General Legislature petitioned Congress for statehood. On March 3, 1845, President John Tyler signed a bill making Florida the 27th state in the Union.

Settlements and statehood notwithstanding, at the middle of the 19th century the Orlando area (named Jernigan for one of its first settler families) was comprised largely of pristine lakes and pine-forested wilderness. There were no roads, and you could ride all day (if you could find a trail) without meeting a soul. The Jernigans successfully raised cattle, and their home and stockade, which was granted a post office in 1850, became a way stop for travelers and the seat of future development. Farmers and cattle ranchers were drawn to the area's verdant grasslands. Before long, a sawmill went up (on the site of today's Orlando Public Library) and a trading post was opened. Other merchants followed, and farms and ranches—which would grow to vast agricultural dynasties—were carved out of the wilderness. In 1856, the boundaries of Orange County were revised, and, thanks to the manipulations of resident James Gamble Speer, a member of the Indian Removal Commission, Fort Gatlin (Jernigan) became its official seat. How the fledgling town came to be named Orlando is a matter of some speculation. Some say Speer renamed the town after a dearly loved friend, whereas other sources say he named it after one of his favorite Shakespearean characters from *As You Like It*. But the most accepted version is that the town was named for prominent plantation owner Orlando Reeves (or Rees), who died in battle with the Seminoles in 1835. The site where he was buried on the shores of Lake Eola came to be known as "Orlando's Grave." Speer is reported to have said, "This place is often spoken of as 'Orlando's Grave.' Let's drop the word 'grave' and let the county seat be called Orlando."

THE 1860S: CIVIL WAR/CATTLE WARS

Throughout the early 1860s, cotton plantations and cattle ranches became the hallmarks of central Florida. Orlando was ringed by a vast cotton empire. Log cabins went up along the lakes, and the pioneers eked out a somewhat lonely existence separated from each other by miles of farmland. But there were troubles brewing in the 31-state nation, which would soon devastate Orlando's planters.

- **1910–25** A land boom hits Florida. Fortunes are made overnight.
- **1926** The land boom goes bust. Fortunes are lost overnight.
- **1929** An invasion of Mediterranean fruit flies devastates Orlando's citrus industry. Its ruined economy is capped by the stock market crash.
- **1939–45** World War II revives Orlando's ailing economy. The city becomes "Florida's Air Capital."
- **1955** Nearby Cape Canaveral becomes a focal point for the space program.
- **1964** Walt Disney begins surreptitiously buying up central Florida farmland, purchasing more than 28,000 acres at a cost of nearly $5.5 million.
- **1965** Disney announces his plan to build in Orlando the world's most spectacular theme park.
- **1968** Kennedy Space Center becomes the launch site for American manned space missions.
- **1971** The Magic Kingdom opens its gates.
- **1972** A new 1-day attendance mark is set on December 27, when 72,328 people visit the Magic Kingdom. It will be broken almost every year thereafter.
- **1973** Shamu ventures into Orlando waters. Sea World opens.
- **1979** Mickey Mouse welcomes the Magic Kingdom's 100-millionth visitor, 8-year-old Kurt Miller from Kingsville, Maryland.
- **1982** Epcot opens to the public with vast hoopla. Participating celebrities include everyone from

continues

Richard Nixon to George Steinbrenner.

- **1984** Donald Duck's 50th birthday is celebrated with a special parade down Main Street that includes 50 live Peking ducks.
- **1988** Walt Disney World celebrates Mickey Mouse's 60th birthday. A special parade *does not* include 50 live mice!
- **1989** WDW launches Disney-MGM Studios Theme Park (offering a behind-the-scenes look at Tinseltown), Typhoon Lagoon (a 56-acre water theme park), and Pleasure Island (an adult-nightclub theme park).
- **1990** Universal Studios opens, offering visitors thrilling encounters with E.T. and King Kong.
- **1993** Sea World continues a major expansion. And Universal Studios unleashes the fearsome *Jaws.*

By 1859, it was obvious that only a war would resolve the slavery issue. In 1861, Florida became the third state to secede from the Union, and the modest progress it had achieved came to a standstill. The Stars and Bars flew from every flagpole, and local men enlisted in the Confederate army, leaving the fledgling town in poverty. A federal blockade made it difficult to obtain necessities, and many slaves fled. In 1866, the Confederate troops of Florida surrendered, the remaining slaves were freed, and a ragtag group of defeated soldiers returned to Orlando. They found a dying cotton industry, unable to function without slave labor or transport to markets. In 1868, Florida was readmitted to the Union.

Its untended cotton fields having gone to seed, Orlando now concentrated on cattle ranching, a business plagued by heavy taxation on herds by the occupation government and one that ushered in an era of lawlessness and violence. Cattle rustling, widely practiced, generated vicious feuds, clogging courtroom calendars and igniting long-running hostilities between warring parties. Like frontier cattle towns out west, post–Civil War Orlando was short on civilized behavior; gunfights, brawls, and murders were commonplace. But as the 1860s drew to a close, large herd owners from other parts of the state moved into the area and began organizing the industry in a less chaotic fashion. Branding and penning greatly reduced rustling, though it never totally eliminated the problem; even a century later, soaring beef prices brought on a rash of cattle thievery as late as 1973!

AN ORANGE TREE GROWS IN ORLANDO

In the 1870s, articles in national magazines began luring large numbers of Americans to central Florida with promises of arable land and a warm climate. In Orlando, public roads, schools, and churches appeared to serve the newcomers, many of whom replanted defunct cotton fields with citrus groves. Orlando was officially incorporated under state law in 1875, setting up definitive boundaries, a city government complete with a mayor, laws and ordinances, a city hall, a jail, and other adjuncts of a municipality. New settlers poured in from all over the country, businesses flourished, and by the end of the year, the town had its first newspaper, the *Orange County Reporter.* The first locomotive of the South Florida Railroad chugged into town in 1880, representing a major step toward growth and prosperity and sparking a building and land boom—the first of many. Orlando got sidewalks and its first bank in 1883—the same year the town voted itself "dry" in hopes of averting the fistfights and brawls that ensued when cowboys crowded into local saloons every Saturday night for rowdy R&R. For many years the city continued to vote itself alternately wet and dry, but in actuality, it made very little difference. Legal or not, liquor was always readily available.

FIRE & ICE

In January 1884, a grocery fire that started at 4am wiped out blocks of businesses, including the offices of the *Orange County Reporter.* But 19th-century Orlando was a bit like a Frank Capra movie. The town rallied round, providing a new location for the paper and presenting its publisher, Mahlon Gore, with $1,200 in cash to help defray losses and $300 in new subscriptions. The paper not only survived but flourished. And the city, realizing the need, created its first fire brigade. By August 1884, a census revealed that the population had grown to 1,666. That same year, 600,000 boxes of oranges were shipped from Florida to points north—most of those boxes originating in Orlando. By 1885, Orlando was a viable town boasting as many as 50 businesses. It was dubbed the "Phenomenal City," after a South Florida Railroad booklet called the city's growth "phenomenal." Which is not to say it was New York. Razorback hogs roamed the streets, and alligator wrestling was a main form of entertainment.

Disaster struck a week after Christmas in 1894, when the temperature plummeted to an unseasonable 24 degrees. Water pipes burst, and orange blossoms froze, blackened, and died. The freeze continued for 3 days, wrecking the citrus crop for the year. Karl H. Abbott, son of the owner of the San Juan Hotel, where northern buyers met to bid on citrus crops, later described the pandemonium that broke out as the thermometer began dipping shortly after noon:

"The buyers hurriedly left the lunch tables and went out of doors to view the weather. The big thermometer in front of the hotel indicated unusual cold. By 2pm the San Juan was in an uproar. Prices had dropped to 'no sale.' Commission merchants were frantically trying to get out of options and heated debates and fistfights started in the lobby. . . . About nine that night a fine-looking gray-haired gentleman in a black coat and Stetson hat walked up the street in front of the hotel and looked at the thermometer, groaned 'Oh my God!' and shot himself through the head."

Many grove owners went bust, and those who remained were hit with a second devastating freeze the following year. Tens of thousands of trees died in the killing frost. Small growers were wiped out, but large conglomerates that could afford to buy up their properties at bargain prices and wait for new groves to mature assured the survival of the industry.

SPECULATION FEVER: GOOD DEALS, BAD DEALS . . .

As Orlando entered the 20th century, citrus and agriculture had surpassed cattle ranching as the mainstay of the local economy. Stray cows no longer had to be shooed from the railway tracks. Streets were being paved and electricity and telephone service installed. The population at the turn of the century was 2,481. In 1902, the city passed its first automobile laws, which included an in-town speed limit of 5 miles per hour. In 1904, the city flooded. And in 1905 it suffered a drought that ended—miraculously or coincidentally—on a day when all faiths united at the local First Baptist Church to pray for rain. By 1910, prosperity had returned, and Orlando, with a population of nearly 4,000, was, in a small way, becoming a tourism and convention center. World War I brought further industrial growth and a real estate boom, not just to Orlando but to all of Florida. Millions of immigrants, speculators, and builders descended on the state in search of a quick buck. As land speculation reached a fever pitch, and property was bought and resold almost overnight, many citrus groves gave way to urbanization. Preeminent Orlando builder and promoter Carl Dann described the action thusly: "It finally became nothing more than a gambling machine, each man buying on a shoestring, betting dollars a bigger fool would come along and buy his option."

Quite suddenly, the bubble burst. A July 1926 issue of the *Nation* provided the obituary for the Florida land boom: "The world's greatest poker game, played with lots instead of chips, is over. And the players are now . . . paying up." Construction slowed to a trickle, and many newcomers who had arrived in Florida to jump on the bandwagon returned to their homes in the north. Though Orlando was not quite as hard hit as Miami—scene of the greediest land grabs—some belt tightening was in order. Nevertheless, the city managed to build a municipal airport in 1928. Then came a Mediterranean fruit fly infestation that crippled the citrus industry. Hundreds of thousands of acres of land in quarantined areas had to be cleared of fruit and vast quantities of boxed fruit destroyed. The 1929 stock market crash that precipitated the Great Depression seemed almost an afterthought to Florida's ruined economy.

. . . AND NEW DEALS

President Franklin D. Roosevelt's New Deal helped the state climb back on its feet. The Works Progress Administration (WPA) put 40,000 unemployed Floridians back to work—work that included hundreds of public projects in Orlando. Of these, the most important was the expansion and resurfacing of the city's airport. By 1936, the tourist trade had revived somewhat, construction was up once again, and the state began attracting a broader range of visitors than ever before. But the event that finally lifted Florida—and the nation—out of the Depression was World War II.

Orlando had weathered the Great Depression. Now it prepared for war with the construction of army bases, housing for servicemen, and training facilities. Almost all new business was geared toward defense. Enlisted men poured into the city, and the airport was again enlarged and equipped with barracks, a military hospital, administration buildings, and mess halls. By 1944, Orlando had a second airport and was known as "Florida's Air Capital"—home to major aircraft and aviation-parts-manufacturing factories. Thousands of U.S. servicemen did part of their hitch in Orlando, and when the war ended, many returned to settle there.

POSTWAR PROSPERITY

By 1950, Orlando—with a population of 51,826—was the financial and transportation hub of central Florida. The city shared the bullish economy of the 1950s with the rest of the nation. In the face of the cold war, the Orlando air force base remained and grew, funneling millions of dollars into the local economy. Florida's population increased by a whopping 78.7% during the decade—making it America's 10th most-populous state—and tourists came in droves, nearly 4.5 million in 1950 alone. One reason for the influx was the advent of the air conditioner, which made life in Florida infinitely more pleasant. Also fueling Orlando's economy was a brand-new industry arriving in nearby Cape Canaveral in 1955—the government-run space program. Cape Canaveral became NASA's headquarters for the Apollo rocket program that eventually blasted Neil Armstrong heavenward toward his famous "giant leap." During the same decade, the Glenn L. Martin Company (later Martin Marietta), builder of the Matador Missile, purchased 10 square miles for a plant site 4 miles south of Orlando. Its advent sparked further industrial growth, and property values soared. More than 60 new industries located in the area in 1959 alone. But even the most

---

In the Words of Walt Disney

Why be a governor or a senator when you can be king of Disneyland?

You can dream, create, design, and build the most wonderful place in the world . . . but it requires people to make the dream a reality.

Happy Anniversary, Mickey and Minnie!

No, it's not really their anniversary (they never really married; perhaps he just couldn't commit). But 1997 is the silver (25th) anniversary of Walt Disney World—an event that will be marked by a yearlong celebration including

- A new parade in which 1,400 guests a day will play a part.
- The transformation of Cinderella Castle, which will be decorated with 25 glowing candles and red and pink "icing" to create the world's biggest birthday cake.
- Festive fairgrounds at Mickey's Starland in the Magic Kingdom, with new attractions such as a child-size roller coaster, a Minnie Mouse House, and big-top tents where Disney characters greet guests.
- Many special privileges and homecoming rallies for returning guests.
- A new Magic Kingdom attraction based on memorabilia and films on Disney's past and future.
- A more-spectacular-than-ever IllumiNations show at Epcot.
- A musical production at the America Gardens Theater in Epcot celebrating 25 years of American music.
- *The Hunchback of Notre Dame* stage show at Disney-MGM Studios, inspired by the company's newest animated feature.

---

optimistic Orlando boosters could not foresee the glorious future that was the city's ultimate destiny.

THE DISNEY DECADES

In 1964, Walt Disney began secretly buying up millions of dollars worth of central Florida farmland. As vast areas of land were purchased in lots of 5,000 acres here, 20,000 there—at remarkably high prices—rumors flew as to who needed so much land and had so much money to acquire it. Some thought it was Howard Hughes; others, the space program. Speculation was rife almost to the very day, November 15, 1965 ("D" Day for Orlando), when Disney himself arrived in town and announced his plans to build the world's most spectacular theme park ("bigger and better than Disneyland"). In a 2-year construction effort, Disney employed 9,000 people. Land speculation reached unprecedented heights, as hotel chains and restaurateurs grabbed up property near the proposed parks. Mere swampland sold for millions. Total cost of the project by its October 1971 opening was $400 million. Mickey Mouse personally led the first visitor into the Magic Kingdom, and numerous celebrities—everyone from Bob Hope to Julie Andrews—took part in the opening ceremonies. In Walt Disney World's first 2 years, the attraction drew 20 million visitors and employed 13,000 people. The sleepy citrus-growing town of Orlando had become the "Action Center of Florida" and the fastest-growing city in the state. A 1972 referendum revitalized downtown Orlando. Additional attractions multiplied faster than fruit flies, and hundreds of firms relocated their businesses in the area. Sea World, a major theme park, came to town in 1973. Walt Disney World has continued to grow and expand, adding Epcot in 1982 and Disney-MGM Studios in 1989, along with water parks, over a dozen "official" resorts, a shopping/restaurant village, campgrounds, a vast array of recreational facilities, and several other adjuncts that are thoroughly described in this book. Universal Studios, which also continues to expand, opened in 1990.

4 Famous Orlandoans

Walter Elias (Walt) Disney (1901–66)   Animation impresario Walt Disney created world-famous cartoon characters Mickey Mouse, Donald Duck, Pluto, and Goofy, among many others. His first full-length cartoon feature was *Snow White and the Seven Dwarfs* (1938). In 1955 he built the 250-acre Disneyland Park in Anaheim, California, which became one of the major tourist attractions in the United States. Many of his plans were realized after his death—among them Orlando's Magic Kingdom, Epcot, and Disney-MGM Studios Theme Park.

Donald Duck (b. 1934)   Member of a prominent thespian family (which includes nephews Huey, Dewey, and Louie, billionaire Uncle Scrooge, and Grandma Duck), Donald has starred in more than 170 cartoons and movies since his 1930s debut as an extra in *The Wise Little Hen.* As recorded in Disney archives, "he bellowed and strutted his way into that production until, bit part or no, he was practically the star of the piece." Though Disney directors have always liked working with the superbly gifted "mad mallard," his career has been somewhat hindered by his terrible temper—most notably his public tantrums when Mickey got his own television show, "The Mickey Mouse Club," in the 1950s. The bellicose duck's most memorable line of dialogue, "Wanna fight?" is said to have inspired Clint Eastwood's "Make my day."

Christian (Buddy) Ebsen (b. 1908)   American actor and dancer specializing in countrified characters. He played second fiddle to Fess Parker in the Davy Crockett movies and was a lead character in the television series *The Beverly Hillbillies.* At 64 he became Barnaby Jones. Ebsen has appeared in many movies, including *Breakfast at Tiffany's.*

Michael Dammann Eisner (b. 1942)   Chairman and CEO of the entire Walt Disney Company since 1984. Though his father made him read for 2 hours each day before watching TV, Eisner started climbing the corporate ladder in the programming departments of CBS, NBC, and ABC. Prior to taking over the helm at Disney, Eisner was president and CEO of Paramount Pictures. In his first decade at the firm, Eisner revitalized Disney's motion picture, television, and theme park operations; opened Disney-MGM Studios Theme Park; moved into commercial television, magazines, and book publishing; and expanded to Europe with Euro Disney.

Goofy (b. 1932)   Goofy first appeared along with Mickey Mouse in a cartoon called *Mickey's Revue.* Though his original name was Dippy Dawg, which later evolved into Dippy the Goof, and finally, Goofy, there has been, over the years, an ongoing controversy as to exactly what kind of animal he is. The claim of Disney representatives that he is supposed to be a human being has never been adequately substantiated. And Goofy himself fueled speculation when he answered a reporter's question about his species in 1992 with the words "Gawrsh! I dunno." Tabloid rumors notwithstanding, this dumb but likable toon is the living embodiment of Murphy's Law—whatever can go wrong will go wrong. But he continues to laugh ("hyuk, hyuk") in the face of adversity.

Mahlon Gore (1837–1917)   Editor and proprietor of the *Orange County Reporter,* businessman, and tireless city booster, Gore came to Orlando from Iowa in 1880 when, he later reported, there were only "200 inhabitants, three stores, a livery stable, and a saloon." Today an Orlando avenue bears his name.

Mickey Mouse (b. 1928)   A prominent Orlando resident since 1971, Mickey also maintains a home in Anaheim, California. Star of more than 120 cartoons and movies, he made his film debut the year of his birth in *Steamboat Willie.* His significant other, Minnie Mouse (no relation), also appeared in the film. Mickey's dad almost named him Mortimer, but his mom (Mrs. Disney) persuaded her husband that Mortimer was too pompous a moniker for a mouse and suggested Mickey. Mickey considers the 1940s, when he starred in *Fantasia,* his "Golden Decade." And he's especially proud that during World War II his name was used as the password of Allied forces on D-Day. Having reached the age of retirement, Mickey has no plans to stop working. "Better to wear out than rust out," says the still teenlike toon.

Jacob Summerlin (1820–93)   Dubbed "King of the Crackers" and "Cattle King of Florida," Summerlin was the first child born in the new state—in a fort where his parents had sought refuge from Seminole attack. He organized Florida cattle owners to supply the Confederate army with beef during the Civil War, engaged in blockade running, financed free public schools, built Orlando's first luxury hotel, and donated his property for parkland around Lake Eola.

Joe Tinker (1880–1948)   Florida building developer, former star shortstop of the Chicago Cubs, and manager of the Cincinnati Reds, Tinker created a baseball team for Orlando that won the 1921 Florida State League championship. He also convinced the Cincinnati Reds to sign a 3-year contract to play in Orlando at the new $15,000 Tinker Field completed in 1923—a ballpark larger than the New York Yankee Field. Tinker was immortalized in Franklin P. Adams's verse *Baseball's Sad Lexicon,* better known as "Tinker to Evers to Chance."

W. W. Yothers (1879–1971)   An entomologist who worked for a quarter of a century in the Orlando area, Yothers is credited with stopping the Mediterranean fruit fly epidemic of 1929–30 and helping control diseases that threatened the citrus industry.

2

Planning a Trip to Walt Disney World & Orlando

Orlando is so packed with attractions that advance planning is crucial. In this chapter, I've compiled everything you need to know before you go. In addition to the information below, see chapters 5 (accommodations) and 7 (attractions) for other tips.

1 Visitor Information

As soon as you know you're going to Orlando, write or call the **Orlando/Orange County Convention & Visitors Bureau,** 8445 International Dr. (in the Mercado Shopping Village), Orlando, FL 32819 (☎ 407/363-5871). The bureau can answer all your questions and will be happy to send you maps, brochures (including the informative *Official Visitors Guide,* the *Area Guide* to local restaurants, and the *Official Accommodations Guide*), and the "Magicard," good for discounts of 10% to 50% on accommodations, attractions, car rentals, and more.

For general information about Walt Disney World—and a copy of the informative *Walt Disney World Vacations*—write or call the **Walt Disney World Co.,** Box 10,000, Lake Buena Vista, FL 32830-1000 (☎ 407/934-7639).

Also contact the **Kissimmee–St. Cloud Convention & Visitors Bureau,** 1925 G. Irlo Bronson Blvd. (U.S. 192)—or P.O. Box 422007—Kissimmee, FL 34742-2007 (☎ 407/847-5000 or 800/327-9159). They'll send maps, brochures, discount coupon books, and the *Kissimmee–St. Cloud Vacation Guide,* which details the area's accommodations and attractions.

If you have Internet access, you can visit Walt Disney World's own Web site at **http://www.disneyworld.com**, which has extensive, entertaining, and regularly updated information. Also access a very informative newsgroup on Usenet called **rec.arts.disney**.

For information about the entire state—including Orlando and Kissimmee—write or call the **Florida Department of Commerce,** Division of Tourism, Visitor Inquiry, 126 Van Buren St., Tallahassee, FL 32399-2000 (☎ 904/487-1462).

2 Money

Disney parks, resorts, shops, and restaurants (but not fast-food outlets) accept the three major credit cards—American Express, MasterCard, and Visa—as well as the Disney credit card.

What Things Cost in Orlando	U.S. $
Taxi from airport to WDW area	38.00
Bus from airport to WDW area (adult fare)	25.00
Double room at Disney's Grand Floridian Beach Resort (very expensive)	265.00–325.00
Double room at Marriott's Orlando World Center (expensive)	159.00–209.00
Double room at Disney's Port Orleans Resort (moderate)	95.00–129.00
Double room at Disney's All-Star Music Resort (inexpensive)	69.00–79.00
Double room at Comfort Inn Maingate, Kissimmee (inexpensive)	33.00–65.00
Seven-course prix-fixe dinner for one at Victoria & Albert's, not including tip or wine (very expensive)	80.00
Three-course dinner at L'Originale Alfredo di Roma in Epcot, not including tip or wine (expensive)	30.00
All-you-can-eat buffet dinner at Akershus in Epcot, not including tip or wine (inexpensive)	17.95
Bottle of beer (restaurant)	2.25
Coca-Cola (restaurant)	1.25
Cup of coffee	1.25
Roll of ASA 100 Kodacolor film, 36 exposures, purchased at Walt Disney World	7.37
Adult 4-Day Value Pass admission to Walt Disney World	124.00
Four-Day Value Pass admission to Walt Disney World for children ages 3–9	97.00
Adult 1-day admission to Sea World	37.95
One-day admission to Sea World for children ages 3–9	31.80
Adult 1-day admission to Universal Studios	37.00
One-day admission to Universal Studios for children ages 3–9	30.00

You can also purchase Disney dollars (currency bearing the images of Mickey, Goofy, and Minnie) available in $1, $5, and $10 denominations; they're good at shops, restaurants, and resorts throughout the Disney realm, as well as Disney stores everywhere. I don't suggest you buy these Disney dollars, because you'll have to cash in leftover bills for real currency upon leaving (a bother), or you'll be stuck with something that, as we say in New York, with a token, will get you on the subway.

You can get cash advances on MasterCard and Visa, cash traveler's checks, cash personal checks of $25 or less (drawn on U.S. banks, upon presentation of a valid driver's license and a major credit card), and exchange foreign currency at branches of the **Sun Bank** on Main Street in the Magic Kingdom (open 9am to 4pm daily; ☎ 407/828-6102) and at 1675 Buena Vista Dr., across from the Disney Village Marketplace (open weekdays 9am to 4pm, until 6pm on Thursday; ☎ 407/828-6106).

ATM machines are conveniently located on Main Street and in Tomorrowland in the Magic Kingdom; at the entrances to Disney-MGM Studios and Epcot; at Pleasure Island; at Disney Village Marketplace; at the All-Star Sports Resort; and at the Crossroads Shopping Center.

3 When to Go

Orlando is essentially a theme park destination, and its busiest seasons are whenever kids are out of school—summer (early June to about August 20), holiday weekends, Christmas season (mid-December to mid-January), and Easter. Obviously, the whole experience is more enjoyable when the crowds are thinnest and the weather is the most temperate. Hotel rooms are also lower priced off-season. Best times: the week after Labor Day until Thanksgiving, the week after Thanksgiving until mid-December, and the 6 weeks before and after school spring vacations. Worst time: summer, when crowds are very large and weather is oppressively hot and humid. I probably shouldn't say this, but I would pull the kids out of school for a few days around an off-season weekend to avoid long lines.

Central Florida Average Temperatures

	Jan	Feb	Mar	Apr	May	June	July	Aug	Sept	Oct	Nov	Dec
High °F	71.7	72.9	78.3	83.6	88.3	90.6	91.7	91.6	89.7	84.4	78.2	73.1
°C	22.0	22.7	25.7	28.7	31.3	32.5	33.2	33.1	32.0	29.1	25.7	22.8
Low °F	49.3	50.0	55.3	60.3	66.2	71.2	73.0	73.4	72.5	65.4	56.8	50.9
°C	9.6	10.0	12.5	15.7	19.0	21.8	22.7	23.0	22.5	18.6	13.8	10.5

ORLANDO AREA CALENDAR OF EVENTS

January

- ✪ **Comp USA Florida Citrus Bowl Game.** This annual college football game, featuring two of the year's top national teams, usually plays to a full house at the Florida Citrus Bowl Stadium, 1 Citrus Bowl Pl. On or close to New Year's Day. Call 407/423-2476 for information, 407/839-3900 for tickets. Tickets ($45) go on sale late October/early November.
- **Walt Disney World Marathon.** This 26.2-mile marathon winding through the resort and theme park areas is open to all, including the physically challenged. The $50 entry fee is included in room price with some Disney resort packages. Pre-registration is required. Call 407/824-4321 for details.

February

- ✪ **Silver Spurs Rodeo.** This is one of the top 20 PRCA rodeos in the nation, featuring professional cowboys and cowgirls in a wide variety of competitions—calf roping, bull and bronc riding, barrel racing, and more. It's held at the Silver Spurs Arena, 1875 E. Irlo Bronson Memorial Hwy. (U.S. 192) in Kissimmee. Third weekend in February. Call 407/847-5000 for details, 407/67-RODEO for tickets. All seats are $15.
- **Kissimmee Valley Livestock Show and Osceola County Fair.** This 6-day county fair—complete with agricultural exhibits, livestock judging, rides, and crafts—takes place at the Kissimmee Valley Agricultural Center, 1901 E. Irlo Bronson Memorial Hwy. (U.S. 192). Admission is $3 for adults, $1 for children ages 4 to 12, under 4 free. Third week of the month. Call 407/846-6046 for details.

- **Mardi Gras Celebration at Pleasure Island,** Walt Disney World. This rollicking Mardi Gras revel is a street party with food, drink, costumes, parades, and entertainment. Call 407/824-4321 for details.

March

- **Houston Astros Spring Training.** Training begins in late February, and there are games through March or early April at Osceola County Stadium, 1000 Bill Beck Blvd., in Kissimmee. Tickets are $5 to $6. Call 407/933-5400 for details and tickets.
- **Kissimmee Bluegrass Festival.** Major bluegrass and gospel entertainers from all over the country perform at this 4-day festival. Beginning the first weekend of the month, at the Silver Spurs Arena, 1875 E. Irlo Bronson Memorial Hwy. (U.S. 192). Tickets are $10 to $17. Multiday packages are available. Call 800/473-7773 for details.
- **Central Florida Fair.** During 11 days in early March (some years, beginning late February), the fair features rides, entertainers, 4-H/livestock exhibits, a petting zoo, and food booths. At the Central Florida Fairgrounds, 4603 W. Colonial Dr. Adults pay $6, children ages 6 to 10 pay $3, under 6 free. Call 407/295-3247 for details.
- **Nestle Invitational.** Arnold Palmer hosts this 7-day, mid-month PGA Tour event at the Bay Hill Club, 9000 Bay Hill Blvd. Daily admission is $28, week-long admission $50. Call 407/876-2888 for details.
- **Spring Flower Festival.** More than 30,000 brightly colored bedding plants, including marigolds, impatiens, and begonias, create beautiful floral topiaries shaped as butterflies, birds, and animals. March through May at Cypress Gardens. Entry included with park admission. Call 941/324-2111 for details.
- **Sidewalk Art Festival.** This major arts festival in Winter Park, drawing artists and artisans from all over North America, takes place in Central Park. Third weekend in March. Call 407/623-3234 or 407/644-8281 for details.

April

- **Orlando Cubs Baseball Season.** The Chicago Cubs farm team plays at Tinker Field, 287 Tampa Ave. South, from April to early September. Admission is $3 to $7. Call 407/245-CUBS for details.
- **Easter Sunrise Service.** An interdenominational service, with music, is presented at the Atlantis Theatre at Sea World, 7007 Sea World Dr. It is hosted by a well-known person each year, most recently Elizabeth Dole. Admission is free. Call 407/351-3600 for details.
- **Easter Sunday** is celebrated in Walt Disney World with an old-fashioned Easter Parade and early opening/late closing throughout the season. Call 407/824-4321 for details.

May

- **Epcot International Flower and Garden Festival.** A month-long event with theme gardens, topiary characters, special floral displays, speakers, and seminars.

June

- **Walt Disney World Wine Festival.** More than 60 wineries from all over the United States participate. Events include wine tastings, seminars, food, and celebrity-chef cooking demonstrations at Disney's Yacht and Beach Club Convention Center. Call 407/827-7200 or 407/824-4321 for details.

- **Walt Disney World All-American College Orchestra and College Band.** The best collegiate musical talent in the country performs at Epcot and the Magic Kingdom throughout the summer. Call 407/824-4321 for details.

July

- **Independence Day.** Walt Disney World's Star-Spangled Spectacular brings bands, singers, dancers, and unbelievable fireworks displays to all the Disney parks, which stay open late. Call 407/824-4321 for details. **Sea World** also features a dazzling laser/fireworks spectacular. Call 407/351-3600 for details.
- **Silver Spurs Rodeo.** Big-time rodeo returns to Kissimmee (see details above in February listings). Some years, late June.

September

✪ **Nights of Joy.** The Magic Kingdom hosts a festival of contemporary Christian music featuring top artists over several weekends, selected annually. This is a very popular event; get tickets early. Admission is about $25 to $30 per night. Exclusive use of Magic Kingdom attractions is included. Call 407/824-4321 for details.

October

- **Halloween Horror Nights.** Universal Studios Florida transforms its studios and attractions for a gigantic "spooktacular" nighttime party during several long weekends prior to Halloween—with haunted attractions, live bands, a psychopath maze, special shows, and hundreds of ghouls and goblins roaming the studio streets and terrifying the populace. Special admission is charged. Call 407/363-8000 for details.
- **Shamu's Halloween Spooktacular.** Sea World hosts a Halloween bash on the holiday weekend with eerie events, a shark tunnel, costume judging, special shows, and more. Call 407/351-3600 for details.
- **Walt Disney World Oldsmobile Golf Classic.** Top PGA tour players compete for a total purse of $1 million at WDW golf courses. Daily ticket prices range from $8 to $15. The event is preceded by the world's largest golf tournament, the admission-free Oldsmobile Scramble. Call 407/824-4321 for details.
- **Walt Disney World Village Boat Show.** Central Florida's largest in-the-water boat show, featuring the best of new watercraft. At the Village Marketplace, over a 3-day weekend early in the month. Call 407/824-4321 for details.

November

- **Mum Festival.** This month-long event at Cypress Gardens features millions of mums, their colorful flowers displayed in beds, "blooming" gazebos, poodle baskets, and bonsai. Entry included with park admission. Call 941/324-2111 for details.
- **Walt Disney World Festival of the Masters.** One of the largest art shows in the south takes place at the Village Marketplace for 3 days, including the second weekend of November. It features top artists, photographers, and craftspeople—winners of juried shows throughout the country. No admission. Call 407/824-4321 for details.
- **Walt Disney World Doll and Teddy Bear Convention.** The top doll and teddy bear designers from around the world travel to WDW to meet with enthusiasts and collectors. Special editions and one-of-a-kind auctions highlight the event. Call 407/824-4321 or 407/560-7232 for details.
- **Walt Disney World Jolly Holidays Dinner Shows.** Late November through mid-December, all-you-can-eat dinner shows are offered at the Contemporary

Resort's Fantasia Ballroom. A cast of over 100 Disney characters, singers, and dancers performs in a delightful old-fashioned Christmas extravaganza. Call 407/W-DISNEY for details and ticket prices.

- **Magic Basketball.** Shaquille O'Neal and his teammates on the Orlando Magic do battle against visiting teams between October and April at the Orlando Arena, 600 W. Amelia St. Ticket prices range from about $13 to $50. Call 407/896-2442 for details, 407/839-3900 for tickets.

- **Poinsettia Festival.** A spectacular floral showcase of more than 50,000 red, white, and pink poinsettia blooms (including topiary reindeer). From late November through mid-January at Cypress Gardens. Entry included with park admission. Call 941/324-2111 for details.

December

- **Burger King Classic Half-Marathon and Hooter's 5K Run.** This annual race, early in December, takes place in downtown Orlando, beginning at Church Street Market, 200 S. Orange Ave. It begins at 8am. Anyone can participate. An entry fee is charged. The event kicks off the Citrus Bowl season. Call 407/423-2476 for information.

- **Walt Disney World Christmas Festivities.** Main Street is lavishly decked out with lights and holly, and visitors are greeted by carolers. An 80-foot tree is illuminated by thousands of colored lights. Epcot and MGM Studios also offer special embellishments and entertainments throughout the holiday season, as do all Disney resorts. Holiday highlights include **Mickey's Very Merry Christmas Party,** an after-dark ticketed event, weekends at the Magic Kingdom, with a traditional Christmas parade and a huge fireworks display. Admission price includes free cookies and cocoa and a souvenir photo. The **Candlelight Procession** at Epcot features hundreds of candle-holding carolers, a celebrity narrator telling the Christmas story, and a 450-voice choir. There are also **Jolly Holidays Dinner Shows**—all-you-can-eat holiday feasts with a show that includes more than 50 Disney characters.

    Call 407/824-4321 for details about all of the above—and more—and call 407/W-DISNEY to inquire about hotel/events packages.

- **Walt Disney World New Year's Eve Celebration.** The **Magic Kingdom** is open until 2am for a massive fireworks exhibition. Other New Year's festivities in the WDW parks include a big bash at **Pleasure Island** featuring music headliners, a special *Hoop-Dee-Doo Musical Revue* show, and guest performances by well-known musical groups at **Disney-MGM Studios** and **Epcot.** Call 407/824-4321 for details.

- **Sea World Holiday Events.** Sea World features a special Shamu show and a luau show called *Christmas in Hawaii.* The 400-foot sky tower is lit like a Christmas tree nightly. Call 407/351-3600 for details.

- **Citrus Bowl Parade.** On an annually selected date in late December, lavish floats—including some from Disney and Sea World—join with local high school bands for a nationally televised parade. Reserved seats in the bleachers are $12. Call 407/423-2476 for details.

- **New Year's Citrus Eve.** The official New Year's Eve celebration of the COMP USA Florida Citrus Bowl takes place at Sea World. Events include headliner concerts (featuring artists such as Lee Greenwood and Tanya Tucker), a laser and fireworks spectacular, a countdown to midnight, and special shows throughout the park. Admission is charged. Call 407/423-2476 for details.

4 Tips for Travelers with Special Needs

FOR THE DISABLED　Write or call the **Florida Governor's Alliance,** 345 S. Magnolia Dr., Suite D-11, Tallahassee, FL 32301 (☎ 904/487-2223 or -2222 TTD), for a free copy of *The Florida Planning Companion for People with Disabilities.* It offers valuable information on accessibility at tourist facilities throughout the state.

At Walt Disney World: WDW does everything possible to facilitate disabled guests. Its many services are detailed in the *Guidebook for Guests with Disabilities.* To obtain a copy prior to your visit, write Guest Letters, P.O. Box 10040, Lake Buena Vista, FL 32830-0040, or call 407/824-4321. Also call that number for answers to any questions regarding special needs. Some examples of Disney services: Almost all Disney resorts have rooms for those with disabilities; there are braille directories inside the Magic Kingdom, in front of the Main Street train station and in a gazebo in front of the Crystal Palace restaurant; there are special parking lots at all three parks; complimentary guided-tour audiocassette tapes and recorders are available at Guest Services to assist visually impaired guests; personal translator units are available to amplify the audio at selected Epcot attractions (inquire at Earth Station); and wheelchairs can be rented at all of the Disney parks. For information about Telecommunications Devices for the Deaf (TDDs), call 407/827-5141.

Some nationwide resources: Mobility International USA, P.O. Box 10767, Eugene, OR 97440 (☎ 503/343-1284), offers accessibility information and has many interesting travel programs for the disabled. Membership ($25 a year) includes a quarterly newsletter called *Over the Rainbow.* Help (accessibility information and more) is also available from the **Travel Information Service** (☎ 215/456-9600) and the **Society for the Advancement of Travel for the Handicapped** (SATH), 347 Fifth Ave., Suite 610, New York, NY 10016 (☎ 212/447-7284). The latter charges $5 to send requested information.

Accessible Journeys (☎ 610/521-0339 or 800/TINGLES) and **Flying Wheels Travel** (☎ 507/451-5005 or 800/535-6790) offer tours for people with physical disabilities. Accessible Journeys can also provide nurse/companions to travelers. **Guided Tour Inc.** (☎ 215/782-1370) has tours for people with physical or mental disabilities, the visually impaired, and the elderly.

Recommended books: A publisher called **Twin Peaks Press,** Box 129, Vancouver, WA 98666 (☎ 360/694-2462), specializes in books for people with disabilities. Write for their *Disability Bookshop Catalog,* enclosing $5.

Amtrak (☎ 800/USA-RAIL) provides redcap service, wheelchair assistance, and special seats with 72 hours' notice. The disabled are also entitled to a discount of 15% off the lowest available adult coach fare. Disabled children ages 2 to 15 can also get a 50% discount on already discounted one-way disabled adult fares. Documentation from a doctor or an ID card proving your disability is required. Amtrak also provides wheelchair-accessible sleeping accommodations on long-distance trains, and service dogs are permissible and travel free of charge. Write for a free booklet called *Amtrak's America* from Amtrak Distribution Center, P.O. Box 7717, Itasca, IL 60143, which has a chapter detailing services for passengers with disabilities.

Greyhound (☎ 800/752-4841) allows a disabled person to travel with a companion for a single fare and, if you call 48 hours in advance, they will arrange help along the way.

FOR SENIORS　Always carry some form of photo ID so that you can take advantage of discounts wherever they're offered. And it never hurts to ask.

...And They Lived Happily Ever After: How to Tie the Knot at Walt Disney World

Walt Disney World offers an almost infinite variety of wedding venues . . . from Paris (at Epcot's France pavilion) to a glass-topped Victorian summer house amid swaying palms on a private island in the Seven Seas Lagoon. Every traditional service and accoutrement is available (flowers, the cake, music, invitations, catering, dazzling decorations, photography, etc.), but it's in theme customizing that Disney really pulls out all the stops. Some examples:

- Anyone can hire a limo to take them to the altar; only here can you arrive in Cinderella's glass coach pulled by six white ponies and attended by footmen and drivers in full regalia!
- Theme your entire wedding on anything from Pocahontas to Pirates of the Caribbean.
- Have Mickey and other Disney characters, not to mention the bride's own fairy godmother, mingle with guests; Mickey (in tails) and a glamorously gowned Minnie often cut in on the couple's first dance.
- Treat all your guests to a cocktail reception cruise.
- Have specified attractions open after hours for exclusive use of your guests . . . even arrange special fireworks shows.
- "Take the plunge," literally, on a plummeting elevator aboard the Twilight Zone Tower of Terror.
- Or marry before an aquarium backdrop of 5,000 denizens of the deep in Epcot's private Living Seas Lounge.

Your guests can enjoy a vacation weekend (they get special rates on rooms) while attending your wedding. For further details on Disney weddings (and honeymoons, of course), call 407/828-3400. The only limit is your own imagination.

If you haven't already done so, consider joining the **American Association of Retired Persons** (AARP) (☎ 202/434-2277). Annual membership costs $8 per person or per couple. You must be at least 50 to join. Membership entitles you to many discounts. Write to Purchase Privilege Program, AARP Fulfillment, 601 E St. NW, Washington, DC 20049, to receive a free list of hotels, motels, and car-rental firms nationwide that offer discounts to AARP members.

Elderhostel is a national organization that offers low-priced educational programs for people over 55 (your spouse can be any age; a companion must be at least 50). Programs are generally a week long, and prices average about $335 per person, including room, board, and classes. For information on programs in Florida, call or write Elderhostel Headquarters, 75 Federal St., Boston, MA 02110-1941 (☎ 617/426-7788) and ask for a free U.S. catalog. Or call the Florida office at 813/864-8312.

Amtrak (☎ 800/USA-RAIL) offers a 15% discount off the lowest available coach fare (with certain travel restrictions) to people 62 or over.

Greyhound also offers discounted fares for senior citizens. Call your local Greyhound office for details.

FOR SINGLE TRAVELERS The best nightlife choices for meeting up with others are **Church Street Station** (in downtown Orlando) and **Pleasure Island** (see details on both, and other clubs, in chapter 9).

Want a fellow traveler? Contact **Travel Companion,** P.O. Box P-833, Amityville, NY 11701-0833 (☎ 516/454-0880), an organization that matches up single travelers with compatible partners. For a fee, you'll be listed in and receive the organization's newsletter, which provides a list of potential companions (you can request same sex or opposite sex).

FOR STUDENTS The key to securing discounts is valid student ID. Be sure to carry such and keep your eyes open for special student prices.

FOR FAMILIES No city in the world is more geared to family travel than Orlando. In addition to its theme parks, recreational facilities provide abundant opportunities for family fun. Every restaurant in town has a low-priced children's menu, and many hotels maintain children's activity centers (see details in chapter 5). A few general suggestions to make traveling with kids easier:

Get the Kids Involved Let them, if they're old enough, write to the tourist offices for information and color brochures. If you're driving, give them a map on which they can outline the route. Let them help decide your sightseeing itinerary.

Packing Although your home may be toddler-proof, hotel accommodations are not. Bring blank plugs to cover outlets and whatever else is necessary.

Accommodations Children under 12, and in many cases even older, stay free in their parents' rooms in most hotels. Look for establishments that have pools and other recreational facilities.

Ground Rules Set up ground rules before leaving home about issues such as bedtime and spending money on souvenirs.

5 Getting There

BY PLANE

THE MAJOR AIRLINES **Delta** has the most flights—over 25%—into Orlando International Airport. It offers service from 200 cities and has a Fantastic Flyer program for kids. Other carriers include **Air Jamaica** (☎ 800/523-5585), **America West** (☎ 800/235-9292), **American** (☎ 800/433-7300), **American Trans Air** (☎ 718/917-6710), **British Airways** (☎ 800/247-9297), **Continental** (☎ 800/231-0856), **Kiwi** (☎ 800/538-5494), **Midway** (☎ 800/446-4392), **Northwest** (☎ 800/225-2525), **Transbrasil** (☎ 800/872-3153), **TWA** (☎ 800/221-2000), **United** (☎ 800/241-6522), **USAir** (☎ 800/428-4322), and **Virgin Atlantic** (☎ 800/862-8621).

FINDING THE BEST AIRFARE Here are some tips for discovering the lowest airfares:

- Since advance-purchase fares are almost always the lowest available, it's a good idea to book your flight as far in advance as possible. Advance-purchase fares can be as much as 75% lower than fares booked the last minute!
- The more flexible you can be about your travel dates and length of stay, the more money you're likely to save.
- Visit a large travel agency to investigate all options. Sometimes a good agent knows about fares you won't find on your own.
- Check newspaper ads (most notably, the Sunday *New York Times* Travel Section) for announcements of short-term promotional fares.
- Fly at off times (for instance, at night) when planes are less likely to be full.
- Inexpensive no-frills flights are offered from the New York area by Kiwi International (☎ 800/538-5494).

PACKAGE TOURS   Frankly, the number and diversity of package tours to Orlando is staggering. But significant savings are available for those willing to do the research. Best bet: Stop at a sizable travel agency and pick up brochures from the below-listed companies (and others). Pore over them at home, comparing offerings to find the optimum package for your trip. Also obtain the *Walt Disney World Vacations* brochure (see details at the beginning of this chapter), which lists the company's own packages. Try to find a package that meets rather than exceeds your needs; there's no sense in paying for elements you won't use. Also, read over the advantages accruing to Disney resort guests in chapter 5; some packages list as selling points services that are automatically available to every Walt Disney World guest.

When you call to reserve your flight, inquire about money-saving packages. For instance, **Delta Dream Vacations,** in several price ranges, include round-trip air transport; accommodations (state and hotel room tax/baggage gratuities included); an air-conditioned intermediate rental car with unlimited mileage or round-trip air-port transfer; a "Magic Passport" that provides unlimited admission to all WDW parks for the length of your stay; one breakfast (which can be a character breakfast); and entry into a selected theme park 1 hour before regular opening time. In pack-ages utilizing Walt Disney World Resorts, you get all the advantages accruing to guests at these properties (see chapter 5 for details). At this writing, 3-night midweek packages begin at $369–$409 per person (based on double occupancy and New York departure; range reflects season). If you put all of those components together on your own, the cost would be much, much higher. In fact, a Delta Dream Vacation can cost less than airfare alone from certain cities. Delta also has Orlando packages for which WDW tickets and resorts are optional. For details, call 800/872-7786.

Additional airline and tour-operator sources for airfare-inclusive packages include **USAir Vacations** (☎ 800/455-0123), **American Airlines Fly Away Vacations** (☎ 800/321-2121), **American Express Vacations** (☎ 800/241-1700), **Travel Impressions** (☎ 800/941-2639), and **Kingdom Tours** (☎ 800/872-8857).

ORLANDO'S AIRPORT   Serving over 22 million passengers each year, **Orlando International Airport** (☎ 407/825-2001) is a thoroughly modern and user-friendly facility with restaurants, shops, a 450-room on-premises Hyatt Regency Hotel, and centrally located information kiosks. All major car-rental companies are located at or near the airport; see "Getting Around" in chapter 4 for more information on rentals.

The airport is 25 miles from Walt Disney World. **Mears Transportation Group** (☎ 407/423-5566) shuttle vans ply the route from the airport (board outside bag-gage claim) to all Disney resorts and official hotels as well as most other area prop-erties. Their comfortable, air-conditioned vehicles operate around the clock, departing every 15 to 25 minutes in either direction. Rates vary with your destination. Round-trip cost for adults is $21 between the airport and downtown Orlando or Interna-tional Drive, $25 for Walt Disney World/Lake Buena Vista or Kissimmee/Hwy. 192. Children ages 4 to 11 pay $14 and $17, respectively. Children 3 and under ride free.

Note: It's always a good idea when you make your reservations to ask about trans-portation options between the airport and your hotel, or, if you're planning to rent a car, ask for driving directions from the airport.

BY CAR

Orlando is 436 miles from Atlanta; 1,312 miles from Boston; 1,120 miles from Chicago; 1,009 miles from Cleveland; 1,170 miles from Dallas; 1,114 miles from Detroit; 1,105 miles from New York City; and 1,261 miles from Toronto.

It's Better with the Bahamas: Combining Your Stay at Disney with a Cruise

Premier Cruise Lines (the Big Red Boat) offers 3- and 4-night luxury ocean cruises to the Bahamas (Nassau and Port Lucaya) in conjunction with 3- or 4-day Orlando theme park vacations. Cruises depart from and return to Port Canaveral, 45 minutes from Walt Disney World. You can add the island segment before or after your stay in Orlando. Participating hotels include Disney resorts. Ships are equipped with swimming pools, Jacuzzis, health clubs, jogging tracks, movie theaters, beauty salons, casinos, bar/lounges, video-game arcades, shops, and nightclubs. Looney Tunes characters (Bugs Bunny, Tweety, Daffy Duck) are your on-board hosts. Package price includes all meals on board ship, an Alamo rental car with unlimited mileage for 7 days, round-trip airfare to/from Orlando, and admission to varied attractions. Rates depend on stateroom and hotel category and the season you're traveling. At this writing, 7-night packages with New York departure start at about $899 per person, based on double occupancy; $589 for children under 9. Call **800/327-7113** for details.

From Atlanta, take I-75 south to the Florida Turnpike to I-4 west.

From points northeast, take I-95 south to I-4 west.

From Chicago, take I-65 south to Nashville and then I-24 south to I-75 south to the Florida Turnpike to I-4 west.

From Cleveland, and take I-77 south to Columbia, South Carolina, and then I-26 east to I-95 south to I-4 west.

From Dallas, take I-20 east to I-49 south to I-10 east to I-75 south to the Florida Turnpike to I-4 west.

From Detroit, take I-75 south to the Florida Turnpike to I-4 west.

From Toronto, take Canadian Route 401 south to Queen Elizabeth Way south to I-90 (New York State Thruway) east to I-87 (New York State Thruway) south to I-95 over the George Washington Bridge, and continue south on I-95 to I-4 west.

AAA (☎ 800/336-4357) and some other automobile club members can call local offices for maps and optimum driving directions.

BY TRAIN

Amtrak trains (☎ 800/USA-RAIL) pull into stations at 1400 Sligh Blvd., between Columbia and Miller streets in downtown Orlando (about 23 miles from Walt Disney World), and 111 Dakin Avenue, at Thurman Street in Kissimmee (about 15 miles from Walt Disney World).

From the Orlando station, you can catch **LYNX** bus no. 34, which departs weekdays at least once an hour between 10:25am and 5:25pm (weekends, take bus nos. 7 or 11 from the stop at the corner of Orange and Columbia avenues, two blocks away). All trips involve a transfer at the downtown bus station—not too much of a hassle because the bus will usually be right there when you arrive. This connecting bus (no. 8) makes stops about every $1^1/_2$ blocks along International Drive, culminating at Sea World, where you can get a taxi (about $28) to Walt Disney World–area hotels. For further details about bus transportation from the Orlando Amtrak station, call 407/841-8240. A taxi from the Orlando Amtrak station to Walt Disney World–area hotels is about $42.

From the Kissimmee Amtrak station, a taxi (about $28 to WDW-area hotels) is your only option.

FARES A limited number of seats on reserved trains are set aside for discount fares. Many people reserve fares months in advance, so the minute you know the dates of your trip, make your reservations so that you can increase your chance of getting a discount. There may be some restrictions on travel dates for discounted fares, mostly around very busy holiday times. To inquire about Amtrak's money-saving packages—including hotel accommodations (some at WDW resorts), car rentals, tours, etc., with your train fare—call 800/321-8684.

AMTRAK'S AUTO TRAIN Amtrak's Auto Train offers the convenience of having a car in Florida without driving it there. The Auto Train begins in Lorton, Virginia—about a 4-hour drive from New York, 2 hours from Philadelphia—and ends up at Sanford, Florida, about 23 miles northeast of Orlando. Once again, reserve early for the lowest fares. The Auto Train departs Lorton and Sanford at 4:30pm daily, arriving at its destination at 9am the next morning. *Note:* You have to arrive 1 or 2 hours before departure time so they can board your car. Call 800/USA-RAIL for details.

BY BUS

Greyhound buses connect the entire country with Orlando. They pull into a terminal at 555 N. Magruder Blvd. (John Young Parkway), between West Colonial Drive and Winter Garden Road, a few miles west of downtown Orlando (☎ 407/292-3422), or in Kissimmee at 16 N. Orlando Ave., between Emmett and Mabbette streets, about 14 miles from Walt Disney World (☎ 407/897-3911). There is van transport from the Kissimmee terminal to most area hotels and motels. From Orlando, you can call for a Mears shuttle van (☎ 407/423-5566), which will cost $12 to $13 one way to a Walt Disney–area hotel, $8 for children ages 4 to 11, free for those under 4 (round-trip fares are less). For the return trip, call from your hotel 24 hours in advance. A taxi to Walt Disney–area hotels will cost about $40. Greyhound's fare structure tends to be complex, but the good news is that when you call to make a reservation, the agent will always give you the lowest-fare options. Once again, advance-purchase fares booked 3 to 21 days prior to travel represent vast savings. Check your phone book for a local Greyhound listing or call 800/231-2222.

3 For Foreign Visitors

This chapter will provide some specifics about getting to Orlando as economically as possible from overseas, plus some helpful information about how things are done in the United States—from mailing a postcard to making a phone call.

1 Preparing for Your Trip

ENTRY REQUIREMENTS

DOCUMENT REGULATIONS   Canadian citizens may enter the United States without visas; they need only proof of residence.

Citizens of the United Kingdom, New Zealand, Japan, and most other western European countries traveling on valid passports may not need a visa for fewer than 90 days of holiday or business travel to the United States, providing that they hold a round-trip or return ticket and enter the United States on an airline or cruise line that participates in the visa waiver program.

(Note that citizens of these visa-exempt countries who first enter the United States may then visit Mexico, Canada, Bermuda, and/or the Caribbean islands and then reenter the States, by any mode of transportation, without needing a visa. Further information is available from any U.S. embassy or consulate.)

Citizens of countries other than those stipulated above, including citizens of Australia, must have two documents: a valid **passport,** with an expiration date at least 6 months later than the scheduled end of the visit to the United States; and a **tourist visa,** available without charge from the nearest U.S. consulate. To obtain a visa, the traveler must submit a completed application form (either in person or by mail) with a $1^1/_2$-inch square photo and demonstrate binding ties to a residence abroad.

Usually you can obtain a visa at once or within 24 hours, but it may take longer during the summer rush from June to August. If you cannot go in person, contact the nearest U.S. embassy or consulate for directions on applying by mail. Your travel agent or airline office may also be able to provide you with visa applications and instructions. The U.S. consulate or embassy that issues your visa will determine whether you will be issued a multiple- or single-entry visa and any restrictions regarding the length of your stay.

MEDICAL REQUIREMENTS   No inoculations are needed to enter the United States unless you are coming from, or have stopped over in, areas known to be suffering from epidemics, particularly cholera or yellow fever.

If you have a disease requiring treatment with medications containing narcotics or drugs requiring a syringe, carry a valid signed prescription from your physician to allay any suspicions that you are smuggling drugs.

CUSTOMS REQUIREMENTS   Every adult visitor may bring in free of duty: 1 liter of wine or hard liquor; 200 cigarettes or 100 cigars (but no cigars from Cuba) or 3 pounds of smoking tobacco; $100 worth of gifts. These exemptions are offered to travelers who spend at least 72 hours in the United States and who have not claimed them within the preceding 6 months. It is altogether forbidden to bring into the country foodstuffs (particularly cheese, fruit, cooked meats, and canned goods) and plants (vegetables, seeds, tropical plants, and so on). Foreign tourists may bring in or take out up to $10,000 in U.S. or foreign currency with no formalities; larger sums must be declared to Customs upon entering or leaving.

INSURANCE

There is no national health system in the United States. Because the cost of medical care is extremely high, we strongly advise every traveler to secure health coverage before setting out.

You may want to take out a comprehensive travel policy that covers (for a relatively low premium) sickness or injury costs (medical, surgical, and hospital); loss or theft of your baggage; trip-cancellation costs; guarantee of bail in case you are arrested; and costs of accident, repatriation, or death. Such packages (for example, "Europe Assistance" in Europe) are sold by automobile clubs at attractive rates, as well as by insurance companies and travel agencies.

MONEY

CURRENCY & EXCHANGE   The U.S. monetary system has a decimal base: one American **dollar ($1)** = 100 **cents (100¢).**

Dollar bills commonly come in $1 ("a buck"), $5, $10, $20, $50, and $100 denominations (the last two are not welcome when paying for small purchases and are not accepted in taxis or at subway ticket booths). There are also $2 bills (seldom encountered).

There are six denominations of coins: 1¢ (one cent, or "a penny"), 5¢ (five cents, or "a nickel"), 10¢ (ten cents, or "a dime"), 25¢ (twenty-five cents, or "a quarter"), 50¢ (fifty cents, or "a half dollar"), and the rare $1 piece.

The exchange bureaus so common in Europe are rare even at airports in the United States, and nonexistent outside major cities. Try to avoid having to change foreign money, or traveler's checks denominated other than in U.S. dollars, at a small-town bank, or even a branch in a big city.

You can exchange foreign currency at Guest Services windows in all three Disney parks, or at City Hall in the Magic Kingdom and Earth Station at Epcot. Currency can also be exchanged at Walt Disney World resorts and at the Sun Bank just across from the Village Marketplace. There are also exchange services at the Orlando International Airport.

TRAVELER'S CHECKS   Traveler's checks denominated in U.S. dollars are readily accepted at most hotels, motels, restaurants, and large stores, though they're much less convenient than using cash or a credit card. But the best place to change traveler's checks is at a bank. Do not bring traveler's checks denominated in other currencies.

Walt Disney World Services for International Visitors

Walt Disney World, which welcomes thousands of foreign visitors each year, has numerous services designed to meet their needs. Unless otherwise indicated, call 407/W-DISNEY for details. Services include

- A special phone number (☎ 407/824-7900) to speak with someone in French or Spanish (other languages are sometimes available as well).
- Personal translator units (in French, German, and Spanish) to translate narrations at some shows and attractions.
- Detailed guidebooks to the three major parks in Spanish, French, German, Portuguese, and Japanese (available at any guest relations location).
- Currency exchange (see above).
- World Key Terminals at Epcot that offer basic park information and assistance with dining reservations in Spanish.
- Resort phones equipped with software that expedites international calls by allowing guests to dial direct to foreign destinations.

CREDIT CARDS   The method of payment most widely used is the credit card: Visa (BarclayCard in Britain), MasterCard (EuroCard in Europe, Access in Britain, Chargex in Canada), American Express, Diners Club, Discover, and Carte Blanche. You can save yourself trouble by using plastic rather than cash or traveler's checks in most hotels, motels, restaurants, and retail stores. American Express, MasterCard, and Visa are accepted for admission to, and all restaurants within, the Disney Parks. You must have a credit card to rent a car. It can also be used as proof of identity (often carrying more weight than a passport), or as a "cash card," enabling you to draw money from banks that accept them.

SAFETY

While the Walt Disney World/Orlando area in general—and the theme parks in particular—are extremely safe, there are some general precautions you can take to minimize your chances of being the victim of crime.

GENERAL   U.S. urban areas tend to be less safe than those in Europe or Japan. Visitors should always stay alert. This is particularly true of large U.S. cities. It is wise to ask the local tourist office if you're in doubt about which neighborhoods are safe. Avoid deserted areas, especially at night. Don't go into any city park at night unless there is an event that attracts crowds. Avoid carrying valuables with you on the street, and don't display expensive cameras or electronic equipment.

Remember also that hotels are open to the public, and in a large hotel, security may not be able to screen everyone entering. Always lock your room door—don't assume that once inside your hotel you are automatically safe and no longer need to be aware of your surroundings.

DRIVING   Safety while driving is particularly important. Question your rental agency about personal safety, or ask for a brochure of traveler safety tips when you pick up your car. Obtain written directions, or a map with the route marked in red, from the agency showing how to get to your destination. And, if possible, arrive and depart during daylight hours.

Recently, more and more crime has involved cars and drivers. If you drive off a highway into a doubtful neighborhood, leave the area as quickly as possible. If you have an accident, even on the highway, stay in your car with the doors locked until you assess the situation or until the police arrive. If you are bumped from behind on the street or are involved in a minor accident with no injuries and the situation appears to be suspicious, motion to the other driver to follow you. *Never* get out of your car in such situations. Go directly to the nearest police precinct, well-lighted service station, or all-night store.

If you see someone on the road who indicates a need for help, do *not* stop. Take note of the location, drive on to a well-lighted area, and telephone the police by dialing 911.

Park in well-lighted, well-traveled areas if possible. Always keep your car doors locked, whether attended or unattended. Look around you before you get out of your car, and never leave any packages or valuables in sight. If someone attempts to rob you or steal your car, do *not* try to resist the thief/carjacker—report the incident to the police department immediately.

2 Getting To & Around the U.S.

GETTING TO THE U.S.   Travelers from overseas can take advantage of the **APEX (Advance Purchase Excursion) fares** offered by all the major U.S. and European carriers.

British Airways (☎ 081/897-4000 from within the U.K.) offers direct flights from London to Miami and Orlando, as does **Virgin Atlantic** (☎ 293/74-77-47 from within the U.K.). Canadian readers might book flights with **Air Canada** (☎ 800/776-3000), which offers service from Toronto and Montréal to Miami and Tampa.

Some large American airlines (for example, TWA, American Airlines, Northwest, United, and Delta) offer travelers on their transatlantic or transpacific flights special discount tickets under the name **Visit USA,** allowing travel between any U.S. destinations at minimum rates. They are not on sale in the United States, and must therefore, be purchased before you leave your foreign point of departure. This system is the best, easiest, and fastest way to see the United States at low cost. You should obtain information well in advance from your travel agent or the office of the airline concerned, since the conditions attached to these discount tickets can be changed without advance notice.

The visitor arriving by air, no matter what the port of entry, should cultivate patience and resignation before setting foot on U.S. soil. Getting through Immigration control may take as long as 2 hours on some days. Add the time it takes to clear Customs, and you'll see that you should make very generous allowance for delay in planning connections between international and domestic flights—an average of 2 to 3 hours, at least.

In contrast, travelers arriving by car or by rail from Canada will find border-crossing formalities streamlined to the vanishing point. And air travelers from Canada, Bermuda, and some places in the Caribbean can sometimes go through Customs and Immigration at the point of departure, which is much quicker and less painful.

GETTING AROUND THE U.S.   Though I give some tips on train and bus passes below, you're going to need a car to get around. It's really only possible to rely on public transportation in the United States in a few urban areas with comprehensive mass transit systems—and Orlando is not among them. To rent a car, you need a major credit card. A valid driver's license is required, and you usually need to be at least 25 years old. Some companies do rent to younger people but add a daily surcharge. Be sure to return your car with the same amount of gas you started out with; rental companies charge excessive prices for gasoline. All the major car-rental companies are represented in Florida (see "Getting Around," in chapter 4).

International visitors can buy a **USA RAILPASS,** good for 15 or 30 days of unlimited travel on Amtrak trains. The pass is available through many foreign travel agents. Prices in 1995 for a 15-day pass were $229 off-peak, $334 peak; a 30-day pass costs $339 off-peak, $425 peak. (With a foreign passport, you can also buy passes at some Amtrak offices in the United States, including locations in San Francisco, Los Angeles, Chicago, New York, Miami, Boston, and Washington, D.C.) Reservations are generally required and should be made for each part of your trip as early as possible.

Visitors should be aware of the limitations of long-distance rail travel in the United States. With a few notable exceptions (for instance, the Northeast Corridor line between Boston and Washington, D.C.), service is rarely up to European standards: Delays are common, routes are limited and often infrequently served, and fares are rarely significantly lower than discount airfares. Thus, cross-country train travel should be approached with caution.

Bus travel in the United States can be both slow and uncomfortable, so this option is not for everyone. Although ticket prices for short hops between cities are often the most economical form of public transit, at this writing bus passes are priced slightly higher than similar train passes. Greyhound, the sole nationwide bus line, offers an **Ameripass** for unlimited travel for 7 days ($259), 15 days ($459), and 30 days ($559).

For further information about travel to Florida, see "Getting There," in chapter 2.

FAST FACTS: For the Foreign Traveler

Automobile Organizations   Auto clubs will supply maps, suggested routes, guidebooks, accident and bail-bond insurance, and emergency road service. The major auto club in the United States, with 983 offices nationwide, is the **American Automobile Association (AAA).** Members of some foreign auto clubs have reciprocal arrangements with AAA and enjoy its services at no charge. If you belong to an auto club, inquire about AAA reciprocity before you leave. AAA can provide you with an International Driving Permit validating your foreign license. You may be able to join AAA even if you are not a member of a reciprocal club. To inquire, call **800/JOIN-AAA.** In addition, some automobile-rental agencies now provide these services, so you should inquire about their availability when you rent your car.

Business Hours   Banks are open weekdays from 9am to 3 or 4pm, although there's 24-hour access to the automatic tellers (ATMs) at most banks and other outlets. Generally, offices are open weekdays from 9am to 5pm. Stores are open 6 days a week, with many open on Sunday, too; department stores usually stay open until 9pm at least 1 day a week.

Climate   See "When to Go," in chapter 2.

Currency & Exchange   See "Money" in "Preparing for Your Trip," earlier in this chapter.

Drinking Laws   See "Liquor Laws" in "Fast Facts," in chapter 4.

Electricity   The United States uses 110–120 volts, 60 cycles, compared to 220–240 volts, 50 cycles, as in most of Europe. In addition to a 100-volt converter, small appliances of non-American manufacture, such as hair dryers or shavers, will require a plug adapter, with two flat, parallel pins.

Embassies and Consulates   All embassies are located in Washington, D.C.; some consulates are located in major cities, and most nations have a mission to the United Nations in New York City. Foreign visitors can obtain telephone numbers for their embassies and consulates by calling "Information" in Washington, D.C. (☎ 202/555-1212).

The Canadian consulate closest to Orlando is at 200 S. Biscayne Blvd., Suite 1600, Miami, FL 33131 (☎ 305/579-1600). There's a British consulate located at 1001 S. Bayshore Dr., Miami, FL 33131 (☎ 305/374-1522); for emergency situations, there is an office in Orlando at the Sun Bank Tower, Suite 2110, 200 S. Orange Ave. (☎ 407/426-7855).

Emergencies   Call **911** to report a fire, call the police, or get an ambulance.

Gasoline (Petrol)   One U.S. gallon equals 3.75 liters, while 1.2 U.S. gallons equal one Imperial gallon. You'll notice there are several grades (and price levels) of gasoline available at most gas stations. And you'll also notice that their names change from company to company. The unleaded ones with the highest octane are the most expensive (most rental cars take the least expensive, "regular" unleaded) and leaded gas is the least expensive, but only older cars can take this, so check if you're not sure.

Holidays   On the following legal national holidays, banks, government offices, post offices, and many stores, restaurants, and museums are closed:

January 1 (New Year's Day)
Third Monday in January (Martin Luther King, Jr. Day)
Third Monday in February (Presidents' Day, Washington's Birthday)
Last Monday in May (Memorial Day)
July 4 (Independence Day)
First Monday in September (Labor Day)
Second Monday in October (Columbus Day)
November 11 (Veteran's Day/Armistice Day)
Last Thursday in November (Thanksgiving Day)
December 25 (Christmas)

Finally, the Tuesday following the first Monday in November is Election Day and is a legal holiday in presidential-election years like 1996.

Languages   Major hotels may have multilingual employees. Unless your language is very obscure, they can usually supply a translator on request. Especially in southern Florida, many people are fluent in Spanish.

Legal Aid   The foreign tourist will probably never become involved with the American legal system. If you are pulled over for a minor infraction (for example, of the highway code, such as speeding), never attempt to pay the fine directly to a police officer; you may wind up arrested on the much more serious charge of attempted bribery. Pay fines by mail, or directly into the hands of the clerk of the court. If accused of a more serious offense, it's wise to say and do nothing before consulting a lawyer. Under U.S. law, an arrested person is allowed one telephone call to a party of his or her choice. Call your embassy or consulate.

Mail   If you want your mail to follow you on your vacation and you aren't sure of your address, your mail can be sent to you, in your name, c/o General Delivery at the main post office of the city or region where you expect to be. The addressee must pick it up in person and produce proof of identity (driver's license, credit card, passport, etc.).

Generally to be found at intersections, mailboxes are blue with a red-and-white stripe and carry the inscription U.S. MAIL. If your mail is addressed to a U.S. destination, don't forget to add the five-figure postal code, or ZIP (Zone Improvement Plan) code, after the two-letter abbreviation of the state to which the mail is addressed (CA for California, FL for Florida, NY for New York, and so on).

Within the United States, it costs 20¢ to mail a standard-size postcard and 32¢ to send an oversize postcard (larger than 4½ by 6 inches, or 10.8 by 15.4 centimeters). Letters that weigh up to 1 ounce (that's about five pages, 8-by-11-inch paper) cost 32¢, plus 23¢ for each additional ounce. A standard postcard to Mexico costs 30¢, a ½-ounce letter 35¢; a postcard to Canada costs 30¢, a 1-ounce letter 40¢. A postcard to Europe, Australia, New Zealand, the Far East, South America, and elsewhere costs 40¢, while a letter is 60¢ for each ½ ounce.

Newspapers and Magazines   National newspapers include the *New York Times, USA Today,* and the *Wall Street Journal.* National news weeklies include *Newsweek, Time,* and *U.S. News & World Report.* All over Florida, you'll be able to purchase the *Miami Herald,* one of the most highly respected dailies in the country. The local newspaper is the *Orlando Sentinel,* and there's a monthly city magazine called *Orlando.*

Radio and Television   Audiovisual media, with five coast-to-coast networks—ABC, CBS, NBC, Fox, and the Public Broadcasting System (PBS)—and the cable network CNN, play a major part in American life. In big cities, televiewers have a choice of at least a dozen channels (including the UHF channels), most of them transmitting 24 hours a day, without counting the pay-TV channels showing recent movies or sports events. All options are usually indicated on your hotel TV set. You'll also find a wide choice of local radio stations, each broadcasting particular kinds of talk shows and/or music—classical, country, jazz, pop, gospel—punctuated by news broadcasts and frequent commercials.

Safety   See "Safety" in "Preparing for Your Trip," earlier in this chapter.

Taxes   In the United States, there is no VAT (Value-Added Tax) or other indirect tax at a national level. Every state, and each city in it, has the right to levy its own local tax on all purchases, including hotel and restaurant checks, airline tickets, and so on. In Florida, sales tax is 6%. Hotel tax in Orlando and Kissimmee (which includes sales tax) is 11%.

Telephone, Telegraph, Telex, and Fax   The telephone system in the United States is run by private corporations, so rates, especially for long-distance service, can vary widely—even on calls made from public telephones. Local calls in the United States usually cost 25¢.

Generally, hotel surcharges on long-distance and local calls are astronomical. You are usually better off using a public pay telephone, which you will find clearly marked in most public buildings and private establishments as well as on the street. Outside metropolitan areas, public telephones are more difficult to find. Stores and gas stations are your best bet.

Most **long-distance** and **international calls** can be dialed directly from any phone. For calls to Canada and other parts of the United States, dial 1 followed by the area code and the seven-digit number. For international calls, dial 011 followed by the country code, city code, and the telephone number of the person you wish to call.

For **reversed-charge or collect calls,** and for **person-to-person calls,** dial 0 (zero, *not* the letter "O") followed by the area code and number you want; an operator will then come on the line, and you should specify that you are calling collect, or person-to-person, or both. If your operator-assisted call is international, ask for the overseas operator.

For local **directory assistance** ("Information"), dial 411; for **long-distance Information,** dial 1, then the appropriate area code and 555-1212.

Like the telephone system, **telegraph** and **telex** services are provided by private corporations like ITT, MCI, and above all, Western Union, the most important. You can bring your telegram in to the nearest Western Union office (there are hundreds across the country) or dictate it over the phone (a toll-free call, 800/325-6000). You can also telegraph money, or have it telegraphed to you, very quickly over the Western Union system.

It's also easy to send a **fax.** Just dial the fax number as you would any phone number. Most hotels have fax service. If yours doesn't, small copy shops found in most neighborhoods provide fax service. They'll send for you for a small fee per page, or, if you make arrangements, they'll receive for you and call you when anything arrives.

Telephone Directory   There are two kinds of telephone directories available to you. The general directory is the so-called *white pages,* in which private and business subscribers are listed in alphabetical order. The inside front cover lists the emergency number for police, fire, and ambulance, and other vital numbers (like the Coast Guard, poison-control center, crime-victims hotline, and so on). The first few pages are devoted to community-service numbers, including a guide to long-distance and international calling, complete with country codes and area codes.

The second directory, printed on yellow paper (hence its name, *yellow pages*), lists all local services, businesses, and industries by type of activity, with an index at the back. The listings cover not only such obvious items as automobile repairs by make of car, or drugstores (pharmacies), often by geographical location, but also restaurants by type of cuisine and geographical location, bookstores by special subject and/or language, places of worship by religious denomination, and other information that the tourist might otherwise not readily find. The yellow pages also include city plans or detailed area maps, often showing postal ZIP codes and public transportation routes.

Time   The United States is divided into four time zones (six, if Alaska and Hawaii are included). From east to west, these are: eastern standard time (EST), central standard time (CST), mountain standard time (MST), Pacific standard time (PST), Alaska standard time (AST), and Hawaii standard time (HST). Always keep changing time zones in mind if you are traveling (or even telephoning) long distances in the United States. For example, noon in New York City (EST) is 11am in Chicago (CST), 10am in Denver (MST), 9am in Los Angeles (PST), 8am in Anchorage (AST), and 7am in Honolulu (HST).

Orlando, like most of Florida, observes eastern standard time; the western part of the state's Panhandle region is on central standard time (its clocks are set an hour earlier). Daylight saving time is in effect from the first Sunday in April through the last Saturday in October (actually, the change is made at 2am on Sunday) except in Arizona, Hawaii, part of Indiana, and Puerto Rico. Daylight saving time moves the clock 1 hour ahead of standard time.

Tipping   This is part of the American way of life, on the principle that you must expect to pay for any service you get. Here are some rules of thumb:

> Bartenders: 10% to 15%
> Bellhops: at least 50¢ per piece; $2 to $3 for a lot of baggage
> Cab drivers: 15% of the fare
> Cafeterias, fast-food restaurants: no tip
> Chambermaids: $1 a day
> Checkroom attendants (restaurants, theaters): $1 per garment
> Cinemas, movies, theaters: no tip
> Doormen (hotels or restaurants): not obligatory
> Gas-station attendants: no tip
> Hairdressers: 15% to 20%
> Redcaps (airport and railroad station): at least 50¢ per piece, $2 to $3 for a lot of baggage
> Restaurants, nightclubs: 15% to 20% of the check
> Sleeping-car porters: $2 to $3 per night to your attendant
> Valet parking attendants: $1

Toilets   Foreign visitors often complain that public toilets are hard to find in most U.S. cities. True, there are none on the streets, but the visitor can usually find one in a bar, restaurant, hotel, museum, department store, or service station—and it will probably be clean (although the last-mentioned sometimes leaves much to be desired). Note, however, a growing practice in some restaurants and bars of displaying a notice that "toilets are for the use of patrons only." You can ignore this sign, or better yet, avoid arguments by paying for a cup of coffee or soft drink. The cleanliness of toilets at railroad stations and bus depots may be more open to question, and some public places are equipped with pay toilets, which require you to insert one or more coins into a slot on the door before it will open.

THE AMERICAN SYSTEM OF MEASUREMENTS

Length

1 inch (in.)			=	2.54cm			
1 foot (ft.)	=	12 in.	=	30.48cm	=	.305m	
1 yard	=	3 ft.			=	.915m	
1 mile (mi.)	=	5,280 ft.				=	1.609km

To convert miles to kilometers, multiply the number of miles by 1.61 (example, 50 mi. × 1.61 = 80.5km). Note that this conversion can be used to convert speeds from miles per hour (mph) to kilometers per hour (km/h).

To convert kilometers to miles, multiply the number of kilometers by .62 (example, 25km × .62 = 15.5 mi.). Note that this same conversion can be used to convert speeds from kilometers per hour to miles per hour.

Capacity

1 fluid ounce (fl. oz.)			=	.03 liter		
1 pint	=	16 fl. oz.	=	.47 liter		
1 quart	=	2 pints	=	.94 liter		
1 gallon (gal.)	=	4 quarts	=	3.79 liters	=	.83 Imperial gal.

To convert U.S. gallons to liters, multiply the number of gallons by 3.79 (example, 12 U.S. gal. × 3.79 = 45.58 liters).

To convert liters to U.S. gallons, multiply the number of liters by .26 (example, 50 liters × .26 = 13 U.S. gal.).

To convert U.S. gallons to Imperial gallons, multiply the number of U.S. gallons by .83 (example, 12 U.S. gal. × .83 = 9.96 Imperial gal.).

To convert Imperial gallons to U.S. gallons, multiply the number of Imperial gallons by 1.2 (example, 8 Imperial gal. × 1.2 = 9.6 U.S. gal.).

Weight

1 ounce (oz.)			=	28.35g				
1 pound (lb.)	=	16 oz.	=	453.6g	=	.45kg		
1 ton	=	2,000 lb.	=			907kg	=	.91 metric ton

To convert pounds to kilograms, multiply the number of pounds by .45 (example, 90 lb. × .45 = 40.5kg).

To convert kilograms to pounds, multiply the number of kilos by 2.2 (example, 75kg × 2.2 = 165 lb.).

Area

1 acre			=	.41ha		
1 square mile (sq. mi.)	=	640 acres	=	259ha	=	2.6km²

To convert acres to hectares, multiply the number of acres by .41 (example, 40 acres × .41 = 16.4ha).

To convert hectares to acres, multiply the number of hectares by 2.47 (example, 20ha × 2.47 = 49.4 acres).

To convert square miles to square kilometers, multiply the number of square miles by 2.6 (example, 80 sq. mi. × 2.6 = 208km²).

To convert square kilometers to square miles, multiply the number of square kilometers by .39 (example, 150km² × .39 = 58.5 sq. mi.).

Temperature

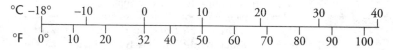

To convert degrees Fahrenheit to degrees Celsius, subtract 32 from °F, multiply by 5, then divide by 9 (example, 85°F − 32 × $^5/_9$ = 29.4°C).

To convert degrees Celsius to degrees Fahrenheit, multiply °C by 9, divide by 5, and add 32 (example, 20°C × $^9/_5$ + 32 = 68°F).

4 Getting to Know Walt Disney World & Orlando

Many visitors to the area never venture beyond the Disney World area, except perhaps to Sea World and Universal Studios, which are close by. For those who do, almost all area hotels offer transportation to the airport and city attractions.

1 Orientation

VISITOR INFORMATION

Contact the **Orlando/Orange County Convention & Visitors Bureau,** 8445 International Dr. (in the Mercado Shopping Village), Orlando, FL 32819 (☎ **407/363-5871**). They can answer all your questions and will be happy to send you maps, brochures (including the informative *Official Visitors Guide,* the *Official Attractions Guide,* and the *Official Accommodations Guide*), and the "Magicard," good for discounts of 10% to 50% on accommodations, attractions, car rentals, and more. Discount tickets to attractions other than Disney parks are sold on the premises, and the multilingual staff can also make dining reservations and hotel referrals. The bureau is open daily except Christmas from 8am to 8pm.

For general information about Walt Disney World—and a copy of the informative *Walt Disney World Vacations*—write or call the **Walt Disney World Co.,** Box 10000, Lake Buena Vista, FL 32830-1000 (☎ **407/934-7639**).

If you're driving, you can stop at the **Disney/AAA Travel Center in Ocala, Florida,** at the intersection of I-75 (exit 68) and FL 200, about 90 miles north of Orlando (☎ **904/854-0770**). Here you can purchase tickets and Mickey ears, get help planning your park itinerary, and make hotel reservations. Hours are 9am to 6pm, until 7pm June through August.

And at the Orlando International Airport, arriving passengers can stroll over to **Greetings from Walt Disney World Resort** (☎ **407/825-2301**), a shop and information center on the third floor in the main lobby just behind the Northwest counter. This facility sells WDW park tickets, makes dinner show and hotel reservations at Disney properties, and provides brochures and assistance. Open daily from 6am to 9pm.

Upon entering WDW grounds, you can tune your radio to 1030 AM when you're approaching the Magic Kingdom, 850 AM

Orlando/Walt Disney World Area Orientation

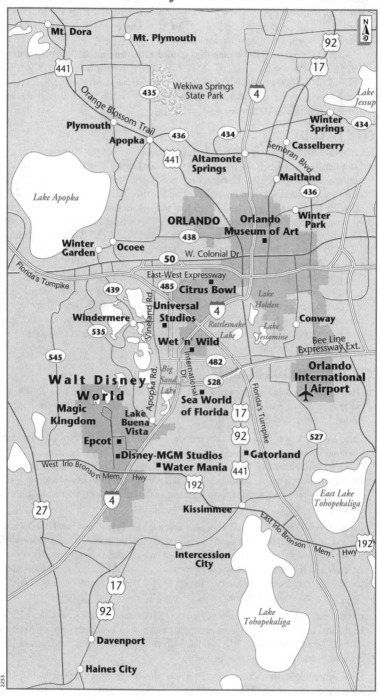

when approaching Epcot. Tune to 1200 AM when departing from the Magic King-dom, 910 AM when departing Epcot. TVs in all Disney resorts and official Disney hotels also have park information stations.

Also contact the **Kissimmee–St. Cloud Convention & Visitors Bureau,** 1925 E. Irlo Bronson Blvd. (P.O. Box 422007), Kissimmee, FL 34742-2007 (☎ **407/847-5000** or 800/327-9159). They'll send maps, brochures, discount cou-pon books, and the *Kissimmee–St. Cloud Vacation Guide,* which details the area's accommodations and attractions.

CITY LAYOUT

Orlando's major artery is **I-4,** which runs diagonally across the state from Tampa to Daytona Beach. Exits from I-4 take you to Walt Disney World, Sea World, Inter-national Drive, U.S. 192, Kissimmee, Lake Buena Vista, Church Street Station, downtown Orlando, and Winter Park. The **Florida Turnpike** crosses I-4 and links up with I-75 to the north. **U.S. 192,** a major east-west artery, stretches from Kissimmee (along a major motel strip) to U.S. 27, crossing I-4 near the Walt Disney World entrance road. Farther north, a toll road called the **Beeline Expressway** (FL 528) goes east from I-4 past Orlando International Airport to Cape Canaveral.

Walt Disney World property is bounded roughly by I-4 and FL 535 to the east (the latter also north), World Drive (the entrance road) to the west, and U.S. 192 to the south. Epcot Center Drive (Hwy. 536/the south end of International Drive) and Buena Vista Drive cut across the complex in a more or less east-west direction; the two roads cross at Bonnet Creek Parkway. Excellent highways and explicit signage make it very easy to find your way around. *Note:* The Disney parks are actually much closer to Kissimmee than to downtown Orlando.

NEIGHBORHOODS IN BRIEF

Walt Disney World   A city unto itself, WDW sprawls over more than 26,000 acres containing theme parks, resorts, hotels, shops, restaurants, and recreational facilities galore. Copious details below.

Lake Buena Vista   This area centers on a hotel village/marketplace owned and operated by Walt Disney World on the eastern edge of Disney property. However, though Disney owns all the real estate, many of the hotels, and some shops and restaurants here, are independently owned. Lake Buena Vista is a charming area of manicured lawns and verdant thoroughfares with traffic islands shaded by towering oak trees.

International Drive   This is another attractive area extending 7 to 10 miles north of the Disney parks between FL 535 and the Florida Turnpike. It, too, centers—for a long way—on a wide thoroughfare with a tree-shaded traffic island. It contains numerous hotels, restaurants, shopping centers, and the Orange County Convention Civic Center and offers easy access to Sea World and Universal Studios. *Note:* Lo-cally, this road is always referred to as I-Drive.

Kissimmee   South of the Disney parks, Kissimmee centers on U.S. 192/Irlo Bronson Memorial Highway—a somewhat tacky strip as archetypical of American cities as Main Street. U.S. 192 is lined with budget motels, lesser attractions, and every fast-food restaurant you can name.

Downtown Orlando   Reached via I-4 east, this burgeoning Sunbelt metropolis is 17 miles northeast of Walt Disney World. Though many tourists never venture downtown, it does have a number of attractions, including noteworthy nightlife.

2 Getting Around

In a city that thrives on its visitor attractions, you won't find it difficult to get around. All hotels offer transport to and from theme parks and other tourist destinations. It's not difficult getting places, but it can be expensive.

THE DISNEY TRANSPORTATION NETWORK If you plan to stay at a Disney resort and visit mostly Disney parks and attractions, there's a very thorough free-transportation network throughout the complex.

Disney resorts and official hotels offer unlimited—and very efficient—complimentary transportation via bus, monorail, ferry, and water taxi to all three parks from 2 hours prior to opening until 2 hours after closing; also to Disney Village Marketplace, Typhoon Lagoon, River Country, Blizzard Beach, Pleasure Island, Fort Wilderness, and other Disney resorts. Disney properties offer transportation to other area attractions as well, though it's not complimentary.

There are a few advantages to using this on-property transportation system: It's free, providing a big saving over car rental, insurance, and gas. You don't have to pay for parking ($5 per day in Walt Disney World). There are never long waits in traffic coming into the parking lots. And if your party wants to split up, you can easily board transport to different areas.

BY CAR

As stated above, if you plan to stay at a Disney resort and visit mostly Disney parks and attractions, you really don't need a car at all. On the other hand, if you're traveling further afield, want to eat at non-Disney restaurants, or just enjoy the independence of your own wheels, you'll want to drive here or rent.

All major rental companies are represented in Orlando and maintain desks at the airport. I was quoted the lowest rates by **Value Rent-A-Car** (☎ 800/GO-VALUE), which also turned out to offer excellent service and 24-hour pickup and return. Some other handy phone numbers: **Alamo** (☎ 800/327-9363), **Avis** (☎ 800/331-1212), **Budget** (☎ 800/527-0700), **Dollar** (☎ 800/800-4000), **Hertz** (☎ 800/654-3131), and **Thrifty** (☎ 800/367-2277).

BY BUS

Mears Transportation Group (☎ 407/423-5566) operates buses to all major attractions, including Cypress Gardens, Kennedy Space Center, Universal Studios, Sea World, Busch Gardens (in Tampa), and Church Street Station, among others. Call for details.

BY TAXI

Taxis line up in front of major hotels, and at smaller properties, the front desk will be happy to call you a cab. Or call **Yellow Cab** (☎ 407/699-9999). Charge is $2.75 for the first mile, $1.50 per mile thereafter.

FAST FACTS: Walt Disney World & Orlando

Ambulances   See "Emergencies," below.

Babysitters   Most Orlando hotels offer babysitting services, and several Disney properties have marvelous child-care facilities with counselor-supervised activity programs on the premises. Disney properties use KinderCare sitters (☎ 407/827-5444), so you can be sure they've been very carefully checked out. If you're not staying at a Disney accommodation, you can call them on your own. Rates for in-room service are: $9 per hour for one child, $10 per hour for two children, $11 per hour for three children, $14 per hour for four children. There is a 4-hour minimum, the first half hour of which is travel time for the sitter. Twenty-four-hour advance notice is required.

Car Rentals   See "Getting Around," earlier in this chapter.

Climate   See "When to Go," in chapter 2.

Convention Center   The Orange County Convention/Civic Center is located at 9800 International Dr. (☎ 407/345-9800).

Crime   See "Safety," below.

Doctors and Dentists   Your best bet is to inquire at your hotel desk. Disney has first-aid centers in all three major parks. There's also a very good 24-hour service in the area called HouseMed (☎ 407/396-1195). HouseMed doctors—who can dispense medication—make "house calls" to all area hotels. HouseMed also operates the Medi-Clinic, a walk-in medical facility (not for emergencies) at the intersection of I-4 and Hwy. 192, open daily from 8am to 9pm (same phone). Call for directions from your hotel. See also "Hospitals" and "Pharmacies," below.

   To find a dentist, call Dental Referral Service (☎ 800/917-6453); they can tell you the nearest dentist who meets your needs. Phones are manned from 5:30am to 6pm daily. Check the yellow pages for 24-hour emergency services.

Emergencies   Dial **911** to contact the police or fire department or to call an ambulance.

Florist   Floral and fruit arrangements can be delivered anywhere on Walt Disney World Resort property by calling 407/827-3505 between 8am and 8pm.

Hospitals   Sand Lake Hospital, 9400 Turkey Lake Rd., is about 2 miles south of Sand Lake Road (☎ 407/351-8550). From the WDW area, take I-4 east to exit 29, turn left at the exit onto Sand Lake Road, and make a left on Turkey Lake Road. The hospital is 2 miles up on your right.

Kennels   All of the major theme parks offer animal-boarding facilities at reasonable fees. At Walt Disney World, there are kennels at Fort Wilderness, Epcot, the Magic Kingdom, and Disney-MGM Studios. If you're traveling with a pet, don't leave it in the car—even with a window cracked—while you enjoy the park. Many pets have perished this way in the hot Florida sun.

Kosher Food   It can be arranged at restaurants at Disney parks and resorts with 24 hours' advance notice. Call 407/WDW-DINE.

Liquor Laws   Minimum drinking age is 21. No liquor is served in the Magic Kingdom at Walt Disney World; however, drinks are available at the other parks.

Lockers   You can rent lockers at all of the Disney parks. Most other theme parks also offer this service. Inquire at Guest Relations.

Lost Children   Every theme park has a designated spot for parents to meet up with lost children. Find out where it is when you enter any park and instruct your children to ask park personnel to take them there if they are lost. Young children should have name tags.

Newspapers and Magazines   The *Orlando Sentinel* is the major local newspaper, but you can also purchase papers of major cities (most notably, the *New York Times*) in most hotel gift shops. Also informative is a city magazine called *Orlando*.

Pharmacies   Walgreen Drug Store, 1003 W. Vine St. (Hwy. 192), just east of Bermuda Avenue (☎ 407/847-5252), operates a 24-hour pharmacy. They can deliver to hotels for a charge ($10 from 7am to 5pm, $15 at all other times).

Photography   Two-hour film processing is available at all three major Disney parks. Look for the Photo Express sign. You can also buy film and rent or buy 35mm, disc, and video cameras in all three parks.

Post Office   The main post office in Lake Buena Vista is at 12541 FL 535, near TGI Friday's in the Crossroads Shopping Center (☎ 407/828-2606). It's open Monday through Friday from 9am to 4pm, Saturday from 9am to noon.

Safety   Whenever you're traveling in an unfamiliar city, stay alert. Be aware of your immediate surroundings. It's a good idea to keep your valuables in a safety-deposit box (inquire at the front desk), though some hotels nowadays are equipped with in-room safes. Do keep a close eye on your valuables when you're in a public place—restaurant, theater, even airport terminal. And don't leave valuables in your car, even in the trunk.

Taxes   Hotel tax in Orlando and Kissimmee is 11%, which includes a state sales tax (6%) that is also charged on all goods except most grocery store items and medicines.

Time   Call 407/646-3131 for the correct time and temperature.

Tourist Information   See "Orientation," earlier in this chapter.

Travel Information   The Delta Air Lines Travel Desk at Disney's Contemporary Resort (on the ground floor of the Tower) provides information on buses, airline reservations, rental cars, and tours to other central Florida attractions.

Weather   Call 407/851-7510 for a weather recording.

5

Accommodations

You'll find a wealth of hotel options in the Walt Disney World area. Beautifully landscaped multifacility resorts are the rule, but there's something to suit every taste and pocketbook. And, of course, you should reserve as far in advance as possible . . . the minute you've decided on the dates of your trip.

HOW TO CHOOSE A HOTEL & SAVE MONEY

Many people assume that motels outside the Disney parks will cost you less than staying on WDW premises, but that isn't always the case.

If you don't have a car, be sure to note the price of hotel shuttle buses to and from Walt Disney World parks. Compute these charges—which can be as high as $12 per person per day—in determining hotel price value. All Disney-owned properties and Disney "official" hotels offer complimentary transportation to and from WDW parks (see details on this, and other advantages of staying at Disney properties, below).

In or out of Walt Disney World, if you book your hotel as part of a package (see chapters 2 and 4 for details), you'll likely enjoy big savings.

Many people don't know that you can bargain with the reservations clerk when booking a hotel. The reason: an unoccupied room nets a hotel zero dollars, and any reasonable offer is better than that. Of course, this only works if you book upon arrival, preferably late in the afternoon when the desk knows there will be empty rooms. It will also work better outside of Walt Disney World.

Another money-saving tip: Reserving via toll-free numbers at chain hotels sometimes puts you into the running for lower rates than reserving at individual properties. And ask about special discounts for students, government employees, senior citizens, military, AAA, and/or corporate clients.

In some hotel listings below, I've mentioned **concierge levels.** In these "hotels within a hotel," guests enjoy a luxurious private lounge (usually with spectacular views) that is the setting for complimentary continental breakfast, hot and cold hors d'oeuvres at cocktail hour, and late-night cordials and pastries. Rooms are usually on high floors and room decor is upgraded. Guests are cosseted with special services (private registration and checkout, a personal concierge, nightly bed turndown) and amenities (upgraded toiletries, bathroom scales, terry robes, hair dryers). Ask for specifics when you reserve. Concierge levels are especially attractive to businesspeople traveling on their own.

Also mentioned under "Facilities" in some cases are **counselor-supervised child-care/activity centers.** Very popular in Orlando, these are marvelous, creatively run facilities where kids enjoy Disney movies, video games, arts and crafts, storytelling, puppet shows, indoor and outdoor activities, and much more. Some centers provide meals and/or have beds where a child can go to sleep while you're out on the town. Check individual hotel listings for these facilities and call to find out exactly what is offered.

RESERVATION SERVICES

Many of the Kissimmee hotels listed soon in "Best Bets" can be booked by calling the **Kissimmee–St. Cloud Convention & Visitors Bureau** at ☎ 800/333-KISS.

Also consider using the services of an Orlando-based organization called **Check-In** (☎ **941/756-4880** or 800/237-1033; fax 941/739-2703). A central booking agency, it has listings for hundreds of condos, resorts, hotels, villas, and luxurious private homes in all price ranges. A minimum stay of 3 nights is required. Check-In doesn't accept credit cards, but it does take personal checks. There's no fee for the service.

HOW TO USE THIS CHAPTER

The hotels listed below are first divided by location, and then by price category alphabetically within a given district. All of the properties I've selected offer easy access to the Walt Disney World parks and other nearby major attractions.

Hotels listed in the **inexpensive** category are those charging $80 or less for a double room (don't blame me, I didn't invent inflation). Properties with $80 to $150 rooms make up the **moderate** category, $150 to $200 I've listed as **expensive,** and anything above that ranks as **very expensive.** Any extras included in the rates (for example, breakfast or other meals) are listed for each property. Categories are approximate, because hotel rates do vary considerably, depending on whether you visit in peak or off-seasons.

1 Best Bets

- **Best for Families:** All of the Disney properties cater to families, with special menus for kids and character meals, video-game arcades, free transport to the parks, and many, many recreational facilities. Camping at woodsy Fort Wilderness (☎ 407/W-DISNEY or 407/824-2900) makes for a special family experience.
- **Best Moderately Priced Hotel:** Disney's Dixie Landings (☎ 407/W-DISNEY or 407/934-6000) and Port Orleans Resort (☎ 407/W-DISNEY or 407/934-5000), offering magnificently landscaped grounds and extensive facilities, are worthy of much higher prices.
- **Best Inexpensive Hotel:** That's easy: Disney's All-Star Music (☎ 407/W-DISNEY or 407/939-6000) and All-Star Sports Resorts (☎ 407/W-DISNEY or 407/939-5000). You can't beat 'em with a stick.
- **Best Budget Motel:** Rock-bottom rates are offered at the Motel 6 on 5731 W. Irlo Bronson Memorial Hwy. (U.S. 192; ☎ 407/396-6333 or 800/4-MOTEL-6). Prices begin at just $25.99 for two, and children under 17 stay free. If you can't get in here, there's another Motel 6 close by. Both are well run and perfectly safe.
- **Best for Business Travelers:** Marriott's Orlando World Center (☎ 407/239-4200 or 800/621-0638) offers full concierge service, 24-hour room service, fine

restaurants and spacious lounges, and an extensive array of business services, not to mention golf, tennis, and other recreational facilities should you find time to relax.

- **Best for a Romantic Getaway:** The 1,500-acre grounds of the Hyatt Regency Grand Cypress (☎ 407/239-1234 or 800/233-1234) are a veritable botanic garden surrounding a swan-filled lake. Couples enjoy stunning accommodations, great service, first-rate restaurants, and every imaginable facility. Also consider the luxurious lodgings—with fireplaces and whirlpool tubs—at the adjoining Villas of Grand Cypress (☎ 407/239-4700 or 800/835-7377).
- **Best Location:** Disney's Grand Floridian Beach Resort (☎ 407/W-DISNEY or 407/824-3000), Polynesian Resort (☎ 407/W-DISNEY or 407/824-2000), or Contemporary Resort (☎ 407/W-DISNEY or 407/824-1000)—all are right on the monorail to whisk you straight to the parks for early opening.
- **Best Service:** The elegant Peabody Orlando (☎ 407/352-4000 or 800/PEABODY) offers 24-hour concierge and room service, nightly bed turndown, and other attentive pampering.
- **Best Pools:** All of the Walt Disney World resorts have terrific swimming pools—generally Olympic-size and often with themes. The pool at the Caribbean Beach Resort (☎ 407/W-DISNEY or 407/934-3400), for instance, replicates a Caribbean fort with stone walls and cannons; it also has a water slide). Outside the Disney complex, the Hyatt Regency Grand Cypress (☎ 407/239-1234 or 800/233-1234) also has a notable pool: a half-acre lagoonlike affair, it flows through rock grottos, is spanned by a rope bridge, and has 12 waterfalls and two steep water slides.
- **Best Health Club:** The Walt Disney World Dolphin (☎ 407/934-4000 or 800/227-1500) has a fully equipped Body By Jake club complete with a weight room overlooking a lake. It contains a full complement of Polaris, Lifestep, Lifecycle, and Liferower equipment; offers aerobics classes throughout the day, personal training, massage, and body wraps; and includes saunas and a large whirlpool.

2 The Perks of Staying with Mickey

Described below are the 15 Disney-owned properties (hotels, resorts, villas, wilderness homes, and campsites) and 9 privately owned properties designated as "official" hotels. All are within the Walt Disney World complex.

In addition to location (they all offer close proximity to the parks), there are a number of advantages to staying at a Disney property or official hotel, especially the former. The following are included at all Disney resorts and official hotels:

- Unlimited complimentary transportation via bus, monorail, ferry, and water taxi to and from all three Disney World parks from 2 hours prior to opening until 2 hours after closing. Unlimited complimentary transport is also provided to and from Disney Village Marketplace, Typhoon Lagoon, River Country, Blizzard Beach, Pleasure Island, Fort Wilderness, and other Disney resorts. Three properties—the Polynesian, Contemporary, and Grand Floridian—are stops on the monorail. This free transport can save a lot of money you'd otherwise have to spend on a rental car or expensive hotel shuttle buses. It also means you're guaranteed admission to all parks, even during peak times when parking lots sometimes fill up.
- Free parking at WDW parking lots (other visitors pay $5 a day).
- Reduced-price children's menus in almost all restaurants.

- Character breakfasts and/or dinners at many restaurants.
- TVs equipped with the Disney channel and Walt Disney World information stations.
- A guest services desk where you can purchase tickets to all WDW theme parks and attractions and obtain general information.
- Use of—and in some cases, complimentary transport to—the five Disney-owned golf courses and preferred tee times at them (these can be booked up to 30 days in advance).
- Access to most recreational facilities at other Disney resorts.
- Mears airport shuttle service.

Additional perks at Disney-owned hotels, resorts, villas, and campgrounds—as well as at the Walt Disney World Swan and Dolphin, but not at other official hotels—include the following:

- Charge privileges at restaurants and shops throughout Walt Disney World.
- Early admission, prior to public opening, to the Magic Kingdom, Epcot, and Disney-MGM on specific days (except at the Dolphin).
- On-premises National Car Rental desk.

WALT DISNEY WORLD CENTRAL RESERVATIONS OFFICE

To reserve a room at Disney hotels, resorts, and villas; official hotels; or Fort Wilderness homes and campsites, contact **Central Reservations Operations,** P.O. Box 10100, Lake Buena Vista, FL 32830-0100 (☎ **407/W-DISNEY**), open Monday through Friday from 8am to 10pm, Saturday and Sunday from 9am to 6pm. Have your dates and credit card ready when you call.

CRO can recommend accommodations that will suit your specific needs as to price, location (perhaps you wish to be closest to Epcot, Magic Kingdom, or Disney-MGM Studios), and facilities such as counselor-supervised child-care centers, a pool large enough for lap swimming, a state-of-the-art health club, on-premises golf or tennis (or other recreational facilities), a kitchen, and so on.

Be sure to inquire about Disney's numerous package plans, which include meals, tickets, recreation, and other features. The right package plan can save you money and time (more of your vacation is planned in advance), and a comprehensive plan is helpful in computing the cost of your vacation in advance.

CRO can also give you information about various park ticket options and make dinner-show reservations for you at the *Hoop-Dee-Doo Musical Revue* or the *Polynesian Luau Dinner Show* when you book your room.

OTHER SOURCES FOR PACKAGES

In addition to the CRO, there are other sources for packages utilizing Disney resorts. These include **Delta Dream Vacations** (☎ 800/872-7786), **USAir Vacations** (☎ 800/455-0123), **American Airlines Fly Away Vacations** (☎ 800/321-2121), **American Express Vacations** (☎ 800/241-1700), **Travel Impressions** (☎ 800/941-2639), and **Kingdom Tours** (☎ 800/872-8857). Best bet: Stop at a sizable travel agency and pick up brochures from all of the above (and others). Pore over them at home, comparing offerings to find the optimum package for your trip.

DISNEY RESORTS IN THE WORKS

Disney resorts have proven so successful that the company is continually expanding its accommodation offerings. Future developments include the following:

The moderately priced 1,980-room **Disney's Coronado Springs Resort,** which will be themed after the American Southwest. Its four- and five-story hacienda-like buildings will have terra-cotta tile roofs and palm-shaded courtyards, and the property itself will house a major 95,000-square-foot convention center and the largest ballroom in the Southeast. Additional facilities will include a white-sand beach, boat rentals, and four swimming pools. It's due to open in the fall of 1997.

A year or two further down the pike is the deluxe 1,000-room **Disney's Mediter-ranean Resort,** which will occupy a prime monorail location on the Seven Seas Lagoon. Its architecture and landscaping will "capture the romance of the sunny resorts of the Greek Islands."

3 Disney Resorts & Official Hotels

DISNEY RESORTS
VERY EXPENSIVE

✪ Disney's Beach Club Resort

1800 EPCOT Resorts Blvd. (off Buena Vista Drive; P.O. Box 10100), Lake Buena Vista, FL 32830-0100. ☎ **407/W-DISNEY** or 407/934-8000. Fax 407/354-1866. 584 rms, 17 suites. A/C MINIBAR TV TEL. $215–$295 double, depending on view and season. Extra person $15. Children under 18 stay free in parents' room. AE, MC, V. Free self- and valet parking.

From its palm-fringed entranceway and manicured gardens to its plush, sun-dappled lobby, the Beach Club resembles a luxurious Victorian Cape Cod resort. A big plus here, especially for families, is Stormalong Bay, a vast free-form swimming pool/waterpark that sprawls over 3 acres between the Yacht and Beach Clubs and flows into a lake; it includes a 150-foot serpentine water slide. So posh is the Beach Club—and so extensive are its sports facilities—that you might consider it for an upscale resort vacation even without the draw of Disney parks nearby. In a similar category are its sister property, the Yacht Club, and the Grand Floridian (see below). Charming rooms—some with balconies— are furnished in bleached woods, decorated in beachy hues, and equipped with ceiling fans, extra phones in the bath, and safes.

Dining/Entertainment: The very elegant Ariel's is open for seafood dinners nightly. Ideal for family dining is the Cape May Café, serving character breakfasts and authentic New England clambake buffet dinners. Other facilities here serve drinks, wines by the glass, light fare, and ice-cream specialties.

Services: 24-hour room service, babysitting, guest services desk, complimentary daily newspaper, boat transport to MGM theme park.

Facilities: Large swimming pool, Jacuzzi, quarter-mile sand beach, boat rentals, fishing, two tennis courts, state-of-the-art health club, volleyball/croquet/bocci ball courts, 2-mile jogging trail, coin-op washers/dryers, unisex hair salon, shops, business center, video-game arcade, Sandcastle Club (a counselor-supervised children's activity center).

✪ Disney's BoardWalk

2101 N. Epcot Resorts Blvd. (off Buena Vista Drive; P.O. Box 10100), Lake Buena Vista, FL 32830-0100. ☎ **407/W-DISNEY** or 407/939-5100 (407/939-6200 for villas). Fax 407/354-1866. 358 rms, 20 suites, 532 villas. A/C TV TEL. $225–$305 double; $380–$450 concierge level; $540–$1,525 suites. Villas: $210–$250 studios; $285–$310 one-bedrooms; $385–$405 two-bedrooms; $780 grand villas. Range depends on view and season. Extra person $15. Children under 18 stay free in parents' room. AE, MC, V. Free self- and valet parking.

Opening shortly after press time (my description here is from a hardhat tour of the construction site, enhanced by press releases), the BoardWalk—occupying 45 acres

Walt Disney World Accommodations

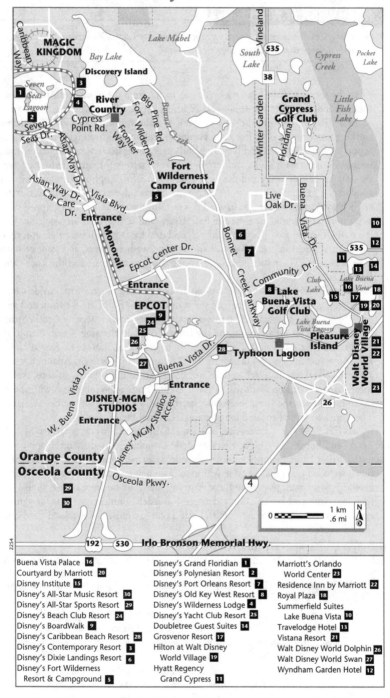

Buena Vista Palace **16**
Courtyard by Marriott **20**
Disney Institute **15**
Disney's All-Star Music Resort **30**
Disney's All-Star Sports Resort **29**
Disney's Beach Club Resort **24**
Disney's BoardWalk **9**
Disney's Caribbean Beach Resort **28**
Disney's Contemporary Resort **3**
Disney's Dixie Landings Resort **6**
Disney's Fort Wilderness
  Resort & Campground **5**

Disney's Grand Floridian **1**
Disney's Polynesian Resort **2**
Disney's Port Orleans Resort **7**
Disney's Old Key West Resort **8**
Disney's Wilderness Lodge **4**
Disney's Yacht Club Resort **25**
Doubletree Guest Suites **14**
Grosvenor Resort **17**
Hilton at Walt Disney
  World Village **19**
Hyatt Regency
  Grand Cypress **11**

Marriott's Orlando
  World Center **23**
Residence Inn by Marriott **22**
Royal Plaza **18**
Summerfield Suites
  Lake Buena Vista **10**
Travelodge Hotel **13**
Vistana Resort **21**
Walt Disney World Dolphin **26**
Walt Disney World Swan **27**
Wyndham Garden Hotel **12**

In the Words of Walt Disney

My operations are based on experience, thoughtful observation, and warm fellowship with my neighbors at home and around the world.

along the shores of Lake Crescent—takes its theme from the plush mid-Atlantic Victorian seaside resorts of the 1920s and 1930s. A large deck with rocking chairs overlooks a village green and the lake beyond, and the stunning 70-foot lobby has a working fireplace. Two- to five-story awninged buildings with shingled rooftops surround private courtyards and New England–style flower gardens, and a quarter-mile boardwalk lined with shops and restaurants is the setting for street performers and vendors (of cotton candy and the like). Extensive nightlife options here make this a good choice for singles and couples. Accommodations, done up in quaint B&B style, are just gorgeous; yours might have a brass or four-poster bed. All are equipped with safes, irons and ironing boards, and hair dryers, and refrigerators are available. Villas, though seemingly pricey, might be a good deal for large families or groups; they additionally offer kitchenettes or full kitchens and washers/dryers, and some contain whirlpool tubs. The resort is within walking distance of Epcot and the Yacht and Beach Clubs.

Dining/Entertainment: Ranged along the boardwalk promenade to provide scenic water views, dining facilities include the upscale Flying Fish Café for steak and seafood; Spoodle's—a casual Mediterranean market-theme eatery serving Greek, Spanish, and Italian fare at all meals; the Big River Grille and Brewing Works (featuring hand-crafted beers and ales); a bakery; and an espresso shop. Lots to do here at night. A 10-piece orchestra plays music from 1940 through Top 40s at the Atlantic Dance, a 1920s-style dance hall. Jellyrolls, a singalong bar, features dueling pianos. And a sports bar airs nonstop worldwide athletic events, hosts radio interviews with sports notables, and has the latest interactive sporting and virtual-reality games on hand. There are also several cocktail lounges and a carousel-theme pool bar.

Services: 24-hour room service, concierge, babysitting, boat transport (to MGM, Epcot, and Epcot resorts), guest services desk, complimentary daily newspaper.

Facilities: Large swimming pool with roller coaster–theme water slide, two additional secluded pools, kiddie pool, whirlpool, two tennis courts, croquet, bike rental, 2-mile jogging path, playground, convention center, full business center, shops, extensively equipped health club, video-game arcade, Community Hall (for games, crafts, recreational equipment rentals), Little Toots (a counselor-supervised child-care activity center).

Disney's Contemporary Resort

4600 N. World Dr. (P.O. Box 10100), Lake Buena Vista, FL 32830-0100. ☎ **407/W-DISNEY** or 407/824-1000. Fax 407/354-1865. 1,041 rms, 80 suites. A/C TV TEL. $195–$240 double; $260–$280 concierge level. Extra person $15. Children under 17 stay free in parents' room. AE, MC, V. Free self- and valet parking.

When it opened in 1971, the Contemporary's aesthetic was cutting-edge. Today its dramatic angular planes, free-form furnishings, and abstract paintings appear, rather charmingly, retro-modern. Centering on a sleek, 15-story A-frame tower, the property comprises 26 acres bounded by a natural lake and the Disney-made Seven Seas Lagoon. Kids are thrilled that the monorail whizzes right through the hotel, and they also enjoy on-premises character meals. Rooms with art deco furnishings (bleached woods with ebony accents) are decorated in neutral hues with splashes of color and cheerful Matisse prints on the walls. Amenities include safes and two phones. The 14th floor of the tower is the concierge level.

Dining/Entertainment: The magnificent 15th-floor California Grill (details in chapter 6) provides panoramic vistas of the Magic Kingdom. Other options here include the Concourse Steakhouse, the garden-theme Contemporary Café (for character breakfasts and prime rib buffet dinners), and several other spots for drinks and light fare.

Services: 24-hour room service, guest services desk, daily newspaper delivery, babysitting, boat transport (to Discovery Island, Fort Wilderness, and River Country), monorail to the Polynesian and Grand Floridian resorts.

Facilities: Two swimming pools, kiddie pool, white-sand beach with volleyball court, shuffleboard, boat rentals, unisex hair salon, six tennis courts (lessons available), shops, Delta Airlines desk, coin-op washers/dryers, full business center, extensive health club, sauna/massage/tanning rooms, video-game arcade, the Mouseketeer Clubhouse (a counselor-supervised child-care/activity center).

✪ Disney's Grand Floridian Beach Resort

4401 Floridian Way (P.O. Box 10100), Lake Buena Vista, FL 32830-0100. ☎ **407/W-DISNEY** or 407/824-3000. Fax 407/354-1866. 900 rms, 34 suites. A/C MINIBAR TV TEL. $265–$325 double, depending on view and season; $450–$470 concierge floors; $500–$1,500 suite. Extra person $15. Children under 18 stay free in parents' room. AE, MC, V. Free self- and valet parking.

The Grand Floridian is magnificent from the moment you step into its opulent five-story lobby (complete with a Chinese Chippendale aviary) under triple-domed stained-glass skylights. Here, amid plush furnishings and potted palms, a pianist entertains during afternoon tea, and an orchestra plays big-band music every evening. This could be a romantic choice for couples and honeymooners (there's even a wedding pavilion here). And if you're into fitness, you'll appreciate the first-rate health club. Though this resort houses a notable convention center and a full business center, they're in a separate building and won't inconvenience independent travelers. Sunny rooms—with private balconies or verandas overlooking formal gardens, the pool, or a 200-acre lagoon—have two-poster beds made up with lovely floral-chintz spreads. In-room amenities include safes and ceiling fans; in the bath, you'll find an extra phone, hair dryer, and terry robe.

Dining/Entertainment: Victoria & Albert's, Orlando's finest restaurant, is described in chapter 6. The lovely Grand Floridian Café, overlooking formal gardens, features southern specialties. The exposition-theme 1900 Park Fare is the setting for character breakfasts and dinners. Flagler's offers northern Italian fare. At the gazebolike Narcoossee's, grilled meats and seafood are prepared in an exhibition kitchen. Intimate and very Victorian, Mizner's Lounge features an international selection of ports, brandies, and appetizers. The Garden View Lounge off the lobby is the setting for ultraelegant afternoon teas. Other options include the Gasparilla Grill (open 24 hours) and a pool bar.

Services: 24-hour room service, nightly turndown, babysitting, on-premises monorail, boat transport to the Magic Kingdom and the Polynesian Resort, free trolley transport around the hotel grounds, shoe shine, massage, guest services desk, complimentary daily newspaper.

Facilities: Large swimming pool, kiddie pool, whirlpool, two tennis courts, boat rentals, waterskiing, croquet, volleyball, playground, jogging trails, fishing excursions, white-sand beach, unisex hair salon, coin-op washers/dryers, shops, state-of-the-art health club, wedding pavilion, video-game arcade, organized children's activities in summer and peak seasons, the Mouseketeer Clubhouse (a counselor-supervised child-care activity center).

Disney's Old Key West Resort

1510 N. Cove Rd. (off Community Drive; P.O. Box 10100), Lake Buena Vista, FL 32830-0100. ☎ **407/W-DISNEY** or 407/827-7700. Fax 407/354-1866. 709 villas. A/C TV TEL. $190–$205 deluxe rooms; $250–$275 one-bedroom vacation home; $355–$375 two-bedroom vacation home; $755 three-bedroom grand villas. Range reflects high and low seasons. AE, MC, V. Free parking.

An understated theme (at least by Disney standards) makes the Old Key West a good choice for those seeking a quieter environment. Architecturally mirroring Key West at the turn of the century, this is a "vacation ownership" (time-share) property. However, you can rent accommodations here when they're not in use by owners. The 156-acre complex is beautifully landscaped. Most accommodations are gorgeous home-away-from-home residences with living rooms (equipped with large-screen TVs and VCRs, smaller sets and extra phones in the bedroom), fully equipped kitchens, furnished patios (offering water, woodland, or fairway views; the property overlooks the Buena Vista Golf Course), and laundry rooms. Many units contain whirlpool tubs in the master suite, and grand villas have stereo systems.

Dining/Entertainment: The Key West–theme Olivia's Cafe, overlooking a canal, serves all meals. There are a few other spots for drinks and light fare.

Services: Babysitting, guest services desk, ferry service to Disney Village Marketplace and Pleasure Island, free bus transport around the grounds, food shopping.

Facilities: Two tennis courts, basketball court, white-sand play area, four swimming pools, whirlpool, kiddie pool, bicycle rental, boat rental, playground, extensive health club, sauna, shuffleboard, horseshoes, volleyball, complimentary use of washers/dryers, general store, video-game arcade, video library. The Community Hall, a recreation center, shows Disney movies nightly and offers various activities.

Disney's Polynesian Resort

1600 Seven Seas Dr. (P.O. Box 10100), Lake Buena Vista, FL 32830-0100. ☎ **407/W-DISNEY** or 407/824-2000. Fax 407/354-1866. 841 rms, 12 suites. A/C TV TEL. $200–$295 double, depending on view and season; $305–$370 concierge floors; $385–$1,100 suite. Extra person $15. Children under 18 stay free in parents' room. AE, MC, V. Free self- and valet parking.

Just below the Magic Kingdom, the 25-acre Polynesian Resort is fronted by lush tropical foliage, waterfalls, and koi ponds. Inside, its skylit lobby is a virtual rain forest of tropical plantings—gorgeous by day, but rather depressingly lit in the evenings. A private, white-sand beach—dotted with canvas cabanas, hammocks, and large swings—looks out on a 200-acre lagoon, and waterfalls, grottoes, and a water slide enhance an immense swimming pool. Large, beautiful rooms—most with balconies or patios—have canopied beds, bamboo and rattan furnishings, and walls hung with Gauguin prints. If you're willing to spend the money, this is a great choice for kids, who will enjoy the extensive Polynesian theme and child-pleasing eateries.

Dining/Entertainment: O'Hana Feast is the setting for character breakfasts and all-you-can-eat island dinners featuring open-pit rock-grilled specialties. Luau Cove hosts Mickey's Tropical Luau and the Polynesian Luau Dinner Show. There are several other restaurants and bars, including a 24-hour ice-cream parlor.

Services: Room service, babysitting, on-premises monorail, boat transport (to the Magic Kingdom, Discovery Island, Fort Wilderness, and River Country), guest services desk, complimentary daily newspaper.

Facilities: Two swimming pools, kiddie pool, boat rental, waterskiing, volleyball, playground, 1¹/₂-mile jogging trail, fishing excursions, coin-op washers/dryers, shops, video-game arcade, the Neverland Club (a counselor-supervised evening activity center for children).

✪ Disney's Yacht Club Resort

1700 Epcot Resorts Blvd. (off Buena Vista Drive; P.O. Box 10100), Lake Buena Vista, FL 32830-0100. ☎ **407/W-DISNEY** or 407/934-7000. Fax 407/354-1866. 630 rms, 12 suites. A/C MINIBAR TV TEL. $215–$295 double, depending on view and season; $360–$395 concierge level. Extra person $15. Children under 18 stay free in parents' room. AE, MC, V. Free self- and valet parking.

Though first-time visitors to Orlando—who generally spend all their time in the parks—don't require extensive recreational facilities, return visitors will appreciate the extensive sports and entertainment options here. This stunning resort—its main five-story, oyster-gray clapboard building evocative of a turn-of-the-century New England yacht club—shares a 25-acre lake, facilities, and gorgeous landscaping with the adjacent Beach Club (described above). The nautical theme carries over to very inviting rooms, decorated in snappy blue and white, with brass sconces, ship lights, and vintage maps on the walls. French doors open onto porches or balconies. Amenities include ceiling fans, extra phones in the bath, and safes. The fifth floor is a concierge level, which will especially appeal to business travelers.

Dining/Entertainment: The plush, pine-paneled Yachtsman Steakhouse grills select cuts of steak, chops, and fresh seafood over oak and hickory. The Yacht Club Galley, a comfortable family restaurant, serves American regional fare. Crew's Cup Lounge airs sporting events and offers light fare and frosted mugs of international ales and beers. And the cozy Ale and Compass Lounge, a lobby bar with a working fireplace, features specialty coffees and cocktails.

Services: 24-hour room service, babysitting, guest services desk, complimentary daily newspaper, boat transport to MGM theme park, tram transport to Epcot.

Facilities: Yacht Club facilities are identical to those of the Beach Club (see above).

EXPENSIVE

✪ Disney's Wilderness Lodge

901 Timberline Dr. (on the southwest shore of Bay Lake, just east of the Magic Kingdom; P.O. Box 10100), Lake Buena Vista, FL 32830-0100. ☎ **407/W-DISNEY** or 407/824-3200. Fax 407/354-1866. 697 rms, 25 junior suites, 6 suites. A/C TV TEL. $159–$215 double, depending on view and season; $270–$290 junior suite; $580–$625 suite. Extra person $15. Children under 18 stay free in parents' room. AE, MC, V. Free self- and valet parking.

This is one of my favorite Disney resorts, and one I think will appeal to adults as much as it does to kids. Its main dining room, Artist Point, could provide the setting for a romantic dinner. Reminiscent of rustic turn-of-the-century national park lodges, this 56-acre resort is surrounded by towering oak and pine forests. Its imposing lobby centers on a massive stone fireplace embedded with replicas of ancient Yellowstone fossils. A geothermal spring flows from the lobby into Silver Creek, which itself empties into beautiful 340-acre Bay Lake. Outside, "volcanic" meadow landscaping is punctuated by bubbling craters, a babbling brook, a cascading waterfall, and a spewing geyser. Five-minute geyser shows take place in the meadow periodically throughout the day, and nightly electric water pageants can be viewed from the shores of Bay Lake. There's a lakefront sand beach, and an immense, serpentine swimming pool is seemingly excavated out of the rocks.

The Disney Institute: The Mouse Grows Up

The Disney Institute, opening shortly after press time, is an exciting new concept designed for adults and older children (10 and up). It will allow guests to custom-design unique Walt Disney World vacations (outside the theme parks), focusing on interactive programs in dozens of diverse areas. These anxiety-free learning experiences (no grades) will be enhanced by noted guest artists and speakers. For instance, Marshall Brickman, Chris Columbus, Siskel and Ebert, Randy Newman, and Morton Gould are among the dozens of well-known directors, critics, singers, and composers Disney has tapped to participate in various Entertainment Arts programs.

Other areas of study will include Sports and Fitness, Lifestyles, Story Arts, Culinary Arts, Design, The Environment, and Architecture. Choices are almost limitless. You might opt for golf or tennis clinics, study animation, indulge in an array of luxurious spa treatments, learn topiary gardening, canoe local waterways, trace your family roots, create puppets, go out on bird-watching expeditions, or try rock climbing. Guests are encouraged to participate in a variety of different programs during their stay.

The Institute—designed to resemble a small town with a village green and architecture suggestive of barns, mills, and country houses—sprawls over 265 acres of lakes, streams, and woodlands. Its resort-style public areas and accommodations (bungalows and one- and two-bedroom townhouses) are gorgeous. An elegant, on-premises restaurant called Seasons—each of its four dining rooms representing a season of the year—features nightly changing menus and cuisines. Other facilities include an 18-hole/par-72 championship golf course, four tennis courts, golf/tennis pros/pro shops, six swimming pools, five whirlpools, a kiddie pool, bike rental/bike trails, three sand volleyball courts, a softball/multipurpose sports field, a rock-climbing wall, boat rentals, a state-of-the-art sports and fitness center, spa services/facilities, two playgrounds, a 3.4-mile jogging course, free washers/dryers, a shop, and BBQ grills/picnic tables. Nightly performances and recitals will take place in a 1,150-seat open-air amphitheater and a 250-seat performance center, and films will be screened weeknights in a 450-seat state-of-the-art movie theater. A counselor-supervised youth center will offer a full roster of daytime programs and activities for children ages 10 to 13 and teens, as well as evening activities for the latter.

The Institute, at 1960 N. Magnolia Way, is adjacent to the Disney Village Marketplace. Based on double occupancy, three-night packages will range from $582–$916, four-night packages $690–$1,135, and seven-night packages $1,208–$1,986. Pricing structure is complex. Rates include all the above listed advantages of staying at a Disney property. For further information on programs and rates, call 407/827-4800 or 800/4-WONDER.

Guest rooms—with patios or balconies overlooking lake, woodlands, or meadow scenery—are furnished in Mission-style and adorned with tribal friezes and landscape paintings of the Northwest. In-room safes are a plus.

Dining/Entertainment: The stunning, lodgelike Artist Point is described in chapter 6. The rustic, western-theme Whispering Canyon Cafe serves up hearty, all-you-can-eat family-style meals in iron skillets. There are additional venues for drinks and light fare.

Services: Room service, guest services desk, babysitting, boat transport to Magic Kingdom and Contemporary Resort, bus transport to MGM, Epcot, and other park areas.

Facilities: Immense swimming pool (see above), kiddie pool with water slide, lakefront sand beach, spa pools, boat rentals, bicycle rental, 2-mile jogging/bike trail with exercise stations, video-game arcade, gift shop, Cub's Den (a counselor-supervised activity center for children ages 4 to 12).

MODERATE

⑤ Disney's Caribbean Beach Resort

900 Cayman Way (off Buena Vista Drive; P.O. Box 10100), Lake Buena Vista, FL 32830-0100.
☎ **407/W-DISNEY** or 407/934-3400. Fax 407/354-1866. 2,112 rms. A/C MINIBAR TV TEL.
$94–$124 double. Extra person $12. Children under 17 stay free in parents' room. AE, MC, V.
Free parking.

Though facilities here aren't as extensive as those at some other Disney resorts, the Caribbean Beach offers especially good value for families. Extensively themed, it occupies 200 lush, palm-fringed tropical acres, with accommodations in five distinct Caribbean "villages" grouped around a large, duck-filled lake. The main swimming pool here replicates a Spanish-style Caribbean fort, complete with water slide, kiddie pool, and whirlpool. There are other pools as well as lakefront white-sand beaches in each village, and a 1.4-mile promenade—popular for jogging—circles the lake. An arched wooden bridge leads to Parrot Cay Island, where there's a short nature trail, an aviary of tropical birds, and a picnic area. Rooms are charming, with pineapple-motif oak furnishings and exquisite floral-print chintz bedspreads. Amenities include coffeemakers and ceiling fans; refrigerators are available at $5 per night. All rooms have verandas, many of them overlooking the lake.

Dining/Entertainment: Facilities include a festive food court, the nautically themed Captain's Tavern for American fare, and a pool bar.

Services: Room service (pizza only), guest services desk, babysitting, complimentary shuttle around the grounds.

Facilities: Video-game arcade, shops, boat rentals, bicycle rental, coin-op washers/dryers, playgrounds.

⑤ Disney's Dixie Landings Resort

1251 Dixie Dr. (off Bonnet Creek Parkway; P.O. Box 10100), Lake Buena Vista, FL 32830-0100.
☎ **407/W-DISNEY** or 407/934-6000. Fax 407/934-5777. 2,048 rms. A/C TV TEL. $95–$129
for up to four in a room. AE, MC, V. Free parking.

Low rates, extensive child-oriented facilities, and a food court make Dixie Landings popular with families, though adults traveling alone might prefer a more sedate setting. Nestled on the banks of the "mighty Sassagoula River" and dotted with bayous, it shares its 325-acre site with the Port Orleans Resort (described below). It includes Ol' Man Island, a woodsy, $3^{1}/_{2}$-acre recreation area containing an immense rustic-theme swimming pool with waterfalls cascading from a broken bridge and a water slide, a playground, children's wading pool, whirlpool, and fishin' hole (rent bait and poles and angle for catfish and bass). Accommodation areas, themed after the Louisiana countryside, are divided into "parishes," with rooms housed in stately colonnaded plantation homes or rural Cajun-style dwellings. The former, fronted by brick courtyards and manicured lawns, are elegantly decorated in Federalist blue and gold, with brass-trimmed maple furnishings. Cajun rooms, on the other hand, are set amid bayous and stands of towering pine; they feature bed frames made of bent branches, patchwork quilts, and calico-print drapes.

Dining/Entertainment: Boatwright's Dining Hall, housed in a replica of an 1800s boat-building factory, serves American/Cajun fare at breakfast and dinner. The Cotton Co-op lounge airs Monday-night football games and offers entertainment (singers and comedians), Tuesday through Saturday nights. A food court and pool bar round out the facilities.

Services: Room service (pizza only), guest services desk, babysitting, boat transport (to Port Orleans, Village Marketplace, and Pleasure Island).

Facilities: Six large swimming pools, coin-op washers/dryers, video-game arcade, bicycle rental, boat rentals, 1.7-mile riverfront jogging/biking path, Fulton's General Store.

⊖ Disney's Port Orleans Resort

2201 Orleans Dr. (off Bonnet Creek Parkway; P.O. Box 10100), Lake Buena Vista, FL 32830-0100. ☎ **407/W-DISNEY** or 407/934-5000. Fax 407/934-5353. 1,008 rms. A/C TV TEL. $95–$129 for up to four in a room. AE, MC, V. Free parking.

This beautiful resort, themed after turn-of-the-century New Orleans, shares a site on the banks of the Sassagoula with Dixie Landings, described above. Its identical room rates and comparable facilities make it, too, a good bet for families. Pastel-hued accommodation buildings, with shuttered windows and lacy wrought-iron balconies, are fronted by lovely flower gardens opening onto fountained courtyards. Pretty cherrywood furnishings, swagged draperies, and walls hung with botanical prints and family photographs make for pretty room interiors. And landscaping throughout the property is a delight, with stately oaks, formal boxwood hedges, azaleas, and fragrant jasmine.

Dining/Entertainment: Bonfamille's Café is open for breakfast and dinner, the latter featuring Creole specialties. Scat Cat's Club, a cocktail lounge off the lobby, airs Monday-night football and features family-oriented live entertainment. A food court and pool bar round out the facilities.

Services: Room service (pizza only), guest services desk, babysitting, boat transport (to Dixie Landings, Village Marketplace, and Pleasure Island).

Facilities: The larger-than-Olympic-size Doubloon Lagoon swimming pool is surmounted by an enormous water slide. Whirlpool, kiddie pool, coin-op washers/dryers, video-game arcade, bicycle rental, boat rentals, 1.7-mile riverfront jogging path, shops.

INEXPENSIVE

⊖ Disney's All-Star Music Resort

1801 W. Buena Vista Dr. (at World Drive and Osceola Parkway; P.O. Box 10100), Lake Buena Vista, FL 32830-0100. ☎ **407/W-DISNEY** or 407/939-6000. Fax 407/354-1866. 1,920 rms. A/C TV TEL. $69–$79 double. Extra person $8. Children under 18 stay free in parents' room. AE, MC, V. Free parking.

Though the unbeatable combination of rock-bottom rates and extensive facilities at Disney's All-Star Music and Sports resorts (see below) is very attractive to families, there is one caveat: rooms are small (a mere 260 square feet). They're ideal for single adults or couples traveling with one child; larger families had best be into togetherness. Nestled among pristine pine forests, this Disney property is part of a 246-acre complex that also includes the adjacent All-Star Sports Resort (see below). Its 10 buildings are musically themed around country, jazz, rock, calypso, or Broadway show tunes. The calypso building, for instance, has a palm-fringed roof frieze and balconies adorned with tropical birds and musical notes, while a convoy of 18-wheelers travels around the country building, which is adorned with fiddles and banjos. Over-sized "icons" in public areas—such as three-story cowboy boots or a walk-through jukebox—are lit by neon and fiber optics at night. Attractive rooms have musically themed bedspreads, paintings, and wallpaper borders. In-room safes are a plus.

Dining/Entertainment: There's a cheerful food court and adjoining bar.

Services: Room service (pizza only), babysitting, guest services desk.

Facilities: Two vast swimming pools, kiddie pool, playground, coin-op washers/dryers, large retail shop, video-game arcade.

⑤ Disney's All-Star Sports Resort

1701 W. Buena Vista Dr. (at World Drive and Osceola Parkway; P.O. Box 10100), Lake Buena Vista, FL 32830-0100. ☎ **407/W-DISNEY** or 407/939-5000. Fax 407/354-1866. 1,920 rms. A/C TV TEL. $69–$79 double. Extra person $8. Children under 18 stay free in parents' room. AE, MC, V. Free parking.

Adjacent to and sharing facilities with the above-listed All-Star Music Resort, this 82-acre property has an elaborate sports theme, with rooms housed in buildings designed around football, baseball, basketball, tennis, and surfing motifs. For instance, the turquoise surf buildings have waves along their rooflines, surfboards mounted on exterior walls, and pink fish swimming along balcony railings. Immense public-area "icons" here include tennis-can stairways and four-story football helmets and whistles. Cheerful rooms feature sports-action-motif bedspreads, paintings, and wallpaper borders; in-room safes are among your amenities. As noted above, however, rooms here are small.

Dining/Entertainment: There's a brightly decorated food court with an adjoining bar.

Services: Room service (pizza only), babysitting, guest services desk.

Facilities: Two vast swimming pools (one surfing themed with two 38-foot shark fins, the other shaped like a baseball diamond with an "outfield" sundeck), kiddie pool, playground, coin-op washers/dryers, shop, video-game arcade.

A DISNEY CAMPGROUND/WILDERNESS HOMES

Disney's Fort Wilderness Resort and Campground

3520 N. Fort Wilderness Trail (P.O. Box 10100), Lake Buena Vista, FL 32830-0100. ☎ **407/ W-DISNEY** or 407/824-2900. Fax 407/354-1866. 784 campsites, 408 wilderness homes. AC TV TEL (homes only). $35–$54 campsite, depending on season, location, number of people, size, and extent of hookup; $180–$215 wilderness home. AE, MC, V. Free self-parking.

This woodsy 780-acre camping resort—shaded by towering pines and cypress trees and crossed by fish-filled streams, lakes, and canals—makes an ideal venue for family vacations. Though it is a tad less central than other Disney properties, its abundance of on-premises facilities more than compensates. Secluded **campsites** offer 110/220-volt outlets, barbecue grills, picnic tables, and children's play areas. There are also **wilderness homes**—rustic, one-bedroom cabins with piney interiors that accommodate up to six people. These have cozy living rooms with Murphy beds, fully equipped eat-in kitchens, picnic tables, and barbecue grills. Guests here enjoy extensive recreational facilities ranging from a riding stable to a nightly campfire program hosted by Chip 'n' Dale.

Dining/Entertainment: The rustic, log-beamed Trails End offers buffet meals, and the cozy Crockett's Tavern features Texas fare. During summer, guests enjoy a dazzling electrical water pageant from the beach, nightly at 9:45pm. And the rambunctious *Hoop-Dee-Doo Musical Revue* takes place nightly in Pioneer Hall.

Services: Guest services desk, babysitting, boat transport (to Discovery Island, the Magic Kingdom, and the Contemporary Resort).

Facilities: Comfort station in each campground area (with restrooms, private showers, ice machines, phones, and laundry rooms), two large swimming pools, white-sand beach, horseback riding (trail rides, pony rides), petting farm, fishing, three sand volleyball courts, ball fields, tetherball, shuffleboard, bike rentals, boat rentals, 1.5-mile nature trail, 2.3-mile jogging path, two tennis courts, two 18-hole championship golf courses, shops, kennel, two video-game arcades.

LAKE BUENA VISTA/OFFICIAL HOTELS

These properties, designated "official" Walt Disney World hotels, are located on and around Hotel Plaza Boulevard. Guests at the below-listed hotels enjoy many privileges (see above). And the location is a big plus—close to the Disney parks and within walking distance of Disney Village Marketplace and Crossroads shops and restaurants, as well as Pleasure Island nightlife.

Note: In addition to the addresses and toll-free phone numbers provided in each listing below, you can also make reservations at any of these official hotels through the Central Reservations Office, P.O. Box 10100, Lake Buena Vista, FL 32830-0100 (☎ **407/W-DISNEY**).

EXPENSIVE

Buena Vista Palace

1900 Buena Vista Dr., just north of Hotel Plaza Boulevard (P.O. Box 22206), Lake Buena Vista, FL 32830. ☎ **407/827-2727** or 800/327-2990. Fax 407/827-6034. 887 rms, 127 suites. A/C MINIBAR TV TEL. $145–$235 double; $219–$250 Crown Level double; $245–$290 one-bedroom suite; $390–$455 two-bedroom suite. Range reflects view and season. Extra person $15. Children under 18 stay free in parents' room. AE, CB, DC, DISC, MC, OPT, V. Free self-parking, valet parking $6 per night.

This 27-acre waterfront resort offers boating, tennis, and other recreational facilities. Additionally, it pampers guests at a European-style spa and houses a first-rate restaurant. Accommodations—most with lake-view balconies or patios—are appealingly decorated and equipped with cable TVs (with Spectravision movie options), safes, bedroom and bath phones, and ceiling fans. There are also luxurious, residential-style one- and two-bedroom suites with living and dining rooms and a 10th-floor concierge level.

Dining/Entertainment: Arthur's 27 (perched on the 27th floor) offers haute-cuisine dinners and panoramic park views, as well as live jazz, piano-bar entertainment, and dancing in an adjoining lounge. In the Outback Restaurant (complete with a three-story indoor waterfall), an Australian storyteller entertains during dinner (steak and seafood are featured). Character breakfasts take place in the Watercress Cafe. Several other venues for dining and drinking include the Laughing Kookaburra Good Time Bar, which offers a selection of 99 beers and hosts happy-hour buffets and live bands for dancing nightly.

Services: 24-hour room service, babysitting, guest services desk (sells tickets and arranges transportation to all nearby attractions), complimentary newspaper, shoe shine/shoe repair.

Facilities: Two large swimming pools, whirlpool, kiddie pool, three tennis courts, boat rentals, 2- and 3-mile jogging paths, sand volleyball court, bike rental, playground, full business center, shops, coin-op washers/dryers, video-game arcade, Kids Stuff (a counselor-supervised child-care program). The spa offers massage, herbal wraps, a fully equipped health club, sauna, whirlpools, a unisex beauty salon, and more.

Hilton at Walt Disney World Village

1751 Hotel Plaza Blvd. (just east of Buena Vista Drive), Lake Buena Vista, FL 32830. ☎ **407/827-4000** or 800/782-4414. Fax 407/827-3890. 787 rms, 27 suites. A/C MINIBAR TV TEL. $150–$260 double, depending on season. Tower rooms $40 additional. Extra person $20. Children of any age stay free in parents' room. Inquire about weekend rates. AE, CB, DC, DISC, JCB, MC, V. Free self-parking, valet parking $6 per night.

Okay, you want to enjoy all the privileges of a Disney resort, but a relentless theme isn't your thing. This property offers traditional Hilton panache. Heralded by a palm-fringed, circular driveway leading up to an imposing waterfall and fountain, it occupies 23 beautifully landscaped acres including two large lakes. Accommodations—done up in soft earth tones with floral-print bedspreads—are equipped with cable TVs (with HBO and Spectravision movie options), coffeemakers, and phones with voicemail and computer jacks. The 9th and 10th floors comprise The Towers, a concierge level.

Dining/Entertainment: Choices include Finn's Grill, a Key West–theme steak and seafood restaurant; Benihana Japanese Steakhouse (for teppanyaki dining and nightly entertaiment, including karaoke); and a cheerful coffee shop. John T's Plantation Bar offers nightly entertainment for dancing. Kids love the Old Fashioned Soda Shoppe for pizzas, burgers, and ice-cream sundaes; it even has video games. And a cedar gazebo is the scene of frequent live poolside entertainment.

Services: 24-hour room service, babysitting, concierge (sells tickets and arranges transport to all other nearby attractions/airport).

Facilities: Two very large swimming pools, whirlpool, children's spray pool, two tennis courts, boat rental, volleyball, water volleyball, badminton, playground, unisex beauty salon, business center, fully equipped health club, sauna, shops, coin-op washers/dryers, video-game arcade, Vacation Station Kids Hotel (a counselor-supervised child-care center).

MODERATE

Courtyard by Marriott

1805 Hotel Plaza Blvd. (between Lake Buena Vista Drive and Apopka-Vineland Road/FL 535), Lake Buena Vista, FL 32830. ☎ **407/828-8888** or 800/223-9930. Fax 407/827-4623. 321 rms, 2 suites. A/C TV TEL. $89–$149 double, depending on view and season. AE, CB, DC, DISC, JCB, MC, V. Free parking.

Courtyard is a moderately priced link in the Marriott chain, with lower prices achieved via limited services. But don't envision a Spartan, no-frills atmosphere. This property was recently renovated to the tune of $4.5 million, and it's looking great. Attractive rooms—most with balconies—have in-room safes, coffeemakers, and cable TVs (with HBO, pay-movie options, and Nintendo); refrigerators are available on request. A full-service restaurant serves American fare at all meals and provides room service. There's also a lobby cocktail lounge, a poolside bar (in season), and an on-premises deli featuring pizza and frozen yogurt. The guest services desk sells tickets and arranges transport to all nearby attractions. Other facilities include two swimming pools, a whirlpool, a kiddie pool, boat rental at nearby Disney Village Marina, a playground, an exercise room, shops, coin-op washers/dryers, and a video-game arcade.

Doubletree Guest Suites Resort

2305 Hotel Plaza Blvd. (just west of Apopka-Vineland Road/FL 535), Lake Buena Vista, FL 32830. ☎ **407/934-1000** or 800/424-2900. Fax 407/934-1011. 229 suites. A/C TV TEL. $129–$235 for up to four people in a one-bedroom suite. Extra person $20. Children under 18 stay free in parents' room. Range depends on view and season. $275–$395 two-bedroom suite. AE, CB, DC, DISC, JCB, MC, V. Free self-parking.

Entered via a cheerful skylit atrium lobby with an aviary of tropical birds and theme-park murals, this seven-story, all-suite hotel is a great choice for families. Children have their own check-in desk, where they receive a free gift. Large one-bedroom suites—which can sleep up to six—are delightfully decorated and include full living rooms, dining areas, and separate bedrooms. Among your in-room amenities are a wet bar, refrigerator, coffeemaker, microwave oven, remote-control cable TVs (with pay-movie options) in the living room and bedroom, a smaller black-and-white TV in the bath, two phones, and a hair dryer.

Dining/Entertainment: The festive Streamers serves buffet and á la carte breakfasts and dinners featuring American fare with Southwestern specialties. A bar lounge adjoins, as does a theater where kids can watch Disney movies while Mom and Dad linger over coffee. Another bar serves the pool.

Services: Room service, babysitting, guest services desk (sells tickets and arranges transport to all nearby attractions).

Facilities: Large swimming pool, whirlpool, kiddie pool with fountain, two tennis courts, boat rental at nearby Disney Village Marina, jogging path, volleyball, playground, exercise room, shops (including a grocery), coin-op washers/dryers, video-game arcade.

Grosvenor Resort

1850 Hotel Plaza Blvd. (just east of Buena Vista Drive), Lake Buena Vista, FL 32830. ☎ **407/ 828-4444** or 800/624-4109. Fax 407/828-8192. 626 rms, 7 suites. A/C TV TEL. $99–$175 for up to four people, depending on view and season. AE, CB, DC, DISC, JCB, MC, OPT, V. Free self-parking, valet parking $5 per night.

In the moderately priced category, the Grosvenor is a comfortable choice with a British Colonial theme and a few unique entertainment options. Occupying 13 lushly landscaped lakeside acres, it centers on a 19-story, peach stucco building fronted by towering palms. Rooms are nicely decorated in attractive resort motif and equipped with remote-control cable TVs with VCRs (movie tapes can be rented), coffeemakers, safes, and minibars (stocked on request); refrigerators can be rented.

Dining/Entertainment: The Baskervilles Restaurant—with a Sherlock Holmes museum on the premises—hosts a Saturday-night mystery dinner–theater and buffet breakfasts and dinners, some with Disney characters. Also here: Moriarty's Pub (offering live entertainment in high season), a 24-hour food court, a pool bar, and a lounge where sporting events are aired on a large-screen TV.

Services: Room service, babysitting, guest services (sells tickets and arranges transport to all nearby attractions), free daily newspaper.

Facilities: Two swimming pools, whirlpool, kiddie pool, exercise room, two tennis courts, boat rental, playground, lawn games, coin-op washers/dryers, shops, video-game arcade.

Royal Plaza

1905 Hotel Plaza Blvd. (between Buena Vista Drive and Apopka-Vineland Road/FL 535), Lake Buena Vista, FL 32830. ☎ **407/828-2828** or 800/248-7890. Fax 407/827-6338. 373 rms, 21 suites. A/C MINIBAR TV TEL. $89–$149 for up to five people in a room; $139–$179 executive king; $119–$159 concierge level; $550 signature suite. Range reflects view and season. AE, CB, DC, DISC, JCB, MC, OPT, V. Free self- and valet parking.

As you read this, the Royal Plaza is completing a multimillion dollar renovation and upgrade, including the refurbishment of all accommodations and public areas. Spiffy new rooms—decorated in soft resort hues with bleached oak furnishings—are equipped with VCRs (movies can be rented), safes, coffeemakers, and hair dryers. Pool-view rooms have patios or balconies, and both executive kings and concierge-level rooms contain Jacuzzis (the former also offer full living rooms). Most unique

---

🏨 Family-Friendly Hotels

Disney Hostelries and Official Hotels *(see p. 46–61)* These offer many advantages for kids, including proximity to Walt Disney World parks, complimentary transportation between the hotel and the parks, and reduced-price children's menus and Disney character appearances in hotel restaurants. Extensive facilities might include lakefront beaches, boating, waterskiing, bike rentals, playgrounds, video-game arcades, swimming pools with waterfalls and slides, and/or organized children's activities.

Disney's Fort Wilderness Resort and Campground *(see p. 55–56)* All of the above and more is offered here, including nightly campfire programs with Chip 'n' Dale, trail rides, pony rides, and a petting farm . . . and you get to go camping.

Residence Inns *(see p. 63, 68, and 74)* Not only do they have swimming pools, children's playgrounds, and other recreational facilities but also accommodations with fully equipped kitchens—a potential money-saver for families. Rates include breakfast. The Lake Cecile hostelry has on-premises barbecue grills and picnic tables and offers fishing, bumper rides, jet skiing, and waterskiing on a scenic lake.

Holiday Inn Sunspree Resort Lake Buena Vista *(see p. 65)* This Holiday Inn has a special check-in desk for kids, and on-premises mascots to welcome them. Rooms are equipped with kitchenettes, and there are themed "kidsuites" available. Kids under 12 eat free in their own restaurant, where movies and cartoons are shown. Numerous organized children's activities are free. The **Holiday Inn Hotel & Suites** *(see p. 66)* offers the identical children's facilities.

---

are a pair of suites decorated, respectively, by Burt Reynolds and Barbara Mandrell, who supplied family photographs, platinum records/acting awards, and other personal memorabilia.

Dining/Entertainment: All new dining facilities are in the works at press time. They will include a Bermuda-theme steak and seafood restaurant, an adjoining lobby bar offering entertainment, a sports bar, a seasonal pool bar, and a family restaurant.

Services: Room service, babysitting, guest services (sells tickets and arranges transport to all nearby attractions), foreign currency exchange.

Facilities: Large, L-shaped swimming pool, whirlpool, four tennis courts, boat rental, fitness center, sauna, coin-op washers/dryers, shop, video-game arcade.

Travelodge Hotel

2000 Hotel Plaza Blvd. (between Buena Vista Drive and Apopka-Vineland Road/FL 535), Lake Buena Vista, FL 32830. ☎ **407/828-2424** or 800/348-3765. Fax 407/828-8933. 321 rms, 4 suites. A/C MINIBAR TV TEL. $99–$169 for up to four people, depending on room size and season. Inquire about packages. AE, CB, DC, DISC, JCB, MC, OPT, V. Free parking.

This 12-acre lakefront property is spiffy and immaculate, with rooms and public areas more upscale than you might expect at a Travelodge. Rates are also higher than the Travelodge norm but represent good value for your money. The reason: This is the company's flagship hotel. Designed to resemble a Barbados plantation manor house, it has a Caribbean resort ambience enhanced by tropical foliage and bright, floral-print fabrics and carpeting. Rooms are particularly inviting, with light bleached-wood furnishings and lovely framed botanical prints and floral friezes. Furnished balconies overlook Lake Buena Vista. Amenities include cable TVs (with Spectravision movie options and Nintendo), coffeemakers, safes, and hair dryers. Free local phone calls are a plus.

Dining/Entertainment: Traders, with a wall of windows facing a wooded area, is open for breakfast and steak and seafood dinners. On the 18th floor, Toppers offers magnificent views of Lake Buena Vista, as well as dancing, music videos, pool tables, and dartboards; it's a great vantage point for watching nightly laser shows and fireworks. There's also a cocktail bar and a casual self-service eatery.

Services: Room service, babysitting, guest services (sells tickets and arranges transport to all nearby attractions), free newspaper weekdays.

Facilities: Large swimming pool, kiddie pool, boat rental, playground, coin-op washers/dryers, shops, video-game arcade.

THE DOLPHIN & THE SWAN

The Dolphin and Swan, both within walking distance of Epcot, occupy some kind of middle ground between Disney properties and official hotels. They offer almost all the perks of Disney-owned properties, such as advance reservations at WDW restaurants and shows, including Epcot establishments, via the hotel concierge. Both are also distinctive for Michael Graves's fantastical architectural style, which people tend to adore or detest.

Walt Disney World Dolphin

1500 Epcot Resorts Blvd. (off Buena Vista Drive; P.O. Box 22653), Lake Buena Vista, FL 32830-2653. ☎ **407/934-4000** or 800/227-1500. Fax 407/934-4099. 1,373 rms, 136 suites; A/C MINIBAR TV TEL. $245–$365 double, depending on view and season; $365–$395 Dolphin Towers floors; $475–$2,750 suite. Extra person $15. Up to two children under 18 stay free in parents' room. Inquire about packages. AE, CB, DC, DISC, JCB, MC, V. Free self-parking, valet parking $6.

Though distinctive architecture is its keynote, sports enthusiasts will also appreciate this resort's extensive health club, boat rentals, and tennis facilities. Designed by whimsical architect Michael Graves, the property centers on a 27-story pyramid with two 11-story wings crowned by 56-foot twin dolphin sculptures. Graves dubs his more-Disneyesque-than-Disney creations "entertainment architecture." Close to a dozen cascading fountains on the property range from a seven-dolphin extravaganza at the entrance to waters rushing across rock-faced grottoes in a fiber-optic "starlit" foyer. A free-form rock-sculpted grotto pool—with waterfalls, a water slide, rope bridge, and three secluded whirlpools—sprawls over 2 acres between the Dolphin and the adjoining Swan. Both properties also share a white sandy beach on Crescent Lake.

There are thousands of works of art in public areas. In the rooms, walls are hung with art prints (Picasso, Matisse, and others), and painted wood furnishings are stenciled with palm trees and pineapples. Amenities include pay movies, desk and bedside phones, safes, coffeemakers, hair dryers, and irons/ironing boards. The Dolphin Towers comprise a 77-room concierge level.

Dining/Entertainment: The elegant Sum Chows serves haute-cuisine pan-Asian dinners. Juan and Only's Bar & Jail offers moderately priced Tex-Mex fare. Harry's Safari Bar & Grille, highlighting steak and seafood, is open for dinner nightly and Sunday character brunch buffets (details in chapter 6). Other venues are the delightful fish-theme Coral Cafe for American fare, an ice-cream/malt shop, a 24-hour cafeteria, Copa Banana, (with a deejay spinning tunes for nightly dancing plus karaoke), a lobby lounge, and a poolside bar.

Services: 24-hour room service, water launch transport to Epcot and Disney-MGM Studios, concierge, guest services desk (sells tickets and arranges transport to all nearby attractions), Japanese tour desk, babysitting.

Facilities: See also facilities at the Swan, below. Water volleyball, boat rentals, four hard-surface night-lit tennis courts, tennis pro shop, fully equipped Body by Jake health club, two beach volleyball courts, miniature golf, 3-mile jogging trail, coin-op washers/dryers, unisex hair salon, shops, full business center, Delta Air Lines desk, large video-game arcade, Camp Dolphin (a counselor-supervised children's activity center, open daily).

Walt Disney World Swan

1200 Epcot Resorts Blvd. (off Buena Vista Drive; P.O. Box 22786), Lake Buena Vista, FL 32830-2786. ☎ **407/934-3000**, 800/248-SWAN, or 800/228-3000 (*Note:* You may get a lower rate by reserving through this latter Westin toll-free number). Fax 407/934-4499. 702 rms, 56 suites. A/C MINIBAR TV TEL. $280–$320 double, depending on view and season; $340–$370 concierge floors; $290–$1,750 suite. Extra person $25. Children under 18 stay free in parents' room. Inquire about packages. AE, CB, DC, DISC, JCB, MC, V. Free self-parking, valet parking $7.

Operated by Westin Hotels & Resorts, this 12-story hotel—its rooftop flanked by 45-foot swan statues and seashell fountains—is adjacent to, and shares a white-sand lakeside beach and facilities with, the above-mentioned Dolphin. The hotels are connected by a canopied walkway. Here Michael Graves has created a festive interior replete with swan fountains, sea horse–motif chandeliers, hallway walls painted with beach scenes, and striped room doors evocative of cabanas. Luxurious accommodations, decorated in cheerful pastels, have furnishings stenciled with parrots and pineapples, swan- and palm-tree-motif lamps, and, like the Swan, walls hung with fine-art prints. In-room amenities include pay movies, desk and bedside phones, and safes. King-bedded rooms have pullout sleeper sofas. The 11th and 12th floors comprise the Royal Beach Club, a concierge level.

Dining/Entertainment: Serving dinner only, the casually elegant Italian-*moderne* Palio has large windows overlooking scenic canals. Strolling musicians entertain while you dine. The delightful Garden Grove Café is the setting for character breakfasts and dinners (details in chapter 6); in the evening it serves steaks and prime rib, and in the morning, a traditional Japanese breakfast is an option. A few other venues include Kimono's, which serves a wide selection of sushi and becomes a karaoke bar after 8:30pm.

Services: 24-hour room service, babysitting, complimentary water launch to Epcot and Disney-MGM Studios, guest services desk, concierge, complimentary daily newspaper, nightly turndown on request.

Facilities: See also facilities at the Dolphin, above. Olympic-size lap pool, children's wading pool, fully equipped health club, full business center, unisex hair salon, children's playground, shops, video-game arcade, Camp Swan (a counselor-supervised child-care/activity center).

4 Other Lake Buena Vista Area Hotels

All of the below-listed are within a few minutes' drive of WDW parks.

VERY EXPENSIVE

✪ Hyatt Regency Grand Cypress

1 Grand Cypress Blvd. (off FL 535), Orlando, FL 32836. ☎ **407/239-1234** or 800/233-1234. Fax 407/239-3800. For villas ☎ **407/239-4700** or 800/835-7377. Fax 407/239-7219. 676 rms, 74 suites, 146 villas. A/C MINIBAR TV TEL. $185–$310 for up to five people in a room; $305–$370 Regency Club; $190–$1,400 one- to four-bedroom villas. Range reflects room size, view, and season. AE, CB, DC, DISC, JCB, MC, V. Free self-parking, valet parking $8 per night.

This dazzling, multifacility resort is in a class by itself. Of all Orlando properties, it's the most alluring for a romantic getaway. Also appealing are its fabulous sports and recreational facilities: a half-acre swimming pool spanned by a rope bridge and flowing through rock grottoes (with 12 waterfalls and two steep water slides), three whirlpools, a white-sand beach, 12 tennis courts, a 45-hole/par-72 Jack Nicklaus–designed golf course, a 9-hole pitch-and-putt golf course, a highly acclaimed equestrian center offering lessons and trail rides, complimentary bicycles, and boat rentals, among others. Tropical plantings in the atrium lobby comprise a small rain forest, with stone-bedded streams and live birds in brass cages. And the grounds (comprising l,500 acres) are dotted with babbling brooks, flower beds, and rock gardens ablaze with bougainvillea and hibiscus. Sailboats and swans glide serenely on 21-acre Lake Windsong. Accommodations are deluxe, decorated in bright tropical hues with wicker furnishings. Amenities include pay-movie options, safes, and, in the bath, hair dryers, robes, scales, and fine toiletries. Two floors comprise the Regency Club, a concierge level. Especially gorgeous are the Mediterranean-style **Villas of Grand Cypress,** all with patios, kitchens, living rooms, and dining rooms; some have working fireplaces and whirlpool baths.

Dining/Entertainment: Hemingway's and the Black Swan are reviewed in chapter 6. At the plush La Coquina, serving "New World" cuisine (it's like continental with international sources), a harpist entertains at dinner and Sunday brunches are exquisite. Other venues include the White Horse Saloon for prime rib dinners and country music; Trellises, a bar/lounge where a jazz ensemble entertains evenings; the lovely, lake-view Cascade, serving American fare at all meals plus Japanese breakfasts; and several poolside and snack bars. The Rock Hyatt Club, adjoining the video-game arcade, offers movies, music, and games for teens 13 to 17.

Services: 24-hour room service, babysitting, concierge (sells tickets to WDW parks and other nearby attractions), free transportation around the grounds, hourly shuttle between the hotel and all WDW parks (round-trip fare is $5 per day), Mears airport shuttle.

Facilities: Golf and tennis instruction/pro shops (the golf school here has been called one of the finest in the country), 45-acre Audubon nature walk, 4.7-mile jogging path, racquetball/volleyball/shuffleboard courts, playground, car rental, unisex beauty salon, full business center, state-of-the-art health club, shops, helicopter landing pad, video-game arcade, counselor-supervised child-care center/Camp Hyatt activity center, teen activities program.

EXPENSIVE

✪ Marriott's Orlando World Center

8701 World Center Dr. (on FL 536 between I-4 and FL 535), Orlando, FL 32821. ☎ **407/239-4200** or 800/621-0638. Fax 407/238-8777. 1,504 rms, 85 suites. A/C MINIBAR TV TEL. $159–$209 for up to five people in a room (range reflects season); pool-view rooms $10 additional per night (14-day advance-purchase rates $129–$169, subject to availability); $265–$2,400 suite. AE, CB, DC, DISC, JCB, MC, OPT, V. Free self-parking, valet parking $8 per night.

Providing the only viable competition for the above-mentioned Hyatt, this sprawling 230-acre multifacility resort, just 2 miles from WDW parks, is a top convention venue that also offers numerous recreational facilties for the tourist. These include three swimming pools (one larger than Olympic size with slides and waterfalls), eight tennis courts, and an 18-hole/par-71 Joe Lee–designed championship golf course. A grand, palm-lined driveway, flanked by rolling golf greens, leads to the main building—a massive, 27-story tower fronted by flower beds and fountains. It houses spacious guest rooms, cheerfully decorated in pastel hues with bamboo and rattan furnishings. All have patios or balconies, and in-room amenities include extensive pay-movie options, irons and ironing boards, safes, and hair dryers in the bathroom.

Step outside the tower and you'll find magnificently landscaped grounds, punctuated by rock gardens, shaded groves of pines and magnolias, and cascading waterfalls; swans and ducks inhabit over a dozen lakes and lagoons spanned by graceful, arched bridges.

Dining/Entertainment: Two of the Marriott's premier restaurants, Tuscany and the Mikado Japanese Steak House, are reviewed in chapter 6. JW's Steakhouse serves sun-dappled breakfasts and lunches on a screened balcony and cozy dinners in a rustic pine interior. Allie's American Grille is a rather elegant family restaurant. And several smaller eateries and bars include the plush Pagoda Lounge for nightly piano bar entertainment and Champion's, a first-rate sports bar.

Services: 24-hour room service, babysitting, concierge, shoe shine, complimentary newspaper weekdays, Mears transportation/sightseeing desk (sells tickets to all nearby attractions, including WDW parks; also provides transport, by reservation, to WDW, other attractions, and the airport), 1-hour film developing. Round-trip fare to WDW parks is $5 per day, free for children under l2.

Facilities: Golf and tennis pro shops/instruction, 18-hole miniature golf course, two volleyball courts, four whirlpools, large kiddie pool, car rental, unisex beauty salon, extensive business center, state-of-the-art health club, coin-op washers/dryers, shops, video-game arcade, Lollipop Lounge (a counselor-supervised child-care/activities center). Inquire as well about organized children's activities—games, movies, nature walks, and more.

✪ Residence Inn by Marriott

8800 Meadow Creek Dr. (just off FL 535 between FL 536 and I-4), Orlando, FL 32821. ☎ **407/239-7700** or 800/331-3131. Fax 407/239-7605. 688 suites. A/C TV TEL. $159–$179 one-bedroom suite (for up to four people); $179–$209 two-bedroom suite (for up to six people). Range reflects season. Rates include full breakfast. AE, CB, DC, DISC, JCB, MC, V. Free parking.

This delightful, all-suite hostelry occupies 50 acres, alternating wooded grounds with neatly manicured lawns, duck-filled ponds, fountains, and flower beds. Guests here enjoy a serene environment that offers the seclusion and safety of a private community (you have to drive through a security gate to enter). They can also avail themselves of the extensive facilities at the adjoining Marriott Orlando World Center (see details above), with room-charge privileges. Tastefully decorated accommodations—with fully equipped eat-in kitchens, private balconies or patios, and large living rooms—are equipped with Spectravision movie options and VCRs (movies can be rented), two phones (kitchen and bedroom), ceiling fans, and safes. Two-bedroom units have two baths.

Dining/Entertainment: A full breakfast is available in the gatehouse each morning, a Pizza Hut is on the premises, and local restaurants deliver food.

Services: Guest services (sells tickets and provides transport to all nearby theme parks and attractions; round-trip to WDW parks is $6), babysitting, complimentary daily newspaper, next-day film developing, free food-shopping service, Mears airport shuttle.

Facilities: Three large swimming pools, two whirlpools, sports court (basketball, badminton, volleyball, paddle tennis, shuffleboard), tennis court, playground, coin-op washers/dryers, shops, two video-game arcades.

Summerfield Suites Lake Buena Vista

8751 Suiteside Dr. (off Apopka-Vineland Road/FL 535), Lake Buena Vista, FL 32836. ☎ **407/238-0777** or 800/833-4353. Fax 407/238-0778. 150 suites. A/C TV TEL. $169–$209 one-bedroom suite (for up to four people); $199–$249 two-bedroom suite (for up to eight people). Range reflects season. Rates include continental breakfast. AE, CB, DC, DISC, JCB, MC, V. Free parking.

This all-suite property, offering free transport to and from the nearby Disney parks, is an excellent choice for families—notable for its friendliness and immaculate accommodations. Spacious, residential-style suites—in buildings surrounding a palm-fringed brick courtyard with umbrella tables, fountains, and gazebos—have fully equipped eat-in kitchens, comfortable living rooms, and a bath for each bedroom. Amenities include bedroom and kitchen phones (with two lines), cable TVs in each bedroom and the living room (with HBO and pay-movie options), VCRs (movies can be rented), and irons and ironing boards.

Dining/Entertainment: Guests enjoy continental breakfast in the pleasant dining room or at umbrella tables in the courtyard; omelets and waffles may be purchased. An on-premises lobby deli (which sells light fare and liquor) also serves the pool area. Many local restaurants deliver to the hotel.

Services: Room service, guest services desk (sells tickets to WDW parks and other nearby attractions, many of them discounted), shuttle to airport/nearby attractions, free daily newspaper, complimentary grocery shopping, babysitting.

Facilities: Large swimming pool, whirlpool, kiddie pool, car rental, full business services, exercise room, coin-op washers/dryers, shop, video-game arcade.

Vistana Resort

8800 Vistana Center Dr. (off FL 535, between I-4 and FL 536), Lake Buena Vista, FL 32830. ☎ **407/239-3100** or 800/877-8787. Fax 407/239-3062. 1,028 two-bedroom villas. A/C TV TEL. $175–$275 for up to six to eight people. Range reflects season. Inquire about packages and weekly rates. AE, CB, DC, DISC, MC, OPT, V. Free self-parking.

This deluxe resort pampers guests with attentive service and a host of recreational facilities. It lies on 135 beautifully landscaped acres encompassing shimmering lakes (home to ducks and black swans) and cascading waterfalls. There are six swimming pools (one of them an immense, free-form affair with a rock waterfall, water volleyball, and water slide), seven outdoor whirlpools (some secluded), 13 tennis courts, and a full health club and recreation center (offering sauna, steam, tanning salon, and massage). Accommodations—stunning two-bedroom, two-bath villas—are decorated in beautiful tropical pastels, with bleached wood, wicker, and bamboo furnishings. All offer full living rooms (with convertible sofas and cable TVs equipped with VCRs), full dining areas (often there's a second dining setup on the patio), fully equipped kitchens, washers and dryers, and patios or balconies (some screened, many overlooking scenic waterways). Some master bedroom baths have whirlpool tubs, and there are ceiling fans in many rooms.

Dining/Entertainment: Open for all meals, the gardenlike Flamingo Cafe & Lounge—with seating at canvas umbrella tables and windows overlooking a weeping willow–shaded pond—specializes in steak, seafood, and pasta; kids love the Flamingo's create-your-own-sundae bar. There's also a casual spot called Zimmie's and a poolside bar.

Services: Babysitting, overnight photo processing, grocery shopping (you can have your room prestocked with food on request). Two guest services desks provide concierge-like assistance, sell tickets (many of them discounted), and arrange transportation to/from all nearby attractions. Transportation to/from Disney parks is free.

Facilities: Five children's wading pools, an 18-hole/par-38 miniature golf course, basketball/sand volleyball/shuffleboard courts, tennis pro shop/instruction, bicycle rental, raft rental, children's playgrounds, game library, outdoor barbecue grills, 1 1/2-mile/12-station jogging path, general store (includes movie-rental library), three video-game arcades. A comprehensive daily activities schedule for adults and children features nature walks, casino nights, Ping-Pong tournaments, arts and crafts, barbe-cues, karaoke, and much, much more.

MODERATE

⑤ Holiday Inn Sunspree Resort Lake Buena Vista

13351 FL 535 (between FL 536 and I-4), Lake Buena Vista, FL 32821. ☎ **407/239-4500** or 800/FON-MAXX. Fax 407/239-7713. 507 rms. A/C TV TEL. $89–$129 for up to four people, depending on season. AE, CB, DC, DISC, JCB, MC, V. Free parking.

About a mile from the Disney parks, this Holiday Inn offers the chain's "no surprises" dependability, while catering to children in a big way. Kids "check in" at their own pint-size desk; receive a free fun bag containing a video-game token coupon, a lolli-pop, and a small gift; and get a personal welcome from animated raccoon mascots, Max and Maxine. Camp Holiday activities—magic shows, clowns, sing-alongs, arts and crafts, and much more—are available at a minimal charge for kids ages 2 to 12. And parents can arrange (by reservation) for Max to come tuck a child into bed. Pretty rooms have kitchenettes with refrigerators, microwave ovens, and coffee-makers. And if you're renting a second room for the children, "kidsuites" here—themed as igloos, space capsules, Noah's Ark, et al.—sleep up to three. Amenities include VCRs (tapes can be rented), hair dryers, and safes.

Dining/Entertainment: Maxine's serves all meals, including steak and seafood dinners. Max's Funtime Parlor offers nightly Bingo and karaoke; it also airs sport-ing events on a large-screen TV. Kids 12 and under eat all meals free, either in a hotel restaurant with parents or in Kid's Kottage, a cheerful facility where movies and car-toons are shown and dinner includes a make-your-own sundae bar.

Services: Room service, babysitting, guest services desk (sells tickets to all nearby attractions, including WDW parks), free scheduled transport to WDW parks (there's a charge for transport to other nearby attractions), telephone grocery shopping, Mears airport shuttle.

Facilities: Large swimming pool, two whirlpools, kiddie pool, Ping-Pong and bil-liards, playground, fitness center, coin-op washers/dryers, shops, car rental, video arcade, Camp Holiday (a counselor-supervised child-care/activity center for ages 2 to 12).

Wyndham Garden Hotel

8688 Palm Pkwy. (between FL 535 and I-4), Lake Buena Vista, FL 32830. ☎ **407/239-8500** or 800/WYNDHAM. Fax 407/239-8591. 164 rms, 3 suites. A/C TV TEL. $74–$104 double, depending on season; $125–$150 suites. Extra person $10. Children under 18 free. AE, CB, DC, DISC, Optima, MC, V. Free self-parking.

This property's location—on a pleasant, tree-lined street and overlooking a lake out back—is a big plus. The Crossroads Shopping Center and Walt Disney World Vil-lage put dozens of shops, services, and restaurants within easy walking distance. And to compete with nearby "official" hotels, the Wyndham Garden offers free shuttle transport to/from Disney parks. A recent massive renovation gave public areas a fresh new look, and rooms have been redecorated with bleached pine furnishings and cheerful resort-theme prints. They're equipped with cable TVs (with pay movies, a tourism-information station, and Nintendo), hair dryers, irons and ironing boards, and coffee makers; some have convertible sofas.

Dining/Entertainment: The Garden Café, serving American fare at breakfast and dinner, has an outdoor poolside seating area and an adjoining bar/lounge.

Services: Room service, complimentary shuttle to/from Disney parks, guest ser-vices desk (sells tickets, many of them discounted, and arranges transport to all nearby attractions), babysitting, complimentary daily newspaper.

Facilities: Nice-size swimming pool and whirlpool, coin-op washers/dryers, exercise room, business center, small video-game arcade.

INEXPENSIVE

⑤ Comfort Inn

8442 Palm Pkwy. (between FL 535 and I-4), Lake Buena Vista, FL 32830. ☎ **407/239-7300** or 800/999-7300. Fax 407/239-7740. 640 rms. A/C TV TEL. $39–$69 for up to four people, depending on season. AE, CB, DC, DISC, MC, V. Free parking.

This is an ideally located, large, and attractively landscaped property with two small manmade lakes amid expanses of manicured lawn and lush greenery. And it offers free transport to WDW parks, which are just 2 miles away. In-room safes are among the amenities in immaculate guest rooms. The Boardwalk Buffet serves reasonably priced buffet meals at breakfast and dinner; kids under 12 eat free. A bar/lounge adjoins. And complimentary tea and coffee are served in the lobby every afternoon. The guest services desk sells tickets (most of them discounted) and provides transport to all nearby theme parks, dinner shows, and the airport. On-premises facilities include two swimming pools, coin-op washers/dryers, a gift shop, and a video-game arcade. Pets are permitted.

5 On U.S. 192/Kissimmee

This very American stretch of highway dotted with fast-food eateries isn't what you'd call scenic, but it does contain many inexpensive hotels within 1 to 8 miles of WDW parks.

MODERATE

⑤ Holiday Inn Hotel & Suites

5678 Irlo Bronson Hwy. (U.S. 192; between I-4 and Poinciana Boulevard), Kissimmee, FL 34746. ☎ **407/396-4488** or 800/FON-KIDS. Fax 407/396-8915. 559 rms, 55 suites. A/C TV TEL. $75–$105 for up to four people; one-bedroom suites with kitchenettes $99–$195. Range reflects season. Inquire about packages. AE, CB, DC, DISC, JCB, MC, V. Free parking.

Just 3 miles from the entrance to the Magic Kingdom, this attractively landscaped, 23-acre property offers identical facilities to the Holiday Inn Sunspree Resort Lake Buena Vista (described earlier), including its own Camp Holiday and all the kid-pleaser features (here the welcoming mascots are Holiday and Holly Hound). There's even a small merry-go-round in the lobby. Accommodations are in two-story, motel-style buildings enclosing courtyard swimming pools. Pets are permitted.

Dining/Entertainment: The Vineyard Cafe serves breakfast and dinner, the latter featuring steak and seafood. There's also a food court and a pool bar proffering frozen tropical drinks. Kids 12 and under eat all meals free, either in a hotel restaurant with parents or in the Gingerbread House, a cheerful facility where movies and cartoons are shown on a large-screen TV and dinner includes a make-your-own sundae bar.

Services: Room service, babysitting, guest services desk (sells tickets to all nearby attractions, including WDW parks), free scheduled transport to WDW parks (there's a charge for transport to other nearby attractions), telephone grocery shopping, Mears airport shuttle.

Facilities: Two Olympic-size swimming pools, two whirlpools, kiddie pool, playground, two tennis courts, sand volleyball, basketball court, coin-op washers/dryers, shops, car rental, two video-game arcades, Camp Holiday (a counselor-supervised child-care/activity center for ages 3 to 12).

Kissimmee Area Accommodations

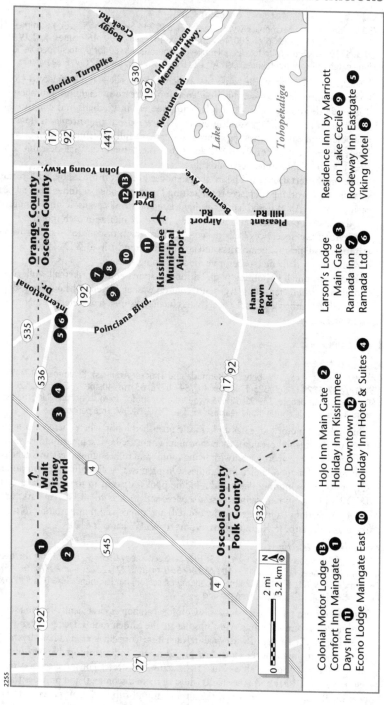

Colonial Motor Lodge **13**
Comfort Inn Maingate **1**

Days Inn **11**
Econo Lodge Maingate East **10**

Holo Inn Main Gate **2**
Holiday Inn Kissimmee Downtown **12**
Holiday Inn Hotel & Suites **4**

Larson's Lodge Main Gate **3**
Ramada Inn **7**
Ramada Ltd. **6**

Residence Inn by Marriott on Lake Cecile **9**
Rodeway Inn Eastgate **5**
Viking Motel **8**

Residence Inn by Marriott on Lake Cecile

4786 W. Irlo Bronson Memorial Hwy. (between FL 535 and Siesta Lago Drive), Kissimmee, FL 34746. ☎ **407/396-2056** or 800/468-3027. Fax 407/396-2909. 159 suites. A/C TV TEL. Studios $119–$129 for up to four people; bilevel penthouses $189 for up to six people. Rates include extended continental breakfast. AE, CB, DC, DISC, JCB, MC, OPT, V. Free parking.

Beautiful landscaping on the banks of 223-acre Lake Cecile—and home-away-from-home accommodations—set this Residence Inn apart from neighboring properties. Tastefully decorated suites offer fully equipped eat-in kitchens and comfortable living room areas. All but studio doubles have wood-burning fireplaces (logs are available), and cathedral-ceiling penthouses contain full baths upstairs and down. Many suites have balconies overlooking the lake. Amenities include cable TVs (VCRs are available on request) and safes.

Dining/Entertainment: The lovely gatehouse lounge off the lobby, with comfy sofas facing a working fireplace, is the setting for an extended continental breakfast each morning. An al fresco bar serves light fare and drinks poolside on a canopied wooden deck. Local restaurants deliver food (there are menus in each room).

Services: Guest services (sells tickets—most of them discounted—and provides transport to all nearby theme parks and attractions; round-trip to WDW parks is $7), complimentary daily newspaper, free food-shopping service.

Facilities: Small swimming pool, whirlpool, sports court (basketball, volleyball, badminton, paddle tennis), playground, coin-op washers/dryers, 24-hour food shop, picnic tables, barbecue grills. Lake activities include fishing, jet skiing, bumper rides, and waterskiing.

INEXPENSIVE

Colonial Motor Lodge

1815 W. Vine St. (U.S. 192, between Bermuda and Thacker Avenues), Kissimmee, FL 34741. ☎ **407/847-6121** or 800/325-4348. Fax 407/847-0728. 83 rms, 40 apts. A/C TV TEL. $22.95–$50 for up to four people; $49.95–$89.95 two-bedroom apt for up to six people. Range reflects season. Rates include continental breakfast. AE, DC, DISC, MC, V. Free parking.

This well-run motor lodge has a pleasantly furnished lobby where there's a complimentary continental breakfast each morning. There are both standard motel rooms and two-bedroom apartments (with living rooms and fully equipped eat-in kitchens) that represent a good choice for families. On-premises facilities include two junior Olympic-size swimming pools and a kiddie pool. Adjacent to the Colonial are an IHOP and a shopping center. Guest services sells tickets to all Disney parks and nearby attractions (some of them discounted) and offers paid transportation to/from them and the airport. Round-trip transport to WDW parks is $12.

Comfort Inn Maingate

7571 W. Irlo Bronson Memorial Hwy. (U.S. 192, between Reedy Creek Boulevard and Sherbeth Road), Kissimmee, FL 34747. ☎ **407/396-7500** or 800/221-2222. Fax 407/396-7497. 281 rms. A/C TV TEL. $33–$65 double, depending on season; garden rooms $6–$10 additional. AE, CB, DC, DISC, JCB, MC, V. Free parking.

Just 1 mile from the Disney parks, this Comfort Inn houses clean, spiffy-looking standard motel accommodations. Most upscale are the garden rooms, facing a lawn with a gazebo; they're equipped with small refrigerators, coffeemakers, and hair dryers. A restaurant on the premises serves low-priced meals, and a comfortable bar/lounge adjoins. There's also a Waffle House right across the street. The guest services desk sells tickets to Disney and other parks (most of them discounted) and provides transport to all nearby attractions and the airport; round-trip to WDW parks costs $7.

Facilities include a swimming pool, playground, coin-op washers/dryers, and video-game arcade.

Days Inn

4104 and 4125 W. Irlo Bronson Memorial Hwy. (U.S. 192, at Hoagland Boulevard North), Kissimmee, FL 34741. ☎ **407/846-4714**, or 800/647-0010, or 800/DAYS-INN. Fax 407/932-2699. 194 rms, 32 efficiency units. A/C TV TEL. $29–$59 for up to four people, depending on season; $37–$63 efficiency unit; $55–$75 Jacuzzi room (for one or two people). Rates may be higher during major events. Rates include continental breakfast. AE, CB, DC, DISC, MC, V. Free parking.

Offering good value for your hotel dollar, these two Days Inn properties—on either side of U.S. 192—share facilities, including two swimming pools, coin-op washers and dryers, and a video-game arcade. A big plus: round-trip fare to WDW parks is free. Several restaurants (which deliver food), a large shopping mall with a 12-theater movie house, and a supermarket are in close walking distance. Rooms at both locations are clean and attractive standard motel units. Best bets are efficiencies with fully equipped kitchenettes at 4104. On the other hand, at 4125 you can ask for a room with a large Jacuzzi, a refrigerator, and a microwave oven. All accommodations offer free HBO, pay-movie options, and in-room safes, and both locations serve free coffee, juice, and doughnuts in their lobbies each morning. Guest services at 4104 sells tickets (many of them discounted) and arranges transport to all nearby attractions, including WDW parks. Airport transfers can be arranged.

⊕ Econo Lodge Maingate East

4311 W. Irlo Bronson Memorial Hwy. (U.S. 192, between Hoagland Boulevard and FL 535), Kissimmee, FL 34746. ☎ **407/396-7100** or 800/ENJOY-FL. Fax 407/239-2636. 173 rms. A/C TV TEL. $29–$79 for up to four people, depending on season. AE, CB, DC, DISC, JCB, MC, V. Free parking.

Ever spent a sleepless night at a motel (the word does derive from "motorist" and "hotel") because of traffic noise? It won't happen here. At this attractively landscaped Econo Lodge, accommodations are set well back from the highway in rustic two- and three-story buildings with cedar balconies and roofing. Well-maintained rooms are equipped with safes, and small refrigerators can be rented. A pool bar serves light fare, including full breakfasts and lunches at umbrella tables under towering live oaks. The guest services desk sells tickets (most of them discounted) and provides transport to all nearby attractions and the airport. Scheduled round-trip transport to/from WDW parks is free. On-premises facilities include a large swimming pool, kiddie pool, volleyball, shuffleboard, horseshoes, coin-op washers/dryers, picnic tables, barbecue grills, and a video-game arcade. This is one of six area hotels under the same ownership, all of which can be booked via the above toll-free number.

Hojo Inn Main Gate

6051 W. Irlo Bronson Memorial Hwy. (U.S. 192, just east of I-4), Kissimmee, FL 34747. ☎ **407/396-1748** or 800/288-4678. Fax 407/649-8642. 358 rms, 9 family suites. A/C TV TEL. $60–$75 for up to four people, depending on season. Children under 19 stay free. Add $10 for an efficiency unit with a kitchenette. $80–$95 family suite. Inquire about packages. AE, CB, DC, DISC, JCB, MC, V. Free self-parking.

Several factors make this Howard Johnson's property a worthwhile choice. Just 2 miles from the Magic Kingdom—and offering free transport to and from the Disney parks—it maintains a special guest services phone number (☎ 800/TOUR-FLA) that you can call in advance of your trip to arrange attraction tickets, paid transportation, car rental, and other vacation needs. Accommodations here are nicely decorated with quilted bedspreads and beach-theme paintings on the walls; amenities include cable

TVs (with pay-movie options and Nintendo) and safes. Efficiency units have fully equipped kitchenettes with small refrigerators, two-burner stoves, and sinks. And family suites have both full kitchens and living rooms with convertible sofas.

Facilities include a medium-size swimming pool, whirlpool, kiddie pool, children's playground, coin-op washers/dryers, video-game arcade, car-rental desk, and pool table. Adjoining the property is a large water park called Watermania and an IHOP where kids under 12 with an adult eat free. On premises, a pool bar serves light fare and drinks, and coffee and tea are served each morning in the lobby. Guest services sells tickets to all Disney parks and nearby attractions (some of them discounted) and offers transportation to/from them and the airport.

⑤ Holiday Inn Kissimmee Downtown
2009 W. Vine St. (U.S. 192 at Thacker Avenue), Kissimmee, FL 34741. ☎ **407/846-2713** or 800/624-5905. Fax 407/846-8695. 200 rms. A/C TV TEL. $38–$89 for up to four people, depending on season; add $15 for an efficiency unit with a kitchenette. Children under 19 stay free in parents' room. AE, CB, DC, DISC, MC, V. Free parking.

Just 8 miles from Walt Disney World, this Holiday Inn gives you a few more facilities than you might expect in its price range. It offers immaculate motel rooms, as well as efficiency units with living room areas and fully equipped kitchens. Pets are permitted. A steakhouse serves all meals and provides room service, and its adjoining bar/lounge features karaoke nights. The guest services desk sells tickets (many of them discounted) to all nearby theme parks and can arrange transportation to/from other nearby attractions and the airport. Round trip to WDW parks is $10. Facilities include two swimming pools (one very large), a kiddie pool, a whirlpool, a playground, a tennis court, a gift shop, coin-op washers/dryers, and a video-game arcade.

⑤ Larson's Lodge Main Gate
6075 W. Irlo Bronson Memorial Hwy. (U.S. 192, just east of I-4), Kissimmee, FL 34747. ☎ **407/ 396-6100** or 800/327-9074. Fax 407/396-6965. 128 rms. A/C TV TEL. $39–$79 double, depending on season; add $15 for an efficiency unit with a kitchenette. Extra person $8. Children under 19 stay free in parents' room. Inquire about packages. AE, CB, DC, DISC, MC, V. Free parking.

With its large, on-premises water park (Watermania), playground, poolside picnic tables, barbecue grills, and cheerful on-site Shoney's restaurant, Larson's Lodge is a good choice for families. Accommodations are equipped with VCRs (movies can be rented), small refrigerators, microwave ovens, and safes. There are also efficiency units with fully equipped kitchenettes. A supermarket is just a few minutes away by car.

The guest services desk sells tickets to all nearby theme parks (many of them discounted), and can arrange transport to other nearby attractions and the airport. Round trip to WDW parks is $8. On-premises facilities include a large swimming pool and whirlpool, shops, coin-op washers/dryers, and a video-game arcade. Guests enjoy a free newspaper and coffee in the lobby each morning and free tennis at the above-mentioned Holiday Inn Kissimmee Downtown. Pets are permitted.

Ramada Inn
4559 W. Irlo Bronson Memorial Hwy. (U.S. 192, between Siesta Lago Drive and Bass Road/Old Vineland Road), Kissimmee, FL 34746. ☎ **407/396-1212** or 800/544-5712. Fax 407/ 396-7926. 114 rms. A/C TV TEL. $23.95–$44.95 for up to four people, depending on season; $6 per night additional for efficiency unit. AE, DC, DISC, MC, V. Free self-parking.

This Ramada offers standard motel rooms; refrigerators are available on request for $6 a night. Efficiency units offer two-burner stoves, extra sinks, and small refrigerators (no eating or cooking utensils are provided). Facilities include coin-op washers/dryers, a swimming pool, children's playground, and picnic tables. The 1950s-style Hollywood Diner—which has an adjoining bar/lounge—serves American fare at all meals. Shuttle service to WDW parks is available for $10 per person, round-trip. Pets are accepted ($6 per night).

Ramada Ltd.

5055 W. Irlo Bronson Memorial Hwy. (U.S. 192, between Poinciana Boulevard and FL 535), Kissimmee, FL 34746. ☎ **407/396-2212** or 800/446-5669. Fax 407/396-0253. 107 rms. A/C TV TEL. $27.95–$45 for up to four people, depending on season. Rates include continental breakfast. AE, DC, DISC, MC, V. Free self-parking.

Less than 4 miles from Walt Disney World parks, this Ramada houses its rooms in a three-story stucco building. Refrigerators are available on request for $6 a night. Facilities include a swimming pool and coin-op washers/dryers. Continental breakfast is served in the lobby each morning. Shuttle service to WDW parks is available for $9 per person, round-trip. Pets are accepted ($6 per night).

Rodeway Inn Eastgate

5245 W. Irlo Bronson Memorial Hwy. (U.S. 192, between Poinciana and Polynesian Isle Boulevards), Kissimmee, FL 34746. ☎ **407/396-7700** or 800/423-3864. Fax 407/396-0293. 200 rms. A/C TV TEL. $31–$55 for up to four people, depending on view and season. Rates may be higher during major events. AE, CB, DC, DISC, JCB, MC, V. Free parking.

The Rodeway's U-shaped configuration of two-story pink stucco buildings forms an attractively landscaped courtyard around a large swimming pool. Families will appreciate picnic tables and a children's play area on the lawn. Rooms are nicely decorated. Lucille's Cafe serves buffet breakfasts, and the comfy Half Time Lounge, where sporting events are aired on a large-screen TV, has a pool table and dartboards. Other facilities include a video-game room, coin-op washers/dryers, and a gift shop. Guest services sells tickets to all WDW parks and nearby attractions (many of them discounted) and offers transportation to/from them and the airport. Round-trip transport to WDW parks is $7.

Viking Motel

4539 W. Irlo Bronson Memorial Hwy. (U.S. 192, between FL 535 and Hoagland Boulevard North), Kissimmee, FL 34746. ☎ **407/396-8860** or 800/396-8860. Fax 407/396-2088. 49 rms. A/C TV TEL. $25–$60 double, depending on season. Extra person $5. Add $10 for kitchenette units. AE, DISC, MC, V. Free self-parking.

Kids love this family-owned property housed in a fantasy castle, with towers topped by little Viking ships. Owners Bert and Christine Langenstroer are from Germany, and they've prettified their motel's Alpine-style balconies with neat flower boxes. Immaculate rooms have peach stucco walls hung with old-fashioned lithograph portraits in oval frames and kitschy landscape paintings. All are equipped with cable TVs (with HBO), safes, and Magic Fingers bed massagers. Some units have refrigerators, and a few offer fully equipped kitchenettes and cozy breakfast nooks. On-premises facilities include coin-op washers/dryers, a shuffleboard court, a Viking-theme playground and sandbox, and a small free-form swimming pool with outdoor tables under thatched umbrellas and barbecue grills on the sundeck. A Waffle House restaurant and a miniature golf course are next door. The guest services desk sells tickets, many of them discounted, to nearby attractions, though it does not carry WDW park tickets. Transportation is, however, available to WDW parks (round-trip fare is $8 per person), other area attractions, and the airport. The Viking is 6 miles from the Magic Kingdom.

6 Accommodations on International Drive

Hotels and resorts listed here are 7 to 10 miles north of the Walt Disney World parks (a quick freeway trip on I-4) and close to Universal Studios and Sea World. Though you won't get away from rambunctious kids anywhere in this town, International Drive properties do tend to be more adult oriented.

Note: There's a moderately priced Courtyard by Marriott (see description of a similar property under "Lake Buena Vista/Official Hotels," above) at 8600 Austrian Court, off International Drive, Orlando, FL 32819 (☎ **407/351-2244** or 800/ 321-2211; fax 407/351-1933).

VERY EXPENSIVE

✪ Peabody Orlando

9801 International Dr. (between the Beeline Expressway and Sand Lake Road), Orlando, FL 32819. ☎ **407/352-4000** or 800/PEABODY. Fax 407/351-0073. 834 rms, 57 suites. A/C MINIBAR TV TEL. $230–$270 for up to three people; $290 for Peabody Club; $425–$1,350 suite. Children under 18 stay free in parents' room; seniors 50 and over pay $89. Inquire about packages and holiday/summer discounts. AE, CB, DC, DISC, JCB, MC, V. Free self-parking, valet parking $6 per night.

This deluxe, 27-story resort (one of Florida's finest) has some especially famous avian residents. Every morning at 11am, five fluffy ducks proudly parade along a red carpet to the beat of John Philip Sousa's *King Cotton* march, their journey culminating at a marble fountain in the lobby where they splash about all day. The hallmark of the Peabody is an ambience of sophistication not found elsewhere in Orlando, and this aura extends to its top-rated restaurants. Luxurious rooms have handsome bamboo and bleached-wood furnishings and walls hung with quality artworks. Amenities include two phones, cable TVs with Spectravision and laser-disc movie setups (there's a vast video library), and, in the bath, cosmetic lights, fine European toiletries, a hair dryer, and a small TV. The concierge-level Peabody Club occupies the top three floors. *Seniors:* Do note the over-50 price above, compensation for wrinkles indeed.

Dining/Entertainment: Dux, the Peabody's elegant signature restaurant; Capriccio, for sophisticated Italian fare; and the casual 24-hour B-Line Diner are detailed in chapter 6. Combos play jazz, blues, and show tunes in the atrium Lobby Bar nightly. The lobby itself is the weekday setting for exquisite afternoon English teas. Sporting events are aired in the cozy, duck-theme Mallards Lounge. And al fresco jazz concerts take place on the fourth-floor recreation level in the spring and fall.

Services: 24-hour room service, 24-hour concierge, nightly bed turndown on request, free daily newspaper, babysitting, transport between the hotel and all WDW parks throughout the day (unlimited daily round-trips cost $6), Mears transportation/ sightseeing desk (sells tickets to all nearby attractions, including WDW parks and dinner shows; also provides transport, by reservation, to attractions and the airport).

Facilities: Olympic-length swimming pool, indoor and outdoor whirlpools, kiddie pool, four tennis courts, golf privileges at four nearby courses, 7-mile jogging path, car rental, Delta Airlines desk, full-service unisex salon, business center, state-of-the-art health club, shops, video-game arcade.

EXPENSIVE

Summerfield Suites

8480 International Dr. (between the Beeline Expressway and Sand Lake Road), Orlando, FL 32819. ☎ **407/352-2400** or 800/833-4353. Fax 407/238-0777. 146 suites. A/C TV TEL.

$159–$199 one-bedroom suite (for up to four people); $179–$239 two-bedroom suite (for up to eight people). Range reflects room size and season. Rates include continental breakfast. AE, CB, DC, DISC, MC, V. Free parking.

This delightful hotel—with potted palms on open-air balconies creating a welcoming resort ambience—is built around a nicely landscaped central courtyard. Like its sister property in Lake Buena Vista (see above), it's notably friendly and well run. Spacious, neat-as-a-pin residential-style suites, very attractively decorated, contain fully equipped eat-in kitchens, comfortable living rooms, and large dressing areas. All offer irons and ironing boards, phones in each bedroom and the kitchen, and satellite TVs (with HBO and pay-movie options) in each bedroom and the living room (the latter with a VCR; rent movies downstairs).

Dining/Entertainment: An extensive continental buffet breakfast is served in a charming dining room (waffles and omelets can be purchased), and the cozy lobby bar is a popular gathering place in the evening. Local restaurants deliver food to the premises.

Services: Babysitting, concierge/tour desk (sells tickets to WDW parks and other nearby attractions), daily newspaper delivery, transport between the hotel and all WDW parks (round-trip fare is $7), shuttle available to the airport and nearby attractions, complimentary grocery shopping.

Facilities: Nice-size swimming pool, whirlpool, kiddie pool, car rental, business services, exercise room, coin-op washers/dryers, 24-hour shop, video-game arcade.

MODERATE

Ⓢ Orlando Marriott

8001 International Dr. (at Sand Lake Road), Orlando, FL 32819. ☎ **407/351-2420** or 800/421-8001. Fax 407/351-5016. 1,062 rms, 16 suites. A/C TV TEL. $79–$120 double, depending on view and season; $110–$300 suite. Extra person $10. Children under 18 stay free in parents' room. AE, DC, DISC, MC, V. Free self-parking.

The grounds at this verdant, 48-acre property—varying neatly manicured lawns and flower beds with fern gullies, lush tropical foliage, and serene lagoons—provide a feeling of resort seclusion that's all the more appealing because you're actually in the heart of a busy area, with proximity to many great restaurants. And rates are very reasonable in light of the facilities you'll enjoy here. Accommodations, housed in pale pink stucco bilevel villas, are attractively decorated in resort mode; half have balconies or patios, and about a fifth contain full kitchens. All offer safes and TVs with pay-movie stations; many are also equipped with hair dryers, electric shoe-shine machines, and irons/ironing boards.

Dining/Entertainment: The tropical-theme Grove specializes in steaks, prime rib, and seafood. The Chelsea Cafe serves American fare at all meals. A club called Illusions features a deejay spinning Top 40 tunes, as well as blackjack, a pool table, and darts. Other choices are Pizza Hut, Kentucky Fried Chicken, and Taco Bell, plus a cozy lobby bar and several poolside bars.

Services: Room service, babysitting, guest services desk (sells tickets, many of them discounted, and arranges transportation to/from WDW parks and all other nearby attractions), 24-hour free tram service around the property, Mears airport shuttle. Round-trip fare to WDW parks is $8.

Facilities: Three swimming pools (one quite large), two kiddie pools, whirlpool, four tennis courts, sand volleyball court, playground, business center, exercise room, 1.4-mile jogging trail, coin-op washers/dryers, car rental, unisex hair salon, shops, two video-game arcades.

⑤ Residence Inn by Marriott

7975 Canada Ave. (just off Sand Lake Road, a block east of International Drive), Orlando, FL 32819. ☎ **407/345-0117** or 800/227-3978. Fax 407/352-2689. 176 suites. A/C TV TEL. $105 studio accommodating up to four people; $115 studio double (up to four people); $165 bilevel penthouse (up to eight people). Rates include extended continental breakfast. AE, DC, DISC, MC, V. Free parking.

Marriott's Residence Inns were designed to offer home-away-from-home comfort for traveling businesspeople, but the concept also works well for families. Accommodation buildings are surrounded by well-tended lawns, shrubbery, and beds of geraniums, and handsomely decorated suites offer full eat-in kitchens and comfortable living room areas. All but studio doubles have wood-burning fireplaces, and two-bedroom penthouses have full baths upstairs and down. Amenities include irons and ironing boards and safes.

Dining/Entertainment: The comfortably furnished gatehouse is the setting for an extended continental breakfast daily, and complimentary beer, wine, and hors d'oeuvres Monday through Thursday from 5:30 to 7pm. If you're traveling alone, it's easy to meet people in this congenial setting. Local restaurants deliver food (there are menus in each room).

Services: Guest services desk (sells tickets—most of them discounted—and provides transport to all nearby theme parks and attractions), complimentary daily newspaper, free food-shopping service (microwave dinners are sold in the lobby), Mears airport shuttle. Round-trip fare to WDW parks is $10.

Facilities: Large swimming pool, whirlpool, basketball court, sand volleyball court, free use of nearby health club, coin-op washers/dryers, food/sundries shop, picnic tables, barbecue grills.

INEXPENSIVE

Country Hearth Inn

9861 International Dr. (between Beeline Expressway and Sand Lake Road), Orlando, FL 32819. ☎ **407/352-0008** or 800/447-1890. Fax 407/352-5449. 150 rms. A/C TV TEL. $59–$139 double, depending on view and season. Extra person $10. Children under 18 stay free in parents' room. Rates include continental breakfast. AE, CB, DC, DISC, MC, V. Free self-parking.

Though it doesn't offer much in the way of resort facilities, the Country Hearth Inn's low rates, great location, and very pretty rooms and restaurant—not to mention wine and cheese receptions for guests several times a week—make this an appealing choice. Centered on a white-trimmed pale-peach octagonal building crowned by a windowed cupola, the inn evokes 19th-century Florida—the leisurely era of riverboat travel and gracious plantations. Ceiling fans whir slowly over verandas and balconies furnished with wicker rocking chairs, and a charmingly landscaped courtyard with neat lawns and flower beds encompasses a large free-form swimming pool backed by verdant woodlands and a wide canal. Charming guest rooms, furnished in handsome maple or mahogany pieces, are adorned with floral friezes and 19th-century folk art. French doors open onto patios, balconies, or courtyards, and baths have art nouveau lighting fixtures. In-room amenities include cable TVs (with HBO and Spectravision movie options), coffeemakers, phones with modem jacks, wood-bladed chandelier ceiling fans, safes, and small refrigerators. Larger deluxe rooms offer sleeper sofas, microwave ovens, and hair dryers.

Dining/Entertainment: The elegant Country Parlor, in the balustraded Victorian lobby, serves moderately priced American fare at all meals; a pianist entertains at Sunday champagne brunches. Equally turn-of-the-century in decor is the Front Porch

Lounge; a popular gathering spot for locals, it features happy hour buffets weekdays from 5:30 to 7pm.

Services: Room service, guest services desk (sells tickets, many of them discounted, and arranges transport to all nearby attractions, including WDW parks), babysitting, Mears airport shuttle. Round-trip fare to WDW parks costs $9.

⑤ Fairfield Inn by Marriott

8342 Jamaican Court (off International Drive, between the Beeline Expressway and Sand Lake Road), Orlando, FL 32819. ☎ **407/363-1944** or 800/228-2800. Fax 407/363-1944. 134 rms. A/C TV TEL. $35–$70 for up to four people. Range reflects season. Rates include continental breakfast. AE, CB, DC, DISC, JCB, MC, V. Free parking.

I love this property's quiet and safe location in a secluded area off International Drive. It nestles in Jamaican Court, a neatly landscaped complex of hotels and restaurants (that means a number of eateries are within walking distance). The rooms are spiffy-looking, and phones are equipped with 25-foot cords and modem jacks. Daily newspapers and local calls are free, as is the continental breakfast served in the lobby each morning.

The guest services desk sells tickets (most of them discounted) and can arrange transport to all nearby theme parks and attractions and the airport; round-trip to WDW parks is $10. A small swimming pool and video-game room are on the premises, and the lobby has a microwave oven for guest use.

7 At the Airport

Hyatt Regency Orlando International Airport

9300 Airport Blvd., Orlando, FL 32827. ☎ **407/825-1234** or 800/233-1234. Fax 407/856-1672. 446 rms, 23 suites. A/C TV TEL. $190 double; $225–$450 suite. Extra person $25. Children under 18 stay free in parents' room. AE, CB, DC, DISC, JCB, MC, V. Self-parking $8, valet parking $11.

If you have to catch an early-morning flight out of Orlando, treat yourself to a night at this gorgeous multifacility hotel right in the airport's main terminal. It's luxurious from the moment you set foot in the plush, 40,000-square-foot palm court atrium lobby. Large, resort-style rooms—off balconies bordered by planters of bougainvillea or philodendrons—are attractively decorated and equipped with large desks, three phones (desk, bedside, and bath), cable TVs (with Spectravision movie, tourism-information, and flight arrival/departure channels), full-size ironing boards/irons, and hair dryers. Rooms are soundproof, so you don't hear planes taking off and landing.

Dining/Entertainment: The elegant Hemisphere Restaurant serves sophisticated American fare at lunch and northern Italian specialties at dinner; a pianist entertains weekend nights. McCoy's Bar & Grill centers on a display kitchen with an oak-burning pizza oven. You can also avail yourself of all the airport eateries, including a food court.

Services: 24-hour concierge/room service, shoe shine, car rental, babysitting, full business center, currency exchange.

Facilities: Airport shopping mall, airline desks, unisex hair salon, swimming pool, fully equipped health club, travel agency.

6 Dining

Since most Orlando visitors spend the majority of their time in the Walt Disney World area, I've focused on the best dining choices there. Also listed are some worthwhile restaurants beyond the realm. Parents will be pleased to note that just about every place in town offers a low-priced children's menu and usually provides some kind of kid's activity (mazes, coloring books, paper dolls) as well. The downside of restaurants that cater to kids is that they're noisy; you can count on at least one howling infant or tantrum-throwing toddler in almost every Orlando eatery. If you're looking for a quiet meal, head for restaurants on International Drive, which are further from Disney parks, and/or patronize more expensive places. Even then, there's no guarantee in this town that there won't be screaming kids among the clientele. See also listings for dinner shows in chapter 9.

Listings are divided by the following price categories: **very expensive** (the average main course at dinner is more than $25) **expensive** ($20 to $25), **moderate** ($10 to $20), **inexpensive** (under $10). Keep in mind that the above categories refer to dinner prices, and some very expensive restaurants offer affordable lunches and/or cheaper early-bird dinners. Also, I'm going by the assumption that you're not stinting when you order. Some restaurants, for instance, have entrées ranging from $12 to $20. In most cases, you can dine for less if you order carefully. My favorite restaurants are marked with a star, those offering particularly good value for the money with a dollar sign.

1 Best Bets

- **Best for Kids:** Kids adore the meals with Disney characters offered at almost all Walt Disney World resorts and elsewhere in the WDW complex (details below). The Sci-Fi Dine-In Theater and the Prime Time Cafe, both at Disney-MGM Studios, are also fun.
- **Best Spot for a Romantic Dinner:** The elegant candlelit Dux at the Peabody Orlando (☎ 407/345-4550) combines a warmly inviting ambience with great food.
- **Best Spot for a Business Lunch:** Much of the restaurant clientele in this town consists of screaming kids (actually, it only takes one to give that impression). Generally, Hemingway's, an upscale, Key West–style restaurant at the Hyatt Regency Grand Cypress

(☎ 407/239-1234), is kid-free, and its intimate dining areas are perfect for business lunches.

- **Best Spot for a Celebration:** Victoria & Albert's, at Disney's Grand Floridian Beach Resort (☎ 407/WDW-DINE), offers a seven-course feast, served in an exquisite setting by a maid and butler.
- **Best Decor:** Victoria & Albert's takes the prize once again, with its plush Louis XIII–style furnishings, brocaded walls, and central dome.
- **Best View:** La Coquina, at the Hyatt Regency Grand Cypress, has big windows overlooking swans and flamingos on Lake Windsong and verdant landscaping. See chapter 5.
- **Best Wine List:** Once again, it's Dux at the Peabody Orlando.
- **Best Value:** Hearty all-you-can-eat family-style meals are served up in iron skillets at the Whispering Canyon Cafe, at Disney's Wilderness Lodge (see chapter 5). And at Romano's Macaroni Grill (☎ 407/239-6676), the ambience and the northern Italian cuisine are first rate and prices are low, low, low.
- **Best American Cuisine:** What could be more all-American than a diner? And the B-Line Diner at the Peabody Orlando (☎ 407/345-4460) is an archetype.
- **Best Chinese Cuisine:** Ming Court (☎ 407/351-9988) features delicacies from all regions of China.
- **Best California Cuisine:** Lucky Orlando. A Wolfgang Puck Café is due to open soon, bringing Spago sophistication to a town that couldn't need it more.
- **Best Barbecue:** Head for Wild Jack's (☎ 407/352-4407), an upscale Wild West–theme restaurant with an open-pit exhibition kitchen; try the smoked brisket here.
- **Best Italian Cuisine:** I'd pick the northern Italian fare at the charming Capriccio, in the Peabody Orlando (☎ 407/352-4000), and also the sedate and elegant Tuscany at Marriott's Orlando World Center (☎ 407/239-4200).
- **Best Seafood:** The 19th-century-style clambake buffet at the Cape May Café at Disney's Beach Club Resort (☎ 407/WDW-DINE) is a feast—seafood stews, clams, mussels, lobster, and more cooked in a rockwood steamer pit.
- **Best Tapas:** Cafe Tu Tu Tango (☎ 407/248-2222) takes the tapas concept international with items ranging from Cajun egg rolls to Thai salad.
- **Best Steakhouse:** At the Yachtsman Steakhouse at Disney's Yacht Club Resort (☎ 407/WDW-DINE), aged prime steaks, chops, and seafood are grilled over oak and hickory.
- **Best Late-Night Dining:** The trendy B-Line Diner at the Peabody Orlando, open round the clock for eclectic fare ranging from filet mignon to a falafel sandwich.
- **Best Character Breakfast:** At the revolving Garden Grill, in the Land Pavilion at Epcot, diners enjoy hearty family-style fare, just-folks country theming, and interesting changes of scenery as the restaurant circles through environments ranging from prairie to rain forest; all this and Minnie and Mickey, too.
- **Best Outdoor Dining:** The terrace at Artist Point (☎ 407/WDW-DINE), the premier restaurant at Disney's Wilderness Lodge, overlooks a lake, waterfall, and scenery evocative of America's national parks.
- **Best People Watching:** It can only be Planet Hollywood (☎ 407/827-7827)!
- **Best Afternoon Tea:** The Garden View Lounge at Disney's Grand Floridian Beach Resort—a plush venue with potted palms and a wall of Palladian windows overlooking formal gardens—serves full afternoon teas from 3 to 6pm daily; a pianist entertains while you dine on tea sandwiches, crumpets, and scones with Devonshire cream. The Peabody Orlando hosts similar afternoon teas on weekdays from 3 to 4:30pm in its gorgeous skylit atrium lobby. Frolicking in a nearby fountain while you sip your Earl Grey are the Peabody's five resident ducks.

•**Best Brunch:** It's a tie: Capriccio at the Peabody Orlando and La Coquina at the Hyatt Regency Grand Cypress, both of which offer lavish buffets of first-rate fare with free-flowing champagne.

2 Restaurants by Cuisine

AMERICAN

Aunt Polly's Landing (Inexpensive, Magic Kingdom)

Buckets (Moderate, Orlando)

Diamond Horseshoe Saloon Revue (Inexpensive, Magic Kingdom)

50's Prime Time Cafe (Moderate, Disney-MGM Studios)

Hollywood Brown Derby (Expensive, Disney-MGM Studios)

King Stefan's Banquet Hall (Expensive, Magic Kingdom)

Liberty Tree Tavern (Expensive, Magic Kingdom)

Pecos Bill Café (Inexpensive, Magic Kingdom)

Plaza Restaurant (Inexpensive, Magic Kingdom)

Prime Time Cafe (Moderate, Disney-MGM Studios)

Sci-Fi Dine-In Theater Restaurant (Moderate, Disney-MGM Studios)

AMERICAN REGIONAL/ CALIFORNIA STYLE

B-Line Diner (Moderate, International Drive)

Black Swan (Very Expensive, Lake Buena Vista)

California Grill (Expensive, Lake Buena Vista)

Fireworks Factory (Moderate, Pleasure Island)

Pebbles (Moderate, Lake Buena Vista)

Planet Hollywood (Moderate, Pleasure Island)

Victoria & Albert's (Very Expensive, Lake Buena Vista)

BARBECUE

Wild Jacks (Moderate, International Drive)

BRITISH

Rose & Crown (Moderate, Epcot)

CAJUN/NEW ORLEANS

Boatwright's Dining Hall (Inexpensive, Lake Buena Vista)

Bonfamille's Cafe (Inexpensive, Lake Buena Vista)

CANADIAN

Le Cellier (Moderate, Epcot)

CHARACTER BREAKFASTS & DINNERS

Artist Point (Expensive, Disney's Wilderness Lodge)

Baskerville's (Moderate Breakfast and Dinner, Grosvenor Resort)

Cape May Café (Expensive, Disney's Beach Club Resort)

Chef Mickey's (Breakfast Expensive, Dinner Moderate; Disney's Contemporary Resort)

Garden Grill (Breakfast Expensive, Lunch and Dinner Moderate; Epcot)

Garden Grove Café (Expensive, Walt Disney World Swan)

Harry's Safari Bar & Grille (Expensive, Walt Disney World Dolphin)

King Stefan's Banquet Hall (Expensive, Magic Kingdom)

Liberty Tree Tavern (Moderate, Magic Kingdom)

Mickey's Tropical Luau
(Moderate, Disney's
Polynesian Resort)

Minnie's Menehune (Expensive,
Disney's Polynesian Resort)

1900 Park Fare (Breakfast
Expensive, Dinner Moderate;
Disney's Grand Floridian
Resort)

Soundstage Restaurant
(Expensive, Disney-MGM
Studios)

Watercress Café (Moderate,
Buena Vista Palace)

CHINESE

Lotus Blossom Cafe
(Inexpensive, Epcot)

Ming Court (Moderate,
International Drive)

Nine Dragons (Moderate,
Epcot)

CONTINENTAL/INTERNATIONAL

Dux (Very Expensive, International Drive)

CUBAN

Rolando's (Inexpensive,
Casselberry)

FOOD COURT

Sunshine Season Food Fair
(Inexpensive, Epcot)

FRENCH

Au Petit Cafe (Moderate,
Epcot)

Bistro de Paris (Expensive,
Epcot)

Chefs de France (Expensive,
Epcot)

Patisserie/Boulangerie
(Inexpensive, Epcot)

GERMAN

Biergarten (Inexpensive, Epcot)

Sommerfest (Inexpensive,
Epcot)

ITALIAN

Capriccio (Moderate,
International Drive)

Enzo's (Inexpensive,
International Drive)

L'Originale Alfredo di Roma
(Expensive, Epcot)

Portobello Yacht Club
(Moderate, Pleasure Island)

Romano's Macaroni Grill
(Inexpensive, Lake Buena
Vista)

Tony's Town Square Restaurant
(Expensive, Magic Kingdom)

Tuscany (Expensive, Lake
Buena Vista)

JAPANESE

Mikado Japanese Steak House
(Expensive, Lake Buena Vista)

Mitsukoshi Restaurant
(Expensive, Epcot)

Yakitori House (Inexpensive,
Epcot)

MEXICAN

Cantina de San Angel
(Inexpensive, Epcot)

San Angel Inn (Moderate,
Epcot)

MOROCCAN

Restaurant Marrakesh
(Moderate, Epcot)

NORWEGIAN

Akershus (Moderate, Epcot)

Kringla Bakeri og Kafe
(Inexpensive, Epcot)

PACIFIC RIM

'Ohana (Moderate, Lake Buena
Vista)

SEAFOOD/STEAKS/CHOPS

Ariel's (Expensive, Lake Buena
Vista)

Artist Point (Moderate,
Lake Buena Vista)

Cape May Café (Inexpensive, Lake Buena Vista)

Coral Reef (Moderate, Epcot)

Fulton's Crab House (Expensive, Pleasure Island)

Hemingway's (Expensive, Lake Buena Vista)

Yachtsman Steakhouse (Expensive, Lake Buena Vista)

TAPAS

Cafe Tu Tu Tango (Moderate, International Drive)

THAI

Siam Orchid (Moderate, International Drive)

3 In Walt Disney World

The following listings encompass restaurants at the Magic Kingdom, Epcot, Disney-MGM Studios, and Disney Village.

AT EPCOT

Though an ethnic meal at one of the World Showcase pavilions is a traditional part of the Epcot experience, I find many of the below-listed establishments just a tad pricey for the value received. Unless money is no object, you might want to consider the numerous lower-priced walk-in eateries at each national pavilion and throughout the park that don't require reservations (for details, check the *Epcot Guidemap* that you get upon entering the park). Or go at lunch, when entrée prices are lower. Almost all of the establishments listed below serve lunch and dinner daily (hours vary with park hours), and, unless otherwise noted, they offer children's meals for $3.99.

Note: Since the clientele at even the fanciest Epcot World Showcase restaurants are coming directly from the parks, you don't have to dress up for dinner.

WORLD SHOWCASE

These restaurants are arranged geographically, beginning at the Canada pavilion and proceeding counterclockwise around the World Showcase Lagoon.

Canada

This self-service buffet—for which no reservations are required—is a good choice for families. Located in the Victorian Hotel du Canada, with its French Gothic facade and steeply pitched copper roofs, **Le Cellier** has a castlelike ambience with seating in tapestried chairs under vaulted stone arches, and amber light emanating from black wrought-iron sconces. Regional dishes include cheddar cheese soup, carved pemeal bacon (a pork loin with a light cornmeal crust), a French Canadian pork- and potato-filled pie called tourtière, chicken and meatball stew, maple syrup pie, and Canadian beers. Entrées cost $7.50 to $9.95 at lunch, $9.95 to $15.95 at dinner. *Note:* The kid's meal of macaroni and cheese might even tempt adults.

United Kingdom

The **Rose & Crown,** entered via a cozy pub, evokes Victorian England with dark oak wainscoting, beamed Tudor ceilings, and English and Scottish folk music. It also offers outdoor seating at tables overlooking the lagoon—a good place to watch IllumiNations. Dinner here might be an appetizer of smoked salmon with Stilton cheese, prime rib with Yorkshire pudding, and a sherry trifle. Wash it all down with a pint of Irish lager, Bass ale, or Guinness stout. Entrées cost $9.25 to $11.75 at lunch, $12.25 to $20.75 at dinner. Traditional tea, with scones, pastries, and finger sandwiches, is served daily at 3:30pm; cost is $9.95. Another option is bar fare (sausage rolls, Cornish pasties, a Stilton cheese and fruit plate), all under $4.50.

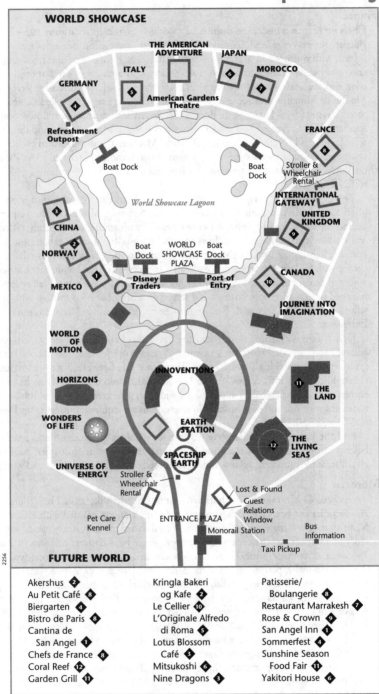

WORLD SHOWCASE

THE AMERICAN ADVENTURE

JAPAN

ITALY

MOROCCO

GERMANY

American Gardens Theatre

Refreshment Outpost

FRANCE

Boat Dock

Boat Dock

Stroller & Wheelchair Rental

World Showcase Lagoon

INTERNATIONAL GATEWAY

CHINA

UNITED KINGDOM

NORWAY

Boat Dock

WORLD SHOWCASE PLAZA

Boat Dock

MEXICO

Disney Traders

Port of Entry

CANADA

JOURNEY INTO IMAGINATION

WORLD OF MOTION

INNOVENTIONS

HORIZONS

THE LAND

WONDERS OF LIFE

EARTH STATION

THE LIVING SEAS

UNIVERSE OF ENERGY

SPACESHIP EARTH

Stroller & Wheelchair Rental

Lost & Found

Guest Relations Window

Pet Care Kennel

ENTRANCE PLAZA

Bus Information

Monorail Station

Taxi Pickup

FUTURE WORLD

2256

Akershus ❷
Au Petit Café ❽
Biergarten ❹
Bistro de Paris ❽
Cantina de San Angel ❶
Chefs de France ❽
Coral Reef ⓬
Garden Grill ⓫

Kringla Bakeri og Kafe ❷
Le Cellier ❿
L'Originale Alfredo di Roma ❺
Lotus Blossom Café ❸
Mitsukoshi ❻
Nine Dragons ❸

Patisserie/ Boulangerie ❽
Restaurant Marrakesh ❼
Rose & Crown ❾
San Angel Inn ❶
Sommerfest ❹
Sunshine Season Food Fair ⓫
Yakitori House ❻

France

Chefs de France is under the auspices of a world-famous culinary triumvirate—Paul Bocuse, Roger Vergé, and Gaston LeNôtre. Its art nouveau/fin-de-siècle interior is agleam with mirrors and brass candelabra chandeliers, etched-glass and brass dividers create intimate dining areas, and tables are elegantly appointed. To start off, I recommend the seafood cream soup with crab dumplings (as featured by Vergé at Moulin de Mougins). Entrée selections at dinner include a superb broiled salmon in sorrel cream sauce à la façcon de Bocuse (it's served with ratatouille and new potatoes) and Vergé's sautéed beef tenderloin with raisins and brandy sauce. And the dessert of choice is LeNôtre's superb soufflé Grand-Marnier. The distinguished chefs also composed the restaurant's wine list, any item of which can be purchased at Au Palais du Vin, a wine shop in the pavilion. Entrées cost $8.95 to $14.95 at lunch, $15.95 to $24.25 at dinner.

The ✪ **Bistro de Paris,** upstairs from Chefs de France and serving dinner only, offers similar fare in a more serene country-French setting. Also under the auspices of Bocuse, Vergé, and LeNôtre, it's rather elegant, with seating in burgundy tufted-leather banquettes, French windows, candlelit white-linen-cloth tables, and art nouveau lighting fixtures. Highlights here include Bocuse's duck foie gras salad appetizer with fresh greens and artichoke hearts, and Vergé's classic bouillabaisse served with garlic sauce and croutons. Another notable entrée: Bocuse's roast red snapper wrapped in thin-sliced potato crust and served on a bed of sautéed spinach with red wine lobster sauce. Stay with Bocuse for dessert; his crème brûlée is unbeatable. Entrées are $20.50 to $26.95.

Lighter fare is available throughout the day at **Au Petit Café,** a sidewalk bistro adjacent to Chefs de France on an awninged terrace overlooking the lagoon. It's a great venue for watching IllumiNations. Traditional cafe fare is featured—ham- and cheese-filled croissants, crêpes, quiche Lorraine, salade niçcoise, and a few heartier entrées such as chicken baked in puff pastry with port wine cream sauce and brochette of prawns with rice and basil butter. No reservations are required. Entrées range from $7.75 to $15.50.

And the **Patisserie/Boulangerie,** its interior redolent of croissants and pastries baking in the oven, offers tempting French treats—gorgeous fruit tarts, pain au chocolât, apple turnovers, eclairs, and much more . . . plus French coffees and wines.

Morocco

The palatial ✪ **Marrakesh**—with its hand-set mosaic tilework, latticed teak shutters, and intricate cut-brass chandeliers suspended from a ceiling painted with elaborate Moorish motifs—represents 12 centuries of Arabic design. Exquisitely carved faux-ivory archways frame the central dining area, where belly dancers perform to *oud, kanoun,* and *darbuka* music. Of all Epcot restaurants, this exotic venue best typifies the international-experience spirit of the park. The Moroccan *diffa* (traditional feast) that lets you sample a variety of dishes is recommended. At dinner it includes a hearty saffron-seasoned harira soup flavored with onions, tomatoes, lentils, and lamb; beef *brewats* (minced beef seasoned with coriander, ginger, cinnamon, and saffron, rolled in thin pastry layers, and fried); roast lamb served with almond- and raisin-studded rice; braised tagine of chicken with green olives and preserved lemon; couscous with seasonal vegetables; Moroccan pastries; and mint tea. Combination appetizer plates are another way to experience culinary diversity. French and Moroccan wines are available to complement your meal. Entrées are $9.95 to $15.95 at lunch, $13.75 to $19.95 at dinner; Moroccan diffa is $29.95 for two at lunch, $49.95 for two at dinner.

How to Arrange Priority Seating at WDW Restaurants

Priority seating is similar to a reservation. It means that you get the next table available when you arrive at a restaurant, but a table is not kept empty pending your arrival. You can arrange priority seating up to 60 days in advance at almost all full-service Magic Kingdom, Epcot, Disney-MGM Studios, resort, and Disney Village restaurants—as well as character meals and shows throughout the complex—by calling **407/WDW-DINE.** Nighttime shows can actually be booked as far in advance as you wish.

Since this priority-seating phone number was instituted in 1994, it has become much more difficult to obtain a table by just showing up. So I strongly advise you to avoid disappointment by calling ahead.

However, if you don't reserve in advance, you can take your chances reserving in the parks themselves:

At Epcot: Make reservations at the Worldkey interactive terminals at Guest Relations in Innoventions East, at Worldkey Information Service Satellites located on the main concourse to World Showcase and at Germany in World Showcase, or at the restaurants themselves.

At the Magic Kingdom: Reserve at the restaurants themselves.

At Disney-MGM Studios: Make reservations at the Hollywood Junction Station on Sunset Boulevard or at the restaurants themselves.

- All park restaurants have nonsmoking interiors; you can smoke on patios and terraces.
- Magic Kingdom restaurants serve no alcoholic beverages, but liquor is available at Epcot and Disney-MGM eateries and elsewhere in the WDW complex.
- All sit-down restaurants in Walt Disney World take American Express, MasterCard, Visa, and the Disney Card.
- Guests at Disney resorts and official properties can make restaurant reservations through guest services or concierge desks.
- All WDW restaurants offer low-priced children's menus.

Japan

The **Mitsukoshi Restaurant** centers on a teppanyaki steakhouse where diners sit at grill tables and white-hatted chefs rapidly dice, slice, stir-fry, and propel cooked food onto your plate with amazing dexterity. Kids especially love watching the chef wield his cleaver and utensils. Since you share a table with strangers, teppanyaki makes for a convivial dining experience. An elaborate dinner for two (of which an abbreviated version is available at lunch) includes a shrimp appetizer, salad with ginger dressing, soup (ask for the *miroshiru*—soybean soup with tofu and mushrooms), grilled fresh vegetables with udon noodles, succulent morsels of grilled beef tenderloin and lobster, steamed rice, choice of dessert (perhaps chestnut cake), and green tea. And even à la carte entrées include plenty of extras. Kirin beer, plum wine, and sake are among your beverage options, along with specialty drinks (some of them nonalcoholic, for kids) such as *tachibana* (light rum, orange curaççao, and mandarin orange juice). Entrées cost $9.25 to $16.50 at lunch, $14.75 to $25.95 at dinner; complete dinner described above costs $39.50 for two at lunch, $59.90 for two at dinner.

Adjoining the teppanyaki rooms is a U-shaped **tempura counter** where you can eat shrimp, scallops, chicken, and fresh vegetables that have been lightly battered and deep-fried. Some sushi and sashimi items are served here as well. Entrées cost $9.25 to $11.95 at lunch, $14.75 to $22.75 at dinner. No reservations required for counter seating.

But for me, the gem of this complex is the peaceful, plant-filled **cocktail lounge** with large windows overlooking the lagoon and torii gate—a very pleasant setting for appetizers (perhaps shrimp tempura or sashimi) and warm sake. Japanese music plays softly in the background. Menu items are $3.95 to $8.25, and no reservations are required. This is a great venue to view IllumiNations.

Finally, housed in a replica of the 16th-century Katsura Imperial Villa in Kyoto is **Yakitori House,** a bamboo-roofed cafeteria serving shrimp tempura over noodles, chicken yakitori, and other Japanese snack-fare items—all of them under $7; a full children's meal is $2.69. Umbrella tables on a terrace overlooking a rock waterfall are a plus.

Italy

Patterned after Alfredo De Lelio's celebrated establishment in Rome, **L'Originale Alfredo di Roma Ristorante** evokes a seaside Roman palazzo with beautiful *trompe l'oeil* frescoes of 16th-century patrician villas inspired by Veronese. The theatricality of an exhibition kitchen, charming Italian waiters, and exuberant strolling musicians create a festive ambience. If you want a quieter setting, ask for a seat on the veranda. De Lelio invented fettuccine Alfredo—and it remains an excellent entrée choice here. Other recommendables are garlicky linguine al pesto and veal scaloppine served with roasted potatoes and vegetables. And there's a sublime tiramisù for dessert. A special vegetarian menu (with excellent grilled veggies, among other items) is available, and the list of Italian wines is extensive. On your way in or out, note the entrance room walls; they're covered with photographs of celebrity diners in Rome, most notably Fairbanks and Mary Pickford, who discovered Alfredo's on their honeymoon and told *tout* Hollywood. Entrées cost $7.25 to $15.95 at lunch, $9.25 to $24.75 at dinner. For an extra $3.75 you can get a side order of pasta with your dinner entrée. A great deal here is a three-course early-bird dinner served from 4:30 to 6pm for $15.75.

Germany

Lit by streetlamps, the **Biergarten** simulates a Bavarian village courtyard at Oktoberfest with autumnal trees, a working water wheel, and geranium-filled flower boxes adorning Tudor-style houses. Waiters are in lederhosen, waitresses in peasant dresses, and entertainment is provided by oom-pah bands, singers, dancers, and a strolling accordionist. Musical shows take place five to seven times a day (depending on the season). Guests are encouraged to dance as the band strikes up polkas and waltzes and to sing along with yodelers and folksingers. All-you-can-eat buffet meals featuring traditional fare (sauerbraten, herring salad, red cabbage, spaetzle with gravy, roasted potatoes, sauerkraut with ham and spicy sausage, pork with fruit, roast chicken, salads) are offered at lunch and dinner. Beverages and desserts are extra. Wash it all down with a stein of Beck's or a glass of Liebfraumilch. Lunch buffets cost $9.95, dinner buffets $14.50.

At **Sommerfest**—a cafeteria with indoor seating backed by a mural of German castles and countryside and courtyard tables overlooking a fountain—you can purchase bratwurst sandwiches with sauerkraut, goulash soup, and desserts such as apple strudel. All items are under $5.

China

One of the most attractive of the World Showcase restaurants, ✪ **Nine Dragons,** with windows overlooking the lagoon, has intricately carved rosewood paneling and furnishings and a beautiful dragon-motif ceiling. Begin your meal here with a selection of dim sum such as honey-glazed spareribs, delicious shrimp toast, pan-fried dumplings (pot stickers) stuffed with pork and vegetables, and ginger-nuanced steamed dumplings stuffed with pork, shrimp, and water chestnuts. Entrées highlight dishes from four regions of China—Mandarin Great Wall duck shredded with green and red peppers and served with pancakes; from Shanghai, a saucy stir-fried boneless chicken with onions, carrots, and green peas; Cantonese tender sliced sirloin and broccoli stir-fried in oyster sauce; and Szechuan deep-fried shrimp ambrosia in a Mao Tai liqueur-spiked fruit sauce. You can order Chinese or California wines with your meal, but I especially love fresh melon juice, either nonalcoholic or mixed with rum or vodka. For dessert, there's red-bean ice cream with fried banana or Chinese pastries. Entrées cost $9.50 to $18.50 at lunch (most are under $15), $10.50 to $23.75 at dinner. A multicourse sampler lunch (soup, spring roll, entrée, pastries, and tea) is $11.50; $39.50 buys an elaborate meal for two at dinner.

Or you can opt for egg rolls, pork-fried rice, and entrées such as stir-fried chicken and vegetables served over noodles at the open-air **Lotus Blossom Café,** a pleasant (and inexpensive) self-service eatery. There are cooking demonstrations near the entrance several times a day.

Norway

Akershus re-creates a 14th-century castle fortress that stands in Oslo's harbor. Its pristine white stone interior, with lofty beamed ceilings and leaded-glass windows, features intimate dining niches divided by Gothic stone archways. Soft lighting emanates from gas lamps, candelabra chandeliers, and flickering sconces. The meal is an immense smorgasbord of traditional *småvarmt* (hot) and *koldtbord* (cold) dishes—smoked pork with honey mustard, strips of venison in cream sauce, gravlax in mustard sauce, smoked mackerel, Norwegian tomato herring, an array of Norwegian breads and cheeses, stuffed pork loin, potato salad, red cabbage, boiled red potatoes, eggs Nordique, and much more. Norwegian beer and aquavit complement a list of French and California wines. And do consider the post-Olympic Lillehammer brandy for an after-dinner drink. Desserts, such as a "veiled maiden"—an applesauce and whipped cream concoction—are à la carte. The lunch buffet costs $11.95 for adults, $4.50 for children ages 4 to 9, age 3 and under free; dinner buffet is $17.95 for adults, $7.50 for children. There are also nonsmorgasbord children's meals for $3.99.

Another facility in this pavilion, the **Kringla Bakeri og Kafe,** offers covered outdoor seating and inexpensive light fare—open-faced sandwiches like smoked salmon stuffed with hard-boiled egg, cheese and fruit platters, waffles sprinkled with powdered sugar, and fresh-baked Norwegian pastries. No reservations are required.

Mexico

The setting for the ✪ **San Angel Inn** is a hacienda courtyard amid dense jungle foliage in the shadow of a crumbling Yucatán pyramid. It is nighttime: Tables are candlelit (even at lunch), and lighting is very low. The Popocatepetl volcano erupts in the distance, spewing molten lava, and you can hear the sounds of faraway birds. Thunder, lightning, and swiftly moving clouds add a dramatic note, but the overall ambience is soothing. The fare is authentic and prepared from scratch. Order an appetizer of *queso fundido* (melted cheese with Mexican pork sausage, served with homemade corn or flour tortillas). Among entrées, specialties include *mole poblano* (chicken simmered with more than 20 spices and a hint of chocolate) and *filete ranchero* (grilled tenderloin of beef served over corn tortillas with sauce ranchero, poblano pepper strips, Monterey jack cheese, onions, and refried beans). Combination platters are available at both meals. There's chocolate Kahlúa mousse pie for dessert, and drink options include Dos Equis beer and margaritas. Entrées are $9.75 to $15.75 at lunch, $13.25 to $23.25 at dinner. A special vegetarian menu lists items from $7.25 to $11.75.

Cantina de San Angel, a cafeteria with outdoor seating at umbrella tables overlooking the lagoon, offers affordable tacos, burritos, and combination plates, along with frozen margaritas; a complete children's meal is $2.69.

FUTURE WORLD

The most notable restaurant in the front section of Epcot is at the Living Seas Pavilion.

Living Seas Pavilion

Dine under the sea at the enchanting **Coral Reef,** where tables ring a 5.6-million-gallon aquarium inhabited by more than 4,000 denizens of the deep. Strains of Debussy's *La Mer* and Handel's *Water Music* playing softly in the background help set the tone. Tiered seating—much of it in semicircular booths—ensures everyone a good view, and diners are given "fish-identifier" sheets with labeled pictures so they can put names to the species swimming by. The menu features (what else?) seafood—creamy lobster bisque, sautéed mahi-mahi in lemon-caper butter, and shrimp satay served atop red pepper pasta. There are also steak and chicken dishes. For dessert, choose frangelico-laced white-chocolate mousse cake served on crème anglaise and crowned with dark chocolate Mickey ears. Coral Reef features premium wines by the glass and matches nightly entrées with selected labels. Entrées cost $12.25 to $19.75 at lunch, $12.25 to $23.75 at dinner—more for lobster or a clambake combination.

The Land

This pavilion's Garden Grill is the setting for character meals described below. It also houses a lower-level food court (a good choice for family dining) called the **Sunshine Season Food Fair,** where vendors proffer an array of low-priced items—barbecued chicken and ribs, homemade soups and fresh salads, immense cinnamon rolls, fresh fruit, pastas, stuffed baked potatoes, sandwiches, oven-fresh cakes and pastries, ice cream, and more. Colorful umbrella tables under a skylit tent-top ring a splashing fountain, and hot-air balloons add to the festive decor.

IN THE MAGIC KINGDOM

There are three major restaurants in the Magic Kingdom offering full-service dining—the **Liberty Tree Tavern, King Stefan's Banquet Hall,** and **Tony's Town Square.** And though there are plenty of fast-food eateries as well, I find a quiet sit-down meal an essential respite from theme park hullaballoo.

MAIN STREET

Inspired by *Lady and the Tramp,* **Tony's Town Square Restaurant** is Victorian plush, with rich cherrywood beams and paneling, a central fountain, cut-glass mirrors, and globe lighting fixtures. Walls are hung with original cels from the movie. There's additional seating in a sunny, plant-filled solarium. Tony's opens early for breakfast (you can eat here while waiting for the other lands to open); menu items range from Lady- and the Tramp-shaped waffles to French toast tossed in cinnamon sugar and served with warm maple or fruit syrup. The rest of the day, the fare is Italian, featuring appetizers such as a five-cheese vegetable pizza and fried calamari with marinara sauce. The lunch menu lists a variety of pastas, calzones, subs, and salads, while at dinner your options range from garlicky sautéed shrimp and seasonal

🏰 Family-Friendly Restaurants

Keep in mind that almost all Walt Disney World restaurants offer very inexpensive kids' meals (usually $3.99), as do most restaurants in this very child-oriented town. Theming that appeals to youngsters and place mats with puzzles and pictures to color are also the norm. Of course, all the character meals described in this chapter delight the kids. Some other notables:

Sci-Fi Dine-In Theater Restaurant *(see p. 90)* A drive-in movie theater at Disney-MGM Studios where you dine in actual convertible cars, eyes glued to a movie screen.

Prime Time Cafe *(see p. 90)* Also at Disney-MGM Studios, this highly themed eatery re-creates the world of 1950s sit-coms, with TV sets airing old shows visible from every table. Homey food, such as meat loaf and mashed potatoes, is also of that era.

Mickey's Tropical Luau *(see p. 106)* Not just a meal but a Polynesian floor show featuring Minnie, Mickey, Pluto, and Goofy along with a cast of South Sea Islanders. At Disney's Polynesian Resort in Luau Cove. Character breakfasts here, too.

Cape May Café Clambake Buffet *(see p. 99)* This old-fashioned nightly clambake at Disney's Beach Club Resort is fun for the whole family.

'Ohana *(see p. 97–98)* Centering on an 18-foot fire pit grill, 'Ohana, at Disney's Polynesian Resort, is a sumptuous island feast enhanced by storytellers, hula hoop contests, and lots of audience participation.

Hoop-Dee-Doo Musical Revue *(see p. 174)* I've never met anyone who didn't have a great time at this whoopin' and hollerin' country-music dinner show in Fort Wilderness's Pioneer Hall. A less expensive variation on the same theme is the **Diamond Horseshoe Saloon Revue** in the Magic Kingdom's Frontierland *(see p. 87)*.

Planet Hollywood *(see p. 92–93)* Kids love all the action and excitement—a fiber-optic ceiling, video walls, hundreds of movie costumes and props on display, and the elusive possibility that they'll actually see someone famous. Long waits on line to get in, however.

---

vegetables over linguine in a light cream sauce to a 12-ounce strip steak/sautéed lobster combination, also served with linguine in garlic cream sauce. Breakfast items cost $2.75 to $7.75; entrées are $7.75 to $15.25 at lunch, $16.25 to $22.75 at dinner.

Near the end of Main Street, to your right as you enter the park, is the pretty **Plaza Restaurant,** with an art nouveau interior. It serves burgers, salads, and sandwiches (tuna and Swiss on whole wheat, a Reuben, hot roast beef double-deckers) that you can wash down with a vanilla, chocolate, or strawberry shake. Or skip the shake and leave room for a hot-fudge sundae. There's waiter service, and reservations are accepted. Open from lunch to park closing. Sundaes are $3.75 to $5.75 (the latter for an elaborate, create-your-own concoction); sandwiches, burgers, and salads cost $7.75 to $10.75.

FRONTIERLAND

Highly recommended is the **Diamond Horseshoe Saloon Revue,** combining a light meal with a 30- to 45-minute western-theme musical revue (details in chapter 7).

The **Pecos Bill Café,** a vast Wild West–theme indoor/outdoor eatery, serves low-priced burgers, hot dogs, chili, and barbecued chicken sandwiches.

I also like **Aunt Polly's Landing** on Tom Sawyer's Island, reached via a short raft trip across the Rivers of America. With its outdoor tables on a porch overlooking the water, it provides a tranquil respite from park hyperactivity. Inexpensive light fare includes sandwiches—peanut butter and jelly, fried chicken, ham and cheese—and soft drinks. And you can relax over refreshing lemonade while the kids explore the island's dark caves and abandoned mines. It's open for lunch only.

LIBERTY SQUARE

The ✪ **Liberty Tree Tavern** replicates an 18th-century pub, with peg-plank oak floors, displays of pewterware in oak hutches, and a vast brick fireplace hung with copper pots in its entranceway. Background music is appropriate to the period, and even the windows have panes of hand-pressed glass, a detail typical of Disney thoroughness. Entrées range from New England pot roast braised in burgundy and served with mashed potatoes and vegetables to a traditional roast turkey dinner with all the trimmings. Precede these with a bowl of creamy New England clam chowder. There's apple crisp topped with vanilla ice cream for dessert. I prefer the food here to King Stefan's (below), and this restaurant is also more likely to be able to seat large parties. Lunch entrées are $9.75 to $14.25. Dinners here are all-you-can-eat character meals (see details below).

In the mood for a light but satisfying meal? I'm partial to the **baked and sweet potato cart** in Liberty Square and the adjacent fruit stand.

AT CINDERELLA CASTLE

King Stefan's Banquet Hall has a Gothic interior with leaded-glass windows and heraldic banners suspended from a vaulted ceiling. The only anachronistic note: Background music is from Disney movies. The menu features hearty cuts of beef such as prime rib and grilled sirloin served with fresh sautéed vegetables and soup. And while you're piling on cholesterol, might as well opt for an appetizer of almond-breaded brie served with wild lingonberry relish. Less caloric entrées include grilled swordfish and a vegetarian plate. There's berry and apple cobbler topped with vanilla ice cream for dessert. *Note:* Cinderella often greets guests in the downstairs entrance hall. Entrées are $10.95 to $16.75 at lunch, $17.50 to $25.75 at dinner. King Stefan's also hosts a daily character breakfast; see details below.

AT DISNEY-MGM STUDIOS

There are more than a dozen eateries in this Hollywood theme park, with movie-lot monikers like the Studio Commissary and Starring Rolls Bakery. The below-listed are my favorites.

The ✪ **Hollywood Brown Derby**, modeled after the famed L.A. celebrity haunt where Louella Parsons and Hedda Hopper held court, evokes its one-time West Coast counterpart with interior palm trees, roomy semicircular leather booths, and derby-shaded sconces. Mahogany-wainscoted walls are hung with 1,600 caricatures of major stars who patronized the California restaurant—everyone from Bette Davis to Sammy Davis. Brown Derby legend abounds: It was at this Hollywood shrine that Clark Gable proposed to Carole Lombard, Wallace Beery poured ketchup over his sponge cake, and Lucille Ball and Jack Haley chucked dinner rolls at each other across the tables! A pianist entertains while you dine. The Derby's signature dish is the Cobb salad, invented by owner Bob Cobb in the 1930s, but, frankly, I don't love it; it's like a salad run through a blender. Dinner entrées come with a choice of soup or salad (select the champagne-nuanced oyster Brie, available à la carte at lunch). Go on to an entrée of baked grouper meunière, served atop pasta in a light, lemony white wine

Magic Kingdom Dining

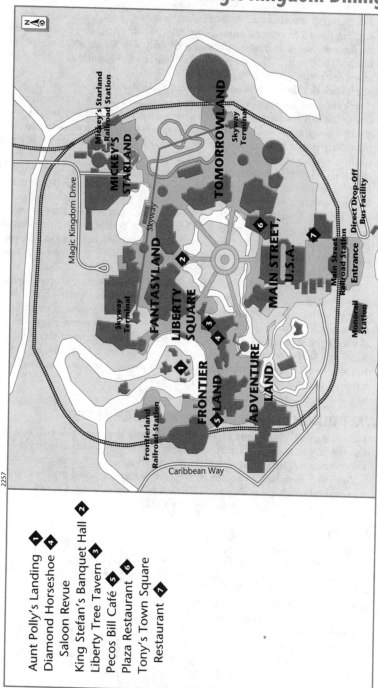

Aunt Polly's Landing ◆1
Diamond Horseshoe
Saloon Revue ◆4
King Stefan's Banquet Hall ◆2
Liberty Tree Tavern ◆3
Pecos Bill Café ◆5
Plaza Restaurant ◆6
Tony's Town Square
Restaurant ◆7

cream sauce. Grapefruit cake with cream cheese frosting is the Derby's signature dessert, but I prefer the white chocolate cheesecake. There's a full bar, California wines are featured, and after-dinner drinks are a specialty. Entrées are $8.95 to $16.50 at lunch, $16.50 to $23.75 at dinner. A good value is a three-course early-bird dinner served from 4 to 5:30pm for $15.75.

The **Sci-Fi Dine-In Theater Restaurant** replicates an archetypical 1950s Los Angeles drive-in movie emporium. Diners are ensconced in flashy, chrome-trimmed convertible cars (complete with fins and whitewalls) under a twinkling starlit sky with the Hollywood hills as a backdrop. Friendly carhops bring your food order and complimentary popcorn. While you eat, you can watch the movie screen, where a mix of zany newsreels (e.g., *News of the Future*) is interspersed with cartoons, horror movie clips (*Frankenstein Meets the Space Monster*), and coming attractions. The food could be better, but the creative theming is ample compensation. Menu items have names like the Towering Terror (barbecued pork ribs with veggies and fries) and Plucked from Deepest Space (a grilled chicken sandwich with Cajun remoulade sauce and fries). Finish up with the Cheesecake That Ate New York. Though the restaurant basically appeals to kids (whose menu items are all under $4), beverages include wine and beer (there's a full bar), as well as milkshakes. Your bill is presented as a speeding ticket. Entrées cost $7.95 to $12.95 at lunch, $9.50 to $22.75 at dinner.

The **50's Prime Time Cafe** places diners in a 1950s time warp/sit-com psychodrama. Eating areas look like homey '50s kitchens, wherein black-and-white TV sets air clips of shows like "My Little Margie" and "Topper." The waitstaff greets diners like family ("Hi Sis, I'll go tell Mom you're home"), and may threaten you with no dessert if you don't eat your veggies, or tell on you for resting your elbows on the table. The food—meat loaf with mashed potatoes, Granny's pot roast, Dad's chili, and such—isn't all that great, but the place is so much fun, you'll love it anyway. Desserts include banana splits and S'mores. Entrées cost $9.95 to $17.50 at lunch, $11.95 to $20.25 at dinner.

WALT DISNEY WORLD VILLAGE/PLEASURE ISLAND

Located about 2^1/$_2$ miles from Epcot off Buena Vista Drive, Walt Disney World Village is a very pleasant complex of cedar-shingled shops and restaurants overlooking a scenic lagoon. Pleasure Island, a nighttime entertainment center, adjoins.

Note: You don't have to pay the entrance fee to Pleasure Island to dine at any of its restaurants. Coming soon to Walt Disney World Village, Orlando's most exciting-ever culinary coup: Wolfgang Puck's Café.

EXPENSIVE

Fulton's Crab House

Aboard the riverboat docked at Pleasure Island. ☎ **407/934-BOAT.** Reservations not accepted. Main courses mostly $13.95–$29.95. AE, MC, V. Daily 4pm–midnight. Free self-parking, valet parking $5. SEAFOOD/STEAKS AND CHOPS.

Fulton's is due to open shortly after press time, aboard a replica of a 19th-century Mississippi riverboat that is permanently moored on the shores of Lake Buena Vista. Its interior, undergoing a renovation at this writing, will be enhanced by authentic nautical artifacts, marine-themed early American lithographs, fishing paraphernalia, and maps. Ceilings will be whimsically adorned with hand-painted constellations, crabs, and fish. There will be a deck for outdoor dining, and the casual Stone Crab Lounge (open 11:30am to 2am) will serve light fare (garlicky steamed clams, oyster-bar selections, peel-and-eat shrimp, cold cracked crab with mustard sauce, and the like). Chef Ron Pollack's daily-changing menus will feature the freshest market

More Walt Disney World Dining

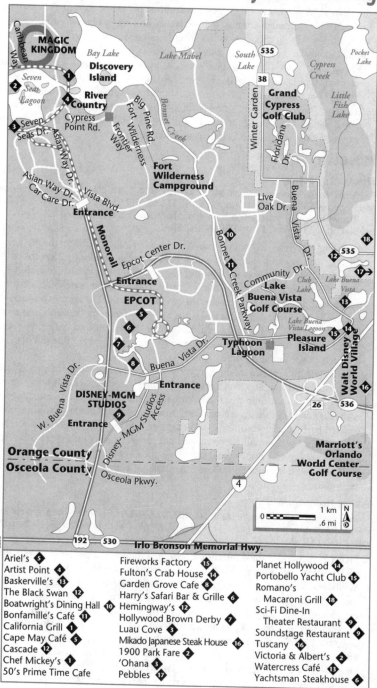

Ariel's 🔟5️⃣
Artist Point 🔟4️⃣
Baskerville's 🔟3️⃣
The Black Swan 🔟2️⃣
Boatwright's Dining Hall 🔟0️⃣
Bonfamille's Café 🔟1️⃣
California Grill 🔟1️⃣
Cape May Café 🔟5️⃣
Cascade 🔟2️⃣
Chef Mickey's 🔟1️⃣
50's Prime Time Cafe

Fireworks Factory 🔟5️⃣
Fulton's Crab House 🔟4️⃣
Garden Grove Cafe 🔟8️⃣
Harry's Safari Bar & Grille 🔟6️⃣
Hemingway's 🔟2️⃣
Hollywood Brown Derby 🔟7️⃣
Luau Cove 🔟3️⃣
Mikado Japanese Steak House 🔟6️⃣
1900 Park Fare 🔟2️⃣
'Ohana 🔟3️⃣
Pebbles 🔟7️⃣

Planet Hollywood 🔟4️⃣
Portobello Yacht Club 🔟5️⃣
Romano's
   Macaroni Grill 🔟8️⃣
Sci-Fi Dine-In
   Theater Restaurant 🔟9️⃣
Soundstage Restaurant 🔟9️⃣
Tuscany 🔟6️⃣
Victoria & Albert's 🔟2️⃣
Watercress Café 🔟3️⃣
Yachtsman Steakhouse 🔟6️⃣

specialties. A meal here might begin with an appetizer of roasted Pacific oysters topped with sourdough crumbs, smoked bacon, and arugula butter. Among entrées, specialties will include a cioppino loaded with seafood in a zesty herbed tomato broth and a clam bake consisting of Maine lobster, clams, mussels, red potatoes, and corn. All fish and seafood dishes can be prepared to your specifications—charcoal grilled, pan roasted, blackened, sautéed, or steamed Asian style. If you don't care for seafood, you might opt for filet mignon with roasted mushrooms and potatoes whipped with fresh corn. Save room for a dessert of milk chocolate crème brûlée. The carefully crafted wine list will change seasonally and offer a good number of by-the-glass selections. Fulton's will also be a character breakfast venue.

MODERATE

Fireworks Factory

1630 Lake Buena Vista Dr., Pleasure Island. ☎ **407/934-8989.** Reservations recommended. Main courses $6.95–$12.95 at lunch, mostly $13.95–$17.95 at dinner. AE, MC, V. Daily 11:30am–11:30pm (dinner served from 4pm); light fare and drinks served until 2am). Free self-parking, valet parking $5. AMERICAN REGIONAL.

According to Disney legend, Captain Merriweather Adam Pleasure, the mythological 19th-century ship merchant and adventurer who developed Pleasure Island, manufactured fireworks as a hobby and staged dazzling spectaculars every July 4th. Pleasure was lost at sea in 1839, but his former corrugated-tin warehouse survives in the form of this "explosively" exuberant casual restaurant. The Factory has exposed-brick walls hung with neon signs and vintage advertisements for fireworks, and missile fireworks are prominently displayed. You can eat downstairs, enjoy the lively scene from a balcony level, or sit outdoors on a patio overlooking Lake Buena Vista. This is a good choice for family dining.

Lunch or dinner, you might start off with an appetizer sampler (spicy chicken wings, shrimp quesadillas, and applewood-smoked baby back ribs). Dinner entrées range from Cajun shrimp pasta to oak-roasted salmon served with roasted tomato/corn relish and angel-hair sweet potatoes. And at lunch you might opt for mesquite-smoked barbecued beef sandwich. For dessert: a giant Toll House cookie served warm, topped with vanilla ice cream and hot fudge. In addition to "explosive" specialty drinks (try a 21 Rum Salute) and wines, the Fireworks Factory offers more than 45 varieties of domestic and imported beer, ale, and stout, including microbrewery selections.

Planet Hollywood

1506 E. Buena Vista Dr., Pleasure Island. ☎ **407/827-7827.** Reservations not accepted. Main courses $7.50–$18.95 (most under $13). AE, DC, MC, V. Daily 11am–2am. Free self-parking, valet parking $5. AMERICAN.

Planet Hollywood crashed meteorlike into the Pleasure Island solar system in 1994, with a lavish opening-night party hosted by stockholders Schwarzenegger, Stallone, Willis, and Moore. A galaxy of stars—Luke Perry, Roseanne, Charlie Sheen, Wesley Snipes, Cindy Crawford, and others—made the scene, and the excitement they generated hasn't dimmed yet. Crowds (mostly teenagers and families) still patiently wait several hours to enter (via a ramp that makes you feel like you're boarding a space ship) the Planet's orbed precincts. Inside, a fiber-optic ceiling creates a planetarium effect; a vast circular video monitor (and 11 other screens) airs film clips, movie previews, and footage of star-studded Planet Hollywood openings; there are light shows; and rock music plays constantly at a fairly high decibel level. The triple-tiered premises also comprise a veritable show-business museum jam-packed with movie and

TV memorabilia, costumes, and props—more than 300 items ranging from Eddie Munster's tricycle to Peter O'Toole's *Lawrence of Arabia* costume. And two shops—one of them topped by a rotating dinosaur—sell vast amounts of Planet Hollywood merchandise.

For all the hoopla, the food's pretty good, and the service is friendly and attentive. You can nosh on appetizers such as hickory-smoked buffalo wings, pot stickers, or nachos. There are also fajitas, burgers, sandwiches, salads, pizzas, pastas . . . not to mention big platters of grilled steak, chicken, ribs, or pork chops. Beverages run the gamut from chocolate malts to exotic specialty drinks with movie-inspired names like "Beetle Juice" and "Die Harder." Try Arnold's mother's apple strudel topped with nutmeg ice cream for dessert.

Portobello Yacht Club

1650 Lake Buena Vista Dr., Pleasure Island. ☎ **407/934-8888.** Reservations not accepted (arrive early to avoid a wait). Main courses $6.95–$9.95 at lunch, $12.95–$22.95 at dinner; pizzas $6.95–$8.95. AE, MC, V. Daily 11:30am–midnight (dinner served from 4pm). Free self-parking, valet parking $5. NORTHERN ITALIAN.

Occupying a Bermuda-style gabled house, the Yacht Club is nautically themed, its interior, though casual, evoking a luxury cruise ship. Walls are plastered with photographs of racing yachts, navigational charts, and yachting flags, and shelves are lined with racing trophies. From the lively, mahogany-paneled bar, you can watch oak-fired pizzas being prepared in an exhibition kitchen. Multipaned windows overlook Lake Buena Vista, as do tables on awninged patios.

Those oak-fired pizzas have crisply thin crusts and toppings such as *quattro formaggi*—mozzarella, romano, Gorgonzola, and provolone—with sun-dried tomatoes. At dinner, you might select a main course of charcoal-grilled half chicken marinated in olive oil, garlic, and fresh rosemary and served with garlicky oven-roasted mashed potatoes and seasonal vegetables. Or choose a pasta dish such as penne with plum tomatoes, Italian bacon, garlic, and fresh basil. There's an extensive list of Italian and California wines. A dessert of crema bruccioto (white-chocolate custard with a caramelized sugar glaze) is recommended.

4 Lake Buena Vista Area

This section is largely composed of notable restaurants at Disney resorts and other area accommodations. Since most of these are gorgeous properties, they're fun to visit. Before or after your meal, take a stroll around the grounds and public areas.

VERY EXPENSIVE

Black Swan

In the Hyatt Regency Grand Cypress Resort, 1 N. Jacaranda (off FL 535). ☎ **407/239-1999.** Reservations recommended. Main courses $25–$34. AE, CB, DC, DISC, JCB, MC, V. Daily 6–10pm. Free self-parking. AMERICAN/CONTINENTAL.

Overlooking the magnificent emerald fairways of this posh resort's golf course, the Black Swan has a lodgelike, split-level interior with a big working fireplace and a cross-beamed knotty-pine cathedral ceiling. Large, pine-framed windows overlook the ninth hole, and that verdant view is echoed within by lovely floral arrangements and planters of greenery. Golfers make up the majority of the clientele. It's not unusual here to see someone rise up excitedly from a table and demonstrate how he eagled the 17th and birdied the 18th hole to win a match. Barring that, dinner entertainment consists of a pianist at a white baby grand.

I began a recent meal here with an appetizer of grilled marinated portobello mushroom nestled on a bed of wilted arugula and topped with a trilogy of wild mushrooms and asiago cheese gratinée. A main dish of roast rack of lamb (thick, juicy slices grilled in an herbed honey-Dijon crust) came with mashed potatoes and rosemary jus. Another, corn-tortilla-crusted breast of chicken, was served with black bean and roasted corn relish and cilantro chili fettuccine. A warm, crisp apple tart on caramel sauce topped with honey-vanilla ice cream and whipped cream provided a fitting finale. The Black Swan has an extensive wine list with many dessert libations (cognacs, ports, etc.).

○ Victoria & Albert's

In Disney's Grand Floridian Beach Resort, 4401 Floridian Way. ☎ **407/WDW-DINE.** Reservations required. Jackets required for men. Prix-fixe meal $80 per person, $25 additional for Royal Wine Pairing. AE, MC, V. Two dinner seatings daily, 6–6:45pm and 9–9:45pm. Free self-parking and validated valet parking. AMERICAN REGIONAL.

It's not often that I'd ever describe a dining experience as flawless, but Victoria & Albert's, the World's most elite restaurant (Walt Disney World, that is), managed to win that adjective from me. Its intimate dining room is plush; diners sink into leather-upholstered Louis XIII–style chairs at exquisitely appointed tables lit by silver-shaded Victorian lamps. A maid and butler provide deft and gracious service, and a harpist plays softly while you dine.

Dinner, a seven-course affair, is described in a personalized menu sealed with a gold wax insignia. The fare changes nightly. On a recent visit, I began with an hors d'oeuvre of Florida lobster tail with aïoli. It was supplanted by a more formal appetizer—vermouth-poached jumbo sea scallops served in a crisp rice-noodle basket on shallot-chive sauce with garnishes of caviar and Chinese tat soi leaves. A shot of peppered vodka added piquancy to a velvety plum tomato bisque sprinkled with smoked bacon and lightly topped with pesto cream sauce. For an entrée, I selected a fan of pinkly juicy sautéed Peking duck breast with wild rice and crabapple chutney. A salad of esoteric greens in an orange sherry vinaigrette cleared the palate for the next course—English Stilton served with pine-nut bread, port wine, and a pear poached in burgundy, cognac, and cinnamon sugar. The conclusion: a sumptuous hazelnut and Frangelico soufflé, followed by coffee and chocolate truffles. This is a highly nuanced cuisine to be slowly savored. There is, of course, an extensive *recherché* wine list. I suggest you opt for the Royal Wine Pairing, which provides an appropriate wine with each course and lets you sample a variety of selections from the restaurant's distinguished cellars.

EXPENSIVE

○ Ariel's

In Disney's Beach Club Resort, 1800 Epcot Resorts Blvd. ☎ **407/WDW-DINE** for priority seating. Main courses mostly $17.95–$24. AE, MC, V. Daily 6–10pm. Free self- and valet parking. SEAFOOD.

Named for the *Little Mermaid* character, this exquisite restaurant overlooking Stormalong Bay is awash in seafoam green, peach, and coral. A prismed 2,000-gallon coral-reef tank is filled with tropical fish, walls are hung with oil paintings of scenes from the movie, and whimsical fish mobiles and glass bubbles dangle from a vaulted ceiling. You'll feel like you're dining in an underwater kingdom.

Appetizers (which supplement a complimentary smoked clam dip) include scrumptious New England silver-dollar crab cakes served with a spicy tartar sauce. Or start off with a Cajun-style shellfish gumbo replete with chunks of shrimp, lobster, and smoky andouille sausage. For your entrée, a traditional Spanish *paella*—an array of

Sitting at the Chef's Table: The Best Seat in the House

There's a special dining option at Victoria & Albert's (see above). Reserve the **Chef's Table** here, and dine in a charming alcove hung with copper pots and dried flower wreaths at an elegantly appointed candlelit table . . . right in the heart of the kitchen! You'll sip champagne with chef Scott Hunnell while discussing your food preferences for the seven- to nine-course menu he'll be creating especially for you. There's a cooking seminar element to this experience; diners get to tour the kitchen and observe the artistry of highly skilled chefs at work. The Chef's Table can accommodate up to six people a night. It's a leisurely affair, lasting 3 or 4 hours. The price is $100 without wine, $125 per person including five wines (I strongly recommend the latter). Let me further whet your appetite: There's a surprise during dinner, but I can't tell you what it is or it won't be one. Chef's Table is immensely popular. Reserve far in advance (even months ahead) by calling 407/WDW-DINE or 407/824-l089.

fresh lobster, scallops, mussels, calamari, and shrimp inside a ring of saffron rice—is highly recommended. A few nonseafood options are offered as well, among them USDA choice New York strip steak grilled over a hickory and oak fire. Desserts include a rich Chambord raspberry chocolate cake, and an extensive award-winning wine list indicates which selections best complement your entrée. A children's menu lists items like chicken nuggets and spaghetti with meat sauce in the $4 to $6 range.

✪ California Grill

At Disney's Contemporary Resort, 4600 N. World Dr. ☎ **407/824-1576** or 407/WDW-DINE for reservations. Main courses $14.75–$27.50. AE, MC, V. Daily 5:30–10pm. CALIFORNIA CUISINE.

You might see Disney CEO Michael Eisner dining here with fellow corporate honchos; it's one of his favorite WDW dining rooms. High above the Magic Kingdom (on the Contemporary Resort's 15th floor), this stunning, California-style restaurant offers scenic views of the park and lagoon below. A zig-zaggy Wolfgang Puckish interior incorporates art deco elements (a cove ceiling, curved pearwood walls, vivid splashes of color, polished black granite surfaces), but the central focus is a dramatic exhibition kitchen with a hearthlike wood-burning oven and rotisserie. Gorgeous flower arrangements and cornucopia-like displays of fruits and vegetables are further embellishments.

Chef Clifford Pleau's menus change seasonally. A sushi sampler makes a good beginning here, as does ravioli filled with goat cheese, shiitake mushrooms, and sun-dried tomatoes. And whole wheat–crusted pizzas might comprise a light entrée. Heartier choices include braised lamb shank (with wild chanterelle risotto and orange-nuanced bread topping) or grilled pork tenderloin served atop polenta with crimini mushrooms and a garnish of crispy fried sage. For dessert, it's hard to surpass the butterscotch crème brûlée with almond biscotti. If you like a close-up view of chefs at work, ask to sit at the kitchen counter. There's a good selection of California wines to complement your meal. And light fare (sushi, quesadillas, spring rolls) is available at the plush adjoining bar lounge.

✪ Hemingway's

In the Hyatt Regency Grand Cypress, 1 Grand Cypress Blvd. (off FL 535). ☎ **407/239-1234.** Reservations recommended. Main courses $7.50–$19.75 at lunch, $19.50–$25 at dinner. AE, CB, DC, DISC, JCB, MC, V. Tues–Sat 11:30am–2:30pm; daily 6–10:30pm. Free self- and validated valet parking. FLORIDA SEAFOOD.

Fronted by a waterfall that cascades into stone-bedded streams, Hemingway's evokes Key West and honors its most famous denizen; walls are hung with sepia photographs of "Papa" and his fishing and hunting trophies. This casually elegant (and generally child-free) restaurant is a good choice for romantic dinners. In a warren of intimate dining areas under a high, weathered-pine ceiling, elegantly appointed tables are lit by gleaming brass hurricane lamps. Weather permitting, you can sit on a screened wooden deck near the waterfall.

Ask not for whom the bell tolls but rather for an appetizer of deep-fried baby squid and grilled eggplant in garlicky herb-seasoned tomato coulis. Follow up with an entrée of golden brown beer-battered coconut shrimp; it's served with roasted potatoes, a colorful array of al dente vegetables, and orange marmalade-horseradish sauce. Also recommended are the deliciously light, moist, and fluffy crab cakes; ask for Cajun tartar sauce with them. For dessert, Key lime pie appropriately reaches its apogee here. The lunch menu offers similar fare, along with paella, sandwiches, and salads. In the adjoining Hurricane Lounge—a most congenial setting with a beautiful oak bar—specialties include a variety of island rums and the Papa Doble, a potent tropical rum and fruit libation invented by Hemingway himself (legend has it he once drank 16 of them at one sitting!).

Mikado Japanese Steak House

In Marriott's Orlando World Center, 8701 World Center Dr. (off FL 536). ☎ **407/238-8664.** Reservations recommended. Main courses $12.95–$28.95. AE, CB, DC, DISC, JCB, MC, OPT, V. Daily 6–10pm. Free self-parking and validated valet parking. JAPANESE.

This gorgeous, 230-acre resort houses a beautiful teppanyaki restaurant. Its serene interior, with intimate seating areas created by shoji screens, has windows overlooking rock gardens, reflecting pools, and a palm-fringed pond. Japanese music helps set the tone. Plan to arrive early and enjoy a cocktail at sunset on the wooden deck overlooking the swimming pool.

Meals here are teppanyaki style—which means you're seated with other patrons at a grill-topped table. For businesspeople dining alone, the socializing that happens naturally here can be a plus. A highly trained chef wheels a cart full of raw food to the table and with dazzling dexterity trims, chops, sautés, and flips it onto your waiting plate. Appetizer selections include softshell crab, smoked salmon and cucumber sushi, and assorted tempura vegetables and shrimp. Entrées—offering various combinations of steak and seafood—come with a complimentary hors d'oeuvre of grilled shrimp or scallops, soup (select the tastier miso), salad, steamed rice (yummy fried rice is available for an additional $2.25), an array of stir-fried vegetables, and green tea. A decanter of warm sake is recommended, and green tea or ginger ice cream makes a refreshing dessert. Low-priced meals are available for children.

✪ Tuscany

In Marriott's Orlando World Center, 8701 World Center Dr. (off FL 536). ☎ **407/239-4200.** Reservations recommended. Main courses $15–$27. AE, CB, DC, DISC, JCB, MC, OPT, V. Daily 6–10pm. Free self-parking; valet parking available. TUSCAN.

The showplace restaurant of a luxury resort, Tuscany has rich cherry- and mahogany-paneled walls hung with gilt-framed Michelangelo prints. White-linen-cloth tables are set with fresh flowers, and diners are comfortably ensconced in roomy tapestried armchairs, booths, and Regency chairs. Soft lighting and opera music complete the ambience.

A pasta appetizer is a good way to begin your meal here—most notably, the gnocchi served with gorgonzola sauce and a garnish of diced plum tomatoes. Impressive entrées—such as rack of lamb in a light demiglace sauce with roasted eggplant purée, white beans, potato croquette, and haricots verts—are aesthetically presented on large white platters. Herbed focaccia bread served with light, garlicky goat cheese accompanies your meal. An extensive European/California wine list includes many by-the-glass selections. Desserts change nightly; I recently enjoyed an exquisite, thin-sliced apple tart served atop crème anglaise and garnished with fresh berries.

✪ Yachtsman Steakhouse

In Disney's Yacht Club Resort, 1700 Epcot Resorts Blvd. ☎ **407/WDW-DINE** for priority seating. Main courses $16.95–$25.50. AE, MC, V. Daily 6–10pm. Free self- and valet parking. STEAK/ CHOPS/SEAFOOD.

The Yacht Club, a gorgeous resort inspired by New England's grand turn-of-the-century summer mansions, houses a fittingly elegant signature restaurant. Lacquered knotty-pine beams, paneling, and plank flooring create a warm, woody feel that is enhanced by burgundy leather-upholstered oak chairs. USDA grain-fed beef—hand selected to ensure top marbling for natural juices and tenderness—is aged, cured, cut, and ground on the premises. You can see these prime cuts on display in a glass-enclosed beef-aging room, and an exhibition kitchen provides a tantalizing glimpse of sizzling steaks, chops, and seafood being grilled over oak and hickory.

You might begin your meal here with an appetizer of garlicky escargots marinated in dry vermouth and served en croûte with rich burgundy sauce. Beef entrées—such as succulent filet mignon, prime rib of beef au jus, or an 18-ounce Kansas City strip steak served on the bone (it's a cattle drive tradition)—are served with baked potato, a board of fresh-baked bread, and a choice of béarnaise or bordelaise sauces. Side dishes, such as a skillet of fresh mushrooms sautéed in cognac and creamed spinach, are noteworthy. Other dishes run the gamut from lamb chops with apple mint butter and rosemary gin sauce to crisp-grilled chicken in apricot brandy sauce. And for the truly intrepid, there's a brownie fudge sundae for dessert. An extensive wine list is available, and a children's menu offers full meals for $3.75 to $6.50.

MODERATE

Artist Point

In Disney's Wilderness Lodge, 901 Timberline Dr. ☎ **407/WDW-DINE** for priority seating. Main courses $14–$21. AE, MC, V. Daily 5:30–10pm. Free self- and valet parking. STEAK AND SEAFOOD/GAME SPECIALTIES.

This stunning resort restaurant centers on western-theme murals inspired by Rocky Mountain School artists Albert Bierstadt and Thomas Moran (they do deviate a bit, however—look for the hidden Mickeys). The illusion that you're dining in a rustically elegant, turn-of-the-century national park lodge is enhanced by large windows overlooking a lake and waterfall. Weather permitting, there's also terrace seating.

The menu changes seasonally. On a recent visit, I enjoyed a Northwest salmon sampler appetizer (smoked pepperlachs, cured gravlax, and pan-seared salmon served with onion/pepper/caper relish). And entrées ranged from a 16-ounce grilled porterhouse steak (served with red-skin potatoes, fire-roasted onions, garlic, and mushrooms) to grilled maple-glazed king salmon served with roasted vegetables, roasted apples, and couscous studded with morsels of sun-dried cherries, pignoli nuts, and smoked onion. Game specials and Pacific Northwestern wines are featured. Desserts—such as chocolate silk bread pudding topped with vanilla ice cream and chocolate sauce—are immense (consider sharing) and delicious.

'Ohana

At Disney's Polynesian Resort, 1600 Seven Seas Dr. ☎ **407/WDW-DINE** for priority seating. Buffet is $19.75 adults, $13 ages 12–16, $8 ages 3–11, under 3 free. AE, MC, V. Daily 5–10pm. PACIFIC RIM.

You'll be welcomed here with warm island hospitality by a server who addresses you as "cousin." 'Ohana means "family" in Hawaiian, and you're about to enjoy a convivial meal with the extended clan. The setting is South Seas exotic, with thatched roofing and tapa-cloth tenting overhead, carved Polynesian columns, and an open kitchen centering on a wood-burning, 18-foot fire-pit grill. There's lots going on at all times. The blowing of a conch shell summons a storyteller, coconut races take place down the central aisle, couples get up and dance to island music, and people celebrating birthdays participate in hula hoop contests as everyone sings "Happy Birthday" to them in Hawaiian. Kids especially love all the hoopla, but if you're looking for an intimate venue, this isn't it.

Soon after you're seated, a lazy susan arrives laden with steamed dumplings in soy/sesame oil, Napa cabbage slaw with honey mustard, black bean and corn relish, and several tangy sauces. And course succeeds course in rapid succession (ask your waiter to slow the pace if it's too fast). The feast includes salad; fresh-baked herbed focaccia bread; grilled chicken, smoky pork sausage, marinated turkey breast, mesquite-seasoned beef, teriyaki ribs, and jumbo shrimp; stir-fried noodles and vegetables; fresh pineapple with caramel sauce; soft drinks; and coffee. Passionfruit crème brûlée is extra, but worth it. A full bar offers tropical drinks, including nonalcoholic ones for kids.

Pebbles

12551 FL 535, in the Crossroads Shopping Center, in Lake Buena Vista. ☎ **407/827-1111.** Reservations not accepted. Sandwiches and salads $4.95–$8.50; main courses mostly $7.95–$15.95. AE, CB, DC, DISC, MC, V. Daily 11am–1am. Free self-parking. CALIFORNIA-STYLE AMERICAN.

Pebbles is one of Orlando's most popular restaurants, especially with a young yuppie crowd. The multilevel dining room centers on a sunken bar under a cross-beamed skylit ceiling, and though it's a large space, white wooden shutters and windowed enclosures create a warren of intimate dining areas. Lush tropical greenery, fountains, and canvas tenting contribute to the garden-party ambience. During the day, sunshine streams in; at night, flickering hurricane lamps provide romantic lighting.

The same menu is offered throughout the day, supplemented by specials. Start off with a "lite bite" of creamy baked chèvre served atop chunky tomato sauce with hot garlic bread. Pebbles offers the option of a casual meal—perhaps a cheddar burger on toasted brioche, honey-roasted spareribs, or a Caesar salad tossed with grilled chicken. Or you can select a more serious entrée such as tender leg of smoked duck that has been rubbed with fennel, glazed with triple sec, and slow roasted to sear in flavorful juices. Dessert of choice: the gold brick sundae—a scoop of vanilla ice cream encased in a candylike chocolate/almond shell and served atop caramel sauce with fresh strawberries. There's a full bar, and many premium wines are offered by the glass.

INEXPENSIVE

Boatwright's Dining Hall

In Disney's Dixie Landings Resort, 1251 Dixie Dr. (off Bonnet Creek Parkway). ☎ **407/WDW-DINE** for priority seating. Breakfast items $4.25–$6.95; main courses $8.25–$14.95; sandwiches $6.95. AE, MC, V. Daily 7–11:30am and 5–10pm. Free self-parking. AMERICAN/CAJUN.

Boatwright's is themed to look like an 1800s boat-building factory, complete with the wooden hull of a Louisiana fishing boat suspended from its lofty beamed ceiling. An uncommonly pretty factory, it has oak-plank floors and two large working brick fireplaces. Kids will enjoy the wooden toolboxes on every table; each contains a salt shaker that doubles as a level, a wood-clamp sugar dispenser, a pepper-grinder-cum-ruler, a jar of unmatched utensils, shop rags (to be used as napkins), and a little metal pail of crayons.

Cajun breakfasts offer intriguing possibilities. French toast here is made with sourdough–sweet potato baguette tossed in rich egg custard, deep-fried, and coated with cinnamon sugar. Another option: a pan of sautéed crawfish, mushrooms, green onions, and tomatoes in mustard cream sauce (served with home-style potatoes topped with two eggs, and an oven-fresh buttermilk biscuit). Start with deep-fried bacon-wrapped oysters and scallops, then follow with an entrée of rich bouillabaisse redolent of oaken cognac or a medley of blackened seafood served over brown-buttered pasta in creamy garlic sauce. For dessert, there's homemade fruit cobbler topped with vanilla ice cream and smothered in whipped cream.

Bonfamille's Cafe

In Disney's Port Orleans Resort, 2201 Orleans Dr. (off Bonnet Creek Parkway). ☎ **407/ WDW-DINE** for priority seating. Breakfast items $4.25–$6.95; main courses mostly $8.25–$14.95; salads and po'boy sandwiches $6.95. AE, MC, V. Daily 7–11:30am and 5–10pm. Free self-parking. AMERICAN/CREOLE.

Named for a character in *The Aristocats,* the charming Bonfamille's is patterned after a fountained French Quarter courtyard. Exposed-brick walls are hung with paintings of New Orleans, big baskets of flowering plants are suspended from beams overhead, and Dixieland jazz plays softly in the background. During breakfast it's light and sunny; in the evening, candle lamps provide soft lighting.

Louisiana-style breakfasts range from fresh hot beignets and café au lait to a skillet of crawfish and andouille sausage topped with zesty Creole sauce and melted sharp cheddar. The latter is served with home-style fried potatoes topped with eggs and a hot buttermilk biscuit. A typical dinner here: an appetizer of chicken wings tossed in spicy Louisiana hot sauce served with celery and blue cheese dip, followed by grilled Atlantic salmon (served with spicy pecan butter, rice, and sautéed vegetables), and a dessert of Bourbon Street pudding with strawberry and caramel bourbon sauces. After dinner, families can head over to the hotel's Scat Cats Lounge, where entertainment—sing-alongs and live music with lots of audience participation—is featured most nights.

ⓢ Cape May Café

In Disney's Beach Club Resort, 1800 Epcot Resorts Blvd. ☎ **407/WDW-DINE** for priority seating. Adults $18.95, ages 7–11 $9.50, ages 3–6 $4.50, under 3 free. Lobster is additional. AE, MC, V. Daily 5:30–9:30pm. Free self- and valet parking. SEAFOOD.

A hearty, 19th-century-style New England clambake buffet is featured nightly at this charming peach and seafoam-green restaurant, where sand sculptures, paintings of turn-of-the-century beach scenes, croquet mallets, and furled striped beach umbrellas evoke an upscale seaside resort. Diners sit in oversized chairs at birchwood tables, and large towel napkins are provided. Aromatic chowder, steamed clams and mussels, corn on the cob, chicken, lobster, and red-skin potatoes are cooked up in a crackling rockweed steamer pit that serves as the restaurant's centerpiece. And these traditional clambake offerings are supplemented by dozens of salads (pasta, seafood, fruit, vegetables), hot entrées (barbecued ribs, smoked sausage, pasta dishes), and a wide array of oven-fresh breads and desserts. There's a full bar.

ⓢ Romano's Macaroni Grill

12148 Apopka-Vineland Rd. (just north of C.R. 535/Palm Parkway). ☎ **407/239-6676** for priority seating. Main courses $4.95–$8.25 at lunch, $6.95–$15.95 at dinner (most under $10). AE, CB, DC, DISC, MC, V. Sun–Thurs 11am–10pm, Fri–Sat 11am–11pm. Free self-parking. NORTHERN ITALIAN.

Though Orlando friends had raved about the Macaroni Grill, I didn't really expect much from a chain restaurant. Upon entering, I was favorably impressed by its cheerful interior, with arched stone walls, shuttered windows, colorful murals of Venice, and lights festively strung overhead. A welcoming glow emanated from the exhibition kitchen where white-hatted chefs were tending an oak-burning pizza oven, and foodstuffs, chianti, flowers, and desserts were aesthetically arrayed on counters.

But the big surprise was the food. Everything was made from the freshest ingredients, and the quality of cuisine would have been notable at three times the price. The thin-crusted pizzas—such as the Mediterranea topped with fresh tomato sauce, shrimp, feta and mozzarella cheeses—were scrumptious, as was a dish of bowtie pasta tossed with grilled chicken, pancetta, and red and green onions in asiago cream sauce. Equally good: an entrée of sautéed chicken with mushrooms, artichoke hearts, capers, and pancetta in lemon butter; it came with spaghettini. There were fresh-baked breads, as well—focaccia and ciabatta (a crusty, country loaf) for sopping up sauces or dipping in extra virgin olive oil. And desserts—especially an apple custard torte with hazelnut crust and caramel topping—kept to the same lofty standard. There's a full bar, premium wines are sold by the glass, and a children's menu offers an entrée and beverage for just $3.25. Bravo Romano!

5 International Drive Area

Some of the best area restaurants are along International Drive, within about 10 minutes of Walt Disney World parks by car.

VERY EXPENSIVE

✪ Dux

In the Peabody Orlando, 9801 International Dr. ☎ **407/345-4550.** Reservations recommended. Main courses $25–$31.95. AE, CB, DC, DISC, JCB, MC, OPT, V. Mon–Sat 6–11pm. Free self-parking and validated valet parking. INTERNATIONAL.

Named for the hotel's signature ducks that parade ceremoniously into the lobby each morning to Sousa's *King Cotton* march, this is one of central Florida's most highly acclaimed restaurants. And since the Peabody is the headquarters hotel for nearby Universal Studios, you're likely to see a celebrity or two among the diners. Upholstered bamboo chairs and cushioned banquettes provide seating at candlelit, white-linen-cloth tables set with flowers and beautiful ceramic show plates. A lavish dessert display table with a floral centerpiece serves as a visual focus, and the textured gold walls are hung with ornately framed mirrors and watercolors representing 72 ducks!

The menu varies seasonally. At a recent dinner, appetizer selections included a unique version of pot stickers—stuffed with portabello mushrooms, scallions, and creamed goat cheese and garnished with asiago twigs. An entrée of Sonoma lamb chops glazed with Hunan barbecue sauce was accompanied by roasted Chinese mushrooms and green onions, with a small "treasure packet" of Pacific rice concealed under the lamb. Also listed that night: grilled Florida black grouper marinated in fearless (read *hot*) West Indian spices and served with a plantain-yam mash and tropical chutney. Dessert was a sublime hazelnut meringue napoleon topped with homemade frangelico ice cream and a dusting of Brazilian cocoa. Dux has an extensive, award-winning wine list.

MODERATE

B-Line Diner

In the Peabody Orlando hotel, 9801 International Dr. ☎ **407/345-4460.** Reservations not accepted. Main courses $2.75–$8.50 at breakfast, $6.50–$10.95 at lunch, $6.95–$19.95 (most under $15) at dinner. AE, CB, DC, DISC, JCB, MC, OPT, V. Daily 24 hours. INTERNATIONALLY NUANCED AMERICAN.

This popular local eatery is of the nouvelle art deco diner genre, which is to say that it's an idealized version of America's ubiquitous roadside establishments. Its interior is agleam with chrome edging that adorns everything from a cove ceiling to peach Formica tables, and the jukebox is stocked with oldies tunes. Gorgeous flower arrangements add upscale panache. Though the B-Line is a sophisticated venue, kids get their own low-priced menu, a duck-theme coloring/activities book, and crayons; they can also enjoy ice-cream sundaes for dessert here.

The seasonally varying menu offers haute versions of diner food such as a superior chicken pot pie, pan-seared pork (with grilled apples, sun-dried cherry stuffing, and brandy honey sauce), or a ham and cheese sandwich on baguette. Other items—such as a falafel sandwich on pita bread with mint yogurt sauce—bear no relation to traditional diner fare. Portions are hearty. A glass display case up front is filled with scrumptious fresh-baked desserts: everything from coffee and chocolate eclairs to white chocolate/Grand Marnier mousse cake. There's a full bar. Self- and validated valet parking are free.

✪ Cafe Tu Tu Tango

8625 International Dr. (just west of the Mercado). ☎ **407/248-2222.** Reservations not accepted. AE, DISC, MC, V. Tapas (tasting portions) $3.75–$7.95. Daily 11:30am–2am. Free self- and valet parking. INTERNATIONAL/TAPAS.

Though one might question the need for yet one more theme experience outside the parks, this zany restaurant is a welcome respite from Orlando's predictable "chain gang." For one thing, there's an ongoing performance-art experience taking place while you dine: One evening, an elegantly dressed couple might tango past your table. Another time, a belly dancer might perform, or a magician might do a few tricks tableside. In addition, there are always artists in a studio area creating pottery, paintings, and jewelry.

Tu Tu's colorful ambience is a lot of fun, but its food is the real draw. The larger your party, the more dishes you can sample; two full plates will sate most appetites. My favorites include Cajun egg rolls (filled with blackened chicken, corn, and cheddar and goat cheese, served with chunky tomato salsa and Creole mustard) and pepper-crusted, seared tuna sashimi with crispy rice noodles and cold spinach in a sesame-soy vinaigrette. International wines can be ordered by the glass or bottle. Great desserts here, too—such as creamy almond/amaretto flan and rich guava cheesecake with strawberry sauce.

✪ Capriccio

In the Peabody Orlando, 9801 International Dr. ☎ **407/352-4000.** Reservations recommended. Main courses mostly $12–$22 (with most pizza and pasta dishes priced below $14); Sun champagne brunch buffet $24.95 for adults, $12.95 for children 4–12, under 4 free. AE, CB, DC, DISC, JCB, MC, OPT, V. Tues–Sun 6–10pm; brunch Sun 11am–2:30pm. Free self-parking and validated valet parking. ITALIAN.

Capriccio's striking Italian *moderne* interior features a gleaming, black-and-white-checkerboard marble-tile floor and black Italian marble tables elegantly appointed with Tuscan-look Villeroy & Boch show plates. An exhibition kitchen occupying an entire wall showcases chefs tending mesquite-burning pizza ovens and grills.

Seasonally changing menus bring verve and imagination to traditional Italian cookery. On a recent visit, I enjoyed an appetizer of fried calamari served with three *aïolis* (garlicky Basque mayonnaises) flavored, respectively, with sun-dried tomato, basil, and saffron. Also scrumptious: a pasta dish of *bucatini* tossed with chunks of mesquite-grilled chicken and mushrooms in a slightly garlicky herbed white wine/pesto sauce and finished with tomato concasse. And an entrée of pan-seared tuna with braised fennel and radicchio was served with lentil flan and a buttery citrus sauce. The kitchen also turns out fabulous pizzas, and oven-fresh breads are accompanied by herb-infused extra virgin olive oil; dip and exult. But save room for Capriccio's desserts, which include the definitive *zuppa inglese*. An extensive, award-winning wine list is available. *Note:* Capriccio also serves a great champagne Sunday brunch.

✪ Ming Court

9188 International Dr. (between Sand Lake Road and the Beeline Expressway). ☎ **407/ 351-9988.** Reservations recommended. Dim sum items mostly $1.95–$2.50; main courses $4.50–$7.95 at lunch, $12.50–$19.95 at dinner. AE, CB, DC, DISC, JCB, MC, V. Daily 11am– 2:30pm and 4:30pm–midnight. Free self-parking. CHINESE REGIONAL.

I was thrilled to find such a fine Chinese restaurant in Orlando, one with a clientele that includes more local food cognescenti than tourists. Ming Court is fronted by a serpentine "cloud wall," crowned by engraved sea-green Chinese tiles (it's a celestial symbol; you dine above the clouds here, like the gods). The candlelit interior is stunningly decorated in soft earth tones. Glass-walled terrace rooms overlook lotus ponds filled with colorful koi, and a plant-filled area under a lofty skylight ceiling evokes a starlit Ming Dynasty courtyard. A musician plays classical Chinese music on a *zheng* (a long zither) at dinner.

The menu offers specialties from diverse regions of China. Begin by ordering a variety of appetizers such as wok-charred Mandarin pot stickers, crispy wontons stuffed with vegetables and cream cheese, and wok-smoked shiitake mushrooms topped with sautéed scallions. Entrées will open up new culinary vistas to even the most sophisticated diners. Lightly battered, deep-fried chicken breast is served with a delicate lemon-tangerine sauce. Szechuan charcoal-grilled filet mignon is topped with a toasted onion/garlic/chili sauce and served with stir-fried julienne vegetables. And crispy, stir-fried jumbo Szechuan shrimp is enhanced by a light fresh tomato sauce nuanced with sake. At lunch, you can order dim sum items in addition to other menu offerings. There's an extensive wine list, and, as a concession to Western palates, Ming Court features sumptuous desserts such as a moist cake layered with Mandarin oranges, key lime, and fresh whipped cream in orange-vanilla sauce.

Siam Orchid

7575 Republic Dr. (between Sand Lake Road and Carrier Drive). ☎ **407/351-0821.** Reservations recommended. Main courses $10.25–$18.95. AE, DC, DISC, MC, V. Daily 5–11pm. Free self-parking. THAI.

Patterned after a palace in northern Thailand, Siam Orchid centers on a platform used to display wood carvings of angels and musicians representing figures from the *Ramayana,* an ancient Hindu epic poem. The split-level dining room, with lofty knotty-pine cathedral ceilings on either side, seats diners in cushioned booths and banquettes and bamboo chairs at white-linen-cloth tables, some of them overlooking a lake. For intimate dining, request a *khun toke*—a private carved teak enclosure that is the Thai answer to Japanese tatami rooms.

Owners Tim and Krissnee Martsching grow many necessary ingredients—fresh chiles, mint, cilantro, lemongrass, and wild lime—in their own garden, and their fare is authentic and delicious. Begin with *tom kha gai* (a savory chicken and mushroom soup) and continue with shared appetizers such as *satay* (grilled skewers of pork or chicken, marinated in coconut cream and mild curry, served with hot peanut sauce) and *tod man* (crispy fried chicken patties flavored with lemongrass, basil, and wild lime leaf). Not to be missed (share an order) is an entrée of *pad Thai* (soft rice noodles tossed with ground pork, fresh minced garlic, shrimp, crab claws, crabmeat, crushed peanuts, and bean sprouts in a tangy-sweet sauce). Curries—such as the royal Thai, replete with chunks of chicken, potato, and onion in a yellow curry sauce—are also a specialty. There's a full bar, and beverage choices include sake, plum wine, and Thai beers. Homemade coconut ice cream topped with crushed peanuts makes a refreshing dessert.

Wild Jacks

7364 International Dr. (between Sand Lake Road and Carrier Drive). ☎ **407/352-4407.** Reservations not accepted. AE, CB, DC, DISC, JCB, MC, V. Main courses $9.45–$17.95. Daily 4:30–11pm. Free self-parking. STEAKS AND BARBECUE.

This upscale but exuberantly western steak and barbecue restaurant has a whimsical decor, including neon beer signs, mounted buffalo heads, and a longhorn steer poised to jump from a giant horseshoe above the copper bar. Soft lighting emanates from massive, wrought-iron wagon-wheel chandeliers, as well as antlered and steer-head-motif fixtures. There's an exhibition kitchen with an open-pit grill. Diners are seated at tables covered with checkered plastic cloths. And the music is country.

Appetizers here are first rate: skewers of tangy barbecued shrimp served over Texas rice (it's studded with corn kernels and red and green peppers), miniature tacos filled with smoked chicken and cheeses, and spicy potato skins topped with melted cheese, chunks of chicken, pico de gallo, sour cream, and guacamole. Best entrée choice is the smoked brisket barbecue, served with salad, warm molasses bread and honey, and your choice of two side dishes—take the jalapeño mashed potatoes and grilled corn on the cob. Steaks and prime rib are other options. For dessert, there's peach cobbler topped with vanilla ice cream sprinkled with cinnamon. The bar has an iced beer well.

INEXPENSIVE

Enzo's

7600 Dr. Phillips Blvd., in the Marketplace Shopping Center (off Sand Lake Road, just west of I-4). ☎ **407/351-1187.** Reservations not accepted. Panini $4.75–$5.95; main courses $4.50–$6.95 at lunch, $8.50–$12.75 at dinner. AE, CB, DC, DISC, MC, V. Mon–Thurs 11:30am–10pm, Fri–Sat 11:30am–11pm. Free self-parking. ITALIAN.

Upon entering this charming little restaurant and Italian charcuterie, you'll walk past display cases filled with antipasti, deli meats, pâtés, and cheeses and shelves stocked with homemade pastas and other fancy foodstuffs. And if that's not enough to whet your appetite, you'll also glimpse chefs tending a pizza oven in an exhibition kitchen. The dining area is cheerful and inviting, with glossy pine-plank floors, peach walls hung with fine art prints, and tables covered with butcher paper (crayons are provided). Italian music (most of it operatic arias) enhances the atmosphere. Enzo's is a casual kind of place, very popular locally.

Pretty much the same menu is available throughout the day. Families troop in for pizzas—either the traditional American kind or Napoli pies with more sophisticated toppings and crisp, delicate crusts. Until 4:30pm, you can also opt for *panini* (sandwiches on crusty Italian bread), with fillings such as Italian sausage, grilled onions, and peppers; they're served with potato salad. A more serious dinner might begin with an appetizer of paper-thin slices of Norwegian salmon and onion served with extra virgin olive oil, capers, lemon, and red peppers. Homemade pastas include fat *bucatini* tossed with mushrooms, fresh-grated Parmesan, prosciutto, bacon, and peas in a robust sauce. And Enzo's most fabulous entrée is *pollo alla cecco* (roasted breast of free-range chicken with rosemary potatoes and an Italian version of ratatouille. Beer and wine are available. For dessert try *zuccotto* (Italian sponge cake soaked in Grand Marnier, layered with fresh fruit and crème anglaise, and topped with chocolate shavings). In busy seasons, arrive off-hours to avoid a wait.

6 Casselberry/Downtown Orlando

Generally, visitors don't drive 40 minutes to downtown Orlando or Casselberry to eat. Buckets, however, is close to major sightseeing attractions in Orlando. Rolando, in Casselberry, is for those of you who want to experience authentic Cuban cuisine while you're in Florida.

For further Orlando eateries, check out the Church Street Station listing in chapter 9.

MODERATE

Buckets

1825 N. Mills Ave. (just across the street from Loch Haven Park museums). ☎ **407/896-4111.** Reservations recommended (required Fri/Sat nights). Main courses $4.95–$10.95 at lunch, $8.95–$17.95 at dinner. AE, CB, DC, DISC, MC, V. Mon–Fri 11am–4pm, Sat–Sun 11:30am–4pm, Sun–Thurs 4–10pm, Fri–Sat 4–11pm; late-night menu Sun–Thurs until midnight, Fri–Sat until 1am. AMERICAN.

This is a great choice when you're visiting Orlando sights such as Leu Gardens and Loch Haven Park museums. Its attractive interior has big, teak-framed windows overlooking Lake Rowena. And weather permitting, it's lovely to sit on the awninged water-view deck. At dinner, there's live entertainment—light jazz or acoustical guitar—Thursday through Saturday.

Lunch items include salads (such as chicken Caesar topped with asiago cheese and almonds), sandwiches (such as smoked turkey breast with mozzarella cheese and tomato salsa), and hot entrées ranging from blackened catch of the day to stir-fried chicken with fresh vegetables and yellow rice tossed with walnuts. At dinner, you might follow up an appetizer of baked seafood-stuffed mushrooms with shrimp scampi served over pasta, jumbo lump crab cakes, barbecued ribs, or grilled filet mignon. And dessert options range from tiramisù to Key lime pie. There's a full bar and an extensive wine list, the latter including many by-the-glass selections.

INEXPENSIVE

⑤ Rolando's

870 E. FL 436 (Semoran Boulevard, between Red Bug Road and U.S. 17-92), in Casselberry. ☎ **407/767-9677.** Main courses $3.25–$4.75 at lunch, mostly $5.75–$11.50 at dinner. AE, DISC, MC, V. Tues–Thurs 11am–9pm, Fri–Sat 11am–10pm, Sun 1–8pm. Reservations not accepted. Free self-parking. Take I-4 east to the East–West Expressway, head east, and make a left on FL 436. CUBAN.

About 40 minutes from Walt Disney World, this inexpensive mom-and-pop eatery serves up huge portions of authentic Cuban fare. Its two dining rooms are pleasant but plain, with Formica tables, stucco walls hung with photographs of Cuba, and pots of philodendrons suspended from the ceiling. Soft lighting adds a smidge of ambience.

I recommend ordering up a bunch of appetizers to share: deep-fried ripe plantains, *papas rellenas*—breaded, deep-fried balls of mashed potato stuffed with spicy *picadillos* (garlicky ground beef cooked with onions, olives, raisins, and green peppers in a tomato sauce)—flavorful Cuban tamales topped with picadillos, and slightly sweet batter-fried corn fritters that are light as air. An entrée of roast chicken is brushed with crushed garlic, white wine vinegar, cumin, and oregano and briefly deep-fried just before serving. Tender, shredded beef is simmered in a richly seasoned, tomato-based sauce with potatoes, olives, peas, pimentos, onions, green peppers, and sweet red peppers. And paella is an option if you call a few hours in advance to order it. Entrées are served with fresh-baked hot rolls, house salad, rice, and plantains or *yuca* (a chewy root plant); take the plantains. For dessert, try the *dulce de tres leche* (a meringue-topped yellow cake mixed with condensed milk, evaporated milk, and cream). At lunch a hearty sandwich of hot Cuban bread stuffed with slices of ham, roast pork, Swiss cheese, and pickles is served with black bean soup. Beer and wine are available.

7 Only in Orlando: Dining with Disney Characters

Especially for the 10-and-under set, it's a thrill to dine in a restaurant where costumed Disney characters show up to greet the customers, sign autographs, pose in family photos, and interact with little kids. And for adults, it's lots of fun to watch the kids going nuts over Mickey or Donald. The following restaurants throughout the Walt Disney World complex offer character breakfasts and dinners. All accept American Express, MasterCard, and Visa. Make reservations as far in advance as possible for these very popular meals.

Note: On selected days, Disney resort guests can arrive earlier at some of the below-listed character breakfasts.

Many of the restaurants listed below are fully described earlier in this chapter. Fulton's Crab House, opening shortly after press time, will also host character breakfasts (see details above); call **407/934-BOAT** for information.

Artist Point, at Disney's Wilderness Lodge, 901 Timberline Dr. (☎ **407/WDW-DINE**), offers daily character breakfasts between 7:30 and 11:30am. The rustic setting—with western murals, a beamed ceiling supported by tree-trunk columns, and large windows providing scenic lake views—was inspired by the grandeur of Rocky Mountain national park country. Goofy, Pluto, and Chip 'n' Dale make the scene. The meal is an all-you-can-eat breakfast buffet priced at $12.95 for adults, $7.95 for children ages 3 to 11.

✪ **Baskerville's,** an elegant, Sherlock Holmes–theme restaurant at the Grosvenor Resort, 1850 Hotel Plaza Blvd. (☎ **407/828-4444**), hosts character breakfasts Tuesday, Thursday, and Saturday mornings from 8 to 10am and character dinners Wednesday evenings from 7:30 to 9:30pm. At either meal, you can order à la carte. Breakfast buffets cost $8.95 for adults, $4.95 for children ages 3 to 11, under 3 free. Dinner buffets, always centering on prime rib and themed around a different cuisine (Italian, Creole, etc.) nightly, also include seafood, chicken, and other meat dishes, along with a full salad bar, side dishes, and an extensive choice of desserts; price is $15.95 for adults, $6.95 for children ages 3 to 11, under 3 free. A la carte, you might order anything from a cheddar burger or Philadelphia cheese steak sandwich to a charbroiled porterhouse steak. Reservations are not accepted; arrive early to avoid a wait.

The **Cape May Café,** at Disney's Beach Club Resort, 1800 Epcot Resorts Blvd. (☎ **407/WDW-DINE**), serves lavish buffet character breakfasts daily from 7:30 to 11am. Food tables are laden with quiches, waffles, roast beef hash, bread pudding, fruit fritters, cheese blintzes, biscuits with sausage gravy, fresh-baked pastries and muffins, and many other goodies. Admiral Goofy and his crew—Chip 'n' Dale and Pluto—(characters may vary) are hosts. Adults pay $12.95, children ages 3 to 11 pay $7.95, under 3 free.

The whimsical **Chef Mickey's,** at Disney's Contemporary Resort, 4600 N. World Dr. (☎ **407/WDW-DINE**), is the setting for character breakfasts from 7:30 to 11:30am daily. A 110-foot buffet table is laden with a huge variety of breakfast dishes. On hand to meet, greet, and mingle with guests are Mickey and various pals. The prix-fixe buffet costs $13.95 for adults and $7.95 for children ages 3 to 11; it's free for kids under 3. Chef Mickey's also hosts ✪ **prime rib buffet character dinners** (including peel-and-eat shrimp, a variety of hot entrées, and a make-your-own sundae bar) nightly from 5 to 9:30pm; price is $16.95 for adults, $7.95 for children ages 3 to 11, under 3 free.

The ✪ **Garden Grill,** in the Land Pavilion at Epcot (☎ **407/WDW-DINE),** is a revolving restaurant with seating in comfortable, semicircular booths. As you dine, your table travels past desert, prairie, farmland, and rain-forest environments. There's a "momma's-in-the-kitchen" theme here: you'll be given a straw hat at the entrance, and the just-folks waitstaff speaks in country lingo. Hearty, family-style meals are hosted by Mickey, Minnie, and Chip 'n' Dale. Extensive American breakfasts (served 8:30 to 11am) are $14.95 for adults, $7.95 for children ages 3 to 9, under 3 free. Lunch and dinner, served, respectively, from 11:15am to 4pm and 4 to 8pm, cost $16.95 for adults and $9.95 for children. The latter meals include several entrées (roast chicken, farm-raised fish, and hickory-smoked steak), smashed potatoes, vegetables, squaw bread and biscuits, salad, beverage, and dessert.

The plant-filled **Garden Grove Café,** at the Walt Disney World Swan, 1200 Epcot Resorts Blvd. (☎ **407/934-3000),** is an airy, three-story domed greenhouse with festive striped canvas awnings, colorful wooden birds perched overhead, and a central terra-cotta fountain. It is the setting for character breakfasts Wednesday and Saturday from 8 to 11am and dinners Monday, Thursday, and Friday from 6 to 10pm. Breakfast offers a choice of à la carte or buffet meals (the latter is $12.50 for adults, $6.95 for children ages 3 to 11, under 3 free). Dinner is à la carte, featuring steak and seafood. Character meals here are hosted by Goofy, Pluto, Pooh, and Tigger.

Harry's Safari Bar & Grille, at the Walt Disney World Dolphin, 1500 Epcot Resorts Blvd. (☎ **407/934-4025),** is jungle themed with stuffed tigers, elephants, and giraffes in residence. Goofy, Pluto, and Chip 'n' Dale host buffet brunches here every Sunday from 8:30am to noon. Adults pay $15.50; it's $9.25 for children ages 3 to 12, under 3 free.

King Stefan's Banquet Hall, in Cinderella Castle in the Magic Kingdom (☎ **407/WDW-DINE),** serves up character breakfast buffets daily from 8 to 10am. Hosts vary, but Cinderella always puts in an appearance. Fare includes eggs, blintzes, Mickey waffles, fresh fruit, cinnamon rolls, juice, and more. Adults pay $14.95, children ages 3 to 9 pay $7.95, under 3 free. It's a great way to start your day in the Magic Kingdom.

✪ The **Liberty Tree Tavern,** in Liberty Square in the Magic Kingdom (☎ **407/ WDW-DINE),** an 18th-century pub, offers character dinners (nightly from 4pm to park closing) hosted by Mickey, Goofy, Pluto, Chip 'n' Dale, and Tigger (some or all of them). Meals, served family style, consist of salad, roast chicken, marinated flank steak, trail sausages, homemade mashed potatoes, macaroni and cheese, rice pilaf, and vegetables. Price is $19.50 for adults, $9.95 for children ages 3 to 11, under 3 free. A dessert of warm apple crisp with vanilla ice cream can be ordered à la carte.

Luau Cove, at Disney's Polynesian Resort, 1600 Seven Seas Dr. (☎ **407/ WDW-DINE),** is the setting for an island-theme character show called **Mickey's Tropical Luau** daily at 4:30pm. It's an abbreviated version of the Polynesian Luau Dinner Show described in chapter 9, "Walt Disney World & Orlando After Dark," featuring Polynesian dancers along with Mickey, Minnie, Pluto, and Goofy. Your prix-fixe meal ($30 for adults, $14 for ages 3 to 11, under 3 free) includes honey-roasted chicken, vegetables, glazed cinnamon bread, and an ice-cream sundae. Guests are presented with shell leis on entering. Reserve far in advance.

The Polynesian also hosts **Minnie's Menehune Character Breakfast** buffets (☎ **407/WDW-DINE**) daily from 7:30 to 10:30am in the Polynesian-theme **'Ohana.** Traditional breakfast foods are prepared on an 18-foot fire pit and served family style. Minnie, Goofy, and Chip 'n' Dale appear, and there are children's parades with Polynesian musical instruments. Adults pay $13.50, children ages 3 to 11 pay $8.25, under 3 free. Reservations are essential.

Disney's elegant Grand Floridian Beach Resort, 4001 Grand Floridian Way (☎ **407/WDW-DINE**), hosts character meals in its festive exposition-theme restaurant, **1900 Park Fare.** The room is decorated with old-fashioned, carved wooden merry-go-round animals, antique toys, and circus-theme paintings. Big Bertha— a French band organ that plays pipes, drums, bells, cymbals, castanets, and xylophone—provides music. Mary Poppins, Winnie the Pooh, Goofy, Pluto, Chip 'n' Dale, and Minnie Mouse appear at elaborate buffet breakfasts served daily between 7:30am and noon. Adults pay $14.95, children ages 3 to 11 pay $9.95, under 3 free. Mickey and Minnie appear at nightly buffets here (featuring prime rib, stuffed pork loin, fresh fish, and more) from 5 to 9pm. Adults pay $19.95, children ages 3 to 11 pay $9.95, under 3 free.

One of the most popular WDW character breakfasts takes place at the **Soundstage Restaurant** at Disney-MGM Studios, adjacent to the Magic of Disney Animation (☎ **407/WDW-DINE**). Selected characters from the movies *Aladdin* and *Pocahontas* sign autographs daily from 8:30 to 10:30am in this warehouse-motif restaurant decorated with movie props and facades. Favorite tunes from both Disney hits play in the background. A vast breakfast buffet is set out. The cost is $12.95 for adults, $7.95 for kids 3 to 9, and free for kids under 3.

The festive and plant-filled **Watercress Café,** at the Buena Vista Palace, 1900 Buena Vista Dr. (☎ **407/827-2727**), has paintings of parrots and flamingos adorning peach stucco walls and large windows overlooking Lake Buena Vista. It's the setting for Sunday morning character breakfasts (8 to 10:30am) featuring Minnie, Goofy, and Pluto. You can order à la carte or buffet meals. The buffet costs $11.95 for adults, $6.95 for kids 4 to 12, under 4 free. Reservations are not accepted; arrive early to avoid a wait.

7

On Your Mark, Get Set, Go!
What to See & Do In &
Around Walt Disney World

We all know what the big attraction is here—the one that put Orlando on the map. With the exception of conventioneers (and I'm sure many of them sneak off to the parks, as well), most people who come to Orlando have come to meet the Mouse.

Walt Disney World, attracting more than 13 million annual visitors, is one of the world's most popular travel destinations. And why not? It provides a welcome retreat to a star-spangled all-American fantasyland where wonderment, human progress, and old-fashioned family fun are the major themes. And these themes are presented in spectacular parades and fireworks displays, 3-D and 360-degree Circle-Vision movies, and adventure-filled journeys through time and space. Though it's not inexpensive, you'll seldom hear people complain about not getting their money's worth. Disney delivers!

The Magic Kingdom opened in 1971. Later additions include Epcot, where guests take exhilarating voyages around the world and into the future; Disney-MGM Studios, centered on "Hollywood Boulevard" and providing a thrilling behind-the-scenes look at motion-picture and TV studios; Pleasure Island, an ongoing street festival in a 6-acre complex of nightclubs and shops, featuring live concerts nightly; Walt Disney World Village, a charming lakeside enclave of shops and restaurants; Typhoon Lagoon, a 56-acre water park where you can catch the world's largest manmade waves or plummet down steep water flumes; River Country, another water park; Blizzard Beach, a new water park that's meant to be "a ski resort in the tropics"; and Discovery Island, an utterly delightful nature preserve and aviary.

The biggest change in the Disney parks this year is the totally renovated Tomorrowland at the Magic Kingdom (details below).

Outside the Disney complex, visitors are lured to two other major theme parks. Universal Studios, a working production facility, is filled with thrilling high-tech rides and attractions and gives visitors a behind-the-scenes look at motion-picture and television development and technology. New to Universal this year will be Terminator 2: 3D Battle Across Time, billed as "the quintessential sight and sound experience for the 21st century!" Nearby, Sea World, whose most famous resident is Shamu, offers 200 acres of marine-oriented shows, rides, and entertainments. Key West at Sea

World, its newest highlight, offers hands-on encounters with denizens of the deep including bottlenose dolphins and endangered turtle species. And theme parks aside, many other museums, gardens, and attractions in the area beckon visitors.

You can't see all the attractions at any of the parks in a single day. Read through the upcoming descriptions, decide which are musts for you, and try to get to them. My favorite rides and attractions are starred.

SUGGESTED ITINERARIES

A Day in the Magic Kingdom

Get to the park well before opening time, tickets in hand. When the gates open, make a dash for ExtraTERRORestrial Alien Encounter in Tomorrowland, which, as the newest major attraction, will have very long lines later in the day.

Then hightail it to Frontierland and ride Splash Mountain—another biggie—before long lines form there. When you come off, it will still be early enough to beat the lines at another major attraction; head over to Adventureland and do Pirates of the Caribbean.

Then relax and take it slow. Complete whatever else interests you in Adventureland. Then walk over to Frontierland and enjoy attractions there until lunchtime. Have lunch while taking in the 12:15 or 1:30pm Diamond Horseshoe Saloon Revue show (they don't take reservations, so arrive early).

After lunch, continue visiting Frontierland attractions as desired or proceed to the Hall of Presidents and the Haunted Mansion in Liberty Square.

By 2:30pm (earlier in peak seasons), you should snag a seat on the curb in Liberty Square along the parade route. After the parade, continue around the park, taking in Fantasyland and Tomorrowland attractions. If SpectroMagic is on during your stay, don't miss it.

If you have little kids (8 and under) in your party, start your day instead by taking the WDW Railroad from Main Street to Mickey's Starland to see the show. Work your way through Fantasyland until lunch at the Diamond Horseshoe. After lunch, visit the Country Bear Jamboree in Frontierland and proceed to Adventureland for the Jungle Cruise, Swiss Family Treehouse, and Tropical Serenade. Once again, stop in good time to get parade seats (in Frontierland). Little kids need to sit right up front to see everything. That's a long enough day for most young children, and your best plan is to go back to your hotel for a nap or swim. If, however, you wish to continue, return to Frontierland and/or Fantasyland for the rides you didn't complete earlier.

If You Can Spend Only 1 Day at Epcot

Epcot really requires at least 2 days, so this is a highlight tour. As above, arrive early, tickets in hand. If you haven't already made lunch reservations by calling 407/WDW-DINE (see chapter 6, "Dining"), make your first stop at the WorldKey terminals in Innoventions East. I suggest a 1pm lunch at the San Angel Inn Restaurant in Mexico. If you don't like Mexican food, move up one pavilion to Norway and reserve for the buffet at Akershus. You can make dinner reservations at the same time. Plan dinner for about 7pm, which will allow you time to eat and find a good viewing spot for IllumiNations (usually at 9pm, but check your schedule).

Spend no more than an hour exploring Innoventions East. Then move on to the Universe of Energy show. Continue to the Wonders of Life Pavilion, where must-sees include Body Wars, Cranium Command, and The Making of Me.

And if time allows—it will depend on line waits at attractions—take in the show at Horizons before heading into World Showcase for lunch. Over lunch, check your show schedule and decide which shows to incorporate into your day.

Then walk around the lagoon, visiting highlight attractions: *Wonders of China, The American Adventure, Impressions de France,* and *O' Canada,* allowing yourself some time for browsing and shopping. After dinner, stay on for IllumiNations.

If You Can Spend 2 Days at Epcot

Ignore the 1-day itinerary above, but do begin your day by making all necessary restaurant reservations—once again for lunch in Mexico or Norway at about 1pm. Make reservations for Day 2 at the same time.

Skip Innoventions East for now and work your way thoroughly through the Universe of Energy, Wonders of Life, Horizons, and World of Motion pavilions, keeping your lunch reservation time in mind.

After lunch, walk clockwise around the lagoon, visiting each pavilion and taking in as many shows as you like (consult your show schedule and try to keep pace as well as possible). Leave IllumiNations for your second day's visit.

Begin your second day exploring Innoventions East and proceed counterclockwise, taking in Spaceship Earth, Innoventions West, The Living Seas (its Coral Reef restaurant is a good choice for lunch), and all the other pavilions on the west side of the park. Cap your Epcot visit with IllumiNations.

A Day at Disney-MGM Studios Theme Park

Since show times change frequently here, it's impossible to really give you a workable itinerary. Upon entering the park, if you haven't already made dining arrangements, stop at the Hollywood Brown Derby (details in chapter 6) and make reservations for lunch. Or you might want to conserve park-touring time by having a light lunch at a casual eatery and saving the Derby for a relaxing dinner.

Nutritional needs accounted for, make a beeline for the Twilight Zone Tower of Terror. While you're waiting in line, plan the rest of your schedule, being sure to include these not-to-be-missed attractions: the Magic of Disney Animation, the Great Movie Ride, Jim Henson's Muppet Vision 3D, and the Monster Sound Show.

If you have girls under 11 in your party, *The Voyage of the Little Mermaid,* and *Beauty and the Beast* will probably be major priorities; for the latter shows, get in line 45 minutes prior to show time. And all kids love the parade; snag a good seat on the parade route 45 minutes ahead of time as well.

Time for more? Do Superstar Television, the Indiana Jones Epic Stunt Spectacular, Star Tours, Inside the Magic, and the Backstage Studio Tour. In peak seasons, stay on for fireworks.

If You Have Extra Days in Town

If you're staying longer than the 4 days accounted for above, you'll probably want to spend at least one of them in the Magic Kingdom and/or Epcot, seeing whatever you've missed. But if you have an additional day:

Adults and families with kids over 10 should head for **Universal Studios,** which is choc-a-bloc with thrilling, hi-tech rides and attractions. Families with younger kids will do better at **Sea World.**

Consider also an excursion to **Cypress Gardens** or the **John F. Kennedy Space Center.**

Still more time? By now you need rest and refreshment. You'll find it at any of the Disney water-theme parks. Spend the morning splashing around, and in the afternoon tour Discovery Island.

Walt Disney World Parks & Attractions

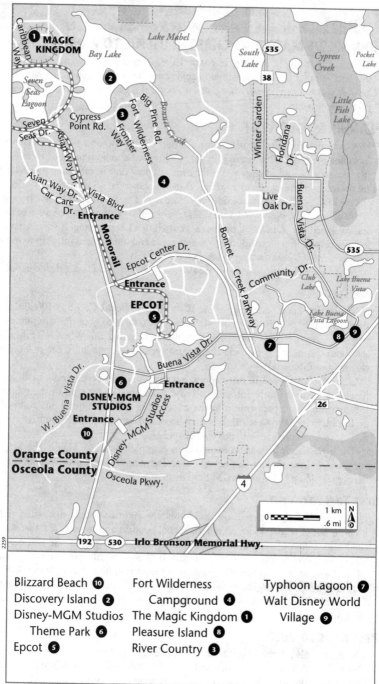

Blizzard Beach ⑩

Discovery Island ②

Disney-MGM Studios
   Theme Park ⑥

Epcot ⑤

Fort Wilderness
   Campground ④

The Magic Kingdom ①

Pleasure Island ⑧

River Country ③

Typhoon Lagoon ⑦

Walt Disney World
   Village ⑨

1 Tips on Visiting Walt Disney World

HOW WE'VE MADE THIS CHAPTER USEFUL TO PARENTS

Before every listing in the three major parks, you'll note the "Recommended Ages" that tells you which age group will most enjoy every ride and attraction. Though most families will want to do everything, you may find this guideline helpful in planning your daily itinerary.

PLANNING YOUR VISIT

How you plan your time at Walt Disney World will depend on a number of factors, including the ages of children in your party, what you've seen on previous visits, your specific interests, and whether you're traveling at a peak time or off-season (when lines are shorter and you can cram more in). Planning, however, is essential.

Unless you're staying for considerably more than a week, you can't possibly experience all the rides, shows, and attractions here—not to mention the vast array of recreational facilities. And you'll only wear yourself to a frazzle trying. It's far better to follow a relaxed itinerary, including leisurely meals and some recreation, than to make a demanding job out of trying to see everything.

Note: Many of these suggestions are also applicable at non-Disney theme parks.

INFORMATION

Before leaving home, call or write the **Walt Disney World Co.,** Box 10000, Lake Buena Vista, FL 32830-1000 (☎ 407/934-7639), for a copy of the very informative *Walt Disney World Vacations*—an invaluable planning aid. When you call, also ask about special events that will be on during your stay (see also "When to Go," in chapter 2 of this book).

Once you've arrived in town, **guest services** and **concierge desks** in all area hotels—especially Disney properties and official hotels—have up-to-the-minute information about happenings in the parks. Stop by to ask questions and pick up literature, including a schedule of park hours and special events. If you have questions your hotel can't answer, call 407/824-4321.

There are also **information locations** in each park—at City Hall in the Magic Kingdom, at Innoventions East near the WorldKey terminals in Epcot, and the Guest Services Building in Disney-MGM Studios.

BEST TIMES TO VISIT

Unless your kid's school has some odd holidays, you can assume that when your brood is out of school, so are all others. School holidays and summer are, therefore, the busiest times of year. Frankly, I think it's worthwhile pulling the kids out of school for a few days to avoid massive crowds. Two especially great times to visit, when the weather is comfortable and there are almost no lines: the week after Labor Day through Thanksgiving and the week after Thanksgiving through mid-December. Worst time is in summer when you have to suffer both long lines and blistering heat.

BEST DAYS TO VISIT

The busiest days at the Magic Kingdom and Epcot are Monday to Wednesday; at Disney-MGM Studios, Thursday and Friday. Surprisingly, weekends are the least busy at all parks. In peak seasons, especially, arrange your visits accordingly.

❓ Did You Know?

- It's not a small world after all! Covering 43 square miles, Walt Disney World is about the size of San Francisco.

- In a recent year, guests at Universal Studios consumed 1,101,245 burgers and 131 miles of hot dogs.

- The manatees at Sea World each eat about 10% of their body weight daily. Their daily diet consists of about 100 pounds of romaine lettuce along with assorted fruits and vegetables, especially apples.

- The pesticide DDT was developed solely in Orlando by a group of government entomologists who were exploring its military uses. Though later abandoned as dangerously toxic, DDT was widely used during World War II.

- The famous Florida sinkhole, appearing in Winter Park in May 1981, consumed several Porsche cars, part of a city street, a home, and a large corner of a public swimming pool. It became a central Florida tourist attraction, with vendors lining up nearby to hawk T-shirts and sinkhole-related merchandise.

CREATE AN ITINERARY FOR EACH DAY

Read the above mentioned *Walt Disney World Vacations* and the detailed descriptions in this book and plan your visit to include all shows and attractions that pique your interest and excitement. It's a good idea to make a daily itinerary, putting these in some kind of sensible geographical sequence, so you're not zigzagging all over the place. Familiarize yourself in advance with the layout of each park.

I repeat this advice—schedule in sit-down shows, recreational activities (a boat ride or swim late in the afternoon can be wonderfully refreshing), and at least some unhurried meals. My suggested itineraries are above.

HOURS

Hours of operation vary somewhat throughout the year.

The **Magic Kingdom** and **Disney-MGM Studios** are generally open 9am to 7pm, with extended hours—sometimes as late as midnight—during major holidays and the summer months.

Epcot hours are generally 9am to 9pm, with Future World open 9am to 7pm, World Showcase 11am to 9pm—once again with extended holiday hours.

Typhoon Lagoon and **Blizzard Beach** are open 10am to 5pm most of the year (with extended hours during some holidays), 9am to 8pm in summer.

River Country and **Discovery Island** are open 10am to 5pm most of the year (with extended hours during some holidays), 10am to 7pm in summer.

Note: Epcot and Disney-MGM sometimes open a half-hour or more before posted time. Keep in mind, too, that Disney resort guests enjoy early admission to all three major parks on designated days.

In the Words of Walt Disney

Family fun is as necessary to modern living as a kitchen refrigerator.

Part of the Disney success is our ability to create a believable world of dreams that appeals to all age groups.

TICKETS

There are several ticket options. Most people get the best value from 4- and 5-day passes. All passes offer unlimited use of the WDW transportation system. Prices quoted below do not include sales tax, and they are, of course, subject to change.

Adult prices are paid by anyone over 10 years of age.

Children's rates are for ages 3 to 9.

Children under 3 are admitted free.

The **4-Day Value Pass** provides admission for 1 day at the Magic Kingdom, 1 day at Epcot, 1 day at Disney-MGM Studios, and 1 day at your choice of any of those three parks; you can use it on any 4 days following purchase, but you cannot visit more than one park on any given day. Adults pay $129, children $103.

The **4-Day Park-Hopper Pass** provides unlimited admission to the three major parks on any 4 days; in other words, you can hop from park to park on any given day. Adults pay $144, children $115.

The **5-Day World-Hopper Pass** provides unlimited admission to the Magic Kingdom, Epcot, and Disney-MGM Studios on any 5 days; you can visit any combination of parks on any given day. It also includes admission to Typhoon Lagoon, River Country, Blizzard Beach, Discovery Island, and Pleasure Island for a period of 7 days beginning the first date stamped. Adults pay $196, children $157.

A **1-day, 1-park ticket for the Magic Kingdom, Epcot, or Disney-MGM Studios** is $38.50 for adults, $31 for children.

A **1-day ticket to Typhoon Lagoon or Blizzard Beach** is $23.95 for adults, $17.95 for children.

A **1-day ticket to River Country** is $14.75 for adults, $11.50 for children.

A **1-day ticket to Discovery Island** is $10.95 for adults, $5.95 for children.

A **1-day ticket to Pleasure Island** is $16.95.

A **combined 1-day ticket for River Country and Discovery Island** is $18.95 for adults, $13.50 for children.

If you are staying at any Walt Disney World Resort or official hotel, you are also eligible for a money-saving **Be Our Guest Pass** priced according to length of stay. It also offers special perks.

If you plan on visiting Walt Disney World more than one time during the year, inquire about a money-saving **annual pass.**

BUY TICKETS IN ADVANCE!

Tickets are, of course, sold at all of the Disney parks, but why stand in an avoidable line? You can purchase 4- or 5-day passes (see details below) prior to your trip by calling **Ticket Mail Order** (☎ **407/824-6750**). There's a $2 postage and handling charge, and you must allow 21 days for processing your request. You can also buy tickets in advance at a Disney Store in your hometown (many malls have them these days). And if you're driving, you can get them at Disney's Ocala Information Center at exit 68 off I-75. *Note:* 1-day tickets can be purchased only at park entrances.

SERVICES & FACILITIES IN THE PARKS
PARKING

Parking—free to guests at WDW resorts—costs $5 per day no matter how many parks you visit. There is a spot for this information on your parking ticket. There are special handicapped lots at each park (☎ 407/824-4321 for details). Don't worry about parking far from the entrance gates; trams constantly ply the route.

LOST CHILDREN

All parks have a place for separated adults and children to meet up. Find out where it is when you come into the park (it's in your park guidemap), and tell your kids to ask a park attendant to take them there if you get separated. Children under 7 should have name tags.

PETS

Don't leave your pet in a parked car, even with a window cracked. The interior of a car becomes incredibly hot baking in the Florida sun. (A dead pet will not enhance your trip.) Pets are not permitted in the parks, but there are four kennels in the WDW complex. Those at the Transportation and Ticket Center in the Magic Kingdom and near the entrance to Fort Wilderness board animals overnight. Day accommodations are offered at kennels just outside the Entrance Plaza at Epcot and at the entrance to Disney MGM-Studios.

. . . AND A FEW LAST PIECES OF ADVICE

Staying at Disney properties simplifies many of the above tasks and procedures. See the full list of perks for Disney and "official" hotel guests in chapter 5.

ARRIVE EARLY!

Unless you're an incorrigible night person, always arrive at the parks a good 30 to 45 minutes before opening time, thus avoiding a traffic jam entering the park and a long line at the gate. Early arrival also lets you experience one or two major attractions before big lines form. In high season, parking lots sometimes fill up and you may even have to wait to get in.

Upon entering any of the three major Disney parks, you'll be given an **entertainment schedule** and a comprehensive **park guidemap** that contains a map of the park and lists all attractions, shops, shows, and restaurants. If by some fluke you haven't obtained these, they are available at the above-mentioned information locations in each park. If, as suggested above, you've formulated an itinerary prior to arrival, you already know the major shows (check show schedules for additional ideas) you want to see during the day and what arrangements you need to make. If you haven't done this, use your early arrival time, while waiting for the park to open, to figure out which shows to attend, and, where necessary, make reservations for them as soon as the gates swing open.

AVOIDING LINES

Some guidebooks to Walt Disney World provide plans of attack that would rival the Allied preparation for World War II. In most cases, these complex methods involve a grim determination and incredible expenditure of energy—both of which are antithetical to your real reason for being here: to have fun. The only sensible methods for avoiding long lines are to come off season and/or to arrive at the parks early and beat the crowd to some of the hottest new rides and attractions. Then relax and go with the flow. Itineraries above offer a few suggestions.

DINING

Try to eat lunch before noon or after 2pm. That way, you can hit popular rides when most people are eating (and lines are a bit shorter) and eat when restaurants are less crowded. Make restaurant reservations far in advance of your trip by calling **407/ WDW-DINE.**

SHOPPING

All of the Disney parks have dozens of shops filled with kid-pleasing items. To avoid a lot of whining and pleading, agree in advance on the amount a child can spend on souvenirs. Leave shopping for the last activity of the day, so that you don't have to lug your purchases around.

LEAVING THE PARKS

If you leave any of the parks and plan to return later in the day, be sure to get your hand stamped upon exiting.

AND REMEMBER TO HAVE FUN!

A theme park provides a unique opportunity to spend some quality time with the kids, but your attitude can make or break the experience. For instance, it's more fun to chat, play games, and tell stories on long lines than to grouse about them. Parents set the tone. So get your priorities in order, and go with the flow.

2 The Magic Kingdom

Centered around Cinderella Castle—its medieval spires are Walt Disney World's most recognizable symbol, after Mickey Mouse—the Magic Kingdom occupies about 100 acres, with numerous attractions, restaurants, and shops in seven theme sections, or "lands."

From the parking lot, you have to take a short monorail or ferry ride to the Magic Kingdom entrance. During peak attendance times, arrive at the Magic Kingdom no later than an hour prior to opening time to avoid long lines at these conveyances. Sections of the parking lot are named for Disney characters (Goofy, Pluto, Minnie, and so on), and aisles are numbered. Be sure to write down where you parked.

Upon entering the park, consult your *Magic Kingdom Guidemap* to get your bearings. It details every shop, restaurant, and attraction in every land. Also consult your **entertainment schedule** to see what's on for the day. There are parades, musical extravaganzas featuring Disney characters, fireworks, band concerts, barbershop quartets, Disney character appearances, and more.

If you have questions, all park employees are very knowledgeable, and City Hall, on your left as you enter, is both an information center and, along with Mickey's Starland (details above), a likely place to meet up with costumed characters.

There's a stroller rental shop just after the turnstiles to your right, and the Kodak Camera Center, near Town Square, supplies all conceivable photographic needs, including camera and camcorder rentals and 2-hour film developing.

MAIN STREET, U.S.A.

Designed to replicate an archetypical turn-of-the-century American street (okay, so it culminates in a 13th-century castle), this is the gateway to the Kingdom. Don't dawdle on Main Street when you enter the park; leave it for the end of the day when you're heading back to your hotel.

Walt Disney World Railroad & Other Main Street Vehicles

Recommended ages: 2–8.

You can board an authentic 1928 steam-powered railroad here for a 15-minute journey clockwise around the perimeter of the park. There are stations in Frontierland and Mickey's Starland. There are also horse-drawn trolleys, horseless carriages, jitneys, omnibuses, and fire engines plying the short route along Main Street from Town Square to Cinderella Castle.

Main Street Cinema
Recommended ages: all ages.

A mannequin is in charge of the ticket booth here, so you can sneak right in without paying. Just kidding—there's no charge for admission. Main Street Cinema is an air-conditioned hexagonal theater where vintage black-and-white Disney cartoons (including the 1928 *Steamboat Willie,* in which Mickey and Minnie debuted) are aired continually on two screens. Viewers have to watch these standing; there are no seats.

Cinderella Castle
Recommended ages: 2–10.

At the end of Main Street, in the center of the park, you'll come to a fairyland castle, 180 feet high and housing a restaurant (King Stefan's Banquet Hall) and shops. Mosaic murals inside depict the Cinderella story, and Disney family coats of arms are displayed over a fireplace. Cinderella herself, dressed for the ball, often makes appearances in the lobby area.

ADVENTURELAND

Cross a bridge to your left and stroll into an exotic jungle of lush tropical foliage, thatch-roofed huts, and carved totems. Amid dense vines and stands of palm and bamboo, drums are beating, and swashbuckling adventures are taking place.

Note: If you're heading toward Adventureland or Frontierland first thing in the morning, wait for the gates to open at the bridge in front of the Crystal Palace, to your left as you enter.

Swiss Family Treehouse
Recommended ages: 4–12.

This attraction is based on the 1960 Disney movie version of Johann Wyss's *Swiss Family Robinson,* about a shipwrecked family of five who created an ingenious

---

❓ Did You Know?

- The movie portion of Universal Studio's *Back to the Future* attraction took 2 years to make and was the most expensive film per minute ever made.
- Mickey Mouse has more than 80 different outfits, ranging from a scuba suit to a tuxedo. Minnie has only 50.
- There are enough Mickey Mouse–ear hats sold each year to cover the head of every man, woman, and child in Pittsburgh.
- You could fit New York's Empire State Building into the Vehicle Assembly Building at the Kennedy Space Center $3^3/_4$ times.
- Shamu, the killer whale at Sea World, eats more than 65,000 pounds of fish a year.
- Every day an average of 100 pairs of sunglasses are turned into the Lost and Found at the Magic Kingdom.
- Since Walt Disney World opened in 1971, the total miles logged by monorail trains would be equal to more than 24 trips to the moon.
- During launch, it takes just 8 minutes for the space shuttle to reach its orbiting speed of 17,500 mph.
- Both Disneyland and Walt Disney World were built on former citrus groves in counties named Orange.

The Magic Kingdom

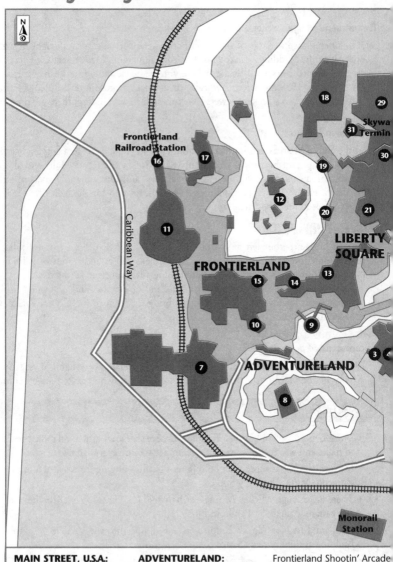

2260

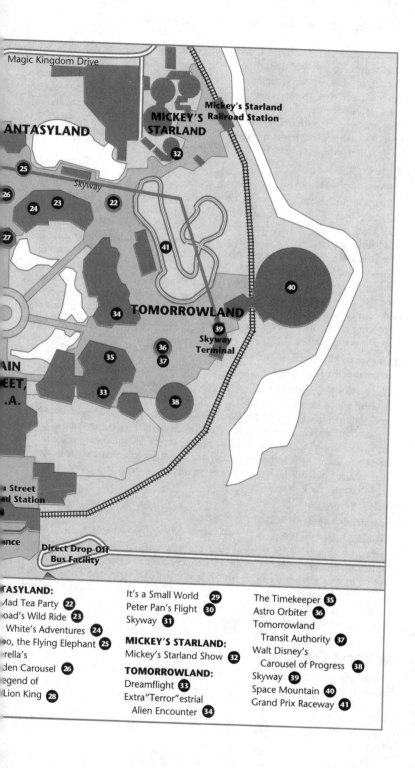

Magic Kingdom Drive

MICKEY'S STARLAND

Mickey's Starland
Railroad Station

ANTASYLAND

Skyway

TOMORROWLAND

Skyway
Terminal

AIN
EET,
.A.

Street
d Station

nce

Direct Drop-Off
Bus Facility

dwelling for themselves in the branches of a sprawling banyan tree. Using materials and furnishings salvaged from their downed ship, the Robinsons created bedrooms, a kitchen, a library, and a living room. Visitors traverse a rope-suspended bridge and ascend the 50-foot tree for a close-up look into these rooms. Note the Rube Goldberg rope-and-bucket device with bamboo chutes that dips water from a stream and carries it to treetop chambers. The "tree" itself, designed by Disney "Imagineers," has 330,000 polyethylene leaves sprouting from a 90-foot span of branches; although it isn't real, it is draped with actual Spanish moss.

Jungle Cruise
Recommended ages: 4–14.

What a cruise! In the course of about 10 minutes, your boat sails through an African veldt in the Congo, an Amazon rain forest, the Mekong River in Southeast Asia, and along the Nile. Lavish scenery, with ropes of hanging vines, cascading waterfalls, and lush tropical and subtropical foliage (most of it real), includes dozens of AudioAnimatronic birds and animals—elephants, zebras, lions, giraffes, crocodiles, tigers, even fluttering butterflies. On the shore, you'll pass a *Raiders*-like Cambodian temple cave fronted by a Buddha and guarded by snakes; a rhino and jackal chasing terrified African beaters up a tree; and a jungle camp taken over by apes. But the adventures aren't all on shore. Passengers are menaced by everything from water-spouting elephants to fierce warriors who attack with spears. The guide keeps up an amusing patter.

✪ Pirates of the Caribbean
Recommended ages: 6–adult.

This is Disney magic at its best. You'll proceed through a long grottolike passageway to board a boat into a pitch-black cave. Therein, elaborate scenery and hundreds of AudioAnimatronic figures (including lifelike dogs, cats, chickens, pigs, and donkeys) depict a rambunctious pirate raid on a Caribbean town. To a background of cheerful "yo-ho-yo-ho" music, the sound of rushing waterfalls, squawking seagulls, and screams of terror, passengers pass through the line of fire in a raging pirate battle and view tableaux of fierce-looking pirates swigging rum, looting, and plundering. This might be scary for kids under 5.

Tropical Serenade
Recommended ages: 2–10.

In a large hexagonal Polynesian-style dwelling, with a thatched roof, bamboo beams, and tapa-bark murals, 250 tropical birds, chanting totem poles, and singing flowers whistle, tweet, and warble. The audience is encouraged to sing along. The show is hosted by four feathered friends named José, Michael, Pierre, and Fritz—all with appropriate national accents—who perch atop an "enchanted" fountain. Highlights include a thunderstorm in the dark (the gods are angry!), a light show over the fountain, and, of course, the famous "in the tiki, tiki, tiki, tiki, tiki room" song. Like it or not, you'll find yourself singing it all day. This is a must for young children.

FRONTIERLAND

From Adventureland, step into the wild and woolly past of the American frontier, where Disney employees (they're called "cast members") are clad in denim and calico, sidewalks are wooden, rough-and-tumble architecture runs to log cabins and rustic saloons, and the landscape is southwestern scrubby with mesquite, saguaro cactus, yucca, and prickly pear. Across the river is Tom Sawyer Island, reachable via log rafts.

In the Words of Walt Disney

Sheer animated fantasy is still my first and deepest production impulse. The fable is the best storytelling device ever conceived. . . . And, of course, animal characters have always been the personnel of fable—animals through which the foibles as well as the virtues of humans can best and most hilariously be reflected.

Never get bored or cynical. Yesterday is a thing of the past.

✪ Splash Mountain
Recommended ages: 10–adult.

Themed after Walt Disney's 1946 film, *Song of the South*, Splash Mountain takes you on an enchanting journey in a hollowed-out log craft along the canals of a flooded mountain, past 26 brilliantly colored tableaux of backwoods swamps, bayous, spooky caves, and waterfalls. Riders are caught up in the bumbling schemes of Brer Fox and Brer Bear as they pursue the ever-wily Brer Rabbit, who, against the advice of Mr. Bluebird, has left his briar-patch home in search of adventure and the "laughing place." The music from the film forms a delightful audio backdrop. Your log craft twists, turns, and splashes—sometimes plummeting in total darkness—all leading up to a thrilling five-story, 45-degree-angle splashdown from mountaintop to briar-filled pond at 40 miles per hour! And that's not the end. The ride continues, and finally it's a Zip-A-Dee-Doo-Dah kind of day. *Note:* You must be 44 inches tall to ride.

✪ Big Thunder Mountain Railroad
Recommended ages: 10–adult.

This mining-disaster-theme roller coaster—its thrills deriving from hairpin turns and descents in the dark, rather than sudden steep drops—is situated in a 200-foot-high redstone mountain with 2,780 feet of track winding through windswept canyons and bat-filled caves. You enter the ride via the ramshackle headquarters of the Big Thunder Mining Company and board a runaway train that careens through the ribs of a dinosaur, under a thundering waterfall, past spewing geysers and bubbling mudpots, and over a bottomless volcanic pool. Riders are threatened by flash floods, earthquakes, rickety bridges, and avalanches. AudioAnimatronic characters (such as the longjohn-clad fellow navigating the floodwaters in a bathtub) and animals (goats, chickens, donkeys, possums) enhance the scenic backdrop, and several-hundred-thousand dollars worth of authentic antique mining equipment adds verisimilitude. *Note:* You must be 40 inches tall to ride.

✪ Diamond Horseshoe Saloon Revue & Medicine Show
Recommended ages: 6–adult.

Sit yourself down in air-conditioned comfort and enjoy a rousing western revue at Dr. Bill U. Later's turn-of-the-century saloon. Marshall John Charles sings and banters with the audience, Jingles the Piano Man plays honky-tonk tunes, there's a magic act, and Miss Lucille L'Amour and her troupe of dancehall girls do a spirited can-can—all with lots of humor and audience participation. There are seven shows daily; plan on going around lunchtime, so you can eat during the show. The menu features deli or peanut butter and jelly sandwiches served with chips.

✪ Country Bear Jamboree
Recommended ages: 4–adult.

I've always loved the Country Bear Jamboree, a 15-minute show featuring a troupe of fiddlin', banjo strummin', harmonica playin' AudioAnimatronic bears belting out rollicking country tunes and crooning plaintive love songs. The chubby Trixie, decked out in a satiny skirt, laments lost love, as she sings "Tears Will Be the Chaser for Your Wine." Teddi Barra descends from the ceiling in a swing to perform "Heart We Did All That We Could." Other star performers include a country-western group called the Five Bear Rugs, Liver Lips McGrowl, and the 7-foot-tall master of ceremonies, Henry. In the rousing show finale, the entire cast joins in a foot-stompin' sing-along. Wisecracking commentary comes from a mounted buffalo, moose, and deer on the wall. A special holiday show plays throughout the Christmas season each year.

Tom Sawyer Island
Recommended ages: 4–14.

Board Huck Finn's raft for a 1-minute float across the river to the densely forested Tom Sawyer Island, where kids can explore the narrow passages of Injun Joe's cave (complete with scary sound effects, like whistling wind), a walk-through windmill, a serpentine abandoned mine, or Fort Sam Clemens, where an AudioAnimatronic drunk is snoring off a bender. Maintaining one's balance while crossing rickety swing and barrel bridges is also fun. Narrow, winding dirt paths lined with oaks, pines, and sycamores create an authentic backwoods island feel. It's easy to get briefly lost and stumble upon some unexpected adventure. You might combine this attraction with lunch at Aunt Polly's restaurant, which serves light fare (fried chicken, sandwiches, and the like) and has outdoor tables on a porch overlooking the river. Adults can rest weary feet over coffee, while the kids explore the island.

Frontierland Shootin' Arcade
Recommended ages: 8–adult.

Combining state-of-the-art electronics with a traditional shooting-gallery format, this vast arcade presents an array of 97 targets (slow-moving ore cars, buzzards, gravediggers) in a three-dimensional 1850s gold-mining town scenario. Fog creeps across the graveyard, and the setting changes as a calm starlit night turns stormy with flashes of lightning and claps of thunder. Coyotes howl, bridges creak, and skeletal arms reach out from the grave. If you hit a tombstone, it might spin around and mysteriously change its epitaph. To keep the western ambience authentic, newfangled electronic firing mechanisms loaded with infrared bullets are concealed in genuine Hawkins 54-caliber buffalo rifles. When you hit a target, elaborate sound and motion gags are set off. Fifty cents buys you 25 shots.

LIBERTY SQUARE

Serving as a transitional area between Frontierland and Fantasyland, Liberty Square evokes 18th-century America with Federal and Georgian architecture, Colonial Williamsburg–type shops, and neat flower beds bordering manicured lawns. Thirteen lanterns, symbolizing the colonies, are suspended from the Liberty Tree, an immense live oak. You might encounter a fife and drum corps marching along Liberty Square's cobblestone streets. The Liberty Tree Tavern here (details in chapter 6) is my favorite Magic Kingdom restaurant.

Hall of Presidents
Recommended ages: 10–adult.

In this red-brick colonial hall, a giant bell suspended in its tower, all American presidents—from George Washington to Bill Clinton (whose actual voice was recorded for this attraction)—are represented by AudioAnimatronic figures who act out important events in the nation's history, from the signing of the Declaration of Independence through the space age. The show begins with a film, projected on a

180-degree, 70mm screen, about the importance of the Constitution. The curtain then rises on the 42 assembled American leaders, and, as each is spotlighted, he nods or waves with presidential dignity. Lincoln then rises and speaks, occasionally even referring to his notes. In a stunning example of Disney thoroughness, painstaking research was done in creating the figures and scenery, with each president's costume reflecting not only period fashion but period fabrics and tailoring techniques! Poet and author Maya Angelou narrates.

✪ Haunted Mansion
Recommended ages: 6–adult.

What better way to exhibit Disney special-effects wizardry than a haunted mansion? Macabre attendants harry groups of visitors past a graveyard, turning them over to a ghost host who encloses them in a windowless, doorless portrait gallery (Are those eyes following you around?) where the floor seems to be descending. Its ambience enhanced by inky darkness, spooky music, eerie howling, and mysterious screams and rappings, this mansion is replete with bizarre scenes and objects: a ghostly banquet and ball, a graveyard band, a suit of armor that comes alive, cobweb-covered chandeliers, luminous spiders, a talking head in a crystal ball, weird flying objects, and much more. At the end of the ride, a ghost joins you in your car. The experience is more amusing than terrifying, so you can take small children inside.

Boat Rides
Recommended ages: 6–adult.

A steam-powered sternwheeler called the *Richard F. Irvine* and two Mike Fink Keel Boats (the *Bertha Mae* and the *Gullywhumper*) depart (the latter, summers and holidays only) from Liberty Square for scenic cruises along the Rivers of America. The passing landscape evokes the Wild West. Both ply the identical route and make a restful interlude for foot-weary parkgoers.

FANTASYLAND

The attractions in this happy land—themed after Disney film classics such as *Snow White, Peter Pan,* and *Dumbo*—are especially popular with young visitors. If your kids are 8 or under, you might want to make it (and Mickey's Starland; details below) your first stop in the Magic Kingdom. *Note:* Mr. Toad's Wild Ride is a bit scary. If your under-5 frightens easily, skip it.

✪ Legend of the Lion King
Recommended ages: 4–12.

This stage spectacular based on Disney's blockbuster motion-picture musical combines animation, movie footage, sophisticated puppetry, and high-tech special effects. The show is enhanced by the Academy Award–winning music of Elton John and Tim Rice. Other voices are provided by Whoopi Goldberg and Cheech Marin as laughing hyenas.

Snow White's Adventures
Recommended ages: 6–14.

This attraction used to focus only on the more sinister elements of Grimm's fairy tale—most notably the evil queen and the cackling, toothless witch—leaving small children screaming in terror. It's been toned down now, with Snow White appearing in a number of pleasant scenes—at the castle courtyard wishing well, in the dwarfs' cottage, receiving the prince's kiss that breaks the witch's spell, and riding off with the prince to live "happily ever after." There are new AudioAnimatronic dwarfs, and the interior colors have also been brightened up and made less menacing. Even so, this could be scary for kids under 7.

Mad Tea Party
Recommended ages: 4–16.

This is a traditional amusement park ride à la Disney, with an *Alice in Wonderland* theme. Riders sit in oversized pastel-hued teacups on saucers that careen around a circular platform, tilt, and spin. In the center of the platform is a big teapot, out from which pops a mouse. Believe it or not, this can be a pretty wild ride—or a tame one. It depends on how much you spin, a factor under your control via a wheel in the cup.

Mr. Toad's Wild Ride
Recommended ages: 6–16.

This ride is based on the 1949 Disney film, *The Adventures of Ichabod and Mr. Toad*, which was itself based on one of my favorite children's classics, the divine *Wind in the Willows*. In colorful cars named for characters (Weasel, Toady, Moley), riders navigate a series of dark rooms, hurtling into solid objects—a fireplace, a bookcase, a haystack—and through barn doors into a coop of squawking chickens. They're menaced by falling suits of armor, snorting bulls, and an oncoming locomotive in a pitch-black tunnel, and are sent to jail (for car theft), to hell (complete with pitchfork-wielding demons), and through a fiery volcano. The ride's interior space is illuminated by invisible ultraviolet light, which makes whites and neons in the scenery glow.

Cinderella's Golden Carousel
Recommended ages: all ages.

It's a beauty, built by Italian wood-carvers in the Victorian tradition in 1917 and refurbished by Disney artists who added 18 hand-painted scenes from the Cinderella story on the wooden canopy above the horses. The carousel organ plays Disney classics such as "When You Wish Upon a Star."

Dumbo, the Flying Elephant
Recommended ages: 2–10.

This is a very tame kiddie ride in which the cars—large-eared baby elephants (Dumbos)—go around and around in a circle gently rising and dipping. But it's very exciting for wee ones.

It's a Small World
Recommended ages: 2–14.

You know the song—and if you don't, you will. It plays continually as you sail "around the world" through vast rooms designed to represent different countries. They're inhabited by appropriately costumed AudioAnimatronic dolls and animals—all singing "It's a small world after all . . ." in tiny doll-like voices. This cast of

In the Words of Walt Disney

Fantasy, if it's really convincing, can't become dated, for the simple reason that it represents a flight into a dimension that lies beyond the reach of time . . . nothing corrodes or gets run down. . . . And nobody gets any older.

We have never lost our faith in family entertainment—stories that make people laugh, stories about warm and human things, stories about historic characters and events, and stories about animals.

thousands includes Chinese acrobats, Russian kazatski dancers, Indian snake charmers in front of the Taj Mahal, French cancan dancers, Irish leprechauns, singing geese and windmills in Holland, Arabs on magic carpets, mountain goats in the Swiss Alps, African drummers and lunging hyenas in the jungle, a Venetian gondolier, and Australian koala bears. Cute. Very cute.

Peter Pan's Flight
Recommended ages: 4–10.

Riding in airborne versions of Captain Hook's ship, passengers career through dark passages while experiencing the story of *Peter Pan.* The adventure begins in the Darlings's nursery and includes a flight over nighttime London to Never-Never Land, where riders encounter mermaids, Indians, a ticking crocodile, the lost boys, Princess Tiger Lilly, Tinkerbell, Hook, Smee, and the rest—all to the movie music "You Can Fly, You Can Fly, You Can Fly." It's fun.

Skyway
Recommended ages: all ages.

Its entrance close to Peter Pan's Flight, the Skyway is an aerial tramway to Tomorrowland that makes continuous trips throughout the day.

MICKEY'S STARLAND

This small land adjacent to Fantasyland, with a topiary maze of Disney characters and a block of "Duckburg" architecture, is accessible from Main Street via the Walt Disney World Railroad. It includes a Walk of Fame à la Hollywood, with Disney character "voiceprints" activated when you step on a star; a hands-on fire station; storefronts that come alive at the push of a button; Grandma Duck's Farm (a petting zoo); funhouse mirrors; a treehouse; and an interactive video area. And Mickey's house is here, too, complete with living room TV tuned to the Disney channel, a shopping list of six kinds of cheese tacked to the refrigerator, and his familiar outfits hanging on a clothesline in the yard. Pluto's doghouse is out front.

The main attraction is **Mickey's Starland Show,** which is presented on a stage behind his house. While waiting to enter the theater, you can watch Disney cartoon videos on monitors in the preshow room. The show—a lively musical—features the Goof Troop, Chip 'n' Dale, a perky hostess named CJ, and a vocal computer-control system called Dude. The story line: The show is about to start, but Mickey is missing! But it all works out in the end. The cheerful cartoon-inspired scenery, audience participation, and dramatic special effects are all designed to appeal to young viewers (ages 2–10). After the show, there's an opportunity to meet Mickey backstage in his dressing room.

TOMORROWLAND

This land focuses on the future—most notably, space travel and exploration. In 1994, the Disney people decided that Tomorrowland (originally designed in the 1970s) was beginning to look like "Yesterdayland." It's now been revamped to reflect the future as a galactic, science fiction–inspired community inhabited by humans, aliens, and robots. A vast state-of-the-art video-game arcade has also been added.

✪ Extra "Terror"estrial Alien Encounter
Recommended ages: 10–adult.

Director George Lucas contributed his space-age vision to this major Tomorrowland attraction. The action begins at the Interplanetary Convention Center, where a mysterious corporation called X-S Tech—a company from a distant planet—

is marketing a "teletransporter" to Earthlings. The device is capable of beaming living beings between planets light-years apart. After a slick corporate presentation, S.I.R., a rather sinister robot, demonstrates the product on Skippy, a cute and fuzzy alien, though not with total success; Skippy ends up discombobulated and with singed fur! Despite this dubious beginning, X-S technicians try to teleport their sinister corporation head, Chairman Clench, to Earth. But the machine malfunctions, sending Clench instead to a distant planet and, inadvertently, teleporting a fearsome extraterrestrial to earth. Lots of high-tech special effects here—from the Alien's breath on your neck to a mist of Alien slime. *Note:* You must be 48 inches tall to ride.

The Timekeeper
Recommended ages: 10–adult.

This Jules Verne/H. G. Wells–inspired multimedia presentation combines CircleVision and IMAX footage with AudioAnimatronics. It's hosted by Timekeeper, a mad scientist robot, and his assistant, 9-EYE, a flying female camera-headed droid and time machine test pilot. In an unpredictable jet-speed escapade, the audience hears Mozart as a young prodigy playing his music to French royalty, visits medieval battlefields in Scotland, watches Leonardo at work, and floats in a hot-air balloon above Moscow's Red Square. There are many other adventures. Timekeeper also throttles his calendar forward—to the 300th anniversary of the French Revolution in 2089. Jeremy Irons, Robin Williams, Michael Piccoli, and Rhea Perlman (9-EYE) do the voice-overs.

✪ Space Mountain
Recommended ages: 10–adult.

In a precursor to the concept of preshows, Space Mountain entertains visitors on its long, long lines with space-age music, exhibits, and meteorites, shooting stars, and space debris whizzing about overhead. These "illusioneering" effects, enhanced by appropriate audio, continue during the ride itself, which is something like a cosmic roller coaster in the inky starlit blackness of outer space. Your rocket climbs high into the universe, before racing—at what feels like breakneck speed—through a serpentine complex of aerial galaxies, making thrilling hairpin turns and rapid plunges. Though the line may seem long, take heart; Space Mountain accommodates 3,000 people an hour. *Note:* You must be 44 inches tall to ride.

Dreamflight
Recommended ages: 10–adult.

The history and wonder of aviation—from barnstorming to space shuttles—is captured in this whimsical fly-through adventure. High-tech special effects and 70mm live-action film footage add dramatic 3-D-style verisimilitude. Guests travel from a futuristic airport up a hillside to witness a flying circus, parachutists, stunt flyers, wing walkers, crop dusters, and aerial acrobats. The action moves on to the ocean-hopping age of commercial flight, as passengers are transported to a Japanese tea garden, Mt. Fuji, and Paris at sunset. Finally, your vehicle is pulled into a giant jet engine and sent into hypersonic flight through psychedelic tunnels of light for a journey to outer space at a simulated speed of 300 mph.

Walt Disney's Carousel of Progress
Recommended ages: 8–adult.

Originally seen at New York's 1964–65 World's Fair, this 22-minute show was revamped in the early 1990s to reflect later technological advances. Shown in a revolving theater, it features an AudioAnimatronic family (including grandparents, a freeloading cousin, and a dog) in humorous tableaux demonstrating a century of

Top 10 Orlando Area Attractions for Grown-ups

1. **Innoventions**   Epcot, generally, is more geared to adults than the other Disney parks, but this display of future technologies is especially intriguing, providing a cogent preview of life in the 21st century.

2. **Disney Institute**   This new Disney concept, which allows guests to custom-design non-theme-park vacations, features exciting programs in diverse areas ranging from gourmet cooking to landscape design.

3. **World Showcase Pavilions**   Experience a round-the-world journey visiting 11 nations in microcosm—with authentically reproduced architectural highlights, restaurants, shops, and cultural performances.

4. **Universal Studios**   Okay, I'm an adult, but sometimes this really is a great place to play.

5. **Swimming with the Manatees**   Sign up for a 5-day program with a manatee biologist for an ecotour on the Crystal River that also includes bird-watching, snorkeling, and informative lectures.

6. **Cypress Gardens**   Stroll 200 acres of gorgeous botanical gardens—roses, bougainvillea, crape myrtles, and magnolias—amid ponds, lagoons, waterfalls, Italian fountains, and manicured lawns.

7. **Kennedy Space Center**   Acquaint yourself with the history, present state, and future of America's space program.

8. **A Day in Winter Park**   This charming town has a museum filled with masterpieces by Louis Comfort Tiffany and other noted 19th-century artists, great upscale shopping, and fine restaurants. Stay overnight at the Langford and arrange a day of beauty at its multifacility spa.

9. **A Resort Vacation**   Top-of-the-line accommodations, fine restaurants, magnificent grounds, golf, tennis, swimming, first-rate health clubs, and other elements of a plush resort vacation are available at the Hyatt Regency Grand Cypress, Marriott's Orlando World Center, the Peabody Orlando, and Disney's Grand Floridian.

10. **Japanese Breakfast**   Cascade, at the Hyatt Regency Grand Cypress, serves up a traditional Japanese breakfast of miso soup, grilled salmon, steamed rice, seaweed, fresh fruit, and green tea. (If only one of you finds this exciting, the other *can* opt for bacon and eggs here as well.)

development in electric gadgetry. The action begins on Valentine's Day in a turn-of-the-century home, where telephones, Victrolas, indoor running water, and gaslight are the marvels of the age; train travel and horseless trolleys are coming into vogue; and there's even talk of "flying contraptions." We travel through time, tracking advances and their detriments (e.g., car travel leads to the commuter rat race), culminating circa the year 2000 on Christmas Eve. Gifts include virtual-reality headgear and a voice-activation system. A preshow featuring Walt Disney traces the history of this production.

Grand Prix Raceway
Recommended ages: 8–16.

This is a great thrill for kids—including pre-driver's-license teens—who get to put the pedal to the metal, steer, and *vroom* down a speedway in an actual gas-powered sports car. Maximum speed on the 4-minute drive around the track is about 7 mph, and kids have to be at least 4 feet, 4 inches tall to drive alone.

Tomorrowland Transit Authority

Recommended ages: all ages.

A futuristic means of transportation, these small five-car trains have no engines. They work by electromagnets, emit no pollution, and use little power (don't ask me to explain it; I didn't do so well in physics). Narrated by a computer guide named Horack I, TTA offers an overhead look at Tomorrowland, including a pretty good preview of Space Mountain. If you're only in the Magic Kingdom for 1 day, this can be skipped.

Skyway

Recommended ages: all ages.

Its Tomorrowland entrance just west of Space Mountain, this aerial tramway to Fantasyland makes continuous round-trips throughout the day.

Astro Orbiter

Recommended ages: 2–10.

This is a tame, typical amusement park ride. The "rockets" are on arms attached to "the center of the galaxy," and they move up and down while orbiting spinning planets.

PARADES, FIREWORKS & MORE

You'll get an *Entertainment Show Schedule* when you enter the park, which lists all goings-on for the day. These include concerts (from steel drums to barbershop quartets), encounters with Disney characters, holiday events, and the three major happenings listed below.

✪ The 3 O'Clock Parade

Recommended ages: all ages.

You haven't really seen a parade until you've seen one at Walt Disney World. This spectacular daily event kicks off at 3pm year-round on Main Street and meanders through Liberty Square and Frontierland. The route is outlined on your *Entertainment Show Schedule.* The only problem: Even in slow seasons, you have to snag a seat along the curb a good half hour before it begins . . . earlier during peak travel times. That's a long time to sit on a hard curb. Consider packing inflatable pillows. But the parade is worth a little discomfort. In addition to Mickey and all his Disney pals— everyone from Minnie to Winnie the Pooh—there are elaborate floats, stunning costumes, dazzling special effects, and a captivating cavalcade of dancers, singers, and other talented performers. Great music, too.

✪ Spectromagic

Recommended ages: all ages.

Along a darkened parade route (the same one as above), 72,000 watts of dazzling high-tech lighting effects (including holography) create a glowing array of pixies and peacocks, sea horses and winged horses, flower gardens and fountains. Roger Rabbit is the eccentric conductor of an orchestra producing a rainbow of musical notes that waft magically into the night air. There are dancing ostriches from *Fantasia,* whirling electric butterflies, flowers that evoke Tiffany glass, bejeweled coaches, luminescent ElectroMen atop spinning whirlyballs, and, of course, Mickey, surrounded by a sparkling confetti of light. And the music and choreography are on par with the technology. It's like nothing you've ever seen before. Once again, very early arrival is essential to get a seat on the curb. SpectroMagic takes place nightly in summer, on selected nights during Christmas and Easter vacation times, and during other special celebrations. Consult your *Entertainment Show Schedule* for details.

✪ Fireworks
Recommended ages: all ages.

Like SpectroMagic, Fantasy in the Sky Fireworks, immediately preceded by Tinker Bell's magical flight from Cinderella's Castle, take place nightly in summer, on selected nights during Christmas and Easter vacation times, and during other special celebrations. Consult your *Entertainment Show Schedule* for details. Suggested viewing areas are Liberty Square, Frontierland, and Mickey's Starland.

3 Epcot

In 1982, Walt Disney World opened its second major attractions park, the world's fair–like Epcot (Experimental Prototype Community of Tomorrow). Its aims are described in a dedication plaque: "May Epcot entertain, inform and inspire. And, above all . . . instill a new sense of belief and pride in man's ability to shape a world that offers hope to people everywhere." Ever growing and changing, Epcot today occupies 260 acres so stunningly landscaped as to be worth visiting for botanical beauty alone—so stop and smell the roses. There are two major sections, Future World and World Showcase.

Epcot is huge, and walking around it can be exhausting (some people say its acronym stands for "Every Person Comes Out Tired"). Don't try to do it all in one day. And conserve your energy by taking launches across the lagoon from the edge of Future World to Germany or Morocco. There are also double-decker buses circling the World Showcase Promenade and making stops at Norway, Italy, France, and Canada.

Unlike the Magic Kingdom, Epcot's parking lot is right at the gate. Sections of the parking lot are named for Epcot themes (Harvest, Energy, etc.), and aisles are numbered.

Stop by the **Guest Relations lobby** to the left of Spaceship Earth to pick up an **Epcot Guidemap** and **entertainment schedule,** and, if you so desire (and haven't already done so by calling **407/WDW-DINE**), make reservations for lunch or dinner at WorldKey terminals just outside the lobby. (Many Epcot restaurants are described in chapter 6.) Then check out your show schedule and incorporate shows you want to see into your itinerary.

Strollers can be rented to your left at the Future World entrance plaza and in World Showcase at the International Gateway between the United Kingdom and France.

FUTURE WORLD

The northern section of Epcot (where you enter the park) comprises Future World, centered on a giant geosphere known as Spaceship Earth. Future World's 10 theme areas, sponsored by major American corporations, focus on discovery, scientific achievements, and tomorrow's technologies in areas running the gamut from energy to undersea exploration.

Spaceship Earth
Recommended ages: 10–adult.

Spaceship Earth, housed in a massive, silvery geosphere 180 feet high and 165 feet in diameter, is Epcot's most cogent symbol. Inside, a show created by sci-fi writer Ray Bradbury, presented by AT&T, and narrated by Jeremy Irons takes visitors on a 14-minute journey through the history of communications beginning 40,000 years ago. We board time-machine vehicles and are drawn into a whirling space-warp vortex to the distant past where an AudioAnimatronic Cro-Magnon shaman recounts the story of a hunt while others record it on cave walls. We advance thousands of years to ancient Egypt, where hieroglyphics adorn the temple walls and writing is recorded on papyrus scrolls (with typical Disney thoroughness, the hieroglyphics are authentic, and words being recorded by a scribe are taken from an actual letter sent by a pharaoh to one of his agents). As our time machine moves ahead, the Greeks have added vowels to the Phoenician alphabet and refined its use. Roman roads expand the network of communications, and the vast Islamic empire furthers the dispersion of manuscripts that enhance knowledge of science, astronomy, and art. In the Middle Ages, we see Benedictine monks painstakingly reproducing classical and religious wisdom by hand, prior to the development of the Gutenberg press in 1456. Man's increasing ability to disseminate ideas becomes a catalyst for the Renaissance. Technologies develop at a rapid pace, enlarging our communications spectrum via steam power, electricity, the telegraph, telephone, radio, movies, and TV. It is but a short step to the age of computers and electronic communications. We are catapulted into outer space to see Spaceship Earth from a new perspective, returning via a kaleidoscopic passageway in a dazzling special-effects finale.

At the end of this journey through time, AT&T invites guests to sample its "global neighborhood" in an interactive computer-video wonderland that includes a motion-simulator ride through the company's electronic network. This exhibit complements Innoventions, detailed below.

✪ Innoventions

Recommended ages: 10–adult.

The pair of crescent-shaped buildings to your right and left just beyond Spaceship Earth house a constantly evolving 100,000-square-foot exhibit that showcases cutting-edge technologies and future products for home, work, and play. Leading manufacturers—IBM, General Electric, AT&T, General Motors, and others—sponsor exhibit areas here, and their representatives are on hand to answer questions. Visitors get a chance to preview electric cars, experience interactive television, and try out more than 200 new computer programs and games. On display are dozens of new high-tech products: video phones, the latest advances in TV remote-control, voice-activated appliances, solar-powered lawn mowers, automatic plant-watering and pet-feeding devices, and many more. At the IBM exhibit, you can access entire libraries via CD Rom, experience Olympic events as they're happening, travel the world, and examine rare manuscripts that were hitherto too fragile for public perusal. Kids will be thrilled to preview new Sega and other interactive computer and video games.

There are several **show areas:** In Dr. Digital's recording studio of tomorrow, audience volunteers with no musical training are chosen to lay down four tracks of an original song. You can be interviewed by Jay Leno on TV. Alec Tronic, a robotic comedian, imitates everyone from Johnny Carson to John Wayne. Bill Nye the Science Guy presents an entertaining multimedia show about how new ideas move from the laboratory to the marketplace. The Masco House of Innoventions demonstrates exciting home-of-the-future products (many of them already on the market), ranging from remote appliance controls to a fireplace that doesn't require a chimney. And at Motorola's "Your Show," a robot host named Sky Cyberguy introduces you to the latest wireless pagers, miniature digital computers, and more. You'll even get a chance to play a virtual-reality game. You can easily spend several hours browsing in the future here.

The two-story **Discovery Center,** located on the right side of Innoventions, includes an information resource area where guests can get answers to all their questions about Epcot attractions in particular and Walt Disney World in general.

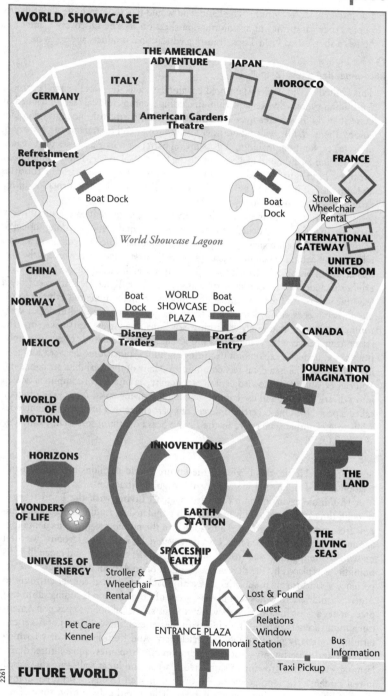

WORLD SHOWCASE

THE AMERICAN ADVENTURE

JAPAN

ITALY

MOROCCO

GERMANY

American Gardens Theatre

Refreshment Outpost

FRANCE

Boat Dock

Boat Dock

Stroller & Wheelchair Rental

World Showcase Lagoon

INTERNATIONAL GATEWAY

UNITED KINGDOM

CHINA

NORWAY

Boat Dock

WORLD SHOWCASE PLAZA

Boat Dock

MEXICO

Disney Traders

Port of Entry

CANADA

JOURNEY INTO IMAGINATION

WORLD OF MOTION

INNOVENTIONS

HORIZONS

THE LAND

WONDERS OF LIFE

EARTH STATION

THE LIVING SEAS

UNIVERSE OF ENERGY

SPACESHIP EARTH

Stroller & Wheelchair Rental

Lost & Found

Guest Relations Window

Pet Care Kennel

ENTRANCE PLAZA

Monorail Station

Bus Information

Taxi Pickup

FUTURE WORLD

2261

For instance, if after visiting The Land, you would like to learn more about hydroponics, they can print out an information sheet on it. The Discovery Center also houses a shop called Field Trips, featuring educational products and software.

✪ The Living Seas
Recommended ages: 12–adult.

This United Technologies–sponsored pavilion contains the world's sixth "ocean," a 5.6-million-gallon saltwater aquarium (including a complete coral reef), inhabited by more than 4,000 sea creatures—sharks, barracudas, parrot fish, rays, and dolphins among them. While waiting on line, visitors pass exhibits tracing the history of undersea exploration, including a glass diving barrel used by Alexander the Great in 332 B.C., and Sir Edmund Halley's first diving bell (1697). A $2^1/2$-minute multimedia preshow highlighting today's undersea technology (sophisticated robotics and computers) is followed by a 7-minute film demonstrating the formation of the earth and seas as a means to support life.

After the films, visitors enter hydrolators for a rapid descent to the sunlit ocean floor. Upon arrival, they board Seacabs that wind around a 400-foot-long tunnel to enjoy stunning close-up views (through acrylic windows) of ocean denizens in a natural coral-reef habitat. The ride concludes in the Seabase Concourse, which is the visitors center of Seabase Alpha, a prototype ocean-research facility of the future. Here exhibits include a $22^1/2$-foot scuba tube used by Seabase Alpha scientists to enter and leave the waters. And seven informational modules contain numerous exhibits focusing on ocean ecosystems, harvestable resources grown in controlled undersea environments, marine mammals (dolphins, sea lions, manatees), earth systems (the relationship between the planet's seas and its landmasses), the study of oceanography from space, undersea exploration (featuring an AudioAnimatronic deep-sea submersible robot), and life in a coral-reef community. Many of these exhibits are hands-on. You can expand your knowledge of oceanography via interactive computers or step into a diver's JIM suit and use controls to complete diving tasks. *Note:* Via a program called Epcot DiveQuest, certified divers can participate in a program that includes a 30- to 40-minute scuba dive in the Living Seas aquarium; for details, call 404/WDW-TOUR.

The Land
Sponsored by Nestlé, this largest of the Future World pavilions highlights man's relation to food and nature in a variety of intriguing attractions.

A 13-minute excursion in a canopied boat, ✪ **Living with the Land** takes us through three ecological environments, each populated by AudioAnimatronic denizens (recommended age group: 12 to adult). In the rain forest—with its dense foliage and tangle of vines, tree ferns, cascading waterfalls, and serene lagoon—we meet up with chattering birds and insects, whooping howler monkeys, and crocodiles. Its humidity is replaced by the dry, oppressive heat of an African desert, where we experience a sandstorm. It subsides as we approach a fog-filled tunnel en route to America's midwestern windswept plains—scene of a thunder and lightning storm that precipitates a grass fire, rousing a swarm of locusts. We sail on, into pastoral American autumn scenery, where a film in a barn theater examines 100 years of American farming from early plows to modern machinery. And from here on, new farming methods and experiments—such as hydroponics, aeroponics, aquaculture, desert farming, even plants growing in simulated Martian and lunar soil!—are showcased in real gardens. The food grown here is utilized in Walt Disney World restaurants. If you'd like a more serious overview, take a 1-hour **guided walking tour** of the growing areas, offered daily. Sign up at the Green Thumb Emporium shop near the entrance to Food Rocks. Adults pay $5, children ages 3 to 9 pay $3, under 3 free. This tour, by the way, is not really geared to children.

Circle of Life: Combining spectacular live-action footage with animation, this 15-minute, 70mm motion picture based on the Disney feature, *The Lion King*, stars Simba (now king of the Pridelands), Timon (the meerkat), and Pumbaa (the warthog) in a cautionary environmental tale. Timon and Pumbaa are building a monument to the good life called Hakuna Matata Lakeside Village, but their project, as Simba points out, is damaging the savannah for other animals. The message: Everything is connected in the great circle of life. Recommended age group: 6–16.

In **Food Rocks,** AudioAnimatronic mock rock performers deliver an entertaining message about nutrition. Neil Moussaka sings "Don't Take My Squash Away from Me," the Refrigerator Police perform "Every Bite You Take," and the Peach Boys harmonize a rendition of "Good Vibrations" ("Good, good, good, good nutrition . . ."), while Excess, a trio of disheveled, obnoxious hard rockers, counters by extolling the virtues of junk food. Rapper Tone Loc (as Füd Wrapper, the show's host), Chubby Checker, Neil Sedaka, Little Richard, and the Pointer Sisters perform the actual voice-over parodies of their music. Recommended age group: 6–14.

Journey into Imagination

In this wondrous pavilion, presented by Kodak and housed in glass pyramids, even the fountains are magical, with arching streams of water that leap into the air like glass rods.

Honey I Shrunk the Audience is a 15-minute 3-D "misadventure" based on the Disney hit films *Honey I Shrunk the Kids* and *Honey I Blew Up the Kid,* with Rick Moranis and Marcia Strassman. The action begins at an Imagination Institute awards ceremony, where zany scientist Dr. Wayne Szalinski is being honored as "Inventor of the Year." The audience, after being menaced by hundreds of mice and a 3-D cat, is shrunk and given a good shaking by a giant 5-year-old. Finally, everyone returns to proper size—everyone but the family dog, who creates the final (not altogether pleasant) special effect. A photo-montage preshow extols the virtues of imagination. Recommended for ages 6 and up.

Behind the Scenes: Special Tours in Walt Disney World

In addition to the above-described greenhouse tour in Epcot's Land pavilion, the Disney parks offer a number of walking tours and learning programs. These include

- the 3-hour **Hidden Treasures of World Showcase,** focusing on the architecture and entertainment offerings of Epcot's international pavilions ($25 per person, ☎ 407/939-8687 for information);
- **Gardens of the World,** a 3-hour tour of the extraordinary landscaping at Epcot led by a Disney horticulturist ($25 per person, ☎ 407/939-8687 for information); and
- the 4-hour **Keys to the Kingdom,** providing an orientation to the Magic Kingdom and a glimpse into the high-tech operational systems behind the magic ($45 per person, ☎ 407/WDW-TOUR).

There are also **learning programs** on subjects ranging from animation to international cultures. For details, call 407/363-6000.

Journey Into Imagination Ride: Visitors board moving cars for a 14-minute ride (recommended for ages 6–14), hosted by a red-bearded adventurer named Dreamfinder and his sidekick, Figment—a mischievous baby dragon with a child-like ability to dream. After a simulated flight across the nighttime sky, we enter the "Imaginarium," where a dream-catching machine is vacuuming up "sparks of imagination, ideas, and natural elements" into a giant storage bag. We then ride past whimsical tableaux in which AudioAnimatronic characters explore the creative worlds of the fine arts, literature, the performing arts (complete with laser-light dancers), science (Dreamfinder's lab is filled with magical gadgetry), and image technology (a.k.a. movies). The ride culminates at Image Works.

Image Works houses dozens of hands-on electronic devices and interactive computers. Here you can activate different musical instruments by stepping on hexagons of colored light (remember Tom Hanks in *Big?*), participate in a TV drama, paint on a magic palette, draw patterns with laser beams, operate a giant kaleidoscope, wend your way through the Rainbow Corridor of a sensor maze, and conduct an electronic philharmonic orchestra. Recommended for ages 6 and up.

World of Motion
Recommended ages: 10–adult.

Closed at this writing for a total revamp (it may be open by the time you read this), this General Motors–sponsored attraction (which will probably also be renamed) will put guests in the driver's seat to experience the thrilling rigors of automobile testing. During a preshow—essentially a GM commercial—guests will learn how the company works to promote automotive safety, reliability, and performance. Then they'll board full-scale, six-passenger test cars and travel upon what appears to be an actual roadway, accelerating on long straightaways, hugging hairpin turns, climbing steep hills, and braking abruptly—often on less-than-perfect road conditions. The ride will culminate with a terrifying high-speed outdoor run along the track's steeply banked "speed loop" that extends far beyond the pavilion facility. Cars will go at a top speed of 65 miles per hour.

Horizons
Recommended ages: 10–adult.

The theme of this pavilion is the future, which presents an unending series of new horizons. We board sideways-facing gondolas for a 15-minute journey into the next millennium. The first tableau honors visionaries of past centuries (like Jules Verne) and looks at outdated visions of the future and classic sci-fi movies. We ascend to an area where an IMAX film projected on two 80-foot-high screens presents a kaleidoscope of brilliant micro and macro images—growing crystals, colonies in space, solar power, a space shuttle launching, DNA molecules, and a computer chip. We then travel to 21st-century cityscapes, desert farms, floating cities under the ocean's surface, and outer space colonies populated by AudioAnimatronic denizens who use holographic telephones, magnetic levitation trains, and voice-controlled robotic field hands. For the return to earth from a space colony, riders have a choice of three futuristic transportation systems—a personal spacecraft, desert Hovercraft, or mini-submarine.

Wonders of Life
Housed in a vast geodesic dome fronted by a 75-foot replica of a DNA molecule, this pavilion, presented by Metropolitan Life, offers some of Future World's most engaging shows and attractions.

Starring zany comedian Martin Short, **The Making of Me** is the sweetest introduction imaginable to the facts of life (recommended for ages 8 and up). In a captivating 15-minute film combining live action with animation, Short travels back in time to witness his parents as children, their meeting at a college dance, their wedding, and their decision to have a baby. Along with him, we view his development inside his mother's womb (via spectacular in-utero photography) and witness his birth. If you've not yet told your kids about sex, you couldn't find a better springboard to that important conversation.

In **Body Wars,** audience members join ex-fighter-pilot Jack Braddock on a medical rescue mission inside the immune system of a human body (recommended for ages 6 and up). Our objective: to save Dr. Cynthia Lair, a miniaturized immunologist who has been accidentally swept into the bloodstream (while studying the body's response to a splinter) and come under attack from white blood cells! After passing through dermatopic purification stations and undergoing miniaturization (to the size of a single cell), visitors board moving theaters for this motion-simulator ride that utilizes special computer-graphics and 70mm motion-picture footage to evoke a wild journey through gale-force winds (in the lungs) and pounding heart chambers. Leonard Nimoy directed.

Cranium Command, a totally delightful multidimensional theater attraction, is suitable for ages 8 and up. Buzzy, an AudioAnimatronic brain-pilot-in-training, is charged with the seemingly impossible mission of controlling the brain of Bobby, a typical 12-year-old boy. A 5-minute animated film introduces the story line and characters. Cranium Command is a training center for brain pilots, in which Buzzy has to prove his ability at the helm. The boy's left brain (logic) is played by Charles Grodin, his right brain (emotion/creativity) by Jon Lovitz, his out-of-control adrenal gland by Bob Goldthwait, his "pumped-up" heart by Kevin Nealon and Dana Carvey (as Hans and Franz of *Saturday Night Live*), and his oft-upset stomach by George Wendt (Norm from *Cheers*). The audience is seated inside Bobby's head as Buzzy guides him through a day of typical preadolescent traumas—running for the school bus, meeting a girl, fighting bullies, and a run-in with the school principal.

Finally, there's **Fitness Fairgrounds,** a large area filled with fitness-related shows, exhibits, and participatory activities that are geared for ages 6 and up. These include an 8-minute multimedia presentation called Goofy About Health (stressed-out Goofy has the *Unhealthy Livin' Blues* until he reforms and extols the joys of healthy living), the Anacomical Players (a live improvisational theater troupe who perform 15-minute health-related comic skits), and Coach's Corner (your tennis, golf, or baseball swing is videotaped and replayed in slow motion, with specific video tips for improvement provided by Chris Evert, Nancy Lopez, and Gary Carter, respectively). You can also do a light workout on a video-enhanced exercise bike here, receive a personalized computer-generated evaluation of your health habits, play sensory games, and take a video voyage to investigate the effects of drugs, tobacco, and alcohol on your heart. There's much, much more. You could easily spend hours here.

Universe of Energy
Recommended ages: 10–adult.

Sponsored by Exxon, this pavilion—its roof glistening with solar panels—aims to better our understanding of America's energy problems and potential solutions via a 35-minute ride-through attraction with visitors seated in solar-powered "traveling theater" cars (hard to explain; you'll see what I mean). Under refurbishment at this writing, its new story line will feature Ellen DeGeneres as an energy expert tutored by Bill Nye the Science Guy to be a *Jeopardy* contestant. On a massive screen in Theater I, an animated motion picture depicts the earth's molten beginnings, its cooling process, and the formation of fossil fuels. You move from Theatre I to travel back 275 million years into an eerie, storm-wracked landscape of the Mesozoic Era, a time of violent geological activity. Here, you're menaced by giant Audio-Animatronic dragonflies, pterodactyls, dinosaurs, earthquakes, and streams of molten lava before entering a steam-filled tunnel deep through the bowels of the volcano to emerge back in the 20th century in Theatre II. In this new setting, which looks like a NASA Mission Control room, a 70mm film projected on a massive 210-foot wraparound screen depicts the challenges of the world's increasing energy demands and the emerging technologies that will help meet them. Your moving seats now return to Theatre I, where swirling special effects herald a film about how energy impacts our lives. It ends on a dramatically upbeat note—with a vision of an energy-abundant future and Ellen as a new *Jeopardy* champion.

WORLD SHOWCASE

Surrounding a 40-acre lagoon at the park's southern end is World Showcase—a permanent community of 11 miniaturized nations, all with authentically indigenous landmark architecture, landscaping, background music, restaurants, and shops. The cultural facets of each nation are explored in art exhibits, dance performances, and innovative rides, films, and attractions. And all of the employees in each pavilion are natives of the country represented.

✪ Canada
Recommended ages: 8–adult.

Our neighbors to the north are represented by diverse architecture ranging from a mansard-roofed replica of Ottawa's 19th-century French-style Château Laurier (here called the Hôtel du Canada) to a British-influenced rustic stone building modeled after a famous landmark near Niagara Falls.

An Indian village—complete with rough-hewn log trading post and 30-foot replicas of Ojibwa totem poles—signifies the culture of the Northwest, while the Canadian wilderness is reflected by a steep mountain (a Canadian Rocky), a waterfall cascading into a whitewater stream, and a "forest" of evergreens, stately cedars, maples, and birch trees. Don't miss the stunning floral displays of azaleas, roses, zinnias, chrysanthemums, petunias, and patches of wildflowers inspired by the Butchart Gardens in Victoria, B.C.

The pavilion's highlight attraction is *O Canada!*—a dazzling, 360-degree Circle-Vision film that reveals Canada's scenic splendor from sophisticated Montréal to the thundering flight of thousands of snow geese departing an autumn stopover near the St. Lawrence River. The film is 18 minutes in length.

Canada pavilion shops carry sandstone and soapstone carvings, fringed leather vests, duck decoys, moccasins, a vast array of Eskimo stuffed animals and Native American dolls, Native American spirit stones, rabbitskin caps, heavy knitted sweaters, and, of course, maple syrup.

United Kingdom
Recommended ages: 10–adult.

Centered on Brittania Square—a formal London-style park, complete with copper-roofed gazebo bandstand and a statue of the Bard—the U.K. pavilion evokes Merry Olde England. Four centuries of architecture are represented along quaint cobble-stoned streets; troubadours and minstrels entertain in front of a traditional British pub; and a formal garden with low box hedges in geometric patterns, flagstone paths, and a stone fountain replicates the landscaping of 16th- and 17th-century palaces.

In the Words of Walt Disney

In my view, wholesome pleasure, sport, and recreation are as vital to this nation as productive work and should have a large share in the national budget.

High Street and Tudor Lane shops display a broad sampling of British merchandise—toy soldiers, Paddington bears, personalized coats of arms, tobaccos and pipes, Scottish clothing (cashmere and Shetland sweaters, golfwear, tams, knits, and tartans), fine English china, Waterford crystal, and pub items (tankards, dartboards, et al.).

A tea shop occupies a replica of Anne Hathaway's thatch-roofed 16th-century cottage in Stratford-upon-Avon, while other emporia represent the Georgian, Victorian, Queen Anne, and Tudor periods. Background music ranges from "Greensleeves" to the Beatles.

✪ France
Recommended ages: 8–adult.

Focusing on La Belle Epoque (1870–1910)—a flourishing period for French art, literature, and architecture—this pavilion is entered via a replica of the beautiful cast-iron Pont des Arts footbridge over the "Seine." It leads to a park with pleached sycamores, Bradford pear trees, flowering crape myrtles, and sculptured parterre flower gardens inspired by Seurat's painting *A Sunday Afternoon on the Island of La Grande Jatte.* A one-tenth replica of the Eiffel Tower constructed from Gustave Eiffel's original blueprints looms above *les grands boulevards,* and period buildings feature copper mansard roofs and casement windows.

The highlight is *Impressions de France.* Shown in a palatial (mercifully sit-down) theater à la Fontainebleau, this 18-minute film is a breathtakingly scenic journey through diverse French landscapes projected on a vast, 200-degree-view wraparound screen and enhanced by music of French composers.

Emporia in the covered shopping arcade, with art nouveau Métro facades at either end, have interiors ranging from a turn-of-the-century bibliothèque to a French château. Merchandise includes French art prints and original art, cookbooks, cookware, wines (there's a tasting counter), fancy French foodstuffs, Madeline and Babar books and dolls, perfumes, and original letters of famous Frenchmen ranging from Jean Cocteau to Napoleon. Another marketplace/tourism center revives the defunct Les Halles, where Parisians used to sip onion soup in the wee hours. The heavenly aroma of a *boulangerie* penetrates the atmosphere, and mimes, jugglers, and strolling *chanteurs* entertain.

Morocco
Recommended ages: 10–adult.

This exotic pavilion—its architecture embellished with intricate geometrically patterned tilework, minarets, hand-painted wood ceilings, and brass lighting fixtures— is heralded by a replica of the Koutoubia Minaret, the prayer tower of a 12th-century mosque in Marrakesh.

The Medina (old city), entered via a replica of an arched gateway in Fez, leads to Fez House (a traditional Moroccan home) and the narrow winding streets of the *souk,* a bustling marketplace where all manner of authentic hand-crafted merchandise is on display. Here you can peruse or purchase pottery, brassware, hand-knotted Berber carpets, colorful Rabat carpets, ornate silver and camel-bone boxes, straw baskets, and prayer rugs. There are weaving demonstrations in the *souk* throughout the day. The Medina's rectangular courtyard centers on a replica of the ornately tiled Najjarine Fountain in Fez, the setting for musical entertainment.

The pavilion's Royal Gallery contains an ever-changing exhibit of Moroccan art, and the Center of Tourism offers a continuous three-screen slide show. Morocco's landscaping includes a formal garden, citrus and olive trees, date palms, and banana plants.

Japan
Recommended ages: 8–adult.

Heralded by a flaming red *torii* (gate of honor) on the banks of the lagoon and the graceful, blue-roofed Goju No To pagoda (inspired by a shrine built at Nara in 700 A.D.), this pavilion focuses on Japan's ancient culture. In a traditional Japanese garden, cedars, yew trees, bamboo, "cloud-pruned" evergreens, willows, and flowering shrubs frame a contemplative setting of pebbled footpaths, rustic bridges, waterfalls, exquisite rock landscaping, and a pond of golden koi. The Yakitori House is based on the renowned 16th-century Katsura Imperial Villa in Kyoto, designed as a royal summer residence and considered by many to be the crowning achievement of Japanese architecture. Exhibits ranging from 18th-century Bunraki puppets to samurai armor take place in the moated White Heron Castle, a replica of the Shirasagi-Jo, a 17th-century fortress overlooking the city of Himeji.

And the Mitsukoshi Department Store (Japan's answer to Macy's) is housed in a replica of the Shishinden (Hall of Ceremonies) of the Gosho Imperial Palace, built in Kyoto in 794 A.D. It sells lacquerware, kimonos, kites, fans, dolls in traditional costumes, origami books, samurai swords, Japanese Disneyana, bonsai trees, Japanese foods, Netsuke carvings, and pottery—even modern electronics. In the courtyard, artisans demonstrate the ancient arts of *anesaiku* (shaping brown rice candy into dragons, unicorns, and dolphins), *sumi-e* (calligraphy), and *origami* (paper folding).

Be sure to include a show of traditional Japanese music and dance at this pavilion in your schedule. It's one of the best in the World Showcase.

✪ The American Adventure
Recommended ages: 10–adult.

Housed in a vast, Georgian-style structure, *The American Adventure* is a 29-minute dramatization of U.S. history, utilizing a 72-foot rear-projection screen, rousing music, and a large cast of lifelike AudioAnimatronic figures, including narrators Mark Twain and Ben Franklin. The "adventure" begins with the voyage of the *Mayflower* and encompasses major historic events. We view Jefferson writing the Declaration of Independence, the expansion of the frontier, Mathew Brady photographing a family about to be divided by the Civil War, the stock market crash of 1929, Pearl Harbor, and the *Eagle* heading toward the moon. John Muir and Teddy Roosevelt discuss the need for national parks, Susan B. Anthony speaks out on women's rights, Frederick Douglass on slavery, Chief Joseph on the situation of Native Americans. While waiting for the show to begin, you'll be entertained by the wonderful Voices of Liberty Singers performing American folk songs in the Main Hall. Note the quotes from famous Americans on the walls here.

Formal gardens shaded by live oaks, sycamores, elms, and holly complement the pavilion's 18th-century architecture. A shop called Heritage Manor Gifts sells signed presidential photographs, needlepoint samplers, afghans and quilts, pottery, candles, Davy Crockett hats, books on American history, historically costumed dolls, classic political campaign buttons, and vintage newspapers with banner headlines like "Nixon Resigns!" An artisan at the shop makes jewelry out of coins.

Note: International cultural performances take place here in the America Gardens Theater.

Italy

Recommended ages: 10–adult.

One of the prettiest World Showcase pavilions, Italy lures visitors over an arched stone footbridge to a replica of Venice's intricately ornamented pink and white Doge's Palace. Other architectural highlights include the 83-foot Campanile (bell tower) of St. Mark's Square, Venetian bridges, and a central piazza enclosing a version of Bernini's Neptune Fountain. A garden wall suggests a backdrop of provincial countryside, and Mediterranean citrus, olive trees, cypress, and pine frame a formal garden. Gondolas are moored on the lagoon.

Shops here carry cameo and filigree jewelry, Armani figurines, kitchenware, Italian wines and foods, Murano and Venetian glass, alabaster figurines, and inlaid wooden music boxes. A troupe of street actors perform a contemporary version of 16th-century commedia dell'arte in the piazza.

✪ Germany

Recommended ages: 8–adult.

Enclosed by towered castle walls, this festive pavilion is centered on a cobblestoned *Platz* with pots of colorful flowers girding a fountain statue of St. George and the Dragon. An adjacent clock tower is embellished with whimsical glockenspiel figures that herald each hour with quaint melodies. The pavilion's outdoor Biergarten—where it's Oktoberfest all year long—was inspired by medieval Rothenberg. And 16th-century building facades replicate a merchant's hall in the Black Forest and the town hall in Frankfurt's Römerberg Square.

Shops here carry Hummel figurines, crystal, glassware, cookware, cuckoo clocks, cowbells, Alpine hats, German wines (there's a tasting counter) and specialty foods, toys (German Disneyana, teddy bears, dolls, and puppets), and books. An artisan demonstrates molding and painting Hummel figures; another paints detailed scenes on eggs. Background music runs from oom-pah bands to Mozart symphonies.

✪ China

Recommended ages: 10–adult.

Bounded by a serpentine wall that snakes around its outer perimeter, the China pavilion is entered via a vast, triple-arched ceremonial gate inspired by the Temple of Heaven in Beijing, a summer retreat for Chinese emperors. Passing through the gate, you'll see a half-size replica of this ornately embellished red and gold circular temple, built in 1420 during the Ming dynasty. Gardens simulate those in Suzhou, with miniature waterfalls, fragrant lotus ponds, groves of bamboo, corkscrew willows, and weeping mulberry trees.

The highlight here is *Wonders of China,* a 20-minute, 360-degree Circle-Vision film that explores 6,000 years of dynastic and communist rule and the breathtaking diversity of the Chinese landscape. Narrated by 8th-century Tang dynasty poet Li Bai, it includes scenes of the Great Wall (begun 24 centuries ago!), a performance by the Beijing Opera, the Forbidden City in Beijing, rice terraces of Hunan Province, the Gobi Desert, and tropical rain forests of Hainan Island. Adjacent to the theater, an art gallery houses changing exhibits of Chinese art.

A bustling marketplace—the Yong Feng Shangdian Shopping Gallery—offers an array of merchandise including silk robes, lacquer and mother-of-pearl-inlay furniture, jade figures, cloisonné vases, tea sets, silk rugs and embroideries, dolls, fans, wind chimes, and Chinese clothing. Artisans here demonstrate calligraphy.

Norway
Recommended ages: 10–adult.

Centered on a picturesque cobblestone courtyard, this pavilion evokes ancient Norway. A *stavekirke* (stave church), styled after the 13th-century Gol Church of Hallingdal, its eaves embellished with wooden dragon heads, houses changing exhibits. A replica of Oslo's 14th-century Akershus Castle, next to a cascading woodland waterfall, is the setting for the pavilion's featured restaurant. Other buildings simulate the red-roofed cottages of Bergen and the timber-sided farm buildings of the Nordic woodlands.

There's a two-part attraction here. **Maelstrom,** a boat ride in a dragon-headed Viking vessel, traverses Norway's fjords and mythical forests to the music of *Peer Gynt*—an exciting journey during which you'll be menaced by polar bears prowling the shore and trolls who cast a spell on the boat. The watercraft crashes through a narrow gorge and spins into the North Sea, where a violent storm is in progress. But the storm abates, and passengers disembark safely in a 10th-century Viking village to view the 70mm film *Norway,* which documents a thousand years of history. Featured images include *Oseberg bat* (a 1,000-year-old Viking ship), a small fishing village, festive national holiday celebrations in Oslo, and soaring jumps at the Holmenkollen ski resort.

Shops feature hand-knit wool hats and sweaters, toys (there's a Lego table where kids can play while you shop), wood carvings, Scandinavian foods, pewterware, and jewelry.

Mexico
Recommended ages: 8–adult.

You'll hear the music of marimba and mariachi bands as you approach the festive showcase of Mexico, fronted by a towering Mayan pyramid modeled on the Aztec temple of Quetzalcoatl (God of Life) and surrounded by dense Yucatán jungle landscaping. Upon entering the pavilion, you'll find yourself in a museum of pre-Colombian art and artifacts.

Down a ramp is a small lagoon, the setting for **El Rio del Tiempo** (River of Time), where visitors board boats for 8-minute cruises through Mexico's past and present. Passengers get a close-up look at the above-mentioned pyramid and the erupting Popocatepetl volcano. Dance performances focusing on the cultures of Mayan, Toltec, Aztec, and colonial Mexico are presented in film segments and by an AudioAnimatronic cast in vignettes ranging from a Day of the Dead skeleton band to children breaking a piñata. Additional film footage focuses on Mexican tourist spots. The show culminates in a Mexico City fiesta with exploding fiber-optic fireworks.

Shops in and around the Plaza de Los Amigos (a "moonlit" Mexican *mercado* with a tiered fountain and streetlamps) display an array of leather goods, baskets, sombreros, piñatas, pottery, embroided dresses and blouses, maracas, jewelry, serapes, paper flowers, colorful papier-mâché birds, and blown-glass objects (an artisan gives demonstrations). La Casa de Vacaciones, sponsored by the Mexican Tourist Office, provides travel information.

ILLUMINATIONS & SHOWS

IllumiNations, a $16^1/_2$-minute spectacular using high-tech lighting effects, darting laser beams, fireworks, strobes, and rainbow-lit dancing fountains, takes place nightly. A backdrop of classical music by international composers (representing World Showcase nations) enhances the drama. Each nation is highlighted in turn. Colorful kites

Find the Hidden Mickeys

Hiding Mickeys in designs began as an inside joke with early Walt Disney World "Imagineers" and became a park tradition. Today, dozens of subtle hidden Mickeys—the world-famous set of ears, profiles, and full figures—are concealed in attractions and resorts throughout Walt Disney World. No one even knows their exact number. See how many you can locate during your visit. A few to look for include the following.

In the Magic Kingdom

In the Haunted Mansion banquet scene, check out the arrangement of plate and adjoining saucers on the table.

In the Africa scene of It's a Small World, note the purple flowers on a vine on the elephant's left side.

While riding Splash Mountain, look for Mickey lying on his back in the pink clouds to the right of the steamboat.

Hint: There are four HMs in The Timekeeper and five in the Carousel of Progress.

At Epcot

In Journey into Imagination, check out the little girl's dress in the lobby film of *Honey I Shrunk the Audience,* one of five HMs in this pavilion.

In The Land pavilion, don't miss the small stones in front of the Native American man on a horse and the baseball cap of the man driving a harvester in the *Circle of Life* film.

As your boat cruises through the Mexico pavilion on the El Rio del Tiempo attraction, notice the arrangement of three clay pots in the marketplace scene.

In Maelstrom, in the Norway pavilion, a Viking wears Mickey ears in the wall mural facing the loading dock.

There are four HMs in Spaceship Earth, one of them in the Renaissance scene, on the page of a book behind the sleeping monk. Try to find the other three.

At Disney-MGM Studios

On the Great Movie Ride, there's an HM on the window above the bank in the gangster scene, and four familiar characters are included in the hieroglyphics wall opposite Indiana Jones.

At Jim Henson's Muppet Vision 3D, take a good look at the "Top five reasons for turning in your 3D glasses" sign, and note the balloons in the film's final scene.

At the Monster Sound Show, check out Jimmy Macdonald's bolo tie and ring, in the preshow video.

In the Twilight Zone Tower of Terror, note the bell for the elevator behind Rod Serling in the film. There are five other HMs in this attraction.

There are also HMs at many Disney resorts. The best place to look for them is at Wilderness Lodge, which has over a dozen that I know about.

---

fly over Japan, the giant Rockies loom over Canada, a gingerbread house rises in Germany, and so on. Find a seat around the lagoon about a half hour before show time.

Live shows, especially those in World Showcase, make up an important part of the Epcot experience. Among others, these might include Chinese lion dancers and acrobats, German oom-pah bands, Caledonian bagpipers, Mexican mariachi bands, Moroccan storytellers and belly dancers, Italian "living statues" and stiltwalkers, colonial fife and drum groups, and much more. Two especially good shows are the Voices of Liberty singers at the American Adventure pavilion and the traditional music and dance displays in Japan. Check your show schedule when you come in and plan your day to include some of them.

4 Disney-MGM Studios

In 1989, Walt Disney World premiered its third kingdom, Disney-MGM Studios, offering exciting movie- and TV-theme shows and behind-the-scenes "reel-life" adventures. Heralded by the 130-foot-high Mouseketeer-hatted "Earffel Tower," its main streets include Hollywood and Sunset boulevards, where you'll encounter starlets, casting directors, and gossip columnists amid art deco movie sets evocative of Hollywood's glamorous golden age. There's also a New York Street lined with Gotham landmarks (the Empire State, Flatiron, and Chrysler buildings) and typical New York characters including wisecracking workmen, peddlers hawking knockoff watches, and cops. More importantly, this is a working movie and TV studio, where shows are in production even as you tour the premises.

Arrive at the park early, tickets in hand. Unlike the Magic Kingdom and Epcot, Disney-MGM's 110 acres of attractions can pretty much be seen in one day. The parking lot is right at the gate. If you don't get a **Disney-MGM Studios Guidemap** and/or **entertainment schedule** when you enter the park, you can pick them up at **Guest Services.** First thing to do is check show times and work out an entertainment schedule based on highlight attractions and geographical proximity. Then, if you haven't done so by calling **407/WDW-DINE,** make restaurant reservations for lunch or dinner (my favorite restaurants here are described in Chapter 6). Strollers can be rented at Oscar's Super Service, inside the main entrance. Major attractions include the following.

✪ Twilight Zone Tower of Terror
Recommended ages: 10–adult.

Legend has it that during a violent storm on Halloween night of 1939, lightning struck the Hollywood Tower Hotel, causing an entire wing—along with an elevator full of people—to disappear. And you're about to meet them as you become the star in a special episode of . . . *The Twilight Zone.* En route to this formerly grand hotel, guests walk past overgrown landscaping and faded signs that once directed them to stables and tennis courts; the vines over the entrance trellis are dead, and the hotel itself is a crumbling ruin. Eerie corridors lead to a dimly lit library, where you can hear a storm raging outside. Suddenly the room is plunged into darkness, and Rod Serling appears on TV. He informs us that the regular elevators being out of order, we'll have to ascend to our rooms via service elevators. These are boarded after a spooky, behind-the-scenes trek through the boiler room. In a dramatic climax, the creaking elevator malfunctions, sending passengers on a terrifying 13-story free-fall plunge into *The Twilight Zone*! *Note:* You must be 40 inches tall to ride.

✪ The Magic of Disney Animation
Recommended ages: 8–adult.

You'll see Disney characters come alive at the stroke of a brush or pencil as you tour actual, glass-walled animation studios and watch artists at work. Walter Cronkite and Robin Williams (guess who plays straight man?) explain what's going on via video monitors, and they also star in a very funny 8-minute Peter Pan–theme film about the basics of animation. It's painstaking work: To produce an 80-minute film, the animation team must complete more than a million individual *cels* (drawings/paintings on clear celluloid sheets) of characters and scenery! Original cels from

Disney-MGM Studios Theme Park

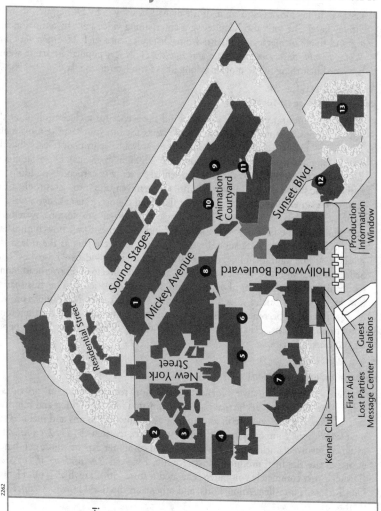

1. Inside the Magic
2. "The Spirit of Pocohontas"
3. Jim Henson's Muppet*Vision 4D
4. Star Tours
5. The Monster Sound Show
6. Superstar Television
7. Indiana Jones Epic Stunt Spectacular!
8. The Great Movie Ride
9. Backstage Studio Tour
10. Voyage of the Little Mermaid
11. The Magic of Disney Animation
12. "Beauty and the Beast"
13. The Twilight Zone Tower of Terror

143

famous Disney movies, and some of the many Oscars won by Disney artists, are on display here. The tour also includes very entertaining video talks by animators and a grand finale of magical moments from Disney classics such as *Pinocchio, Snow White, Bambi, Beauty and the Beast,* and *Aladdin.* This very popular attraction should be visited first thing in the morning; long lines form later in the day.

Backstage Studio Tour
Recommended ages: 10–adult.

This 25-minute tram tour takes you behind the scenes for a close-up look at the vehicles, props, costumes, sets, and special effects used in your favorite movies and TV shows. You'll see costumers at work in the wardrobe department (Disney has the world's largest costume collection—more than 2 million garments), house facades of *The Golden Girls* and *Empty Nest* on Residential Street, and carpenters building sets in the scenic shop. All very interesting until the tram ventures into Catastrophe Canyon, where an earthquake in the heart of desert oil country causes canyon walls to rumble, and riders are threatened by a raging oil fire, massive explosions, torrents of rain, and flash floods! Then you're taken behind the scenes to see how filmmakers use special effects to create such disasters. Almost as interesting as the ride is the preshow. While waiting on line, you can watch entertaining videos—hosted by Tom Selleck and Carol Burnett—of well-known actors and directors, on overhead monitors: Penny Marshall talking about the piano scene in *Big,* Richard Dreyfuss sharing how he landed the role in *Jaws* that launched his movie career, Mel Brooks on why he was "forced" to become a director/producer, and many more. After the tram tour, visit Studio Showcase, a changing walk-through display of sets and props from popular and classic movies.

✪ The Making of . . .
Recommended ages: 8–adult.

This attraction, which always focuses on the most recent Disney hit, provides a behind-the-scenes look at the making of an animated film. Intriguing and informative, it takes you into video-edit and audio-postproduction rooms and includes interviews with the composers, actors, animators, artists, researchers (*The Lion King,* for instance, involved a field trip to East Africa), and computer experts whose combined efforts create the final product. Most recently, I viewed *The Making of Toy Story* (Disney's first completely computer-generated feature film), in which Tom Hanks, Don Rickles, Tim Allen, Annie Potts, and other stars discussed how they conceived their roles.

Inside the Magic
Recommended ages: 10–adult.

Movie and TV special effects and production facets are the focus of this behind-the-scenes walking tour of studio facilities. You'll see how a naval battle—complete with burning ships, torpedos, and undersea explosions—is created and then view the results on videotape. Two young volunteers from the audience help demonstrate how miniaturization was achieved in *Honey, I Shrunk the Kids.* You'll visit three studio soundstages (on some tours, you'll get to see movies or TV shows being filmed from a soundproof catwalk); view a short comedy called *The Lottery* starring Bette Midler and learn how its special effects were achieved; and head to the Walt Disney Theater where, blessed relief, you'll get to sit down and enjoy a behind-the-scenes look at the company's latest animation feature. To find the entrance to this attraction, follow the big pink footsteps of Roger Rabbit.

✪ Voyage of the Little Mermaid
Recommended ages: 4–adult.

Hazy lighting, creating an underwater effect in a reef-walled theater, helps set the mood for this charming musical spectacular based on the Disney feature film. The show combines live performers with more than 100 puppets, movie clips, and innovative special effects. Sebastian sings the movie's Academy Award–winning song, "Under the Sea"; the ethereal Ariel shares her dream of becoming human in a live performance of "Part of Your World"; and the evil, tentacled Ursula, 12 feet tall and 10 feet wide, belts out "Poor Unfortunate Soul." It all has a happy ending, as most of the young audience knows it will; they've seen the movie.

✪ Theater of the Stars
Recommended ages: 4–adult.

This 1,500-seat covered amphitheater is currently presenting a 25-minute live Broadway-style production of *Beauty and the Beast,* based on the Disney movie version. Musical highlights from the show range from the rousing "Be Our Guest" opening number to the poignant title song featured in a romantic waltz-scene finale complete with the release of white doves. A highlight is "The Mob Song" scene in a dark forest, in which villagers led by Gaston (the beast's rival for Belle) and armed with axes, hoes, and pitchforks set out on a rampage to "kill the beast," setting up the emotional climax. Sets and costumes are lavish, production numbers spectacular. Consider going to the last show; it makes for a feel-good (and sit-down) ending to your day. Arrive early to get a good seat.

When is someone going to do a version of this tale in which the beast is a woman and a man loves her for her inner qualities?

Note: Beauty and the Beast has been enjoying a long run here; a new show, based on a more recent Disney hit, may be in progress by the time you visit.

✪ Jim Henson's Muppet Vision 3D
Recommended ages: 4–adult.

This delightful film starring Kermit and Miss Piggy combines Jim Henson's puppets with Disney AudioAnimatronics and special-effects wizardry, 70mm film, and cutting-edge 3-D technology. Wow! The coming-right-at-you action includes flying Muppets, cream pies, cannonballs, high winds, fiber-optic fireworks, bubble showers, even an actual spray of water. Kermit is the host, Miss Piggy sings "Dream a Little Dream of Me," Statler and Waldorf critique the action (which includes numerous mishaps and disasters) from a mezzanine balcony, and Nicki Napoleon and his Emperor Penguins (a full Muppet orchestra) provide music from the pit. Kids in the first row get to interact with the characters. In the preshow area, guests view an entertaining Muppet video on overhead monitors and see movie props belonging to Muppet superstars. Note the cute Muppet fountain out front, and the Muppet take on a Rousseau painting inside.

Star Tours
Recommended ages: 8–adult.

A wild galactic journey based on the *Star Wars* trilogy (George Lucas collaborated on its conception), this action-packed adventure uses dramatic film footage and flight-simulator technology to transform the theater into a vehicle careening through space. We enter a preshow area—where R2-D2 and C-3PO are running an intergalactic travel agency—and board 40-passenger "spacecraft" for a voyage to the Moon of Endor. En route, we encounter robots, aliens, and droids, among them our inexperienced pilot, RX-24. No sooner has he extricated our spaceship from an asteroidlike tunnel of frozen ice fragments than he's drawn into combat with a massive Imperial Star Destroyer. The ship lurches out of control, and passengers experience sudden drops, violent crashes, and oncoming laser blasts. The harrowing ride ends safely, and we exit into a *Star Wars* merchandise shop.

✪ The Great Movie Ride
Recommended ages: 10–adult.

Film footage and AudioAnimatronic replicas of movie stars are used to re-create some of the most famous scenes in filmdom on this thrilling ride through movie history. You'll relive magic moments from the 1930s through the present—Bergman and Bogart's classic airport farewell in *Casablanca*, Rhett carrying Scarlett up the stairs of Tara for a night of passion, Brando bellowing "Stellllaaaa," Sigourney Weaver fending off slimy *Alien* foes, Gene Kelly singin' in the rain, Johnny Weissmuller's trademark Tarzan yell and vine-swing across the jungle, and many more. Action is enhanced by dramatic special effects, and your tram is always highjacked en route by outlaws or gangsters. "Fasten your seat belts. It's going to be a bumpy night." The setting for this attraction is a full-scale reproduction of Hollywood's famous Mann's Chinese Theatre, complete with handprints of the stars out front.

✪ Monster Sound Show
Recommended ages: 10–adult.

Four "Foley artists" (Foley is the Hollywood sound-effects system named for its creator, Jack Foley) are chosen from the audience to create sound effects for a 2-minute comic Gothic thriller starring Chevy Chase and Martin Short. We see the film three times, first with professional sound, then without sound as volunteers frantically try to create an appropriate track, and finally with the sound effects they've provided. Errors in timing and volume make it all quite funny, as a knock at the door or crashing glass comes just a few seconds too late. The show features some of the 20,000-plus ingenious gadgets created by sound master Jimmy Macdonald during his 45 years with Disney Studios. David Letterman narrates a terrific video preshow, including one of his famous "top-10" lists, in this case "most entertaining sounds" (number 10: "A sweaty fat guy getting up out of a vinyl beanbag chair").

In a postshow area called Soundworks, guests can attempt to reproduce flying saucer sounds from the film *Forbidden Planet*, dub the voice of Roger Rabbit, and create the gallop of the Headless Horseman in *Legend of Sleepy Hollow*.

Superstar Television
Recommended ages: 10–adult.

This 30-minute show takes guests through a broadcast day that spans television history. During the preshow, "casting directors" choose a few dozen volunteers from the audience to reenact 15 famous television scenes (arrive early and station yourself near the stage if you want to snag a role). The broadcast day begins with a 1955 black-and-white "Today" show featuring Dave Garroway (the date is July 18, the morning after Disneyland opened) and continues with a classic *I Love Lucy* episode (the

---

In the Words of Walt Disney

A family picture is one the kids can take their parents to see and not be embarrassed.

I don't like downbeat pictures, and I cannot believe that the average family does either . . . when I go to the theater, I don't want to come out depressed.

---

candy factory), a scene from *General Hospital,* the *Ed Sullivan Show, Bonanza, Gilligan's Island,* Walter Cronkite doing the news (Neil Armstrong's moon landing), a *Three Stooges,* sequence (a volunteer gets a pie in the face), *Cheers, Golden Girls, Home Improvement, Howard Cosell's Sportsbreak,* the *Tonight Show,* and *Late Night with David Letterman.* Real footage is mixed with live action, and though occasionally a star is born, it's more often fun watching amateur actors freeze up, flub lines, and otherwise deviate from the script.

✪ Indiana Jones Epic Stunt Spectacular
Recommended ages: 6–adult.

Visitors get a glimpse into the world of movie stunts in this dramatic, 30-minute show that re-creates major scenes from the *Indiana Jones* series. It takes place in a vast, 2,000-seat covered amphitheater.

The show opens on an elaborate Mayan temple backdrop. Indiana Jones crashes dramatically onto the set in a free fall, and, as he searches with a torch for the golden idol, he encounters booby traps and spears popping up from the ground before being chased by a rolling boulder. The set is then dismantled to reveal a colorful Cairo marketplace where a sword fight ensues, and the action includes virtuoso bullwhip maneuvers, lots of gunfire, and a truck bursting into flames. An explosive finale takes place in a desert scenario.

The action is enhanced by movie theme music and entertaining narrative, and throughout, guests get to see how elaborate stunts are pulled off. During the preshow, volunteers are chosen to participate as extras.

PARADES, SHOWS, FIREWORKS & MORE

The colorful **Toy Story parade,** based on the movie, features all of its adorable toy-chest characters. Of course, the Green Army Men love a parade (they strew green confetti from a float); "defender of the universe" Buzz Lightyear appears on a float surrounded by a cadre of adoring Martian drones; the Barrel of Monkeys torment Mr. Potato Head, pulling out his eyes; and the finale float is a wagon overflowing with toys and carrying top toy Cowboy Woody and Rex—all to a musical backdrop of Randy Newman's "You've Got a Friend in Me" and "Strange Things (Are Happening to Me)." The parade takes place daily; check your entertainment schedule for route and times.

The **Sorcery in the Sky** fireworks show is presented nightly during summer and peak seasons. Check your entertainment schedule to see if it's on.

The **Visiting Celebrity** program features frequent appearances by stars such as Betty White, Burt Reynolds, Joan Collins, Leonard Nimoy, and Billy Dee Williams. They appear at attractions, record their handprints in front of the Chinese Theatre, and appear at question-and-answer sessions with park guests. Check your entertainment schedule to see if it's on. Kids ages 10 and up will enjoy it.

The *Honey, I Shrunk the Kids* **Movie Set,** an 11,000-square-foot playground based on the film, is located near New York Street. Everything in it is larger than life and will appeal to kids ages 2–10. A thicket of grass is 30 feet tall, mushroom caps are three stories high, and a friendly "ant" makes a suitable seat. Play areas—enhanced by sounds such as the buzzing of giant crickets and bees—include a massive cream cookie, a 52-foot garden hose (with leaks), cereal loops 9 feet in diameter (cushioned for jumping), a waterfall cascading from a leaf to a dell of fern sprouts (the sprouts form a musical stairway, activated when guests step from sprout to sprout), a root maze with a flower-petal slide, a "filmstrip" slide in a giant Kodak film can, and a huge spider web with 11 levels to climb.

Centering on a gleaming $14^1/_2$-foot bronze Emmy, the **Academy of Television Arts & Sciences Hall of Fame Plaza,** adjacent to SuperStar Television, honors TV legends. Bronze statues of television luminaries Carol Burnett, Sid Caesar, James Garner, Andy Griffith, Barbara Walters, Rod Serling, Bill Cosby, Mary Tyler Moore, Red Skelton, Danny Thomas, and Milton Berle are displayed, along with one of Walt Disney. This is really for adults; kids may not know all these names yet. Additional statues will be added each year. ATAS holds its annual Hall of Fame induction ceremonies at the Disney-MGM Studios.

Ace Ventura—When Nature Calls is a 20-minute show featuring a Jim Carrey lookalike who roars onto the set in an old jalopy, coming to a crashing halt. He performs his typically zany antics, does stunts, and gives wiseass answers to an interviewer. After the show, he poses for photos and signs autographs. For ages 6–14.

5 Other WDW Attractions

TYPHOON LAGOON

Ahoy swimmers, floaters, run-aground boaters!
A furious storm once roared 'cross the sea
Catching ships in its path, helpless to flee . . .
Instead of a certain and watery doom
The winds swept them here to TYPHOON LAGOON.

Such is the Disney legend relating to ✪ **Typhoon Lagoon,** which you'll see posted on consecutive signs as you enter the park. Located off Lake Buena Vista Drive, halfway between Walt Disney World Village and Disney-MGM Studios, this is the ultimate in water theme parks. Its fantasy setting is a palm-fringed tropical island village of ramshackle, tin-roofed structures, strewn with cargo, surfboards, and other marine wreckage left by the "great typhoon." A storm-stranded fishing boat dangles precariously atop the 95-foot-high Mt. Mayday, the steep setting for several major park attractions. Every half hour the boat's smokestack erupts, shooting a 50-foot geyser of water into the air.

In summer, arrive no later than 9am to avoid long lines. The park is often filled to capacity by 10am and closed to later arrivals. Beach towels and lockers can be obtained for a minimal fee, and all beach accessories can be purchased at Singapore Sal's. Light fare is available at two eateries—Leaning Palms and Typhoon Tillie's Galley and Grog—a beach bar called Let's Go Slurpin' sells beer and soft drinks, and there are also picnic tables (consider bringing picnic fare; you can keep it in your locker until lunchtime). Guests are not permitted to bring their own flotation devices into the park. A full day's worth of water attractions and activities includes the following:

Typhoon Lagoon

This large and lovely lagoon, the size of two football fields and surrounded by white sandy beach (complete with volleyball setup), is the park's main swimming area. The chlorinated water's turquoise hue evokes the Caribbean. Large waves for surfing and bobbing crash against the shore every 90 seconds. A foghorn sounds to warn you when a wave is coming. Young children can wade in the lagoon's more peaceful tidal pools—Blustery Bay or Whitecap Cove.

Castaway Creek

Hop onto a raft or inner tube and meander along this 2,100-foot lazy river. Circling the lagoon, Castaway Creek tumbles through a misty rain forest, past caves and secluded grottoes. It has a theme area called Water Works, where jets of water spew from shipwrecked boats and a Rube Goldberg assemblage of broken bamboo pipes and buckets spray and dump water on passersby. There are exits along the route where you can leave the creek; if you do the whole thing, it takes about a half hour. Tubes are complimentary.

Water Slides

Humunga Kowabunga consists of two 214-foot Mt. Mayday water slides that drop you down the mountain before rushing into a cave and out again at 30 mph. Three longer (about 300 feet each) but less steep slides—Jib Jammer, Rudder Buster, and Stern Burner—take you on a serpentine route through waterfalls and bat caves, past nautical wreckage at about 20 mph before depositing you in a bubbling catch pool; each offers slightly different views and thrills. There's seating for nonparticipatory parents whose kids have commissioned them to "watch me."

Whitewater Rides

Mt. Mayday is the setting for three whitewater rafting adventures—Keelhaul Falls, Mayday Falls, and Gangplank Falls—all of them offering steep drops, coursing through caves, and passing lush scenery. Keelhaul Falls has the most winding spiral route, Mayday Falls the steepest drops and fastest water, while the slightly tamer Gangplank Falls uses large tubes so the whole family can ride together.

Shark Reef

Guests are given free snorkel equipment (and instruction) for a 15-minute swim through this 362,000-gallon simulated coral-reef tank populated by about 4,000 rainbow parrotfish, queen angelfish, yellowtail damselfish, rock beauties, blue tang, puddingwife fish, and other colorful denizens of the deep. Underwater scenery includes shipwrecked boats, and there's a rock waterfall at one end. If you don't want to get in the water, you can observe the fish via portholes in a walk-through area. Shark Reef is housed in a sunken upside-down tanker.

Ketchakiddie Creek

Many of the above mentioned attractions require guests to be at least 4 feet tall. This section of the park is a kiddie area exclusively for those *under* 4 feet. An innovative water playground, it has bubbling fountains to frolic in, mini–water slides, a pint-size whitewater tubing adventure, spouting whales and squirting seals, rubbery crocodiles to climb on, grottoes to explore, and waterfalls to loll under.

BLIZZARD BEACH

Blizzard Beach is Disney's newest water park—a 66-acre "ski resort" in the midst of a tropical lagoon. The park centers on a 90-foot snow-capped mountain (Mt. Gushmore), which swimmers ascend via chairlifts, and the on-premises restaurant resembles a ski lodge. It's located on World Drive, just north of the All-Star Sports and Music resorts. Arrive at—or before—park opening to avoid long lines and to be sure you get in. Beach towels and lockers are available for a small charge, and you can buy beach accessories at the Beach Haus.

Mt. Gushmore attractions include

- **Summit Plummet.** Starting 120 feet up, this is a speed slide/thrill ride that makes a 55 mph plunge straight down to a splash landing at the base of the mountain.
- **Slush Gusher.** Another Mt. Gushmore speed slide (a bit tamer than the above) that travels along a snow-banked mountain gully.
- **Teamboat Springs.** The world's longest white-water raft ride, with six-passenger rafts twisting down a 1,200-foot series of rushing waterfalls.

- **Toboggan Racers.** An eight-lane water slide that sends guests racing head first over exhilarating dips as they descend a snowy slope.
- **Snow Stormers.** Three flumes descending from the top of Mt. Gushmore and following a switchback course through ski-type slalom gates.
- **Runoff Rapids.** An inner-tube run, where guests can careen down four different twisting, turning flumes—sometimes in total darkness.
- **Chair Lift.** Converted ski lifts, complete with snow skis on their underside, that carry guests to the top of the mountain.

A nice-size sandy beach below Mt. Gushmore offers the following:

- **Tike's Peak.** A scaled-down kiddie version of Mt. Gushmore attractions.
- **Melt-Away-Bay.** A 1-acre free-form wave pool fed by melting-snow waterfalls.
- **Cross Country Creek.** Inner tubers can float lazily along this meandering 2,900-foot creek, which circles the entire park, but beware: It will take you inside a mysterious cave.
- **Ski Patrol Training Camp.** Designed for preteens, it features a rope swing, a T-bar drop over water, slides (including the wet and slippery Mogul Mania), and a challenging ice-floe walk along slippery floating icebergs.

RIVER COUNTRY

One of the many recreational facilities at the Fort Wilderness Resort campground, this mini–water park is themed after Tom Sawyer's swimming hole. Kids can scramble over boulders that double as diving platforms for a 330,000-gallon pool. Two 16-foot water slides also provide access to the pool. Attractions on the adjacent Bay Lake, which is equipped with ropes and ships' booms for climbing, include a pair of flumes—one 260 feet long, the other 100 feet—that corkscrew through Whoop-N-Holler Hollow; White Water Rapids, which carries inner tubers along a winding, 230-foot creek with a series of chutes and pools; and the Ol' Wading Pool, a smaller version of the swimming hole designed for young children.

There are pool and beachside areas for sunning and picnicking, plus a 350-yard boardwalk nature trail through a cypress swamp. Beach towels and lockers can be obtained for a minimal fee. Light fare is available at Pop's Place. To get here without a car, take a launch from the dock near the entrance to the Magic Kingdom or a bus from its Transportation and Ticket Center.

DISCOVERY ISLAND

This lush, tropical 11½-acre zoological sanctuary—just a short boat ride away from the Magic Kingdom entrance, the Contemporary Resort, or Fort Wilderness Resort—provides a tranquil counterpoint to Disney World dazzle.

Plan to spend a leisurely afternoon strolling its scenic mile-long nature trail, which, shaded by a canopy of trees, winds past gurgling streams, groves of palm and bamboo, ponds and lagoons filled with ducks and trumpeter swans, a bay that is a breeding ground for brown pelicans, and colonies of rose-hued flamingos. Peacocks roam free, and aviaries house close to 100 species of colorful exotic birds, including macaws, cockatoos, roseate spoonbills, scarlet ibis, kookaburras, bald eagles, toucans, parrots, partridges, king vultures, East African crowned cranes, and white-crested hornbills. Discovery Island denizens also include Patagonian cavies (they're a kind of guinea pig), alligators and caimans, Galápagos tortoises, small primates, and muntjac miniature deer from Southeast Asia.

Two different bird shows and a reptile show are scheduled several times throughout the day; they take place outdoors with seating on log benches. Guests can also look through a viewing area to see the nursery complex of the island's animal hospital, where baby birds and mammals are often hand-raised.

6 Universal Studios

Universal Studios Florida, 1000 Universal Studios Plaza (☎ **407/363-8000**), is a working motion-picture and television-production studio that invites the public in for a glimpse behind the scenes. As you stroll along "Hollywood Boulevard" and "Rodeo Drive," you'll pass more than 40 full-scale sets and large props from famous movies (from the hedges used in *Edward Scissorhands* to New York's Central Park). On hand to greet visitors are Hanna-Barbera characters (Yogi Bear, Scooby Doo, Fred Flintstone, and others). While waiting on line, you'll be entertained by excellent preshows. Work out a show schedule when you arrive.

ESSENTIALS

ADMISSION   A 1-day ticket costs $37 for ages 10 and over, $30 for children 3 to 9. A 2-day ticket is $55 for ages 10 and over, $44 for children 3 to 9. An annual pass (admission for a full year) is $89 for ages 10 and over, $70 for children 3 to 9. Ages 2 and under free. Parking costs $5 per vehicle, $6 for RVs and trailers.

OPEN HOURS   Universal Studios is open 365 days a year from 9am; closing hours vary seasonally. Call before you go.

DIRECTIONS   Take I-4 east, making a left on Sand Lake Road, then a right onto Turkey Lake Road, and follow the signs.

MAJOR ATTRACTIONS

After 75 years of moviemaking, Universal knows how to create a supercolossal theme park experience. Steven Spielberg is the park's creative consultant, and thrilling rides and attractions utilize cutting-edge technology—such as OMNIMAX 70mm film projected on seven-story screens—to create unprecedented special effects. Top attractions include the following.

A Day in the Park with Barney

This musical show is set in a parklike theater-in-the-round with sets portraying fields of wildflowers, trees lit by tiny colored lights, clouds, and blue sky. The popular purple one, Baby Bop, and BJ use song, dance, special effects (it rains and snows on the audience), and interactive play to deliver an environmental message. Guests are greeted by Mr. Peekaboo and his eccentric parrot, Bartholomew, in a preshow area festooned with Barney-hued bouganvillea. And after the show—which is exited via an innovative play area and a Barney store—they can meet Barney and get his autograph. For young children, this could be the highlight of the day.

Terminator 2: 3D Battle Across Time

He's back . . . at least he will be soon—in an attraction billed as "the quintessential sight and sound experience for the 21st century!" Opening shortly after press time, this new Jim Cameron production (which features the *Terminator 2* cast) will combine 70mm 3-D film (utilizing three 23-by-50-foot screens) with live stage action and thrilling technical effects. The story line: The year is 2029, and the earth is once again threatened by the evil Cyberdyne Systems corporation.

E.T. Adventure

This is the movie sequel Spielberg said he'd never make. Visitors are given a passport to E.T.'s planet, which needs his healing powers to rejuvenate it. You'll soar with E.T.

on a mission to save his ailing planet, through the forest and into space, aboard a star-bound bicycle—all to the accompaniment of that familiar movie theme music.

Back to the Future

The year is 2015. The incompetent but evil Biff has penetrated Doc Brown's Laboratory of Future Technology, imprisoned Doc, and taken off in the DeLorean. On a mission to save the time machine from Biff, visitors blast through the space-time continuum, plummeting into volcanic tunnels ablaze with molten lava, colliding with Ice Age glaciers, thundering through caves and canyons, and are briefly swallowed by a dinosaur, in a spectacular multisensory adventure. Actors Christopher Lloyd (Doc) and Tom Wilson (Biff) appear on video.

Kongfrontation

It's the last thing the Big Apple needed. King Kong is back! As you stand in line—in a replica of a grungy, graffiti-scarred New York subway station—CBS newsman Roland Smith reports on Kong's terrifying rampage. Everyone must evacuate to Roosevelt Island. So it's all aboard the Roosevelt Island tram. Cars collide and hydrants explode below, police helicopters hover overhead putting us directly in the line of fire, the tram malfunctions, and, of course, we encounter Kong, 32 feet tall, 13,000 pounds, with over 100 facial expressions. He emits banana breath in our faces and menaces passengers, dangling the tram over the East River. A great thrill—or just another day in New York.

Earthquake, The Big One

You board a BART train in San Francisco for a peaceful subway ride, but just as you pull into the Embarcadero station, there's an earthquake—the big one—8.3 on the Richter scale! As you sit helplessly trapped, vast slabs of concrete collapse around you, a propane truck bursts into flames, a runaway train comes hurtling at you, and the station floods (60,000 gallons of water cascade down the steps). Your feet will get wet. Earthquake is preceded by several interesting preshows narrated by Charlton Heston, during which the audience is briefed for roles as extras and taken behind the scenes to see how special effects were achieved.

Ghostbusters

There are so many ghosts these days, Ghostbusters just has to sell franchises. Lewis Tully delivers a zany, high-pressure sales pitch to the audience, and volunteers come up on stage and get slimed. Tully demonstrates flushing ghosts into the Ectoplasmic Container Chamber and discusses starter kits in three price ranges. But the ghosts—wouldn't you know it—break loose from Gozer's Temple, and demons lunge at the audience.

Jaws

You're in the charming New England town of Amity. Did you really think it was safe to go back in the water? Guests are assured the waters are shark-free, but as your boat heads out to the open seas, an ominous dorsal fin appears on the horizon. What follows is a series of terrifying face-to-glistening-jaw attacks from a 3-ton, 32-foot-long, great white shark who tries to sink its teeth into passengers. Just when you feel safe in the deserted boat house, "Jaws" breaks through the walls, sending oars, lobster traps, and buoys hurtling through the air. And there's more trouble ahead. The boat is surrounded by a 30-foot wall of flame from burning fuel. I won't tell you how it ends, but here's a hint: The pungent stench of charred shark flesh comes into it.

Nickelodeon Studios Tour

Kids get a bang out of touring the studios of their own cable network, the premises of which are fronted by a slime geyser. Along the tour route, guests get a look at the soundstages where shows such as *Clarissa Explains It All* are produced; view concept pilots for Nick shows; visit the kitchen where Gak and Green Slime are produced (you can touch and taste, if you like); play games typical of Nickelodeon shows; and try out new Sega video games. There's lots of audience participation, and a volunteer will get slimed.

Wild, Wild, Wild West Show

Stunt people demonstrate falls from balconies, gun and whip fights, dynamic explosions, and other oater staples.

Beetlejuice Graveyard Revue

Dracula, Wolfman, the Phantom of the Opera, Frankenstein and his bride, and Beetlejuice put on a funky—and very funny—rock music show with pyrotechnic special effects and MTV-style choreography.

FUNtastic World of Hanna-Barbera

This motion-simulator ride takes guests careening through the universe in a spaceship piloted by Yogi Bear to rescue Elroy Jetson. Prior to this wild ride, you'll learn about how cartoons are created. After it, in an interactive area, you can experiment with animation sound effects—boing! plop! splash!

. . . AND MORE TO SEE & DO

Other Universal Studios attractions include the following.

The **Gory, Gruesome & Grotesque Horror Makeup Show,** all about makeup and special effects in movies such as the transformation scenes from *An American Werewolf in London, The Fly,* and *The Exorcist.* The lobby of the theater houses **Jurassic Park Behind the Scenes,** an exhibit comprising props, costumes, and videos from the movie, most notably the 26-foot-long ailing triceratops.

Lucy: A Tribute, honoring America's queen of comedy, consists of a vast collection of Lucy–Desi memorabilia, home movies, costumes, props, awards, fan letters, a scale model of the *I Love Lucy* soundstage, and a Lucy computer trivia game.

Fievel's Playland, based on the Spielberg movie, is a very innovative western-theme playground with giant props and sets (in which kids experience being mouse-size), including a 200-foot-long water ride, a 30-foot spider web to climb, and a Gulliver-size harmonica that makes music as kids glide down the keys.

At **Murder She Wrote,** you're on the set with Angela Lansbury trying to solve a crime involving a rare black pearl. Via computer, the audience gets to make postproduction executive decisions—choose the murder weapon, the murderer, and Jessica's dinner companion. Robert Wagner narrates the preshow.

At **Alfred Hitchcock's 3-D Theatre,** a volunteer is chosen from the audience to play Norman Bates. The attraction is a tribute to the "master of suspense," who directed 53 films, eight of them for Universal. The late Tony Perkins narrates a reenactment of the famous shower scene from *Psycho,* and *The Birds,* as if it weren't scary enough, becomes an in-your-face 3-D movie.

Across from the Hitchcock Theatre is **T-Rex Attack!,** a photo-op with the jeep and a T-Rex from *Jurassic Park.*

An explosive, 10-minute nighttime show on the lagoon called **Dynamite Nights Stuntacular** features daredevil boat pilots (the story line involves a strike force chasing drug dealers), an impressive display of pyrotechnics, shoot-em-up battles, and a 60-foot stunt boat jump into a three-story inferno of raging fire! It always takes place at the end of the day. The pier in front of Richter's at Lombard's Landing offers the best views; arrive early to get a good spot. *Note:* Young children tend to be frightened by the noise.

Beethoven, Lassie, Benji, Mr. Ed (descendants of, actually), and other animal superstars perform their famous pet tricks in the **Animal Actors Show.**

During **Screen Test Home Video Adventure,** a director, crew, and team of "cinemagicians" put visitors on the screen in an exciting video production.

Over 25 **shops** in the park sell everything from Lucy collectibles to Bates Motel towels, and **restaurants** run the gamut from Mel's Drive-In (of *American Graffiti* fame), to the Hard Rock Café, to Schwab's.

7 Sea World

This popular 200-acre marine-life park, at 7007 Sea World Dr. (☎ **407/351-3600**), explores the mysteries of the deep in a format that combines entertainment with wildlife-conservation awareness. Its beautifully landscaped grounds, centering on a 17-acre lagoon, include flamingo and pelican ponds (more than 1,500 birds, primarily waterfowl, make their home in the park) and a lush tropical rain forest. Sea World's involvement in marine-life research, education, animal rescue and release programs, and preserving and breeding endangered species is impressive. Shamu, a killer whale, is the star of the park. Work out a show schedule as soon as you enter.

ESSENTIALS

ADMISSION A 1-day ticket costs $37.95 for ages 10 and over, $31.80 for children 3 to 9. A 2-day ticket is $42.95 for ages 10 and over, $36.80 for children 3 to 9. Discounted admissions in conjunction with Busch Gardens in Tampa are available; call for details or inquire at the gate. Parking costs $5 per vehicle, $7 for RVs and trailers.

OPEN HOURS The park is open 365 days a year, 9am to 7pm, later during summer and holidays, when there are additional shows at night.

DIRECTIONS Take I-4 to the Beeline Expressway (Hwy. 528) and follow the signs.

MAJOR ATTRACTIONS

Wild Arctic

Enveloping guests in the beauty, exhilaration, and danger of a polar expedition, Wild Arctic combines a high-definition adventure film with high-tech flight-simulator technology to evoke a flight over the frozen North. After a hazardous jet helicopter journey—albeit one affording breathtaking Arctic panoramas—guests emerge at a remote research base built around the skeleton of a British ship that once searched the Northwest Passage and has been frozen in the ice for 150 years. In this frigid Arctic environment of ice floes, snow-covered rocky outcroppings, surge pools, and boulders, seals and polar bears (including Sea World star residents Klondike and Snow) romp, lumbering walruses haul themselves up from the sea to sprawl on icy perches, white beluga whales surface, and salmon sparkle in clear, cold water.

In 28 stations designed to provide tableaux vivants of life in the Arctic, guests participate in record-gathering aboard the shipwreck, explore polar bear dens, log on to ArcticNET, and pop their heads through openings in a simulated ice floe.

Mermaids, Myths & Monsters

This nighttime multimedia spectacular is a must-see, featuring fireworks and hologram-like imagery against a towering 60-foot screen of illuminated water. King Neptune rises majestically from the deep, as do terrifying sea serpents, storm-tossed ships, and frolicking mermaids. It's thrilling!

Big Splash Bash

The show begins as an old-fashioned seaside-theme musical but goes high-tech with fiber-optic fireworks and lightning (in a sequence about the destruction of Atlantis) and later includes a Bermuda Triangle–theme laser light show. Bright neon fish, seahorses, and other denizens of the deep do a jazzy "dance" to Fats Waller's "This Joint Is Jumpin'." The finale is a rousing rock gospel sequence with a fabulous dancing-waters display.

Terrors of the Deep

This exhibit houses 220 specimens of venomous and otherwise scary sea creatures in a tropical-reef habitat. Immense acrylic tunnels provide close encounters with slithery eels, three dozen sharks, barracudas, lionfish, and poisonous pufferfish. A theatrical presentation focusing on sharks puts across the message that pollution and uncontrolled commercial fishing make humankind the ultimate "terror of the deep."

Manatees: The Last Generation?

For centuries, seagoing cultures have been fascinated by the gentle manatee, which some believe is the basis for mermaid myths (though you'd have to be at sea a long, long time for a manatee to suggest a woman). Today the Florida manatee is in danger of extinction, with as few as 2,000 remaining. Underwater viewing stations, innovative cinema techniques, and interactive displays combine to create an exciting format for teaching visitors about the manatee and its fragile ecosystem. In a winding tropical $3^1/_2$-acre lagoonlike setting, visitors view the world from a manatee's perspective, perceiving what the creatures hear, see, and feel. Also on display here are hundreds of other native fish as well as alligators, turtles, and shorebirds, and there's a nursing pool for manatee mothers and their babies.

Key West at Sea World

This lush 5-acre tropical paradise of palms, hibiscus, and bougainvillea is set in a Caribbean village offering island cuisine, street vendors, and entertainers. The attraction comprises three naturalistic animal habitats: **Stingray Lagoon,** where visitors enjoy hands-on encounters with harmless southern diamond and cownose rays (you can buy them treats and feed them; their diet consists of clams, shrimp, smelt, and squid); **Dolphin Cove,** a massive habitat for bottlenose dolphins set up for visitor interaction; and **Sea Turtle Point,** home to threatened and endangered species such as green, loggerhead, and hawksbill sea turtles.

Key West Dolphin Fest

At the Whale and Dolphin Stadium, a big partially covered open-air stadium, whales and Atlantic bottlenose dolphins perform flips and high jumps, swim at high speeds, twirl, swim on their backs, and give rides to trainers—all to the accompaniment of calypso music.

Sea World Theatre: Window to the Sea

A multimedia presentation—which begins with a ballet of dancing waters shimmering in a rainbow of colored lights—takes visitors behind the scenes at Sea World and explores a variety of marine subjects. These include an ocean dive in search of the rare six-gilled shark, a killer whale giving birth, babies born at Sea World (dolphins, sea horses, penguins, walruses), dolphin anatomy, and underwater geology.

Shamu: World Focus

Sea World trainers develop close relationships with killer whales, and in this partly covered open-air stadium, they direct performances that are extensions of natural cetacean behaviors—twirling, waving tails and fins, rotating while swimming, and splashing the audience (sit pretty far back if you don't want to get soaked). Trainers also ride the whales. An informative video, narrated by Jane Seymour and projected on a vast 16-by-20-foot monitor, adds an underwater perspective to the show. The stadium includes a research and breeding area where you might see killer whale calves. The evening show here, called *Shamu: Night Magic*, utilizes rock music and special lighting effects; I suggest attending it instead of the daytime show. It's a fun way to wind up your day at Sea World.

Shamu: Close Up!, an adjoining exhibit, lets you get close to the killer whales and talk to trainers; don't miss the underwater viewing area here.

Gold Rush Ski Show

This wacky waterski exhibition features a cantankerous prospector and a talented team of cowboy waterskiers performing long-distance jumps, water ballet (performed by the miners' mail-order brides), flips, and backward and barefoot skiing. Their antics are accompanied by rollicking hoedown music and dance.

Penguin Encounter

This display of hundreds of penguins and alcids (including adorable babies) native to the Antarctic and Arctic regions also serves as a living laboratory for protecting and preserving polar life. On a moving walkway, you'll view six different penguin species congregating on rocks, nesting, and swimming underwater. If you want to observe their antics for a longer period, there is a viewing area for that purpose. The attraction is augmented by video displays about penguins and an additional area for puffins and *murres*—flying Arctic cousins of penguins.

Hotel Clyde and Seamore

Two sea lions, along with a cast of otters and walruses, appear in this fishy *Fawlty Towers* comedy with a conservation theme.

Shamu's Happy Harbor

This innovative 3-acre play area provides facilities for kids to climb a four-story net tower with a 35-foot crow's nest lookout, fire water cannons, play steel drums, swing on tires, operate remote-controlled vehicles, navigate a water maze, do a ball crawl, and propel themselves upward on an air bounce. One section is especially for children under 42 inches tall.

. . . AND MORE TO SEE & DO

Pacific Point Preserve is a $2^1/2$-acre setting with beaches and ocean waves that duplicates the northern Pacific coast. It is home to California sea lions and harbor and fur seals.

A **Tropical Reef** aquarium is fronted by a tide pool of touchables—sea anemones, starfish, sea cucumbers, and sea urchins. Inside, the 160,000-gallon manmade coral reef is home to 1,000 brightly hued tropical fish—including blue surgeon fish, sergeant majors, porkfish, French angelfish, guitarfish, and conch—displayed in 17 vignettes of undersea life.

A **Hawaiian dance troupe** entertains with island songs and dances in an outdoor facility at Hawaiian Village; if you care to join in, grass skirts and leis are available.

You can ascend 400 feet to the top of the **Sea World Sky Tower** for a revolving 360-degree panorama of the park and beyond (there's an extra charge of $3 per person for this activity).

And at the $5^1/2$-acre **Anheuser-Busch Hospitality Center**—set amid tropical lagoons, waterfalls, and lush landscaping—you can view turn-of-the-century brewery equipment and a restored beer wagon, try free samples of Anheuser-Busch beers (there are soft drinks for kids) and snacks, and stroll through the stables to watch the famous Budweiser Clydesdale horses being groomed. There's indoor and terrace seating overlooking a lake. Anheuser-Busch is the owner of Sea World.

The **Aloha! Polynesian Luau Dinner and Show**—a musical revue featuring South Seas food, song, and fire dancing—takes place nightly at 6:30pm. Park admission is not required. Cost is $29.65 for adults, $20.10 for children ages 8 to 12, $10.55 for children 3 to 7, under 3 free. Reservations are required (☎ **407/363-2559** or 800/227-8048).

There are, of course, numerous restaurants, snack bars, and food kiosks throughout the park. My favorites are the Bimini Bay Café—a very pleasant, full-service restaurant featuring seafood and basic American fare—and Mango Joe's, specializing in fajitas and offering alfresco seating at umbrella tables overlooking the lagoon. Dozens of shops carry marine-related gifts, toys, clothing, diving gear, and souvenirs, as well as wilderness/conservation-oriented items.

Visitors can take a 90-minute **behind-the-scenes tour** of the park's breeding, research, and training facilities and/or attend a **45-minute presentation** about Sea World's animal behavior and training techniques. Cost for either tour is $5.95 for ages 10 and over, $4.95 for children 3 to 9, 2 and under free.

8 Other Area Attractions

IN KISSIMMEE

Kissimmee sights are close to the Walt Disney World area—about a 10- to 15-minute drive.

✪ Cypress Island

1541 Scotty's Rd., Kissimmee. ☎ **407/935-9202.** Admission $24 adult for an all-day pass, including boat ride; $17 children 3–12; under 3 free. Call for rates for additional activities. Daily 9am–5pm. Take U.S. 192 east, make a right at Shady Lane, and follow the signs.

About 12 miles from Walt Disney World, you can get a feel for old-time Florida at Cypress Island, located on Lake Tohopekaliga, the second-largest lake in central Florida. Throughout the 1800s, the 200-acre island was a Seminole fort site, and it was the childhood home of Cacoochee, one of the last great chiefs of that tribe.

Visitors reach the island via an excursion boat that offers an ecotour narrative en route (there are frequent departures throughout the day). On arrival, you can explore (on foot or in a safari cart) 2 miles of pristine signposted nature trail lined with ancient live oaks and cypress. Another island attraction is abundant wildlife. Emus, peacocks, Sicilian donkeys, Barbados mountain sheep, African pygmy goats, and llamas freely roam grassy savannahs, and avian residents include American bald eagles, osprey, blue herons, white egrets, hummingbirds, cranes, cardinals, ibis, hawks, and owls. Bring your camera and binoculars.

By prior reservation, you can also arrange airboat and swamp buggy rides, waterskiing, jet-skiing, tubing, and horseback riding here. And there are nighttime gator safaris (led by experienced guides) through marshy areas of the lake. On-premises facilities include volleyball, horseshoes, picnic tables, a country store, and a concession that sells barbecued burgers and other fare.

Flying Tigers Warbird Air Museum

231 Hoagland Blvd. (off U.S. 192, one traffic light west of Armstrong Boulevard and Yates Road). ☎ **407/933-1942.** Admission $6 adults, $5 seniors over 60 and children 6–12, under 6 free. Daily 9am–5 or 6pm (hours vary seasonally).

Flying Tigers is actually a World War II aircraft restoration facility where vintage planes are rebuilt and test-flown. Seventy-five percent of the displays—which run the gamut from 1920s antiques to 1970s fighter jets—are permanent; the rest are in shop on a temporary basis.

On guided tours, which depart at intervals throughout the day, you'll visit the rebuilding facility where planes in various stages of assemblage are being restored. Exhibits include a U.S. Navy pilot trainer, many World War II bombers (including B-17s), Navy helicopters, torpedo bombers, cargo planes, and a rare World War II Paisacki Hup 1, as well as actual bombs, military jeeps and command cars from World War II and the Korean War, a large display of World War II memorabilia, and much, much more.

Visitors can sit in the cockpit of a jet fighter simulator, or—for a more realistic Red Baron fantasy experience—arrange to go up in a 1935 three-seat open biplane (call ahead for information on the latter, as well as other flight and piloting opportunities, some for families).

Gatorland

14501 S. Orange Blossom Trail (U.S. 441; between Osceola Parkway and Hunter's Creek Boulevard). ☎ **407/855-5496** or 800/393-JAWS. Admission $11.95 adults, $9.56 seniors over 65, $8.95 children 3–11, under 3 free. Daily 8am–dusk. Free parking.

Founded in 1949 with a handful of alligators living in huts and pens, Gatorland today features thousands of alligators and crocodiles on a 70-acre spread. Breeding pens, nurseries, and rearing ponds are situated throughout the park, which also displays monkeys, snakes, deer, goats, birds, sheep, Florida lake turtles, a Galapagos tortoise, and a bear. A 2,000-foot boardwalk winds through a cypress swamp and a 10-acre breeding marsh with an observation tower. Or you can take the free Gatorland Express Train around the park.

There are three shows scheduled throughout the day—Gator Wrestlin', the Gator Jumparoo, and Snakes of Florida. Facilities include an open-air restaurant (where you can try smoked gator ribs and nuggets), a shop (Gatorland also functions as an alligator-breeding farm for meat and hides; you'll find a wide array of alligator leather products here, not to mention canned gator chowder), and a picnic area.

✪ Green Meadows Petting Farm

1368 S. Poinciana Blvd. (off U.S. 192 between Polynesian Boulevard and S.R. 535). ☎ **407/846-0770**. Admission $13 adults, children under 3 free. Daily 9:30am–5:30pm, with tours departing throughout the day until 4pm.

Though kids of any age will enjoy it, if your children are 8 or younger, a visit to this delightful 40-acre farm—home to over 200 animals—will give you better value for your money than any major theme park. On guided 2-hour farm tours, visitors view, learn about, and in some cases feed or pet, sheep, goats, exotic chickens, turkeys, ducks, llamas, pigs, donkeys, ostriches, peacocks, and bison. Kids especially love to see the baby animals, and for parents, it's really fun to watch the kids in this setting. Everyone also gets a turn to milk a cow, and a hayride, miniature train ride, and pony ride are included in the entrance fee.

Call before you go to find out about special events such as shows, pumpkin harvesting, and barn dances. There's a large shaded picnic area, so pack your lunch and make a day of it.

Splendid China

Formosa Gardens Boulevard (off West Irlo Bronson Memorial Highway/U.S. 192, between Entry Point Boulevard/Sherbeth Road and Black Lake Road). ☎ **407/396-7111**. Admission $23.55 adults, $13.90 children 5–12, under 5 free. Daily from 9:30am. Free parking. Closing hours vary seasonally; call ahead.

This 76-acre outdoor attraction features more than 60 miniaturized replicas of China's most noted manmade and natural wonders, spanning 5,000 years of history and culture. Visitors enter via a bustling commercial street in the "water city" of Suzhou (the Venice of the East) circa A.D. 1300 to view a short orientation film about China. Park highlights include a half-mile-long copy of the 4,200-mile Great Wall; the Forbidden City's 9,999-room Imperial Palace, built in 1420; Tibet's sacred Potala Palace, former mountain home of the Dalai Lama; carved Buddhist grottoes with statuary dating from A.D. 477 to A.D. 898; the massive Leshan Buddha, carved out of a mountainside between A.D. 713 and A.D. 803; the Stone Forest of Yunan, a natural formation of towering limestone peaks; and the Mongolian mausoleum of Genghis Khan.

Live shows (acrobats, martial-arts demonstrations, storytelling, dance, puppetry, and more) take place throughout the day on stages around the park, in the indoor 800-seat Golden Peacock Theater, and in a 900-seat open-air amphitheater; check your entertainment schedule when you come in.

Over a dozen shops sell Chinese merchandise. Food concessions, a gourmet restaurant, and a Chinese cafeteria are on the premises.

Two-hour guided walking tours, departing several times a day, cost $5 per person (children under 12 free), and 1-hour golf-cart tours ($45 per six-person cart) depart every half hour. Or you can board a free tram that circles the park, stopping at major points for pick-up and drop-off. There is also recorded commentary at each attraction.

Water Mania

6073 W. Irlo Bronson Memorial Hwy. (U.S. 192), just east of I-4. ☎ **407/396-2626**. Admission $22.95 adults, $17.95 children 3–12, under 3 free. Open daily mid-Feb to the end of Nov. Closed Dec–mid-Feb. Hours vary seasonally (call before you go). Parking $3.

This conveniently located 36-acre water park offers a variety of aquatic thrill rides and attractions. You can boogie-board or body-surf in continuous-wave pools, float lazily along an 850-foot river, enjoy a whitewater tubing adventure, and plummet down spiraling water slides and steep flumes. Or dare to ride the Abyss—an enclosed tube slide that corkscrews through 300 feet of darkness, exiting into a splash pool. There's a rain forest–theme water playground for children. A miniature golf course and wooded picnic area—with arcade games, a beach, and volleyball—adjoin.

A World of Orchids

2501 Old Lake Wilson Rd. (C.R. 545), off U.S. 192. ☎ **407/396-1887**. Admission $8.95 adults, 15 and under free. Daily 9:30am–5:30pm. Closed New Year's Day, July 4, Thanksgiving, and Christmas.

Lovers of horticulture will enjoy touring this conservatory filled with tropical trees (including 64 varieties of palms and 21 of bamboo), ferns, lush tropical foliage, and, most notably, thousands of orchids—many of them rare—magnificently abloom at all times. Streams, waterfalls, koi ponds, and birds enhance this little enchanted garden. Also on the premises: a nature walk through a wooded area, aquariums of exotic fish, and a small aviary. Free guided tours are given by resident horticulturalists at 11am and 3pm weekdays, 11am and 1 and 3pm on weekends.

Note: If this is the kind of attraction you enjoy, be sure to also visit Harry P. Leu Gardens in Orlando (details below).

ON INTERNATIONAL DRIVE

Like Kissimmee attractions, these are about a 10- to 15-minute drive from the Disney area.

Ripley's Believe It or Not! Museum

8201 International Dr. (1½ blocks south of Sand Lake Road). ☎ **407/345-0501**. Admission $9.95 adults, $6.95 children 4–11, under 4 free. Daily 9am–11pm.

It's always fun to peruse a Ripley collection of oddities, curiosities, and fascinating artifacts from faraway places. Among the hundreds of items and mannequins on display here are a 1,069-pound man, a two-headed kitten, a five-legged cow, a ³/₄-scale model of a 1907 Rolls-Royce made from a million matchsticks, a mosaic of the *Mona Lisa* created from 1,426 pieces of toast, torture devices from the Spanish Inquisition, a Tibetan flute made from human bones, an Ecuadorean shrunken head, a painting on a grain of rice, a "disappearing" nude bather (they do it with mirrors), Ubangi women with wooden plates in their lips, and Burmese Padaung women who stretch their necks up to 15 inches long by wearing heavy brass rings around them. There are exhibits on Houdini and Florida sinkholes, and a film documents people swallowing unusual items . . . coathangers, a lightbulb, and, most notably, a padlock, ring, and keys (when the latter three items are—ahem!—evacuated, the ring is locked into the padlock!). Museum visitors are greeted by a hologram of Robert Ripley.

Wet 'N Wild

6200 International Dr. (at Republic Drive). ☎ **407/351-wild** or 800/992-WILD. Admission $22.95 adults, $17.95 children 3–9, under 3 free. Open 365 days a year. Hours vary seasonally (call before you go). Parking $3. Take I-4 east to Exit 30A and follow the signs.

When temperatures soar, head for this 25-acre water park and cool off by jumping waves, careening down steep flumes, and running rapids. Among the highlights: Fuji Flyer, a six-story, four-passenger toboggan ride through 450 feet of banked curves; The Surge, one of the longest, fastest multipassenger tube rides anywhere in the southeast, with 580 feet of exciting banked curves; Bomb Bay (enter a bomblike casing 76 feet in the air for a speedy vertical flight straight down to a target pool); Black Hole (step into a spaceship and board a two-person raft for a 30-second, 500-foot, twisting, turning, space-themed reentry through total darkness propelled by a 1,000-gallon-a-minute blast of water!); Raging Rapids, a simulated white-water tubing adventure with a waterfall plunge; and Lazy River, a leisurely float trip.

There are additional flumes, a vast wave pool, a large and innovative children's water playground where the above rides are re-created in miniature, a sunbathing area, and a picnic area. Food concessions are located throughout the park, lockers and towels can be rented, and you can purchase beach accessories at the gift shop.

IN ORLANDO

All of the above-listed Orlando attractions are close to one another, making for a pleasant day's excursion. Loch Haven Park is about 35 minutes by car from the Disney area. You can probably also incorporate Winter Park sights in the same day (see chapter 10 for details).

✪ Harry P. Leu Gardens

1920 N. Forest Ave. (between Nebraska Street and Corrine Drive). ☎ **407/246-2620.** Admission $3 adults, $1 children 6–16, under 6 free. Daily 9am–5pm. Leu House tours Tues–Sat 10am–3:30pm, Sun–Mon 1–3:30pm. Closed Christmas. Take I-4 east to Exit 43 (Princeton Street), follow Princeton Street east, make a right on Mills Avenue and a left on Virginia Drive; look for the gardens on your left.

This delightful, 50-acre botanical garden on the shores of Lake Rowena offers a serene respite from theme park razzle-dazzle. Meandering paths lead through forests of giant camphors, moss-draped oaks, palms, cycads, and camellias (one of the world's largest collections, comprising some 2,000 plants in 50 species; they bloom October through March). Exquisite formal rose gardens (the largest in Florida, displaying 75 varieties) are enhanced by Italian fountains, a gazebo, and statuary. Other highlights include orchids, azaleas, desert plants, beds of colorful annuals and perennials, and a 50-foot floral clock. The gardens were created by Orlando businessman Harry P. Leu, who donated his 49-acre estate to the city in the 1960s.

Free 20-minute tours of the Leu House, built in 1888 and restored to reflect the period between 1910 and 1930, take place on the hour and half hour. The house is a decorative-arts museum filled with Victorian, Chippendale, and Empire pieces and other furnishings and objets d'art. It takes about 2 hours to see the house and gardens. Inquire about lectures and workshops, including some for children.

Orange County Historical Museum

812 E. Rollins St. (between Orange and Mills Avenues), in Loch Haven Park. ☎ **407/897-6350.** Admission $2 adults, $1.50 seniors 65 and over, $1 children 6–12, under 6 free. Monday admission is by donation. Mon–Sat 9am–5pm, Sun noon–5pm. Closed Martin Luther King Day, Memorial Day, July 4, Labor Day, Thanksgiving, Christmas, and New Year's Day. Take I-4 east to Exit 43 (Princeton Street) and follow the signs to Loch Haven Park.

Sharing a building with the Orlando Science Center (details below), this museum focuses on central Florida history, beginning with prehistoric projectile points, a Timucuan canoe, and tooled animal bones from hunting cultures that existed here 12,000 years ago.

Other exhibits include displays of Seminole pottery and clothing; items from a pioneer kitchen; artifacts from an 1892 courthouse; a chronicle of the citrus industry and the role it played in the development of central Florida; and re-creations of a turn-of-the-century country store, a Victorian parlor, and the old *Orlando Sentinel* composing room. Also on the premises is Fire Station No. 3, a restored 1926 firehouse containing historic fire trucks, equipment, and memorabilia. The permanent collection is supplemented by changing exhibits of local, national, and international significance.

Orlando Museum of Art

2416 N. Mills Ave. (in Loch Haven Park off Hwy. 17-92). ☎ **407/896-4231.** Admission $4 adults, $2 children 4–11, under 4 free. Tues–Sat 9am–5pm, Sun noon–5pm. Art Encounter hours are Tues–Fri and Sun noon–5pm, Sat 10am–5pm. Free parking. Closed Mon, New Year's Day, Memorial Day, July 4, Labor Day, Thanksgiving, and Christmas. Take I-4 east to Exit 43 (Princeton Street) and follow the signs to Loch Haven Park.

Founded in 1924, the Orlando Museum of Art displays its permanent collection of 19th- and 20th-century American art, pre-Colombian art dating from 1200 B.C. to A.D. 1500, and African art on a rotating basis. These holdings are augmented by long-term loans focusing on Mayan archaeology and art of the African sub-Saharan region. Art Encounter is an interactive hands-on area for young children, where they might weave on a giant loom, piece together a pre-Colombian pot, or play African instruments. And temporary exhibits here range from Hudson River School landscapes to works of Andy Warhol. Inquire about guided tours, workshops for adults and children, gallery talks, and other activities.

At this writing, a 31,000-square-foot expansion is underway that will allow for major exhibitions.

Orlando Science Center

810 E. Rollins St. (between Orange and Mills Aves.), in Loch Haven Park. ☎ **407/896-7151.** Admission $6.50 for adults, $5.50 for children 3–11, under 3 free. Mon–Thurs and Sat 9am–5pm, Fri 9am–9pm, Sun noon–5pm. Closed Thanksgiving and Christmas. Take I-4 east to Exit 43 (Princeton Street) and follow the signs to Loch Haven Park.

The Orlando Science Center specializes in hands-on interactive exhibits. In its Tunnel of Discovery, you can play with an echo tube, encase yourself in a giant soap bubble, create a tornado, or learn about anatomy from an immense soft-sculpture doll named

Stuffee. Nature Works focuses on the flora and fauna of four Florida habitats—cypress swamp, sand pine scrub, sinkhole lake, and pine flatwood. In Water Works, an area for prekindergarten through fourth grade, children can learn how water moves objects by building dams and canals, crawl under a glass-bottom turtle tank, touch starfish and sponges, and examine discovery drawers filled with fossils, plants, insects, and bones. In addition, you can search for cardinals in a bird-watching area, find out what the weather is back home, take in a free planetarium show, or touch live frogs and turtles during daily reptile and amphibian demonstrations.

About 50% of the museum is given over to changing exhibits on subjects ranging from dinosaurs to exotic insects. A cafe serves light fare at outdoor umbrella tables, and a gift shop carries many interesting science projects for children. Inquire about workshops for children and nighttime planetarium shows and laser-show rock concerts.

Note: A vast new facility, which may be open by the time you read this, will quadruple current exhibition space. At that time, admission prices will probably be raised.

9 Outdoor Activities

Recreational facilities of every description abound in Walt Disney World and the surrounding area. These are especially accessible to guests at Disney-owned resorts, official hotels, and Fort Wilderness Resort and Campground, though many other large resort hotels also offer comprehensive facilities (see details in chapter 5). The Disney facilities listed below are all open to the public, no matter where you're staying. For further information about WDW recreational facilities, call **407/824-4321.** Guests at Disney properties can inquire when making hotel reservations or at guest services/concierge desks.

BICYCLING

Bike rentals (single and multispeed bikes for adults, tandems, and children's bikes) are available from the **Bike Barn** (☎ **407/824-2742**) at Fort Wilderness Resort and Campground. Rates are $3 per hour, $10 per day; overnight rentals are $15. Both Fort Wilderness and Disney's Village Resort offer good bike trails.

BOATING

Walt Disney World, with its many manmade lakes and lagoons, owns the nation's largest fleet of pleasure boats. At the **Walt Disney World Village Marina,** you can rent Water Sprites, canopy boats, and 20-foot pontoon boats. For information, call **407/828-2204.**

The **Bike Barn** at Fort Wilderness (☎ **407/824-2742**) rents canoes ($4 per hour, $10 per day) and paddleboats ($5 per half hour, $8 per hour).

See hotel facilities listings in chapter 5 for additional boating options.

FISHING

Fishing excursions on Lake Buena Vista—mainly for largemouth bass—may be arranged from 2 to 14 days in advance by calling the **Walt Disney World Village Marina** (☎ **407/828-2204**). No license is required. The fee is $137 for up to five people for 2 hours, those rates including gear, guide, bait, and tax.

A less-expensive alternative: rent fishing poles at the **Bike Barn** (☎ **407/824-2742**) to fish in Fort Wilderness canals. No license is required.

FLYING

The **Flying Tigers Warbird Air Museum** offers rides in a 1934 open-cockpit barnstormer and hands-on dual-instruction adventures in a historic World War II fighter trainer. Call ☎ **407/933-1942** for details.

A slightly more offbeat experience is offered by **Fighter Pilots USA.** Ever dreamed of suiting up, jumping into a fighter plane, and engaging in high-speed one-on-one dogfighting? This is your chance to experience the excitement of aerial combat. Actual F-16 pilots are your instructors. To schedule a "mission," call ☎ **407/931-4333** or **800/56-TOPGUN.** No license is required. Cost is $795 per person.

GOLF

Walt Disney World operates five championship 18-hole, par-72 golf courses and one nine-hole, par-36 walking course. All are open to the general public and offer pro shops, equipment rentals, and instruction. For tee times and information, call **407/824-2270** up to 7 days in advance (up to 30 days for Disney resort and official property guests). Call ☎ 407/W-DISNEY for information about golf packages.

Also consider calling **Golfpac** (☎ **407/260-2288** or 800/327-0878), an organization that packages golf vacations (with accommodations and other features) and prearranges tee times at over 40 Orlando-area courses. The further in advance you call (I'm talking months here), the better your options.

HAYRIDES

The hay wagon departs from Pioneer Hall at **Fort Wilderness** nightly at 7 and 9:15pm for hour-long, old-fashioned hayrides with singing, jokes, and games. Cost is $6 for adults, $4 for children ages 3 to 10, under 3 free. Children under 12 must be accompanied by an adult. No reservations; it's first-come, first-served.

HORSEBACK RIDING

Disney's Fort Wilderness Resort and Campground offers 50-minute scenic **trail rides** daily, with four to six rides per day. Cost is $17 per person. Children must be at least 9 years old. For information and reservations up to 5 days in advance, call **407/824-2832.**

ICE-SKATING

Rock on Ice! Skating Arena, in the Dowdy Pavilion, 7500 Canada Ave., between Sand Lake Road and Carrier Drive (☎ **407/352-9878**), is a gorgeous, Olympic-size indoor rink with high-tech lighting and sound systems. A deejay spins Top 40 tunes. There are ice-skating games with prizes throughout the day. Facilities include video games, a snack bar, and a complete skate shop offering a large selection of figure skating and hockey equipment. Rental skates are $2. Admission is $4.50 to $6, depending on the season. Hours vary seasonally; call ahead.

To get here from the Disney World area, take International Drive north, turn right at Sand Lake Road and left on Canada Avenue. It's about a 10-minute drive.

JOGGING

Many of the Disney resorts have scenic jogging trails. For instance, the **Yacht and Beach Club** resorts share a 2-mile trail, the **Disney Institute** has a 3.4-mile course with 32 exercise stations, the **Caribbean Beach Resort's** 1.4-mile promenade circles a lake, **Dixie Landings** has a 1.7-mile riverfront trail, and **Fort Wilderness's**

Hot Links: Orlando's Top Golf Courses

Like most of Florida, Orlando is a golfer's paradise, with 123 courses within a 45-minute drive of downtown . . . courses designed by Arnold Palmer, Jack Nicklaus, Tom Fazio, Pete Dye, Robert Trent Jones, and other major players. Its most famous courses include

- the legendary **Arnold Palmer's Bay Hill Club,** 9000 Bay Hill Blvd. (☎ **407/876-2429** or 800/523-5999), site of the Nestlé Invitational. Its 18th hole, nicknamed the Devil's Bathtub, is supposed to be the toughest par-4 on the tour;
- **Falcon's Fire Golf Club,** 3200 Seralago Blvd., in Kissimmee (☎ **407/239-5445**), a challenging Ree Jones course with 136 bunkers and water on 10 holes; and
- **Walt Disney Resorts** facilities (see details above), comprising 99 holes. Their most famous hazard is a sand trap on Magnolia Course's 6th hole in the shape of Mickey Mouse.

Also notable are two beautifully landscaped facilities: the award-winning 45-hole/par-72 Jack Nicklaus–designed course at the **Villas of Grand Cypress** (☎ **407/239-4700** or 800/835-7377) and the 18-hole/par-71 Joe Lee–designed championship course at **Marriott Orlando World Center** (☎ **407/239-4200** or 800/621-0638). See details on both properties in chapter 6.

tree-shaded 2.3-mile jogging path has exercise stations about every quarter mile. Pick up a jogging trail map at any Disney property's guest services desk.

SWIMMING WITH THE MANATEES

An organization called **Oceanic Society Expeditions** (☎ **415/441-1106** or 800/326-7491) offers a "Swim with the Manatees" program in the Crystal River area, 2 hours east of Orlando. A manatee biologist leads 5-day Monday-to-Friday trips aboard a 12-person skiff, which include swimming with manatees, bird-watching, snorkeling, slide presentations, and an excursion to a facility for the care of injured and orphaned wildlife. Cost is $985, including accommodations, excursions, and most meals. Reserve as far in advance as possible.

TENNIS

Seventeen lighted tennis courts are located throughout the Disney properties. Most are free and available on a first-come, first-served basis. If you're willing to pay, courts can be reserved up to several months in advance at two Disney resorts: the **Contemporary** (☎ **407/824-3578**) and the **Grand Floridian** (☎ **407/824-2433**). Both charge $12 per hour; you can also reserve lesson times with resident pros. The Contemporary offers a large pro shop, a ball machine, rebound walls, and equipment rentals.

WATER PARKS/SWIMMING

See section 5 of this chapter, "Other WDW Attractions," for information on River Country, Typhoon Lagoon, and Blizzard Beach, as well as water parks listed in section 8, "Other Area Attractions," above.

WATERSKIING

Waterski trips (including boats, drivers, equipment, and instruction) can be arranged at Walt Disney World by calling ☎ **407/824-2621.** Make reservations up to 14 days in advance. Cost is $82 per hour for up to five people.

10 Spectator Sports

As we go to press, construction is underway on the multimillion-dollar **Walt Disney World International Sports Center,** a 200-acre facility. It will include a 7,500-seat baseball stadium; a 5,000-seat field house featuring six basketball courts, a fitness center, and training rooms; major league practice fields and pitcher mounds; four softball fields; 12 tennis courts, including a 2,000-seat stadium center court; a track-and-field complex; a golf driving range; and much more. The center is scheduled to open in 1997.

The **Orlando Centroplex** administers six public sports and entertainment facilities in the downtown area. These include three major sporting arenas: the Florida Citrus Bowl, the Orlando Arena, and Tinker Field.

BASEBALL

From April to September, the **Orlando Cubs**—the Chicago Cubs' Class AA southern league affiliate—play at Tinker Field, 287 S. Tampa Ave., between Colonial Drive (Hwy. 50) and Gore Street (☎ **407/245-CUBS** for information and to charge tickets). Tickets are $3 to $7. To get there, take I-4 east to the East–West Expressway and head west to Hwy. 441; make a left on Church Street and follow signs. Tinker Field adjoins the Citrus Bowl. Parking is $2.

BASKETBALL

The 17,500-seat Orlando Arena, (the "O-rena"), 600 W. Amelia St., between I-4 and Parramore Avenue (☎ **407/896-2442** for information, 407/839-3900 to charge tickets), is home to the **Orlando Magic** during their October-to-April season. Led by star center (and marketing phenomenon) Shaquille O'Neal, the team has become a perennial playoff power. Tickets to games (about $13 to $50) have to be acquired far in advance; they usually sell out by September before the season starts. To get there, take I-4 east to Amelia Avenue, turn left at the traffic light at the bottom of the off-ramp, and follow signs. For up-to-the-minute parking information, turn your car radio to 1620 AM.

FOOTBALL

The Florida Citrus Bowl, 1 Citrus Bowl Pl., at West Church and Tampa streets (☎ **407/473-2476** for information, 407/839-3900 to charge tickets), hosts the annual **Comp USA Florida Citrus Bowl** game, college football games, and NFL preseason games. Tickets to all football events are hard to come by, but you may have some luck if you try far enough in advance. To get there, take I-4 east to the East–West Expressway and head west to Hwy. 441, make a left on Church Street, and follow the signs. Parking is $5.

GREYHOUND RACING

The **Sanford-Orlando Kennel Club,** 301 Dog Track Rd., between FL 427 and U.S. 17/92, in Longwood (☎ **407/831-1600**), offers a pleasant way to spend a day or evening, especially if you opt to watch the races over lunch or dinner in the glassed-in clubhouse restaurant. The restaurant is moderately priced and has a full bar; reservations are suggested. There are a variety of ways to bet on the greyhounds; if you've never done it before, pick up a free brochure that explains trifectas, quinelas, boxing, and wheeling and also shows you how to read your ticket. You can also buy tip sheets here recommending computer and expert picks. Each meet includes 14 races. You must be at least 18 years old to enter the track. This facility also offers simulcast wagering of greyhound, thoroughbred, and harness racing at other Florida tracks and at Aqueduct.

Admission is $1, plus $1 admission to the clubhouse restaurant. Parking is free, preferred parking (closer to the entrance) is $1, and valet parking is $2.

It's open from November to early May. Nighttime races are held Monday through Saturday at 7:30pm; matinees are Monday, Wednesday, and Saturday at 12:30pm. From the Walt Disney World area, take I-4 east, make a right at Maitland Boulevard, go north on 17/92, and make a left onto Dog Track Road. It's about a 40-minute drive.

Seminole Greyhound Park, 2000 Seminola Blvd., just east of U.S. 17/92, in Casselberry (☎ **407/699-4510**), offers a very similar setup to the above. Its attractive third-floor restaurant, Osceola Terrace, has tiered seating with big picture windows overlooking the track and TV monitors enhancing the view at higher tables. Prices are moderate, and there's a full bar; reservations are suggested. Each meet here includes 14 or 15 races. Children are welcome but must be at least 18 years old to enter the betting area.

Admission is $1, free for seniors 55 and over at matinees, $2 for clubhouse seating, $3 for restaurant seating. Children under 18 pay half price throughout. Parking is free, preferred parking (closer to the entrance) is $1, and valet parking is $2.

Open May to October. Nighttime races are held Monday through Saturday at 7:30pm; matinees are Monday, Wednesday, and Saturday at 1pm. From the Walt Disney World area, take I-4 east, make a right at Exit 48 (FL 436), a left at U.S. 17/92, and a right on Seminola Boulevard, which dead-ends at the track. It's about a 40-minute drive.

Unfortunately, when past their racing prime, these graceful greyhounds are often callously put to death by track owners. There have always been animal-rescue agencies promoting greyhound adoption, but their effectiveness greatly increased in the early 1990s when the ASPCA and the American Greyhound Council joined together to support existing programs and to get the word out that greyhounds make intelligent (they're easy to train), gentle (they're good around kids), and loving—not to mention very handsome—pets. And since they've lived with other greyhounds their entire lives, they adapt well to your other dogs. If you're interested in adopting (and possibly saving the life of) a greyhound, call **212/876-7700,** ext. GREY, or 800/366-1472.

JAI ALAI

Orlando Jai-Alai, 6405 S. U.S. 17/92, at S.R. 436 in Fern Park (☎ **407/339-6221**) offers the action-packed Basque sport of jai-alai (it's the world's fastest game).

It's played on a 180-foot court with three walls. The ball is hurled at speeds of up to 150 miles an hour from baskets strapped to the players' wrists, and the object of the game is to throw the ball with such force, spin, and/or placement that the opponent is unable to return it before it bounces twice. A score of seven points wins. There are two opposing singles or doubles teams on the court at all times.

Your program offers extensive information about how the game is played and how to wager, and the public-address announcer explains what is happening on the court.

Best bet is to watch the action from the moderately priced, and very attractive, open-air Terrace Restaurant, with some tables as close as 20 feet from the court. There's a color TV monitor at every table. Fare is American/continental; there's a full bar; reservations are suggested. Children 39 inches and taller are admitted into the fronton with parents, but not allowed in the betting area.

Note: The fronton also features intertrack wagering; you can place bets here on thoroughbred and harness races as well as Miami jai-alai.

Admission is $1, reserved seats are $2, restaurant seating is $3, and box seats are $3 to $5. Seniors 55 and older get free admission to matinees. Parking is free; valet parking is $1.50. Open year-round Wednesday to Sunday. Evening games are held at 7:30pm Wednesday to Saturday, matinees at noon Thursday and Saturday, and at 1pm Sunday. From the Walt Disney World area, take I-4 east, make a right at Exit 47A (Maitland Exchange), a right at U.S. 17/92, and look for the fronton 2 miles along on your right. It's about a 40-minute drive.

8

Shopping

You probably didn't come down here to shop, but I doubt you'll leave without a purchase or two. All Orlando-area theme parks abound with emporia, in addition to which Walt Disney World has its own shopping complex.

Just about every shop throughout Walt Disney World carries what I call "Disneyana": plush Mickey Mice, *Little Mermaid* T-shirts, et al. But you may be surprised that many Disney shops also target the serious collector. Shops in all WDW parks will deliver purchases to Disney resorts and official hotels.

1 Shopping in Walt Disney World

THE MAGIC KINGDOM
MAIN STREET AREA

The vast **Disneyana Collectibles** carries limited-edition movie cels, antique Disney clocks and porcelain figures, collectible dolls, and items such as a 1947 Donald Duck cookie jar that today is worth $2,000! Why did I ever let Mom throw out my old toys?

The **Emporium,** in Town Square, houses the park's largest selection of Disneyana, everything from Mickey-logo golf balls to Dumbo cookie jars. Note the Animatronic window displays.

Basically an old-fashioned candy store, the **Market House** also has an interesting line of pipes and tobaccos, as well as Disney-theme kitchenware . . . Mickey cupcake papers, ice-cube molds, and cookie cutters.

Over at the **Harmony Barber Shop,** where nostalgic men's grooming items are sold (moustache wax, spice colognes, shaving mugs), a barbershop quartet called The Dapper Dans performs on the hour all day (except at 3pm).

Autographed sports memorabilia and team clothing—Joe Namath–signed footballs, Pittsburgh Steeler T-shirts, Bulls jerseys, a Babe Ruth autographed 1936 World Series program, and the like—are available at the **Main Street Athletic Club.**

At **Crystal Arts,** you can watch craftspeople create the intricate animals, cut-glass vases and bowls, and other glittering items sold here. And at the adjoining **Shadow Box,** silhouette artists create cutout portraits of customers on black paper.

At the end of Main Street, the **King's Gallery,** inside Cinderella Castle, is cluttered with family crests, tapestries, suits of armor, and other medieval wares, as well as miniature carousels. An artisan here demonstrates *damascening*, a form of metal engraving that originated in Damascus circa A.D. 600.

ADVENTURELAND

The exotic **Traders of Timbuktu** carries carved wooden and soapstone animals, masks, and cowhide drums from Kenya, among other ethnic wares.

Plaza del Sol Caribe, a Mexican mercado, has piñatas, baskets, straw hats, stuffed and papier-mâché toucans and parrots, and much more.

For the Indiana Jones look, check out the clothing and accessories at **Elephant Tales.** The little **Tiki Tropic Shop** carries surfer-theme merchandise.

Shell mobiles and hangings, plus a wide selection of straw hats, are sold at the **Zanzibar Shell Shop. Island Supply,** a Disney version of The Nature Company, offers nature-theme books, posters, toys, bird feeders, and more.

And both the **House of Treasure** and the adjoining **Lafitte's Portrait Deck** retail pirate merchandise: hats, Captain Hook T-shirts, ships in bottles, and toy muskets and daggers; the latter has a pirate ship photo setup.

FRONTIERLAND

Mosey into the **Frontier Trading Post** for western-look leather items, cowboy boots and hats, western shirts, coonskin caps, turquoise jewelry, belts, and toy rifles. **Prairie Outpost & Supply** sells Native American items such as drums, headdresses, and bows and arrows, many of them related to Pocahontas.

Visit the **Briar Patch,** under Splash Mountain, for Uncle Remus and Winnie the Pooh merchandise.

LIBERTY SQUARE

Olde World Antiques' high-quality inventory might range from an 18th-century pine hutch to 19th-century Staffordshire Chinoiserie willow-pattern platters (There's talk of changing it to a Christmas-year-round shop.) The adjoining **Silversmith** carries Revere-style silver and pewter butter dishes, candlesticks, bowls, trays, jewelry, and picture frames.

The **Yankee Trader** is a charming country store, its shelves stocked with Lion King and Winnie the Pooh cookie jars, Mickey cookie cutters, and fancy food items.

And over at **Heritage House,** you can purchase parchment copies of famous American documents as well as actual historic framed letters (one signed by President Andrew Johnson in 1864 was priced at $2,350). Old campaign buttons, Civil War hats, and presidential signatures are here, too. A craftsperson on the premises makes jewelry cut from coins.

FANTASYLAND

It's always the holiday season at **Mickey's Christmas Carol,** supply central for Disney-motif ornaments, caroller dolls, Mickey Christmas stockings, and charming Christmas-theme music boxes.

And little girls will adore **Tinker Bell's Treasures,** its wares comprising Peter Pan merchandise, costumes (Tinker Bell, Snow White, Cinderella, Pocahontas, and others), and collector dolls.

TOMORROWLAND

Kids love browsing over **Merchant of Venus's** space-theme *Alien Encounter* and *Star Wars* merchandise. Also here: **Mickey's Star Traders,** a large Disneyana shop.

EPCOT

The most fascinating shops are found in **World Showcase** pavilions, which comprise an international bazaar selling everything from Berber rugs to Japanese kimonos. You'll find descriptions of merchandise available in these pavilions in World Showcase listings in chapter 7, section 3.

DISNEY-MGM STUDIOS

There's some really interesting shopping here. The **Animation Gallery** carries collectible cels, books about animation, arts and crafts kits for future animators, and collector figurines.

Sid Cahuenga's One-of-a-Kind sells autographed photos of the stars, original movie posters, and star-touched items such as a bracelet that once belonged to Joan Rivers.

Over at **Cover Story,** you can have your photograph put on the cover of your favorite magazine, anything from *Forbes* to *Psychology Today* to *Golf Digest.* Costumes are available.

Celebrity 5 & 10, modeled after a 1940s Woolworth's, has movie-related merchandise: *Gone With the Wind* memorabilia, MGM Studio T-shirts, movie posters, Elvis mugs, and more.

And major park attractions all have complementary merchandise outlets selling Indiana Jones adventure clothing, *Little Mermaid* stuffed characters and logo-wear, *Star Wars* souvenirs, and so on.

DISNEY VILLAGE MARKETPLACE

Just 2¹/₂ miles from Epcot, this complex of restaurants and shops, on the shores of Buena Vista Lagoon makes for a very pleasant browse. Designed to evoke a quaint seaside town, the Marketplace (☎ **407/828-3058**) is enhanced by innovative fountains, character topiaries, theme gardens, children's play areas, and waterside seating. It has about 20 weathered-wood and shingled shops offering a wide variety of giftware, Disneyana (**Mickey's Character Shop** has one of the largest collections anywhere), toys, logo/designer/resort clothing, Christmas-year-round merchandise (9,000 square feet of it), books, jewelry, crystal, housewares, country/folk crafts, shells, wines and spirits, and sports shoes and apparel.

Highlights include the **Art of Disney** shop, retailing upscale collectibles . . . cels, toys, and one-of-a-kind furnishings such as a Mickey Mouse armchair and hassock; **Toys Fantastic,** featuring the latest Mattel playthings and a play table for kids; and **Discover,** a nature store selling birdhouses and feeders, wind chimes, mounted butterflies, and the like.

Artisans demonstrate crafts such as glass-blowing, pottery-making, silhouette-cutting, and caricaturing at various locations throughout the complex, and many special events—ranging from boat shows to a major art festival—take place here. There's plenty of free parking; valet parking is $5.

See chapter 6 for Marketplace (and adjoining Pleasure Island) restaurant suggestions. You can also rent mini-speedboats and pontoons at the marina here. And the vast **Gourmet Pantry** carries reasonably priced fixings—cold fried chicken breast, salads (perhaps lobster, couscous, Asian chicken, or tortellini), sandwiches on fresh-baked breads, wines, Godiva chocolates, and pastries—for a waterfront picnic at an umbrella table. The Marketplace is open daily from 9:30am to 11pm.

CROSSROADS OF LAKE BUENA VISTA

Also under Walt Disney World auspices, this retail center at Exit 27 off I-4 (☎ **407/ 827-7300**) is anchored by a 24-hour Goodings supermarket with a full-service pharmacy. Other shops sell sportswear, electronics, books, cards, gifts, shoes, and Disney merchandise. There's also a post office, and restaurants/fast-food outlets include, among others, T.G.I. Friday's, Johnny Rockets, Pebbles (see chapter 6), Pizzeria Uno, and Red Lobster. Shops are open daily 10am to 10pm. It's just like a shopping center in the real world.

2 Orlando Area Malls

FACTORY OUTLETS

Belz Factory Outlet World, 5401 W. Oak Ridge Rd., at the north end of International Drive (☎ **407/354-0126** or 407/352-9600), is the largest of these, with 180 stores in two huge, enclosed malls and four shopping annexes. It offers an immense range of merchandise at savings up to 75% off retail prices. There's even a carousel for the kids.

Among its emporia: 18 shoe stores (including Bass, Bally, and Capezio); 14 housewares shops (including Fieldcrest/Cannon, Corning, Oneida, and Mikasa); and more than 60 clothing shops for men, women, and children (including London Fog, Van Heusen, Jonathan Logan, Guess Jeans, Aileen, Danskin, Jordache, Leslie Fay, Carole Little, Harvé Benard, Calvin Klein, and Anne Klein). You can also shop for books and records, electronics, sporting goods, health and beauty aids, jewelry, toys, gifts, accessories, lingerie, and hosiery here. Open Monday through Saturday from 10am to 9pm, Sunday from 10am to 6pm.

Close to the above is the **Quality Outlet Center,** on International Drive a block east of Kirkman Road (☎ **407/423-5885**). It has about 20 outlets, including Arrow, American Tourister, Corning-Revere (glassware and cookware), Florsheim shoes, Magnavox, Laura Ashley, Adidas, Great Western Boots, Totes, Le Creuset (cookware), Linens 'N Things, Mikasa, Royal Doulton, and Villeroy & Boch. Once again, big savings. Open Monday through Saturday from 9:30am to 9pm, Sunday from 11am to 6pm.

Continuing a quarter of a mile north on International Drive, you'll come to the **International Drive Value Center,** under the same auspices as the Quality (same phone, same hours). Its 15 stores include T. J. Maxx, other women's clothing stores, Old Navy Clothing Company (a Gap concept), Lane Bryant, Linea Garbo (Italian shoes), Converse, Perfumania, Books A Million, and Bed, Bath, & Beyond.

Manufacturer's Outlet Mall, U.S. 192, a mile east of FL 535 in Kissimmee (☎ **407/396-8900**), houses about 35 stores, including Van Heusen, Nike, London Fog, Fieldcrest/Cannon, Bass Apparel, Geoffrey Beene, American Tourister, Westport (women's fashions), Acme Boot, and Levis. Open Monday through Saturday from 10am to 9pm, Sunday from 11am to 5pm.

INTERNATIONAL DRIVE AREA MALLS

The Mercado, 8445 International Dr., just south of Sand Lake Road (☎ **407/345-9337**)—a Mediterranean-style shopping center with brick and cobblestone streets, terra-cotta-roofed buildings, brightly colored awnings, and splashing fountains—is home to the Orlando/Orange County Visitor Information Center. A video-game arcade here keeps the kids amused while you shop, and there's live entertainment evenings (jazz, country rock, and reggae bands) in the central courtyard.

More than 60 specialty shops include Swings 'N' Things (everything from hammocks to wind chimes), Kandlestix (handcrafted candles), American Cola Company (Coca-Cola and Anheuser-Busch memorabilia), House of Ireland (china, crystal, claddagh jewelry), Historic Families (find your family's coat of arms), Earth Matters (conservation/ecology-theme merchandise), Lady Bug (needlecrafts), the Magic Shop (novelties, tricks, and pranks), and the Looking Glass (blown glass). It makes good browsing, and there are over a dozen restaurants and bars on the premises.

Stop by guest services to get a free "Privilege Card" for discounts at mall stores. Guest services also offers airline ticketing, discounted attraction tickets (including Disney parks), car rental, help with accommodations, and more. Open daily from 10am to 10pm, until 11pm late spring through the end of August.

The **Florida Mall,** 8001 S. Orange Blossom Trail, at Sand Lake Road (☎ 407/ 851-6255), is your basic massive shopping mall with more than 200 shops, restaurants, and services. Centered on a 500-room Sheraton Hotel, it is anchored by six department stores—Belk Lindsey, two Dillard's stores, J. C. Penney, Gayfers, and Sears. In addition, there are more than 10 jewelry shops, about 50 clothing and accessory shops (including mall regulars such as Benetton, Warner Bros. Studio Store, The Gap/Gap Kids, The Limited, and Victoria's Secret), over a dozen shoe stores, bookstores, electronics stores, eateries (among them, a food court), and much, much more. Open Monday through Saturday from 10am to 9:30pm, Sunday from 11am to 6pm.

Walt Disney World & Orlando After Dark

9

My hat's off to those of you who after a long day traipsing around amusement parks still have the energy to venture out at night in search of entertainment. You'll find plenty to do. And this being a kid's world, many evening shows are geared to families.

In addition to the below-listed suggestions, check the "Calendar" section of Friday's *Orlando Sentinel* for up-to-the-minute details on local clubs, visiting performers, concerts, and events—and many are world-class.

Tickets to many performances are handled by **TicketMaster.** Call **407/839-3900** to charge tickets.

1 What's New in 1997 (and What's in the Works)

Many new developments on the nightlife scene are in the works at this writing.

Disney is expanding Pleasure Island (details below), to include Dan Aykroyd's **House of Blues,** which will offer live music (blues, R&B, jazz, and country) nightly and offer a New Orleans–style menu; **Lario's,** created by Gloria Estefan and her husband Emilio, which, like its popular Miami Beach sister club, will feature sizzling Latin American rhythms; **Disney's Entertainment Theater,** a new performing arts venue to showcase Disney productions and visiting headliners; and 14 new screens at the already-extant multiplex **AMC Theatres,** bringing its total to 24 and making it the largest such complex in the state.

The luxurious **Disney's BoardWalk Resort,** opening as we go to press, will have several on-premises clubs, including **Atlantic Dance** (a classic dance hall with a 10-piece orchestra playing music from the '40s through the '90s) and **Jellyrolls** (a dueling-piano bar similar in concept to Blazing Pianos, described below).

There are also exciting developments underway at Universal Studios Florida, where a multibillion-dollar expansion (due for completion in January 1998) will include a dynamic, high-energy 12-acre entertainment complex called **E-ZONE.** Occupying a two-tiered promenade with authentic streetscapes, a 4-acre lagoon, waterfalls, and lush landscaping, E-ZONE will include a **Hard Rock Cafe** (the biggest and baddest on the planet) with a 2,000-seat live concert venue; **Shaq's Place,** a 31,000-square-foot sports bar and nightclub featuring a high-tech game room, sports-oriented skill games, and a dance floor that looks like a basketball court (there will be occasional live performances by hit recording artists, and Shaq himself will make appearances); **B.B. King's Blues Club,** a replica of the singer's popular Memphis supper/dance club, featuring live performances by R&B artists and a restaurant highlighting southern specialties (B.B. and other major stars will drop in to jam); **Pat O'Brien's,** a New Orleans dueling-pianos transplant that claims to be the original of the genre; a 16-screen **Cineplex Odeon** movie theater (a cutting-edge projection and sound system are promised, along with "a totally unique moviegoing environment"); and a **floating outdoor theater** to be used for special shows and concerts.

2 Walt Disney World Dinner Shows

Two distinctly different dinner shows are hosted by Walt Disney World. Other nighttime park options include SpectroMagic, fireworks, and IllumiNations (details in chapter 7).

Hoop-Dee-Doo Musical Revue

Disney's Fort Wilderness Resort and Campground, 3520 N. Fort Wilderness Trail. ☎ **407/ W-DINE.** $36 adults, $18 children 3–11. Taxes and gratuities extra. Show times at 5, 7:15, and 9:30pm nightly. Free self-parking.

Fort Wilderness's rustic log-beamed Pioneer Hall is the setting for this 2-hour footstompin', hand-clappin', down-home musical revue. It's a high-energy show, with 1890s costumes, corny vaudeville jokes, rousing songs, and lots of good-natured audience participation.

During the show, the audience chows down on an all-you-can-eat barbecue dinner, including chips and salsa, salad, smoked ribs, country-fried chicken, corn on the cob, baked beans, loaves of fresh-baked bread with honey butter, and a big slab of strawberry shortcake for dessert. Beverages (coffee, tea, beer, sangría, and soda) are included.

Reservations are required. If you catch an early show, stick around for the Electrical Water Pageant at 9:45pm, which can be viewed from the Fort Wilderness Beach.

Polynesian Luau Dinner Show

Disney's Polynesian Resort, 1600 Seven Seas Dr. ☎ **407/WDW-DINE.** $33 adults 21 and over, $25 ages 12–20, $17 children 3–11. Taxes and gratuities are extra. Show times 6:45 and 9:30pm nightly. Free self- and valet parking.

This delightful 2-hour dinner show is a big favorite with kids, who are all invited up on the stage. It features a colorfully costumed cast of entertainers from New Zealand, Tahiti, Hawaii, and Samoa performing authentic hula, warrior, ceremonial, love, and fire dances on a flower-bedecked stage. The show also includes a Hawaiian/Polynesian fashion show.

It all takes place in an open-air theater (dress for nighttime weather) with candlelit tables, red-flame lanterns suggesting torches, and tapa-bark paintings adorning the walls. Arrive early; there's a preshow highlighting Polynesian crafts and culture (lei making, hula lessons, and more).

The all-you-can-eat meal includes a big platter of fresh island fruits, barbecued chicken, corn on the cob, other vegetables, roasted red potatoes and sweet potatoes, pull-apart cinnamon bread, beverages, and a tropical ice cream sundae.

Reservations are required. There's also a 4:30pm version daily (see character meal listings in chapter 6).

3 Entertainment Complexes: Pleasure Island & Church Street Station

Pleasure Island

In Walt Disney World, adjacent to Walt Disney World Village. ☎ **407/934-7781.** Free admission before 7pm, $14.95 after 7pm. Admission included in the 5-Day World-Hopper Pass. Clubs daily 8pm–2am, shops 10am–1am. Free self-parking, valet parking $5.

This Walt Disney World theme park is a rollicking, 6-acre complex of nightclubs, restaurants, shops, and movie theaters (details in section 4, later in this chapter) where, for a single admission price, you can enjoy a night of club-hopping until the wee hours.

Due to double in size in the near future (see above), the park is designed to evoke an abandoned waterfront industrial district with clubs in "converted" ramshackle lofts, factories, and warehouses, but the streets are festive with brightly colored lights and balloons. Dozens of searchlights play overhead, and rock music emanates from the bushes. You'll be given a map and show schedule when you enter the park; take a look at it, and plan your evening around shows that interest you.

The mood here is always festive. For one thing, every night at Pleasure Island is New Year's Eve, celebrated on the stroke of midnight with a high-energy street party, live entertainment, a barrage of fireworks, and showers of confetti.

You can feel perfectly secure sending your teenage kids here for the evening, though they must be 18 to get in unless accompanied by a parent or legal guardian.

The on-premises clubs do come and go. At this writing they include the following.

Pleasure Island Jazz Company: This big, barnlike club—purported to be an abandoned waterfront carousel factory—features contemporary and traditional live jazz. Performers are mostly locals, but about once a month there are big names such as Kenny Rankin, Lionel Hampton, Maynard Ferguson, the Rippingtons, and Billy Taylor. Light fare, international coffees, and a variety of foreign and domestic wines are available.

Mannequins Dance Palace: Housed in a vast dance hall with a small-town movie-house facade, Mannequins is supposed to be a converted theatrical mannequin warehouse (remember, you're still in Disney World). It's a high-energy club with a large rotating dance floor. Three levels of bars and hangout space are festooned with elaborately costumed mannequins and moving scenery suspended from overhead rigging. A deejay plays contemporary tunes at ear-splitting decibel level, and there are high-tech lighting effects. You must be 21 to get in, and they're very serious about it. They even carded me, and I learned to dance to the Platters.

Neon Armadillo Music Saloon: You guessed. This trilevel club is country—with neon beer signs, rustic tables mounted on beer barrels, walls hung with spurs and saddles, and a spur-shaped neon chandelier. Live country bands play nightly, and dancers whirl around the floor doing the Texas two-step or cotton-eyed Joe (lessons are given Sunday from 7 to 8pm). Sometimes name stars come in and take the stage. The staff is in cowboy/cowgirl garb. A specialty at the bar is Jell-O shooters—Jell-O cubes laced with rum, vodka, and other alcoholic beverages. You can also order southwestern fare here such as chili and fajitas.

Adventurers Club: The most unique—and my personal favorite—of Pleasure Island's clubs occupies a multistory building that, according to Disney legend, was designed to house the vast library and archeological trophy collection of island founder and compulsive explorer Merriweather Adam Pleasure. It's also head-

---

Blazing Pianos: A Perfect Hell for the Shy

A rambunctious crowd of all ages hangs out at this popular sing-along club, where a talented cast of singers and musicians—on fire-engine-red grand pianos—perform classic rock tunes, do a bit of comedy, and try to embarrass audience members. Most of the songs they select are on the lively side—"Great Balls of Fire," "The Twist," "Jailhouse Rock," and the like, as well as TV theme songs.

Audience members occasionally get up on the stage—or are dragooned there—to dance. And probably once a night everyone stands up to perform "Hand Jive." Blazing Pianos promotes audience participation to the max; it's an exhibitionist's paradise, and perhaps unbearable for the sensitive (you might be spotlighted if they see you're not singing!). The ambience is slick and upscale; special effects include smoke, mirror balls, and strobe lights. A fairly extensive bar menu lists items such as fried calamari and buffalo wings, plus gourmet desserts.

Blazing Pianos is located in the Mercado at 8445 International Blvd., just south of Sand Lake Road (☎ **407/363-5104**).

Admission is $5. Though it opens earlier, the action begins about 9:30pm and continues until 2am nightly. No one under 21 is admitted weekend nights. Sunday through Thursday, children are welcome, and it makes for a fun family outing.

---

quarters for the Adventures Club, which Pleasure headed up until he vanished at sea in 1941. The plushly furnished club is chock-full of artifacts—early aviation photos, hunting trophies, shrunken heads, Buddhas, Indian goddesses, spears, and a mounted "yakoose" (half yak, half moose) who occasionally speaks. He's not the only one. In the eerie Mask Room, strange sounds are often heard, and more than 100 masks move their eyes, jeer, and make odd pronouncements. Also on hand are Pleasure's zany band of globe-trotting friends and club servants, played by skilled actors who interact with guests and always stay in character. Improvisational comedy shows take place throughout the evening in the main salon, diverse 20-minute cabaret shows/events in the library (during which "volunteers" are dragooned from the audience). You could easily hang out here all night imbibing potent tropical drinks in the library and at the bar—where elephant-foot barstools rise and sink mysteriously.

Comedy Warehouse: Housed in the island's former power plant, the Comedy Warehouse—another favorite of mine—has a rustic interior with tiered seating. A very talented troupe performs 45-minute improvisational comedy shows based on audience suggestions. There are five shows a night, and bar drinks are available. Arrive early.

Rock & Roll Beach Club: Once the laboratory in which Pleasure developed a unique flying machine, this three-story structure today houses a dance club where live bands play "classic rock from the '60s through the '90s." There are bars on all three floors, including one serving international beers. The first level contains the dance floor. The second and third levels offer air hockey, pool tables, basketball machines, pinball, video games, darts, and a pizza and beer stand.

8 Trax: This 1970s-style club, with about 50 TV monitors airing diverse shows and videos over the dance floor, occupies three levels, all with bars. Period movie posters (*Bananas, Star Wars*) adorn the walls, and the top-floor lounge is vaguely psychedelic in decor. A deejay plays disco music, and guests engage in games of Twister.

In addition, live bands—including occasional big-name groups—play the **West End Plaza** outdoor stage and the **Hub Stage;** check your schedule for show times.

You can star in your own music video at **SuperStar Studios.** And there are carnival games, a video-game arcade, virtual reality games, a Velcro wall (don a jumpsuit over your clothes, bounce on a trampoline, and stick yourself on), and an Orbitron (a "21st-century workout machine," originally developed for NASA, that lets you experience weightlessness). **Shops and eateries** (with outdoor umbrella tables) are found throughout the park. **Planet Hollywood** (see chapter 6 for details) is adjacent.

Church Street Station

129 W. Church St. (off I-4, between Garland and Orange Avenues in downtown Orlando). ☎ **407/422-2434.** Free admission prior to 5pm after which you have to pay $16.95. Clubs are open nightly until 2am, shops until 11pm. There are several parking lots nearby (call for specifics). Valet parking, at Church Street and Garland Avenue, is $6. Take I-4 east to Exit 38 (Anderson Street), stay in the left lane, and follow the blue signs. Most hotels offer transportation to and from Church Street, and, since you'll probably be drinking, I advise it.

Though not part of Walt Disney World, Church Street Station in downtown Orlando operates on a similar principle to Pleasure Island (in fact, it started the concept).

Occupying a cobblestoned city block lined with turn-of-the-century buildings (real ones), it, too, is a shopping/dining/nightclub complex offering a diverse evening of entertainment for a single admission price. There are 20 live shows nightly; consult your show schedule upon entering.

Stunning interiors are the rule here. It's worth coming by just to check out the magnificent woodwork, stained glass, and thousands of authentic antiques. And capitalizing on the traffic Church Street generates, many other clubs have opened in the immediate area, further enlarging your bar-hopping potential.

Entry to restaurants, the Exchange Shopping Emporium, and the Midway game area is free. Highlights include:

Rosie O'Grady's Good Time Emporium: This 1890s-style gambling hall–cum-saloon, with beveled- and leaded-glass panels, etched mirrors, and vast globe chandeliers suspended from a high pressed-tin ceiling, is filled with interesting antiques. The train benches came from an old Florida rail station, backbar mirrors from a Glasgow pub, and bank teller's cages from a 19th-century Pittsburgh bank. Dixieland bands, banjo players, singing waiters, and cancan dancers entertain nightly. Light fare (deli sandwiches, chili dogs) is available. The house specialty drink is a rum and fruit concoction called the Flaming Hurricane (served in a souvenir glass).

Apple Annie's Courtyard: Adjoining Rosie's, this brick-floored establishment, domed by arched trusses from an early 19th-century New Orleans church, evokes a Victorian tropical garden. The room is further embellished by 12-foot hand-carved filigree mirrors created in Vienna circa 1740 and magnificent 1,000-pound chandeliers suspended from an ornate vaulted cherrywood ceiling. An 18th-century French communion rail serves as the front bar. Seating is in wicker peacock chairs at English pub tables. Patrons sip potent tropical fresh fruit and ice-cream drinks while listening to folk and bluegrass music.

Lili Marlene's Aviator's Pub & Restaurant: Its plush oak-paneled interior is embellished with World War I memorabilia, stained-glass transoms, and accoutrements from an 1850 Rothschild townhouse in Paris, the latter including a walnut fireplace and wine cabinets. Eclectic seating ranges from hand-carved oak pews that came from a French church to a place at a large drop-leaf mahogany table where Al Capone once dined. Model airplanes and marvelous Victorian chandeliers are suspended from a beamed pine ceiling with a stained-glass skylight. The menu features premium aged steaks, prime rib, and fresh seafood.

Phineas Phogg's Balloon Works: This whimsical bar, with hot-air balloons and airplanes over the dance floor, is a high-energy club playing loud, pulsating music. It doubles as a virtual ballooning museum housing photographs and artifacts from historic flights, including Orlando native Joe Kittinger—first man to cross the Atlantic in a gas balloon. Every Wednesday from 6:30 to 7:30pm, beers cost just 5¢ here. No one under 21 is admitted.

Cheyenne Saloon and Opera House: This stunning trilevel balconied saloon, crowned by a lofty stained-glass skylight, is constructed of golden oak lumber from a century-old Ohio barn. Quality western art is displayed throughout, including many oil paintings and 11 Remington sculptures. Balcony seating, in restored church pews, overlooks the stage—setting for entertainment ranging from country bands (some big names) to clogging exhibitions—and the dance floor. The menu features steaks, barbecued chicken and ribs, and hickory-smoked brisket.

Orchid Garden Ballroom: This stunning space, with ornate white wrought-iron arches and Victorian lighting fixtures suspended from an elaborate oak-paneled ceiling, is the setting for an oldies dance club. A deejay plays rock 'n' roll classics like "Great Balls of Fire" and "Let's Go to the Hop," interspersed with live bands. As the evening progresses, so do the musical decades.

Crackers Oyster Bar: Brick columns, oak paneling, and a gorgeous antique oak and mahogany bar characterize this cozy, late 1800s-style dining room. Fresh Florida seafood is featured, along with more than 50 imported beers. You can nibble on appetizers such as oysters Rockefeller, smoked fish dip, and steamed mussels. Or opt for more serious entrées ranging from crab cakes rémoulade to paella.

In addition, the 87,000-square-foot Exchange houses the carnival-like **Commander Ragtime's Midway of Fun, Food and Games** (including an enormous video-game arcade), a food court, and more than 50 specialty shops. You can rent a horse-drawn carriage out front for a drive around the downtown area and Lake Eola. And hot-air balloon flights can be arranged (☎ **407/841-8787**).

4 More Entertainment

LITTLE HOUSE OF HORRORS

Terror on Church Street

135 S. Orange Ave. (at Church Street in downtown Orlando, a block from Church Street Station). ☎ **407/649-FEAR** or 407/649-1912. Admission $12 adults, $10 children under 17. Mon–Thurs and Sun 7pm–midnight, Fri–Sat 7pm–1am. Most hotels offer transportation to the area. There are several lots nearby (call for specifics). You can use Church Street Station's valet parking ($6) at Church Street and Garland Avenue. Take I-4 east to Exit 38 (Anderson Street), stay in the left lane, and follow the blue signs to Church Street Station parking.

Terror on Church Street is a multimedia, high-tech house of horrors incorporating innovative special effects and 23 highly theatrical sets on two floors. On a labyrinthine 25-minute tour of the darkened premises, guests are menaced by cleaver- and chain-saw-wielding maniacs, ghoulish monks, assorted cadavers, vicious dogs, Freddie Kreuger, and Dracula, among others—all convincingly portrayed by actors. Children under 10 are not admitted without an adult. A gift shop on the premises sells stick-on warts and burn scars, coffin banks, and the like.

A SPORTS BAR

Champions

In Marriott's Orlando World Center, 8701 World Center Dr. ☎ **407/239-4200.** Free admission. Open nightly until 2am. Free self-parking, valet parking $7.

Champions is a sports-bar chain—one so appealing, it's easy to see why the concept has succeeded. Its interior is chockablock with $25,000 worth of signed sports photos, posters, and artifacts such as Lou Gehrig's baseball bat, a golf bag autographed by Dallas Cowboys coach Jimmy Johnson, and (of local interest) a wet suit belonging to Cypress Gardens' famed barefoot waterski star, Banana George. Some nights a dejay plays music (mostly Motown and oldies) for dancing. Otherwise, entertainments include three pool tables, video games, foosball, darts, coin-op football and basketball, and blackjack tables. In addition, sporting events are aired on large-screen TVs and on smaller monitors around the room (a calendar at the entrance lists all game times). Champions offers a fairly extensive bar-food menu.

Note to single women: Men outnumber women about five to one, so this is a good place to meet guys—if you can distract them from the sports action on the screen.

MORE DINNER SHOWS

American Gladiators Orlando Live!

Gladiator Arena, 5515 W. Irlo Bronson Memorial Hwy (U.S. 192, between I-4 and FL 535), Kissimmee. ☎ **407/390-0000** or 800/BATTLE-4. Snack show: adults $27.95, children 3–12 $15.95, under 3 free; dinner show: adults $39.95, children 3–12 $21.50. Sun–Thurs 7:30pm, Fri–Sat 6:30 and 9:30pm; the two-show weekend time schedule is also in effect mid-Feb–mid-Apr, the third week of June–the third week of Aug, and Christmas week.

This 90-minute, action-packed show features qualified contenders battling in areas such as assault, breakthrough and conquer, joust, powerball, the wall, and whiplash. If you don't know what all that means, watch it on TV before you decide whether or not it's your thing. Shows at 6:30 and 7:30pm include a full chicken dinner, while snack fare is served at the later show.

Wild Bill's Wild West Dinner Extravaganza

5260 U.S. 192 (just east of I-4). ☎ **407/351-5151** or 800/883-8181. Admission $33.95 adults, $19.95 children 3–11, under 3 free. Shows take place nightly at 7pm, with 9:30pm shows on selected nights.

Located at Fort Liberty, a 22-acre western-theme shopping/dining/entertainment complex, this rambunctious dinner show takes place in a big barnlike wooden building. You'll be given a cardboard cowboy hat when you sit down, which identifies you as a shepherd or cowherd for audience-participation activities (there are a lot of these). The show includes rousing song-and-dance numbers ("Annie Get Your Gun," "Oklahoma," "Back in the Saddle Again"); rodeo roping, knife-throwing, and archery demonstrations; sing-alongs; a cancan; and Comanche ceremonial and war dances. All the children in the audience get to go up on the stage.

Dinner—served on pewterware—is a hearty four-course meal consisting of salad, soup, beef stew, fried chicken, barbecued pork ribs, biscuits with honey butter, corn, beans, a baked potato, and hot apple pie. Beer, wine, and Coca-Cola are included.

MOVIES

Pleasure Island AMC Theater

In Walt Disney World adjacent to the Pleasure Island nightclub complex. ☎ **407/827-1300.** Matinees $4.50 adults, $3.75 seniors and children 2–13, under 2 free; twilight shows (4:30–6pm) $3.25 for all seats; evening shows $6.50 adults, $4.50 students, $3.75 seniors (over 55) and children 2–13, under 2 free.

This 10-screen AMC theater complex—equipped with state-of-the-art Dolby-digital sound systems and 70mm projection capability—extends the variety of nighttime entertainment available to Disney World guests and will soon extend it further; it's adding 14 new screens to become Florida's largest multiplex! A bridge connects the theater complex with Pleasure Island clubs. New Disney films premiere here, and first-run films are shown; check the *Orlando Sentinel* for show times.

5 Major Concert Halls & Auditoriums

Three large entertainment facilities, administered by the Orlando Centroplex, host the majority of big-name performers playing the Orlando area.

The **Florida Citrus Bowl,** 1610 W. Church St., at Tampa Street (☎ **407/849-2020** for information, **407/839-3900** to charge tickets), with 70,000 seats, is the largest. This is the setting for major rock concerts and headliners like Billy Joel, Elton John, The Eagles, Guns n' Roses, Paul McCartney, Metallica, and the Rolling Stones. To reach the Citrus Bowl, take I-4 east to the East–West Expressway and head west to Hwy. 441; make a left on Church Street and follow the signs. Parking is $5.

The 17,500-seat **Orlando Arena** at 600 W. Amelia St., between I-4 and Parramore Avenue (☎ **407/849-2020** for information, **407/839-3900** to charge tickets) also hosts major performers (Elton John, Bruce Springsteen, Billy Joel, Bette Midler) in addition to an array of family-oriented entertainment: Ringling Bros. Barnum & Bailey Circus every January, *Discover Card Stars on Ice* in February, Tour of World Figure-Skating Champions in April or May, and *Walt Disney's World on Ice* in September. To reach the arena, take I-4 east to Amelia Avenue, turn left at the traffic light at the bottom of the off-ramp, and follow signs. Parking is $5.

The area's major cultural venue is the **Bob Carr Performing Arts Centre,** 401 W. Livingston St., between I-4 and Parramore Avenue (☎ **407/849-2020** for information, **407/839-3900** to charge tickets). Concert prices vary with performers, ballet tickets are $15–$35, opera tickets $12–$45, Broadway Series $24.50–$46.50. This 2,500-seat facility is home to the **Orlando Opera Company** and the **Southern Ballet Theater,** both of which have October-to-May seasons. The **Orlando Broadway Series** (September to May) features original-cast Broadway shows such as *Carousel,* The Who's *Tommy, Damn Yankees,* and *Cats.* Also featured at the Bob Carr are concerts and comedy shows; a recent year's performers included Patti LaBelle, Lyle Lovett, Julio Iglesias, and Crosby, Stills, and Nash. To get here, take I-4 east to Amelia Avenue, turn left at the traffic light at the bottom of the off-ramp, and follow signs. Parking is $5.

Side Trips from Walt Disney World & Orlando

10

Get away from the glitter and glitz that characterizes most Orlando attractions. Stroll through Cypress Gardens—a serene botanical paradise that was central Florida's first major tourist draw; find out what NASA is up to over at the Kennedy Space Center; head to Winter Park, a charming upscale town with some exquisite attractions; or check out the self-proclaimed "World's Most Famous Beach" and "World Center of Racing," Daytona Beach.

1 Cypress Gardens

40 miles SW of Walt Disney World, 45 miles SW of Orlando

Founded in 1936 when Dick and Julie Pope hired a crew of laborers to dig canals and drain swamps, ✪ **Cypress Gardens,** located on FL 540 at Cypress Gardens Boulevard in Winter Haven (☎ **941/ 324-2111** or 800/282-2123), came into being as a 16-acre public garden along the banks of Lake Eloise with cypress-wood-block pathways and thousands of tropical and subtropical plants. Today it has grown to over 200 acres, with ponds and lagoons, waterfalls, classic Italian fountains, topiary, bronze sculptures, and manicured lawns. Ancient cypress trees shrouded in Spanish moss form a backdrop to ever-changing floral displays of 8,000 varieties of plants from more than 90 countries. Southern belles in Scarlett O'Hara costumes stroll the grounds or sit on benches under parasols in idyllic, tree-shaded nooks. They symbolize Florida's old-fashioned southern hospitality.

In the late winter and early spring, more than 20 varieties of bougainvillea, 40 of azalea, and hundreds of roses burst into bloom. Crape myrtles, magnolias, and gardenias perfume the late-spring air, while brilliant birds of paradise, hibiscus, and jasmine brighten the summer landscape. And in winter, the goldenrain trees, floss silk trees, and camellias of autumn give way to millions of colorful chrysanthemums and red, white, and pink poinsettias.

GETTING THERE

Take I-4 west to U.S. 27 south, and proceed west on to FL 540. If you don't have a car, inquire about public transportation at your hotel.

EXPLORING THE GARDENS

Strolling the grounds is, of course, the main attraction (there are over 2 miles of winding botanical paths, and half of the park's acreage is devoted to floral displays), but this being central Florida, it's not the only one.

Shows are scheduled several times each day. The world-famous **Greatest American Ski Team** performs daring freestyle jumps, swivel skiing, barefooting, ski ballet, and slalom exhibitions on Lake Eloise in a show augmented by an awesome hang-gliding display. **Moscow on Ice Live!** is the Russian answer to America's Ice Capades. And **Variété Internationale** features specialty acts from all over the world.

And there's still more. An enchanting exhibit called **Wings of Wonder** surrounds visitors with more than 1,000 brightly colored free-flying butterflies (representing more than 50 species) in a 5,500-square-foot Victorian-style glass conservatory filled with tropical plantings, orchids, and waterfalls.

Electric boats navigate a maze of lushly landscaped canals in the original botanical gardens area. You can ascend 153 feet to the **Island in the Sky** for a panoramic vista of the gardens and a beautiful chain of central Florida lakes.

Carousel Cove, with eight kiddie rides and arcade games, centers on an ornate turn-of-the-century-style carousel. It adjoins another kid pleaser, **Cypress Junction,** an elaborately landscaped model railroad (scenery includes everything from a burning house to Mount Rushmore) that travels 1,100 feet of track with up to 20 trains moving at one time.

Cypress Roots, a museum of park memorabilia, displays photographs of famous visitors (Elvis on water skis, Tiny Tim tiptoeing through the roses) and airs ongoing showings of *Easy to Love* starring Esther Williams (it was filmed here). Another museum commemorates the **age of radio,** with a display of hundreds of vintage radios, radio memorabilia, and recordings of radio shows and music from the 1920s to the 1950s.

Wind up your visit with a relaxing 30-minute narrated **pontoon cruise** on scenic Lake Eloise, past virgin forest, bulrush, and beautiful shoreline homes. En route, you're likely to spot cormorants, osprey, ducks—maybe even an alligator or two. There's a $4-per-person charge.

Admission to Cypress Gardens is $27.95 for ages 10 and over, $17.45 for children 3 to 9, free for kids under 3. There are discounts for seniors. Cypress Gardens is open 365 days a year, from 9:30am to 5:30pm, with extended hours during peak seasons. Parking is free.

WHERE TO DINE

Your options range from a food court to the **Crossroads Restaurant,** a cheerful full-service facility serving American fare and offering alfresco seating at umbrella tables on a terrace. I also like the more casual **Lakeview Terrace,** with covered outdoor seating overlooking Lake Eloise; it offers great views of the ski show.

Fresh strawberries are sold throughout the park in season. And if you care to pack a basket, there are picnic tables. Over a dozen shops sell everything from quaint country-store merchandise to gardening books and paraphernalia.

2 Winter Park

20 miles N of Walt Disney World, 5 miles N of Orlando

The beautiful lakefront community of Winter Park was created in the early 1880s as "a first-class place" for "men and women of intelligence, culture, character, taste and means." Developers Loring A. Chase and Oliver E. Chapman priced their lots accordingly. The town was incorporated in 1887. To this day it remains an affluent haven—Florida's answer to Greenwich, Connecticut. You can visit on a day-trip, or you can spend a relaxing night or two here away from theme park hubbub.

Its attractions include a lovely Beverly Hills–like shopping strip (Park Avenue) lined with posh boutiques and art galleries; golf courses; fine old homes along winding, tree-shaded streets; shimmering lakes and canals (Winter Park has been called the "Venice of America"); Central Park, a large village green with lush lawns, stately moss-draped live oaks, and rose gardens; and a museum housing a treasure trove of Tiffany windows, lamps, and objets d'art. And though (actually, *because*) refined Winter Park takes no official notice of the fact, the town attracts numerous celebrities looking for a quaint and quiet retreat. Don't be surprised if you run into Gerald Ford or Paul Newman in a local shop.

ESSENTIALS

GETTING THERE   Take I-4 east to Fairbanks Avenue (Exit 45), exit right and proceed east for about a mile, turn left on Park Avenue, and follow signs to public parking.

Amtrak service (☎ **800/USA-RAIL**) is available from Orlando and Kissimmee (see chapter 2 for locations). The Winter Park station is located right in the center of town at 150 W. Morse Blvd. (☎ **407/645-5055**).

Take LYNX bus no. 4 from the Osceola Square Mall at Columbia Street and Hoagland Avenue in Kissimmee. It will take you to the Orlando downtown terminal where you can transfer to bus no. 1 or 9, either of which makes several stops along Park Avenue in Winter Park. Call **407/841-8240** for schedule.

VISITOR INFORMATION   For further information about Winter Park, contact the **Chamber of Commerce,** 150 N. New York Ave., just north of Morse Boulevard (P.O. Box 280), Winter Park, FL 32790 (☎ **407/644-8281**). Hours are 9am to 4pm Monday through Friday.

PARKING   Street parking is sometimes difficult. There are convenient and free municipal lots on South New York Avenue on either side of Morse Boulevard.

SEEING THE SIGHTS

Stroll Winter Park's main street, browse its boutiques, visit its museums, play a few rounds of golf, and take a leisurely lake cruise. Do note that most of the town's museums are closed on Monday.

✪ Charles Hosmer Morse Museum of American Art

445 Park Ave. (between Canton and Cole avenues). ☎ **407/645-5311**. Admission $3 adults, $1 students of any age. Tues–Sat 9:30am–4pm, Sun 1–4pm. Closed Mon, Memorial Day, July 4, Labor Day, Thanksgiving, Christmas, and New Year's Day.

Anyone who loves the sinuous, nature-inspired art nouveau genre (and who doesn't?) will be amazed and thrilled by this gem of a gallery. It alone justifies a trip to Winter Park.

It was founded by Hugh and Jeannette McKean in 1942 to display their peerless collection (more than 4,000 pieces), including 40 magnificent windows and 21 paintings created by Louis Comfort Tiffany! In addition, there are non-Tiffany windows by William Morris, Frank Lloyd Wright, Frederick Stymetz Lamb, and 15th- and 16th-century German masters; leaded lamps by Tiffany and Emile Gallé; paintings by John Singer Sargent, Samuel F. B. Morse, Maxfield Parrish, Thomas Hart Benton, and Arthur B. Davies; jewelry designed by Tiffany, Lalique, and Fabergé; sculptures by Hiram Powers and Daniel Chester French (of Lincoln Memorial fame); prints by

Cézanne, Childe Hassam, Rembrandt, Whistler, Winslow Homer, Mary Cassatt, and Grant Wood; photographic works by Tiffany and other 19th-century artists; and art nouveau furnishings by Tiffany, Gallé, and others. The collection, which is shown on a rotating basis, also includes Tiffany memorabilia—letters, furnishings, personal effects, and photographs used by his studio as source materials.

And furniture and accessories by Gustav Stickley and his contemporaries—plus a major collection of American art pottery—make the Morse's arts and crafts collection one of the most important in the Southeast.

Be sure to peek into the gift shop, where unique items include art nouveau gift wraps, Maxfield Parrish stationery, and much more.

Cornell Fine Arts Museum

At the eastern end of Holt Avenue, on the campus of Rollins College at Lake Virginia. ☎ **407/646-2526.** Free admission. Tues–Fri 10am–5pm, Sat–Sun 1–5pm. Free parking in adjacent lot "H." Closed Mon, July 4, Thanksgiving, Christmas Eve, Christmas Day, New Year's Eve, and New Year's Day.

Rollins College was the first home of Hugh and Jeannette McKean's (see listing above) Tiffany glass. Today, with close to 4,000 square feet of exhibition space, it houses an impressive century-spanning collection that includes works by Hiram Powers, Childe Hassam, Tiffany, Thomas Sully, William Glackens, Reginald Marsh, Leonard Baskin, and the studio of Peter Paul Rubens. Also displayed here: 19th-century silver, 17th-century Dutch Delftware, French rococo decorative panels, and Chippendale furniture. Traveling exhibits supplement the collection.

A SCENIC BOAT TOUR

Since 1938, tourists have been boarding pontoons at the eastern end of Morse Boulevard for leisurely hour-long cruises on Winter Park's beautiful chain of natural lakes. The ride traverses Lake Osceola (which flows north into the St. John's River), Lake Virginia, and Lake Maitland, winding through canals built by loggers at the turn of the century and tree-shaded fern gullies lined with bamboo and lush tropical foliage.

You'll view magnificent lakeside mansions and villas (Margaret Mitchell used to winter on Lake Maitland), pristine beaches, cypress swamps, ancient trees draped with Spanish moss, and dozens of marsh birds—white herons, grackle, cormorants, osprey, and gallinule, possibly even an American bald eagle. The captain regales passengers with local lore. It's a delightful trip. You can also rent canoes and small fishing boats here.

For information, call **407/644-4056.** The price is $6 for adults, $3 for children ages 2–11 (children under 2 ride free). Weather permitting, tours depart daily between 10am and 4pm, every hour on the hour, except on Christmas.

WHERE TO STAY

Though you could visit Winter Park on a day excursion from Orlando, do consider an overnight stay at one of the following properties.

Langford Resort Hotel

300 E. New England Ave. (at Interlachen Avenue), Winter Park, FL 32789. ☎ **407/644-3400.** Fax 407/628-1952. 209 rms, 9 suites. A/C TV TEL. $75–$95 double; $100–$200 suite. Extra person $10. Children 17 and under stay free. Rooms with kitchenettes $10 extra. AE, DC, MC, V. Free self-parking.

In pre-Disney days, Winter Park was one of central Florida's most-visited resorts, and the Langford was the place to stay. Vaughn Monroe entertained in the lounge, and the guest roster listed people like Eleanor Roosevelt, Mamie Eisenhower, Lillian Gish, Vincent Price, and Dina Merrill. Ronald and Nancy Reagan celebrated their 25th wedding anniversary here.

Today, though it's no longer glamorous, this friendly, family-run resort does offer extensive resort facilities at very reasonable rates. Most notably, its on-premises spa offers sauna, steam, massage (shiatsu, Swedish, and deep athletic), body wraps, seaweed wraps, salt glows, facials, manicures, pedicures, and day-of-beauty packages. And its central location, on a lovely street shaded by tall oaks draped with Spanish moss, is another plus. Room decor varies. Many rooms have balconies and/or fully equipped kitchenettes with two-burner stoves and small refrigerators.

Dining/Entertainment: The nautical/tropical Bamboo Room serves reasonably priced American fare; steak and seafood are featured at dinner. The adjoining Del Prado bar/lounge provides piano bar entertainment and complimentary hors d'oeuvres from 5 to 8pm nightly and dancing to live band music Tuesday through Saturday from 8pm to midnight. The elegant Empire Room offers a lavish buffet champagne Sunday brunch and Saturday-night mystery dinner theater.

Services: Concierge (sells tickets, many of them discounted, to Walt Disney World and other Orlando attractions), room service, *Orlando Sentinel* delivered to your room daily, babysitters.

Facilities: Olympic-size swimming pool, kiddie pool, car-rental desk, small video-game arcade, unisex hair salon. Golf and tennis are close by.

Park Plaza Hotel

S. 307 Park Ave. (at New England Avenue), Winter Park, FL 32789. ☎ **407/647-1072** or 800/228-7220. Fax 407/647-4081. 16 rms, 11 suites. A/C TV TEL. $90–$135 double; $150–$185 suite. During special events, rates may be higher. Rates include continental breakfast. AE, DC, MC, V. Free self- and valet parking.

Centrally located in the heart of the Park Avenue shopping and restaurant district, this small, elegant hotel dates to 1921. Owners John and Sandra Spang bought the property in 1975 and did an exquisite renovation, fitting out rooms bed-and-breakfast style with antique furnishings, Persian rugs, patchwork quilts, and beautiful floral-print bedspreads. Wide wooden Bermuda shutters on the windows and wood-bladed ceiling fans add tropical ambience and homey touches include live plants in white wicker baskets and magazines in the rooms.

Most rooms open onto a wicker-furnished, plant-filled balcony, and many have cozy parlor areas. Especially lovely is the Balcony Suite, which has Victorian-reproduction wallpaper and a brass bed made up with a Ralph Lauren spread, throw pillows, and white dust ruffle. There are also four luxurious honeymoon suites with oversized oak beds and private balconies. In-room amenities include complimentary fruit baskets at check-in.

The hotel's Park Plaza Gardens restaurant (see "Where to Dine," below) adjoins. The front desk offers concierge-like service. Other amenities here include room service, complimentary daily newspaper, and nightly bed turndown; transport to/from Disney parks and Orlando airport can be arranged. A beauty shop is just behind the property, and, for a fee, guests can use the nearby Winter Park Wellness Center, an extensively equipped health club. A complimentary continental breakfast with fresh-squeezed orange juice and fresh-baked muffins is served daily in the European-style lobby (or in your room). Golf and tennis are close by.

WHERE TO DINE

There are so many fine restaurants in Winter Park that Orlandoans often drive over just to dine and stroll the tree-lined streets. My first listing is in Altamonte Springs, a few minutes' drive from Winter Park.

VERY EXPENSIVE

Maison & Jardin

430 S. Wymore Rd. (off I-4 Exit 48 between FL 436 and Maitland Boulevard), in nearby Altamonte Springs. ☎ **407/862-4410.** Reservations recommended. Brunch $19.50 prix fixe; main courses $17.95–$28.50. AE, CB, DC, DISC, MC, V. Mon–Sat 6–10pm; Sun (Oct to mid-June only) 11am–2pm and 6–9pm. Free self-parking. CONTINENTAL.

One of Florida's most highly acclaimed restaurants, Maison & Jardin was architecturally inspired by a mansion in southern France that dates to Roman times—hence the pedimented neoclassic exterior, manicured formal gardens, and imposing doors with brass-lion knockers. The exquisite interior is furnished with museum-quality pieces and objets d'art—Austrian crystal chandeliers, Venetian and French chinoiserie cabinets, and mirrors in gilt frames from a 17th-century Venetian palazzo. I especially like the Gazebo Room, which evokes the ambience of a 17th-century Mediterranean château. Elegantly appointed tables are candlelit throughout.

A featured appetizer is blinis à la Russe with your choice of caviars; it's flamed tableside in brandy and served with frosted vodka. Also very recommendable: baked escargots en croûte topped with spinach, Boursin cheese, and garlic cream sauce. The chef does a beautiful job with frequent game specials, such as elk sautéed with morel mushrooms in a brandy cream sauce and served over pasta. I also recommend seafood entrées here—perhaps poached Norwegian salmon in a basil beurre blanc sauce. The menu changes seasonally, so your options may vary from the above.

The extensive, award-winning wine list is international in scope, with many selections available by the glass or half bottle. Desserts range from fresh raspberries with whipped cream to elaborate flaming finales such as bananas Foster and crêpes Suzette; there are also more than 40 postprandial cognacs and brandies.

Sunday brunch, including free-flowing complimentary champagne, is composed of an appetizer (perhaps chilled smoked Norwegian salmon) and a choice of entrées ranging from eggs Benedict to New Zealand rack of lamb, salad, and dessert; a Dixieland band entertains the first Sunday of every month.

Park Plaza Gardens

319 S. Park Ave. (between Lyman and New England Avenues). ☎ **407/645-2475.** Reservations recommended. Main courses $7.95–$12.95 at lunch (sandwiches and salads $5.95–$8.95), $19.95–$26.95 at dinner. AE, CB, DC, DISC, MC, Optima, V. Mon–Sat 11:30am–3pm; Mon–Thurs 6–10pm, Fri–Sat 6–11pm; Sun 11am–3pm and 6–9pm. Free parking at city lot at New England and South New York Avenues. CONTEMPORARY AMERICAN/FLORIDA SEAFOOD.

This charming patio garden restaurant—with tables shaded by a striped canvas awning and seating amid a small forest of ficus trees—offers the feeling of outdoor dining in air-conditioned comfort. During the day, sunlight streams in through a skylit ceiling; at night, tables are romantically candlelit. Exposed-brick walls hung with changing exhibits serve as gallery space for local artists. There are also cafe tables on Park Avenue.

Chef Luis Colon's culinary creations—served on large white platters—are as exquisitely presented as they are delicious. Good beginnings here include smoked duck pâté drizzled with goat cheese cream and velvety lobster bisque beautifully marbleized with crème fraîche. Entrées include broiled sea bass wrapped in banana leaves, served with bulgur wheat pilaf and wild berry preserves. Also excellent are the rack of lamb dijonnaise with rosemary-thyme sauce and crisp, cherrywood-smoked Muscovy duck served with sweet-potato haystack. For dessert, ebony and ivory is a sweet dream—espresso chocolate mousse and thin, semisweet chocolate leaves on a mirror of marbleized white chocolate sauce with blackberry garnish. The well-chosen wine list offers many by-the-glass selections, and there's page after page of after-dinner cordials, cognacs, ports, sherries, and brandies.

The lunch menu adds pasta, sandwich, and salad options. Brunch—including complimentary champagne, mimosa, or Kir royale—includes an appetizer, soup or salad, and entrées ranging from a seafood frittata topped with creamy velouté and caviar to sesame-seared Maui snapper glazed with Hawaiian fruit chutney and served on a bed of rice.

MODERATE

✪ La Venezia Cafe

142 Park Ave. S. (between Morse Boulevard and Welbourne Avenue). ☎ **407/647-7557.** Reservations not accepted. Breakfast pastries $1.75; main courses $5.95–$9 lunch/brunch, $5.95–$18.50 at dinner; prix-fixe afternoon teas $7, $10, and $15. AE, DISC, MC, V. Mon–Thurs 7am–11pm, Fri–Sat 7:30am–midnight, Sun 8am–11pm. Parking on street only. ITALIAN/ COSMOPOLITAN COFFEE HOUSE.

La Venezia Cafe is a highlight of a Winter Park visit, for continental breakfast, British-style afternoon tea, or a full meal. It's a charming place, with flower-bedecked tables (white-linen-cloth and candlelit at night) and cream stucco walls hung with photographs of Italy. There's an open-air patio overlooking Central Park here, but the pièce de résistance is inside: a collection of six authentic Tiffany windows.

La Venezia fresh-brews 52 different kinds of coffee and offers an extensive choice of gourmet teas. Come by in the morning for a steaming pot of fragrant Ethiopian Yrgacheffe with a fresh-baked croissant, jalapeño corn bread, or brown-sugar-topped streusel coffee cake. At lunch and dinner, menu options include delicious salads (I love the chicken curry tossed with greens, mango chutney, raisins, coconut, and peanuts), sandwiches, pizzas, pastas, quesadillas, and quiches. The evening meal also features more serious entrées, such as pistachio-crusted baked salmon served with wild mushrooms in pink champagne butter sauce.

Other enticements here are flavored coffees, coffee/ice-cream drinks and frappes, and a wide selection of liqueurs, aperitifs, and international beers. And save some room for oven-fresh desserts like buttered rum apple pie and amaretto-praline buttercream torte. A $15 afternoon tea includes finger sandwiches, freshly baked scones and pastries, berries, tea, and champagne.

INEXPENSIVE

The Briarpatch

252 Park Ave. N. (at Garfield Avenue). ☎ **407/628-8651.** Reservations not accepted. Breakfast $2.95–$6.95, lunch and dinner main courses and sandwiches $4.95–$8.95. AE, MC, V. Mon–Thurs 7am–9pm, Fri–Sat 7am–10pm, Sun 8am–5pm. Street parking only. AMERICAN.

A delightful way to start your day in Winter Park is with breakfast on the Briarpatch's open-air patio overlooking Central Park. If it's raining or chilly, the rustic gardenlike interior is also alluring. Breakfast fare includes great coffee and fresh-baked biscuits, muffins, and cinnamon buns. Other options are buttermilk pancakes, a Brie and parsley omelet, a bagel with Nova and cream cheese, or hot oatmeal with berries and bananas.

Later in the day, come by for sandwiches, salads, stuffed baked potatoes, burgers, or pasta dishes—or for cappuccino with fresh-baked desserts such as Kahlua praline cream squares and mile-high chocolate layer or carrot cake.

11

Beach Vacations Near Walt Disney World

1 Daytona Beach: The Birthplace of Speed

50 miles NE of Orlando

The self-proclaimed "World's Most Famous Beach" is even more celebrated as "The Birthplace of Speed" and "World Center of Racing." It has been a mecca for car-racing enthusiasts since the days when automobiles were called horseless carriages. Early automobile magnates Ransom E. Olds, Henry Ford, the Stanley brothers (of steamer fame), and Louis Chevrolet—along with motor-mad millionaires like the Vanderbilts, Astors, and Rockefellers—wintered in Florida and raced their vehicles on the hard-packed sand beach.

The era of stock-car racing began in 1936 with a new beach race course, a host of daredevil drivers, and thousands of cheering fans. In 1947, driver and race promoter Bill France founded the National Association for Stock Car Auto Racing (NASCAR), headquartered at Daytona Beach. Today it is the world's largest motorsports authority, sanctioning the Daytona 500 and other major races at tracks throughout the United States. The final stock-car race on the beach took place in 1958.

A year later, France's dream of a multimotorsports facility, the Daytona International Speedway, was realized. At press time, the Speedway is completing an $18-million expansion to include **Daytona USA**—a state-of-the-art motorsports entertainment attraction.

Of course you don't have to be a racing aficionado to enjoy Daytona. It has 23 miles of sandy beach 500 feet wide at low tide (you can still drive and park—but not race—on the sand; maximum speed allowed is 10 mph).

The town is mobbed with college students during spring break—the annual beach blanket Babylon—and during Bike Week in February, thousands of leather-clad motorcycle buffs make the scene.

But barring spring break and major Speedway events, Daytona is a laid-back beach resort, offering boating, tennis, golf, water sports, and the opportunity to stroll the sands, swim, and soak up some sunshine.

ESSENTIALS

GETTING THERE If you're coming from north or south, take I-95 and head east on International Speedway Boulevard (U.S. Hwy.

92). From Tampa or Orlando, take I-4 east and follow Daytona Beach signs to I-95 north to U.S. Hwy. 92. From northwest Florida, take I-10 east to I-95 south to U.S. Hwy. 92.

From Orlando, **Daytona–Orlando Transit Service (DOTS)** (☎ 904/257-5411 or 800/231-1965) provides van transport between the two cities. They offer 12 round-trips daily. One-way fare is $26 for adults, round-trip $46; children under 12 pay half price. The service brings passengers to the company's terminal at 1598 N. Nova Rd., or, for an additional fee, to beach hotels. In Orlando, the vans depart from the airport.

American, Continental, Delta, and USAir fly into **Daytona Beach International Airport** (☎ 904/248-8030). A taxi from the airport to most beach hotels runs between $8 and $12.

The closest **Amtrak** station (☎ 800/USA-RAIL) is in De Land, 23 miles southwest of Daytona.

Greyhound buses connect Daytona with most of the United States. They pull into a very centrally located terminal at 138 S. Ridgewood Ave. (U.S. 1) (☎ 904/255-7076 or 800/231-2222).

VISITOR INFORMATION   The **Daytona Beach Area Convention & Visitors Bureau,** 126 E. Orange Ave., just west of the Silver Beach Bridge (P.O. Box 910), Daytona Beach, FL 32115 (☎ 904/255-0415 or 800/854-1234), can help you with information on attractions, accommodations, dining, and events. They also maintain a branch at the Speedway.

GETTING AROUND   You can drive and park directly on the beach here. There is a $5 access fee between February 1 and November 30; the rest of the year it's free.

Votran, Volusia County's public transit system, runs buses throughout major areas of town between 6am and 7pm, Monday through Saturday; Sunday 6:30am to 7pm. Adults pay 75¢, children under 17 and seniors pay 35¢, and children under 6 accompanied by an adult ride free.

SPECIAL EVENTS

Also check with the Daytona Beach Area Convention & Visitors Bureau (see above) to find out what else is happening in town during your stay.

FEBRUARY

Nineteen days of **Speedweeks** events (taking place the first 3 weeks of February) get underway with the **Rolex 24** (a 24-hour endurance road race for sports cars), which draws international entries. Following that, top names in NASCAR stock-car racing compete in the **Busch Clash, Arca 200, Gatorade Twin 125-mile Qualifying Races, International Race of Champions (IROC), Florida 200,** and **Goody's 300,** culminating in the **Daytona 500,** which is always held on the Sunday prior to the third Monday in February. All events take place at the Daytona International Speedway. Call **904/253-7223** for ticket information. For the Daytona 500, especially, tickets must be purchased far—even as much as a year—in advance. They go on sale January 1 of the prior year.

MARCH

Bike Week/Camel Motorcycle Week is the rallying point for an international gathering of motorcycle enthusiasts for 11 days early in the month. Major races at the Speedway (featuring the world's best road racers, motocrossers, and dirt trackers) include the **Daytona 200 by Arai Motorcycle Classic,** the **Daytona Supercross by Honda,** and the **AMA Grand National Kickoff.** The last day of Bike Week, the

Annual Motorcycle Parade with thousands of riders leaves Bellair Plaza on A1A and continues to the Speedway. Call **904/255-0145** for details.

For 3 weeks in March, college students from all over the United States and Canada flock to Daytona Beach for **Spring Break**—endless partying, wet T-shirt and bikini contests, free concerts, volleyball tournaments and other games on the beach, hotel pool deck parties, etc. A career fair adds a more serious note. Call **904/255-0981** for details.

Late in the month (sometimes early April), the **Spring Speedway Spectacular,** a car show and swap meet at the Daytona International Speedway, features a wide variety of collector vehicles. In addition, displays include automotive toys and memorabilia, auto-theme art, and a crafts sale. Admission is charged. Call **904/255-7355** for details.

MAY

During the **Greater Daytona Beach Striking Fish Tournament** on Memorial Day weekend, some 250 boats from all over the Southeast compete for more than $75,000 in cash and prizes in seven fishing categories. Call **904/255-0415** for details.

JULY

The **Pepsi 400** race, marking the halfway point in the NASCAR Winston Cup Series for stock cars, is held the first Saturday in July at 11am at the Daytona International Speedway. Call **904/253-7223** for details.

The **Florida International Festival,** a 17-day musical event taking place every other year (in odd-numbered years), features concerts by major classical and pop musicians from all over the world—everything from the London Symphony Orchestra to Trisha Yearwood, as well as preconcert lectures, jazz bands, ballet, and special concerts for children. Events are scheduled at the Peabody Auditorium, Ocean Center, and other local performance places in late July, possibly early August. Call **904/257-7790** for details and ticket information.

OCTOBER

During 4 days in mid-October, road-racing stars compete at the Daytona International Speedway in the **CCS Motorcycle Championship Biketoberfest.** Events include a program of CCS "Races of Champions" National Championship Sprints for a variety of road-racing classes, as well as Formula USA and North American Sports Bike Series Finals and the Harley Davidson Twin Sports World Final. Call **904/253-7223** for ticket information. Call **800/854-1235** for additional Biketoberfest activities—parties, parades, concerts, and more.

NOVEMBER

The **Daytona Beach Fall Speedway Spectacular,** featuring the Annual Turkey Rod Run, is the Southeast's largest combined car show and swap meet, with thousands of street rods and classic vehicles on display and for sale. It takes place at the International Speedway on Thanksgiving weekend. Events include an auto-parts swap meet, a collector vehicle auction, and a nonautomotive crafts show. Admission is charged. Call **904/255-7355** for details.

DECEMBER

World Karting Association Enduro World Championships, the biggest karting event in the country, takes place between Christmas and New Year's at the Daytona International Speedway. Call **904/253-7223** for details.

ENJOYING THE BEACH & SEEING THE SIGHTS

The Speedway and the beach are, of course, Daytona's major attractions.

In addition, if you're interested in deep-sea fishing and/or whale watching, contact **Critter Fleet,** 4950 S. Peninsula Dr., Ponce Inlet (☎ **904/767-7676**). You can also fish from the **Main Street Pier,** near the Adam's Mark (☎ **904/253-1212**) or the **Sun Glow Fishing Pier,** 3701 S. Atlantic Ave. (☎ **904/756-4216**). Both offer bait and fishing gear, and no license is required.

The **Daytona Beach Golf Club,** 600 Wilder Blvd. (☎ **904/258-3119**), is the city's largest course, with 36 holes. **Shenandoah Stables,** 1759 Tomoka Farms Rd., off U.S. Hwy. 92 (☎ **904/257-1444**), offers daily trail rides and horseback-riding lessons between 10am and 5pm. For jet-ski rentals, contact **Daytona High Performance–MBI,** 925 Sickler Dr., at the Seabreeze Bridge (☎ **904/257-5276**). Additional water-sports equipment, as well as bicycles, beach buggies, and mopeds, can be rented along the beach in front of major hotels. A good place to look is in front of the Adam's Mark.

✪ Daytona International Speedway

1801 W. International Speedway Blvd. (U.S. 92, at Bill France Boulevard). ☎ **904/253-RACE** for tickets, 904/254-2700 for information. Auto events $30–$150; motorcycle events $6–$35; go-cart events under $10. Big events sell out months in advance (the Daytona 500 at least a year in advance), so plan far ahead and also reserve accommodations well before your trip. Parking is free for grandstand seating; infield parking charges vary with the event. Daily. Closed Thanksgiving and Christmas Day.

Opened in 1959 with the first Daytona 500, this 480-acre "World Center of Racing" is practically the raison d'être for Daytona Beach—certainly the keynote of the city's fame. It presents about eight weekends of major racing events annually, featuring stock cars, sports cars, motorcycles, and go-carts, and is also used for automobile testing. Its grandstand, a mile long, seats over 110,000.

Major annual races are described above in the "Special Events" calendar. For further information, write to Daytona International Speedway, P.O. Box 2801, Daytona Beach, FL 32120-2801.

To learn more about racing, head for the **World Center of Racing Visitors Center** at the east end of the Speedway and NASCAR office complex. Open daily from 9am to 5pm, the center is also the departure site for entertainingly narrated 25-minute guided tram tours of the facility. Admission is $5 for adults, free for children 6 and under. Tours depart daily every 30 minutes between 9:30am and 4pm, except during races and special events. Also at the center are a large gift shop; a snack bar; the Gallery of Legends, where the history of motorsports in the Daytona Beach area is documented through photographs and memorabilia; and the Budweiser Video Wall, tracing the history of racing in the Daytona Beach area. You can feel the thunder while listening to a 20-minute Surround-Sound audio presentation called *The Daytona 500: From Dawn to Determination.* The center also stocks information on area accommodations, restaurants, attractions, and nightlife.

Opening on Speedway grounds shortly after press time is the 50,000-square-foot **Daytona USA**—a state-of-the-art interactive motorsports entertainment attraction that will vividly present the history, color, and excitement of stock-car, go-cart, and motorcycle racing in Daytona. Visitors will be able to "participate" in a pit stop on a NASCAR Winston Cup stock car, design and test their own stock car using computer-aided technology, have video talks with favorite competitors, view an action-packed 70mm film, and play radio or television announcer by calling the finish of a race. Many racing artifacts will be on display. The facility will be open daily except Christmas from 9am to 6pm. Admission for adults will be about $10, with reductions for children and seniors.

Museum of Arts and Sciences

1040 Museum Blvd. (off Nova Road). ☎ **904/255-0285.** Admission $4 adults, $1 children and students with ID, free for kids under 6; planetarium shows, $1. Tues–Fri 9am–4pm, Sat–Sun noon–5pm. Closed New Year's Day, Thanksgiving, and Christmas Day. Take International Speedway Boulevard west, make a left on Nova Road, and look for a sign on your right.

Housing art, history, and natural-science exhibits, this eclectic museum dates to 1956, when Cuban dictator Fulgencio Batista donated his vacation home and art collection to the city. In 1971, the museum relocated to its present building. The Cuban collection—mostly paintings—spans two centuries from 1759 to 1959. "Masterworks of American Art" includes art and furnishings from the Pilgrim period, abolitionist paintings, works by Gilbert Stuart and Samuel Morse, Federalist furnishings, and Tiffany silver. In the Karshan Center of Graphic Arts, you'll view 18th- and 19th-century European prints, turn-of-the-century art nouveau posters, and lithographs by artists ranging from William Blake to Degas. There's a prehistory of Florida section. And "Africa: Life and Ritual" documents African peoples from over 30 cultures in 15 countries. A contemporary sculpture garden and a 1-mile nature trail are on the grounds. Planetarium shows take place at 1 and 3pm daily.

Ponce de León Inlet Lighthouse

4931 S. Peninsula Dr., Ponce Inlet. ☎ **904/761-1821.** Admission $4 adults, $1 children under 12. May–Aug, daily 10am–9pm; Sept–Apr, daily 10am–5pm (last admission an hour before closing). Closed Christmas. Follow Atlantic Avenue south, make a right on Beach Street, and follow the signs.

Built in the mid-1880s, this is, at 175 feet, the second-tallest lighthouse in the United States. The present beacon, visible for 16 nautical miles, flashes every 10 seconds. In the 1970s, this brick-and-granite coastal sentinel and its original outbuildings were restored and added to the National Register of Historic Places. The head lighthouse keeper's cottage—which was used as a barracks during World War II—today houses a museum of exhibits on navigational aids, marine biology, deep-sea fishing, and ocean exploration. The first-assistant keeper's house is furnished to reflect turn-of-the-century occupancy. Other buildings contain lighthouse-related displays and artifacts and a theater where a 12-minute video on the history of this particular lighthouse is shown (visit it first). In the boatyard, you can board the 46-foot oak-and-cypress *F. D. Russell* tugboat, built in 1938. There's an adjoining playground and picnic area with tables and barbecue grills.

A Tiny Cruise Line River Excursions

401S. Beach St., at Halifax Harbor. ☎ **904/226-2343.** Cruises $8.50–$13.50 adults, $6–$8 children 4–12, free for kids under 4. Weather permitting, cruises depart Mon–Sat Apr–Sept at 11:30am, 1-hour cruises at 2 and 3:30pm; closed Mon the rest of the year (call for reservations and also inquire about sunset cruises).

Take a leisurely cruise on the Halifax River aboard the 14-passenger, 25-foot *Fancy,* a replica of the old fantail launches used at the turn of the century. Captain Jim regales passengers with river lore and points out dolphins, manatees, herons, diving cormorants, pelicans, egrets, osprey, oyster beds, and other natural phenomena en route. Morning tours make a 20-minute stop at River Park, where there are picnic tables should you care to bring lunch.

I don't recommend bringing children under 8 on these tours; they get bored in a confined space and totally wreck the tranquil river cruise atmosphere for other passengers.

WHERE TO STAY

Daytona Beach hotels fill to the bursting point during major races at the speedway, whenever college students are on break, and during other special events. At these times room rates skyrocket, if you can find a room at all, and there's often a minimum-stay requirement. If you're planning to be in town at one of these busy times (see "Special Events," above in this section), reserve far in advance.

All of the accommodations listed below are on or near the beach and close to the Speedway.

BEACHFRONT HOTELS & MOTELS

Moderate

✪ Adam's Mark Daytona Beach Resort

100 N. Atlantic Ave. (between Earl Street and Auditorium Boulevard), Daytona Beach, FL 32118. ☎ **904/254-8200** or 800/872-9269. Fax 904/253-0275. 377 rms, 25 suites. A/C MINIBAR TV TEL. $99–$295 double, the high end reflecting special events; $250–$1,000 suite. Additional person $20 extra. Children under 18 stay free in parents' room. AE, CB, DC, DISC, MC, V. Free parking in lot across the street; valet parking $8 per night.

This is Daytona's most central beachfront hotel—and one of its most luxurious—designed so that every room proffers a gorgeous ocean view. In season, its beach and boardwalk are the site of concessions offering parasailing, bicycle rentals, motorized four-wheelers, surfboards, boogie boards, cabanas, and umbrellas. Accommodations are decorated in pleasing resort colors with bleached-oak furnishings. Rooms on the Executive Level (16th floor) feature VCRs, and, in the baths, black-and-white TVs, hair dryers, and extra phones.

Dining/Entertainment: Coquinas is the hotel's premier dining room, featuring steak and seafood dinners. The pretty Parkside Oceanfront Café, with picture windows overlooking the beach and umbrella tables outside, serves all meals. There's also a pool bar, a complex of small beachfront restaurants and bars with outdoor cafe seating, and the Clocktower Lounge for nightly entertainment.

Services: Concierge, room service, free newspapers at bell desk.

Facilities: Indoor/outdoor swimming pool, two whirlpools, steam and sauna, kiddie pool, sand volleyball court, playground, video-game arcade, coin-op washers/dryers, complete health club, gift shops.

✪ Daytona Beach Hilton Oceanfront Resort

2637 S. Atlantic Ave. (between Florida Shores Boulevard and Richard's Lane), Daytona Beach, FL 32118. ☎ **904/767-7350** or 800/525-7350. Fax 904/760-3651. 212 rms, 2 suites. A/C TV TEL. Per person $79–$139 standard, $89–$149 ocean view, $99–$164 oceanfront. Extra person $15. Children of any age stay free in parents' room. AE, CB, DC, DISC, JCB, MC, V. Free parking.

This property and the above-described Adam's Mark are Daytona's premier hotels. The Hilton welcomes guests in an elegant lobby with comfortable seating areas amid potted palms. Large balconied guest rooms are furnished in French provincial oak pieces, with pretty Matisse-like print fabrics and beach-theme art. All are equipped with safes, coffeemakers, irons and full-size ironing boards, hair dryers, small refrigerators, and satellite TVs with pay-movie options. All rooms provide ocean and/or river views.

Dining/Entertainment: The airy oceanfront Blue Water Grille—one of Daytona's most beautiful restaurants—serves all meals. Seafood, steaks, and pastas are featured, and patio dining is an option. A comfy bar/lounge with game tables adjoins; it's the setting for nightly entertainment—a pianist or jazz combo. In summer, reggae bands play poolside, and there's a pool bar.

Services: Room service, free daily newspaper.

Facilities: Large pool, kiddie pool, whirlpool, hair salon, gift shop, video-game room with pool table, coin-op washers/dryers, fitness room, walkway across A1A.

Inexpensive

Days Inn

1909 S. Atlantic Ave. (at Flamingo Avenue), Daytona Beach, FL 32118. ☎ **904/255-4492** or 800/224-5056. Fax 904/238-0632. 184 rms, 7 efficiencies. A/C TV TEL. $45–$65 double; $65–$85 efficiency for one or two. During special events, $100–$125 double; $135–$145 efficiency for one or two. Additional person $10 extra. Children under 12 stay free in parents' room. AE, CB, DC, DISC, MC, V. Free parking.

At this nine-story beachfront hotel, the pretty peach and teal rooms all offer ocean views. All have balconies, and some contain small refrigerators and microwave ovens. Large oceanfront efficiencies have fully equipped kitchens.

Facilities include a swimming pool/kiddie pool/sun deck overlooking the beach, an on-premises restaurant serving breakfast only, and a video-game room.

Days Inns nationwide offer a Super Saver rate of just $29 to $49 single or double if you reserve 30 days in advance via the toll-free phone number. This deal is, of course, subject to availability, but it's worth a try. If you can't get in here, there are five other Days Inns in town, all conveniently located beachfront properties. Call **800/329-7466** for details.

BED & BREAKFASTS

Captain's Quarters Inn

3711 S. Atlantic Ave. (about a quarter mile south of Dunlawton Avenue), Daytona Beach, FL 32127. ☎ **904/767-3119** or 800/332-3119. Fax 904/767-0883. 26 suites. A/C TV TEL. $80–$100 suite for one or two; $145–$185 oceanfront penthouse suite. During special events, $175 suite for one or two; $275 oceanfront penthouse suite. Additional person $5 extra. Children under 17 stay free in parents' suite. Lower rates available for weekly and monthly stays. AE, DISC, MC, V. Free parking.

This five-story beachfront inn has spacious suites, most with ocean or river views and all with living/dining room areas and fully equipped kitchens. Country-look bedrooms, furnished in oak antique reproductions, utilize charming floral-print wall coverings and fabrics. French doors open onto balconies or patios furnished with wooden rockers. Accommodations are equipped with remote-control cable TVs (two per unit) and VCRs (movies can be rented). The penthouse suite has a fireplace, a spa tub, and a big picture window overlooking the ocean.

On-premises facilities include a country crafts/gift shop, a heated swimming pool, a sundeck with loveseat swings and barbecue grills, and coin-op washers and dryers. The Galley Restaurant, which has an outdoor deck overlooking the ocean, is open for breakfast and lunch daily. Daily newspapers are complimentary.

❂ Coquina Inn

544 S. Palmetto Ave. (at Cedar Street), Daytona Beach, FL 32114. ☎ **904/254-4969** or 800/805-7533. Fax 904/254-4969. 7 rms. A/C TV. Fri–Sun $80–$110 double; Mon–Thurs $69–$89 double; $150–$175 during special events. Additional person $10 extra. No children under 12 accepted. Rates include full breakfast. AE, MC, V. Free parking.

This charming terra-cotta-roofed coquina and cream-stucco house sits on a tranquil, tree-shaded street half a block west of the Halifax River and Harbor Marina. Guests can relax before a working fireplace in a lovely parlor. The crystal-chandeliered dining room is the setting for breakfasts, served on fine china and including a choice of quiches, homemade muffins and scones, fresh fruit, juice, tea and coffee. Classical music is played in public areas.

Each room is exquisitely decorated, most with area rugs strewn on oak floors and ceiling fans overhead. For instance, the Jasmine Room features a working coquina fireplace and a canopied mahogany bed. And in the Hibiscus Room, a black iron bed embellished with gold leaf is made up with a pretty floral chintz spread, and French doors lead to a private plant-filled balcony overlooking an ancient live oak draped with Spanish moss. All rooms are provided with bubble bath and candles. Portable phones are available on request. Complimentary tea and sherry are served in the parlor throughout the day. Beach cruiser bikes are offered at no cost (the beach is just a mile away), and several restaurants are within easy walking distance.

✪ Live Oak Inn

444–448 S. Beach St. (at Loomis Avenue), Daytona Beach, FL 32114. ☎ **904/252-4667.** 12 rms. A/C TV TEL. $70–90 double. Additional person $10 extra. Rates may be higher during peak events. Rates include extended continental breakfast. AE, MC, V. Free parking. No children under 10.

Occupying two adjoining restored 19th-century houses with a front lawn enclosed by a white picket fence, this charming B&B hostelry is surrounded by centuries-old live oaks. An inviting front porch with white wicker rocking chairs faces the street. The guest rooms—seven with private sun porches or balconies—are delightfully decorated, with area rugs strewn on polished oak floors and wood-bladed fans whirring slowly overhead. Plants, old family photographs, and baskets of potpourri and dried flowers add to the ambience. Yours might be furnished with an Eastlake bed. Or perhaps you'll get a Victorian sleigh bed with a patchwork quilt and a private, plant-filled sun porch furnished with Adirondack chairs. Rooms look out on the Halifax Harbor Marina or a garden. All are stocked with books and magazines and equipped with VCRs; baths have Victorian soaking tubs or Jacuzzis.

Breakfast is served on an enclosed porch with lace-curtained windows overlooking a yacht basin (or a similar dining area in the other house). Public areas also include a fine steak/seafood/pasta restaurant with a warm, inn-like interior and outdoor seating on a wooden deck—worth visiting on its own. Other amenities here: fax and copy machines for guest use, complimentary drinks and flowers at check-in, and terry robes. Delmar and Jessie Glock are your personable owners/hosts. No smoking is permitted in the house.

WHERE TO DINE
EXPENSIVE

✪ Alexander's Blue Note Supper Club

123 W. Granada Blvd. (between North Ridgewood Avenue and U.S. 1). ☎ **904/673-5312.** Reservations recommended. Main courses $5.95–$8.95 at lunch, $17.95–$24.95 at dinner. AE, MC, V. Mon–Sat 11:30am–3pm and 6–10pm; bar open for lunch fare in the interim and late-night snacks. FRENCH/CONTINENTAL.

This charming, inn-like restaurant is Daytona's most sophisticated venue. Several small dining rooms sport floral wallpapers and lace- and balloon-curtained windows. In the central Bacchus Room, its walls hung with Louis Icart prints, you can view the wine cellar via a glass door. Wednesday through Saturday, a pianist plays standards (Cole Porter et al.) on a baby grand.

The menu changes frequently. If it's available, order the tangy cheddar soup spiked with sherry. Other appetizers here might include French pâtés or baked escargot in buttery-garlicky Pernod sauce. Classic haute-cuisine entrées range from steak au poivre flamed tableside in brandy cream sauce to grilled sea scallops in a beurre blanc citrus sauce. Sorbet is served between courses, and appropriate wines are recommended with each entrée. Dessert might be a very rich black velvet chocolate cake or cherries jubilee. The lunch menu lists sandwiches, salads, pastas, and a few entrées such as pan-blackened filet mignon.

Alexander's offers an extensive international wine list (with many by-the-glass selections) and a good choice of single-malt scotches and draft beers. The adjoining bar/lounge is deservedly popular (see "The Club & Bar Scene," below for details).

Chart House

1100 Marina Point Dr. (off Beach Street). ☎ **904/255-9022.** Reservations recommended. Main courses mostly $15.95–$24.95. AE, CB, DC, DISC, MC, V. Sun–Thurs 5–9:30pm, Fri–Sat 5–10:30pm. CONTINENTAL/STEAK/SEAFOOD.

The plant-filled Chart House is of octagonal design, with palm trees growing toward a lofty skylit bamboo ceiling. Ship models and a service staff in Hawaiian shirts enhance the restaurant's tropical/marine ambience. And windowed walls overlooking the Halifax River and a marina ensure every diner a water view. Consider having dessert or after-dinner drinks in the plush bar/lounge downstairs or on an open-air riverside deck with umbrella tables.

You might want to bypass appetizers here, since your main course includes a very extensive salad bar, a basket of hot sourdough and seven-grain squaw bread, and a baked potato or Chart House wild rice. For your entrée, select shrimp or chicken Santa Fe dusted with cumin, paprika, and cayenne, grilled in butter, and served with tangy bleu-cheese dip. Steak, prime rib au jus with creamed horseradish sauce, and surf-and-turf combinations are also options. Mud pie is the dessert of choice. The bar offers exotic tropical drinks, and an international wine list highlights American vineyards. Service is excellent.

MODERATE

○ Anna's Italian Trattoria

304 Seabreeze Blvd. (at Peninsula Drive). ☎ **904/239-9624.** Reservations recommended. Main courses mostly $8.50–$14; early-bird dinners (served 5–6:30pm) $5–$8. AE, DISC, MC, V. Daily 5–10pm. Closed Sun in winter. ITALIAN.

At this friendly little trattoria, the Triani family has created a warm atmosphere enhanced by cheerful Italian music. Everything is homemade—from the creamy Italian dressing on your house salad to the basket of hot crusty bread, the latter ideal for sopping up the tangy dressing of a scungilli salad appetizer. A scrumptious pasta dish is the fettuccine alla campagniola—pasta tossed with strips of sautéed eggplant and chunks of sausage in tomato-cream sauce. Nonpasta recommendables include salmon scampi and risotto alla Anna (the latter is similar to a Spanish paella). Portions are hearty, and there's a good selection of Italian wines to complement your meal. Both the tiramisù and the homemade ricotta cheesecake are excellent dessert choices.

You can park free in a lot on Seabreeze Boulevard, across Peninsula Drive.

○ Aunt Catfish's

4009 Halifax Dr. (at the west end of the Port Orange Bridge). ☎ **904/767-4768.** Reservations not accepted, but you can—and should—call ahead for priority seating. Main courses $4–$8 at lunch, mostly $8–$13.50 at dinner; early-bird dinners $7–$10.50. Reduced prices for children and seniors. Sun brunch $9 for adults, $5.50 for children 4–12, free for kids under 4. AE, DC, DISC, MC, V. Mon–Sat 11:30am–9:30pm, Sun 9am–9:30pm (brunch Sun 9am–2pm; early-bird dinners daily noon–6:30pm). Closed Christmas. SOUTHERN/SEAFOOD.

This country-cozy southern restaurant represents one of the best values I've ever encountered. The homey setting is appealing: Tables are topped with laminated horse-feed sacks, weathered-looking wood-paneled walls are hung with historic photographs of the Daytona Beach area, and decorative elements include antique clothes wringers and corn huskers. During the day, ask for a window seat overlooking the Halifax River.

The food is great, and there's plenty of it. For one thing, all main courses include hush puppies, a chunk of watermelon, unbelievable yummy hot cinnamon rolls, a side dish (perhaps baked Mexican potato skins), and unlimited helpings from an extensive salad bar, which in addition to salads is laden with such down-home fare as cheese grits, cinnamon apples, fresh-baked cornbread, and hominy. A great main-dish choice is the Florida cracker sampler platter—a spit-roasted quarter chicken with cranberry-orange relish, crab cakes served in hollandaise sauce, fried shrimp, and fried catfish fingerlings. Lightly breaded fried oysters here are also highly recommendable. There's a full bar, though you might prefer fresh-squeezed lemonade. For dessert, split a boatsinker fudge pie with Häagen-Dazs coffee ice cream dipped in a coat of hardened chocolate and topped with whipped cream.

The lavish Sunday brunch buffet provides temptation to overindulgence. Lunch choices include burgers, sandwiches, and a soup and salad buffet in addition to ribs, chicken, and seafood dishes.

✪ The Cellar

220 Magnolia Ave. (between Palmetto and Ridgewood Avenues). ☎ **904/258-0011.** Reservations for large lunch parties only. Main courses $5.50–$6.95 at lunch, $9.95–$15.95 at dinner. AE, CB, DC, DISC, MC, V. Lunch Mon–Fri 11am–3pm, dinner Thurs–Sat 6–10pm. AMERICAN.

Housed in a National Historic Register Victorian home built in 1907 for Warren G. Harding, The Cellar couldn't be more charming. It's low-ceilinged interior, with cabbage-rose carpeting, posies of fresh flowers on every table, and backlit stained-glass windows draws a genteel luncheon crowd plus a few businessmen willing to brave a tearoomy-feminine ambience in the pursuit of good food. Classical music enhances the setting. There's also outdoor seating at umbrella tables on a covered garden patio.

Everything here is homemade, including soups and fresh-baked breads and desserts. Cellar crab cakes—available at lunch and dinner—are fluffy and delicious, drizzled with remoulade sauce and served with seasoned rice and fresh vegetables. Other dinner options range from seafood fettuccine in cream sauce to tenderloin of pork roasted in rosemary and flamed tableside in applejack brandy. At lunch, a salad sampler—great chunky chicken salad, tabbouleh tuna salad, and herbed potato salad—is a good bet; order some banana bread on the side. Wine and beer are available. Flambéed desserts such as cherries jubilee and bananas foster are featured, though I prefer the luscious cappuccino cake.

INEXPENSIVE

✪ Down the Hatch

4894 Front St., Ponce Inlet. ☎ **904/761-4831.** Reservations not accepted; call ahead for priority seating. Main courses mostly $7.95–$12.95; sandwiches $3.25–$5.25; early-bird menu (served 11:30am–5pm) $4.95–$6.95. Reduced prices for children. AE, MC, V. Daily 7am–10pm. Closed Thanksgiving and Christmas. Take FL A1A south, make a right on Beach Street, and follow the signs. SEAFOOD.

Occupying a half-century-old fish camp on the Halifax River, Down the Hatch serves up fresh fish and seafood (note their shrimp boat docked outside). During the day, picture windows provide scenic views of a passing parade of boats and shorebirds, and you might even see dolphins frolicking. At night, arrive early to catch the sunset over the river and also to beat the crowd at this very popular place. In summer, light fare is served outside on an awninged wooden deck.

Start your meal with an order of piquant buffalo shrimp served with chunky home-made bleu-cheese dressing. Main dishes include fried or broiled fresh fish such as red snapper or grouper, and there's an excellent crab Imperial broiled in tarragon-mayonnaise sauce. If seafood isn't your thing, filet mignon and prime rib are aged on the premises. There's a full bar. Down the Hatch also offers a complete break-fast menu—everything from waffles to three scrambled eggs with fried fish, potatoes, and biscuits.

DAYTONA BEACH AFTER DARK
THE CLUB & BAR SCENE

Alexander's Blue Note Supper Club
123 N. Granada Blvd. (between North Ridgewood Avenue and U.S. 1), in Ormond Beach. ☎ 904/673-5312.

The cathedral-ceilinged art deco bar/lounge of this upscale restaurant is very popu-lar with local businesspeople and sophisticates. The white-linen-cloth tables are lit by brass oil lamps. A pianist entertains Wednesday through Saturday from 7pm on a white baby grand; other nights there's recorded music from the '30s and '40s—jazz, big band, and swing.

You can order from the extensive wine list, have an appetizer or dessert, try one of the cafe's many single-malt scotches (I recommend the smoky Lagvulin), cognacs, or draft beers . . . or order up a fine cigar. The bar is cigar-friendly, but open win-dows keep the smoke level down. Open Monday through Saturday until somewhere between midnight and 2am, depending on the crowd. At happy hour, weekdays 4–8pm, most drinks are half price.

Coliseum
176 N. Beach St. (at Bay Street). ☎ 904/257-9982. Cover $5–$8, which also entitles you to admission to The Spot (see below).

Heralded by a pedimented Doric colonnade, this upscale Roman-theme dance club occupies a converted movie theater. Inside, a raised dance floor is flanked by Ionic columns, and Roman-style bas-reliefs and sculpture adorn the walls. A deejay plays Top-40 tunes; 16 monitors project music and ambience videos; and nightly laser shows are high-tech, utilizing 3-D and sophisticated graphic-arts effects.

The crowd is mostly 20-something with occasional glitterati, rock musicians, and local athletes in attendance. Tom Cruise partied here during the filming of *Days of Thunder,* and *90210's* Ian Ziering was a recent visitor. During spring break there are special events.

The Coliseum is open nightly to 3am. Parking is free behind the club on Bay Street; usually there's ample street parking as well.

Razzles
611 Seabreeze Blvd. (between Grandview and South Atlantic Avenues). ☎ 904/257-6236. Cover before 10pm, $6–$8 with free drinks; after 10pm, $5 for 18- to 20-year-olds, $3 for those 21 and over.

At this large and popular dance club, a deejay plays Top-40 tunes and high-energy music until 3am nightly. The setting is archetypical, with lots of neon tubing, the requisite monitors flashing music videos, and sophisticated lighting effects over the dance floor. There's plenty to keep you occupied when you're not dancing here—10 pool tables, a blackjack table, air hockey, electronic darts, pinball, and video games.

The crowd is young—early 20s. There's free parking behind the club on Grandview between Seabreeze and Oakridge boulevards.

The Spot

176 N. Beach St. (at Bay Street). ☎ **904/257-9982.** Cover $5–$8, which also entitles you to admission to The Coliseum (see above).

Under the same ownership as the above-mentioned Coliseum, The Spot shares its address and phone as well. Billing itself as a premier sports bar, it has large-screen TVs in every corner, which, along with over 30 smaller monitors, air major worldwide sporting events via satellite. This cavernous club centers on a U-shaped bar trimmed in turquoise neon. The walls are decorated in a painted collage of baseball cards, car-racing photos, sports paraphernalia, and American flags. Amusements include football, air hockey, video games, pinball machines, a one-on-one basketball court, eight regulation pool tables, dartboards, and bar games. Light fare (hot wings, good pizza, salads) is available. Monday-night football parties include raffles for tickets to local sporting events. Open nightly until 3am. Parking is free behind the club on Bay Street; usually there's ample street parking as well.

THE PERFORMING ARTS

At the 2,552-seat **Peabody Auditorium,** 600 Auditorium Blvd., between Noble Street and Wild Olive Avenue (☎ **904/255-1314**), Daytona Beach's Civic Ballet performs *The Nutcracker* every Christmas and sponsors another ballet every spring. The Daytona Beach Symphony Society arranges a series of six classical concerts between December and April. During the same season, Concert Showcase features pop artists such as James Taylor, Henry Mancini, and Steve Lawrence and Eydie Gorme, as well as full Broadway-cast stage shows. The London Symphony Orchestra has been performing here for over 25 years during the semiannual Florida International Festival.

Under the same city auspices is the **Oceanfront Bandshell** (☎ **904/258-3169**), on the boardwalk next to the Adam's Mark Hotel. The city hosts a series of free big-band concerts at the bandshell every Sunday night from early June through Labor Day. It's also the scene of spring-break concerts.

Prices at the Peabody vary with the performances. Bandshell concerts are usually free. Parking is $3 in a lot adjacent to the Peabody.

2 Kennedy Space Center

60 miles E of Walt Disney World, 45 miles E of Orlando

Operated by NASA, the ✪ **John F. Kennedy Space Center** (☎ **407/452-2121**) has been the launch site for all U.S. manned space missions since 1968. Astronauts departed earth at this site en route to the most famous "small step" in history—man's first voyage to the moon. All space shuttle launches have also been staged from this site.

A nonoperational area of the Kennedy Space Center is the 140,000-acre **Merritt Island National Wildlife Refuge** (☎ **407/861-0667**). This pristine wilderness of dense woods, unspoiled beaches, fish-filled waterways, marshlands, and mud flats provides refuge for numerous bird species, deer, bobcats, otters, sea turtles, manatees, alligators, and other native Florida wildlife—more than 500 species in total. To find out about guided nature walks and interpretive programs (November through March only), sea turtle watches in June and July, and year-round wildlife drives and self-guided hikes (trails range from a quarter of a mile to 5 miles), call or visit the

Visitor Information Center, which is 4 miles east of Titusville on FL 402. It is open Monday through Friday from 8am to 4:30pm, Saturday from 9am to 5pm, and Sunday (November through March only) from 9am to 5pm; closed all federal holidays. (*Note:* You won't have time to tour nature trails and see the Space Center in the same day.)

GETTING THERE

Take the Beeline Expressway (Hwy. 528) east; where the road divides, go left on FL 407; make a right on FL 405; and follow signs. If you don't have a car, inquire about public transportation at your hotel.

LEARNING ABOUT AMERICA'S SPACE PROGRAM

At the **Visitor Center,** the past, present, and future of space exploration are explored on bus tours of the facility and in movie presentations and numerous exhibits. It takes at least a full day to see and do everything.

Arrive early and make your first stop at **Information Central** (it opens at 9am) to pick up a schedule of events/map and for help in planning your day. Nearby, space-related exhibits and interactive computers allow visitors to "meet the astronauts," access current mission information, and look into the history of spaceflight. *Note:* A massive renovation in visitor facilities—underway at this writing, and due for completion by the end of 1997—will dramatically alter the experience, making it more of an interactive adventure.

On the 2-hour **Red Tour,** you'll board a double-decker bus to explore the complex. En route, your driver will point out significant buildings such as the laboratories where instruments are calibrated and maintained; the headquarters building, administrative hub for all Space Center activities; astronauts' living quarters prior to a launch; and the building where hardware bound for the launchpad is inspected and tested prior to use. You'll view a film about the *Apollo 11* mission in a simulated launch control firing room. The countdown, launch, and planting of a flag on the moon are thrilling even at second hand. In an adjoining room, related exhibits include an *Apollo 11* command service module (home for the three crew members during their round-trip) and a lunar module (their home on the lunar surface). The tour continues to Complex 39 Space Shuttle launchpads (where a stop is made for exploration) and the massive Vehicle Assembly Building, where space shuttles are assembled. In volume, the VAB is the world's second-largest building, with doors 456 feet high. Visitors get a close-up look at an actual *Apollo/Saturn V* moon rocket—America's largest and most powerful launch vehicle. Also on view are massive, 6-million-pound Crawler Transporters that carry space shuttles to their launchpads.

Tours depart at regular intervals beginning at 9:45am, with the last tour leaving in the late afternoon (call for details). Purchase tickets at the Ticket Pavilion as soon as you arrive. *Note:* Itinerary variations may occur subject to launch schedules.

Though most visitors are sated by the Red Tour, a second 2-hour **Blue Bus Tour** (call for departure schedule) visits the Cape Canaveral Air Station. On this tour, you'll see where America's first satellites and astronauts were launched in the Mercury and Gemini programs, view launchpads currently being used for unmanned launches, visit the original site of Mission Control, and stop at the Air Force Space Museum, which houses a unique collection of missiles and space memorabilia.

Satellites and You is a 45-minute voyage through a simulated future space station. In Disneyesque fashion, the attraction combines AudioAnimatronic characters with innovative audiovisual techniques to explain satellites and their uses. Passing through futuristic airlock spacecraft doors à la *Star Trek,* visitors enter work chambers with names like Central Module Alpha 1 and 2. In each chamber, you'll learn something new about today's satellite technology and its uses in diverse areas. Farther along, the role of satellites in creating a global village focuses on the rapid dissemination of information worldwide. The final program explains how the space program is involved in improving the quality of life on earth.

In the **Galaxy Center building,** three spectacular IMAX films projected on 5 1/2-story screens are shown continually throughout the day in twin theaters. *Destiny in Space,* narrated by Leonard Nimoy, features unique exterior views of the space shuttle in flight around Earth, footage from the Hubble space telescope servicing mission, and thrilling flyovers of Mars and Venus. In *The Dream Is Alive*—featuring in-flight footage from three space shuttle missions—viewers join astronauts in preflight training, aboard the space shuttle in orbit, and on a breathtaking launch and landing. And *Blue Planet* is an environmentally themed look at Spaceship Earth from the vantage point of outer space.

The Galaxy Center also houses a NASA art exhibit; a walk-through replica of a future space station, a manned research laboratory that will be orbiting the earth by 1999; and an exhibit called "Spinoffs from Space." The latter—which is hosted by hologram characters—displays some of the 30,000 spinoffs that have resulted from space-program research, including improved consumer products ranging from football helmets to cordless tools, and advances in medicine, computer sciences, energy, public safety, transportation, agriculture, and the environment.

The **Gallery of Manned Spaceflight,** a large museum, houses hardware and models relating to significant space projects such as the Mercury missions (1958–63), Gemini 9 (a two-man mission in 1966), the Apollo–Soyuz Test Project (the world's first international space venture), and Skylab. It also contains interesting exhibits on lunar exploration and geology. You can view a moon rock and have a photograph taken of yourself in a lunar rover.

Spaceport Theater presents films and live demonstrations on topics ranging from how space shuttles are prepared for launch to activities of astronauts in space.

The **Astronauts Memorial**—a 42.5-by-50-foot black granite "Space Mirror" dedicated May 9, 1991—honors the 16 American astronauts who have lost their lives in the line of duty.

Aboard **Explorer,** a full-size replica of a space shuttle orbiter, visitors can experience the working environment of NASA astronauts. Adjoining it are two refurbished solid rocket boosters.

A **playground** housed in a large geodesic dome features educational astronaut/ space-related play equipment, along with a ball crawl, a maze, and a super slide.

And the **Rocket Garden** displays eight actual U.S. rockets.

There are two **cafeterias**—the Orbit and the Lunch Pad—on the premises. The gift shop carries a wide array of innovative space-related books, toys, games, videotapes, astronaut flight suits, NASA and space logo clothing, and more.

Admission to the Kennedy Space Center is free. Tickets for either bus tour cost $7 for adults, $4 for children ages 3 to 11, and free to children under 3. IMAX film tickets are $4 for adults, $2 for children ages 3 to 11, and free to children under 3. The Kennedy Space Center is open daily from 9am to dusk; it's closed on Christmas. Parking is free.

SEEING A LAUNCH

Today a rocket soaring skyward is not an uncommon sight, but it's still one that fills most observers with awe. If you'd like to see a launch, call **407/452-2121** for current launch information, ext. 260 to make reservations. Tickets for viewing cost

$7 for adults, $4 for children ages 3 to 11, under 3 free. You can reserve tickets up to 7 days before a launch, but they must be picked up at least 2 days before the launch. A special bus takes observers to a site just 6 miles from the launchpad.

3 Canaveral National Seashore & Cocoa Beach

Adjoining the grounds of the Kennedy Space Center, **Canaveral National Seashore** (☎ **904/428-3384** for information), is a protected stretch of coastline that's a magnet for birdwatchers, who have spotted hundreds of species of shore birds and waterfowl here. There's a visitor's center on A1A, and wooden boardwalks lead from each of the parking areas to the pristine beaches, perfect for swimming and sunbathing. A marked hiking trail leads to an ancient Native American mound, where there are picnic tables. Note that it's forbidden to walk on the dunes or pick the sea grass. The preserve also contains Mosquito Lagoon, where you might spot alligators and sea turtles.

As you drive through **Cocoa Beach,** there's no way you'll miss the glaringly original building housing the **Ron Jon Surf Shop,** at 4151 North Atlantic Ave. (☎ **407/ 799-8888**), set beside the A1A highway, a block from the beach. It's a Hollywood version of Art Deco gone wild, with tropical colors and lights. Inside, you'll find everything you need to make you look like a surfer. The shop also rents beach bikes, boogey boards, surfboards, and in-line skates by the hour, day, or week.

If you want to stay in Cocoa Beach, your options include the **Cocoa Beach Hilton,** 1550 North Atlantic Ave. (☎ **407/799-0003**); the **Holiday Inn Cocoa Beach Resort,** 1300 North Atlantic Ave. (☎ 407/783-2271 or 800/2-BOOK US), which lies on 30 oceanfront acres; and **The Inn at Cocoa Beach,** 4300 Ocean Beach Blvd. (☎ **407/799-3460** or 800/343-5307), offering large rooms with ocean views. Nearby, the **Radisson Resort at the Port,** 8701 Astronaut Blvd., Cape Canaveral (☎ 407/784-0000 or 800/333-3333), is the closest major hotel to Port Canaveral (where a few major cruise-ship companies are based) and the Space Station, though it's not on the beach.

Contact the **Cocoa Beach Chamber of Commerce**, 400 Fortenberry Rd., Merritt Island, FL 32952 (☎ **407/459-2200**), for information about Cocoa Beach, Cape Canaveral, Merritt Island, and a half-dozen other communities nearby.

4 Tampa

200 miles SW of Jacksonville, 254 miles NW of Miami,   *by Cindy Dupre*
63 miles N of Sarasota

The miles of wide, sandy beaches extending throughout Pinellas, Manatee, and Sarasota counties put the Tampa Bay area on the tourist map. They extend the length of the Gulf of Mexico shoreline and include offshore barrier islands, some of which remain pristine and untouched by development. Today the revival of the European travel market and increased air service to the newly renovated Tampa and St. Petersburg–Clearwater international airports have brought new energy to the area.

Tampa is the business hub of the Bay Area, and is the home of the region's top attractions—Busch Gardens, the Florida Aquarium, and the Museum of Science and Industry. Until recently there was never much going on in Tampa after hours, but the rebirth of Ybor City, an ethnic enclave rich in Spanish and Cuban architecture and tradition, has changed all that. This new hot spot doesn't even get started until after midnight and then keeps jumping into the wee hours.

Yes, millions of visitors do invade the Tampa Bay area each winter. The roads become clogged, the restaurants jammed. But it's a manageable frenzy, not half as crazy as Miami at the height of the tourist season.

And yes, summers can be hot and rainy, and occasional outbreaks of Red Tide can plague the coastline. In the winter, unpredictable cold snaps may ruin your quest for the perfect tan. But it's not just hype to say that the climate here is picture-perfect most of the time, providing year-round opportunities for golf, tennis, swimming, sailing, waterskiing, jet skiing, canoeing, fishing, and camping. And don't forget those magnificent beaches!

Tampa is a great place to use as a home base on Florida's west coast. Travel 20 miles west toward the Gulf of Mexico and you're exploring the wide sandy beaches of Pinellas County. Head 12 miles north and you can play golf or tennis where the top pros train. Travel 80 miles east and you're in the heart of Orlando's theme parks. Or stay in Tampa itself and sail, windsurf, and waterski on the local rivers, lakes, and bay.

Though the recent closing of the local Anheuser-Busch brewery caused quite a commotion, Busch Gardens continues to be Tampa's no. 1 tourist attraction, hands down. Slated to open in the summer of 1996, the new 7-acre area known as "Egypt" is the largest expansion in the history of Busch Gardens.

In the spring of 1996 the New York Yankees opened a $30-million, 31-acre spring-training complex across from Tampa Stadium. Legends Field was a smash success; many fans claim that there's not a bad seat in the house. And in October 1996 the Tampa Bay Lightning National Hockey League franchise is scheduled to unveil its new $153-million home in the previously dead Channel district of downtown: The Ice Palace Arena is a 660,000-square-foot palace of glass that will seat visitors for hockey, basketball, and center-stage events like the circus, ice shows, and major concerts.

At press time, football fans were still waiting to hear the fate of the Buccaneers. Businessman Malcolm Glazer bought the team for a record $192 million but was threatening to move the team if the city didn't build a new stadium. Locals claim that a new stadium is too expensive, yet losing the team could be equally costly.

The area's newest major attraction, the Florida Aquarium, opened in March 1995 at the Garrison Seaport Center. Visitors can view over 5,300 animals and plants representing 600 species native to Florida. Despite the universally positive reaction, attendance has not been as high as hoped. Aquarium officials blame the lack of other activities around the downtown waterfront location; as a result, they're encouraging development in hopes of creating an environment similar to that around Baltimore's Harborplace and National Aquarium.

At press time, future plans for restaurants, retail stores, and clubs were on the drawing board, all part of this attempt to breathe new life into Tampa's downtown. Tampa has one of the fastest-growing cruise ports in the country, with thousands of visitors arriving for before- and after-cruise visits to the area, and with this growth in mind, the Tampa Bay Port Authority is proceeding with plans for an entertainment complex. Already one of the state's major hubs for business and banking, Tampa is growing and developing at an astonishing rate.

ESSENTIALS

GETTING THERE   The Tampa area is linked to the Interstate system and is accessible from I-275, I-75, I-4, U.S. 19, U.S. 41, U.S. 92, U.S. 301, and many state highways.

Tampa & St. Petersburg Area Orientation

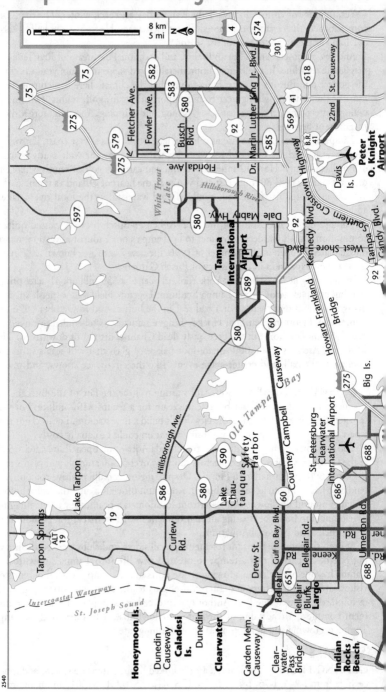

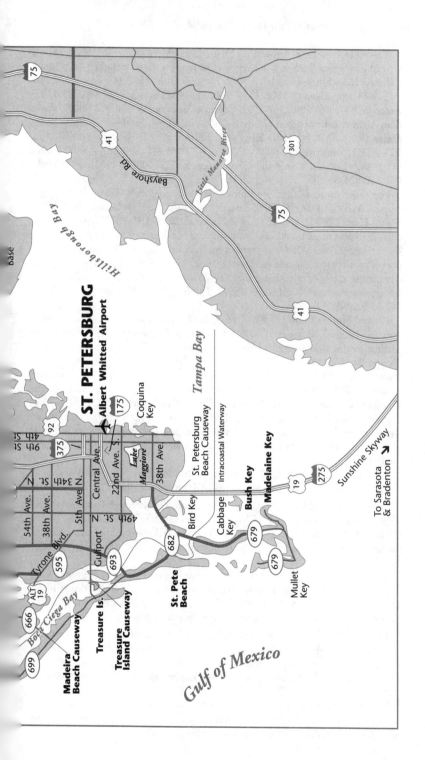

Tampa International Airport, off Memorial Highway and Fla. 60, 5 miles northwest of downtown Tampa, is served by most major airlines, including **Air Canada** (☎ 800/268-7240 in Canada, or 800/776-3000 in the U.S.), **Air South** (☎ 800/247-7688), **American** (☎ 800/433-7300), **America Trans Air** (☎ 800/225-2995), **America West** (☎ 800/235-9292), **Cayman Airways** (☎ 800/422-9626), **Canadian Airlines International** (☎ 800/426-7000), **Continental** (☎ 800/525-0280), **Delta** (☎ 800/221-1212), **Kiwi** (☎ 800/538-5494), **Northwest** (☎ 800/225-2525), **Southwest** (☎ 800/435-9792), **TWA** (☎ 800/221-2000), **United** (☎ 800/241-6522), **USAir** and **USAir Express** (☎ 800/428-4322), and **ValuJet** (☎ 800/825-8538).

Five major car-rental firms are represented on the grounds of Tampa International Airport: **Avis** (☎ 813/396-3500), **Budget** (☎ 813/877-6051), **Dollar** (☎ 813/396-3640), **Hertz** (☎ 813/874-3232), and **National** (☎ 813/396-3782). Most of these companies also maintain offices downtown and in other parts of Tampa such as the Busch Gardens area. Many car-rental companies have premises just outside the airport. The firms that provide van travel to/from the airport and often post the most competitive rates include **Alamo** (☎ 813/289-4323), **A-Plus** (☎ 813/289-4301), **Enterprise Payless** (☎ 813/289-6554), **Thrifty** (☎ 813/289-4006), and **Value** (☎ 813/289-8870).

Central Florida Limo (☎ **813/396-3730**) operates van service between the airport and hotels. The fare is $7 to $15 for up to two passengers, depending on the destination (for most downtown hotels it would be $11). Taxi service is provided by **Tampa Bay Cab** (☎ 813/251-5555), **Yellow Cab Taxis** (☎ 813/253-0121), and **United Cabs** (☎ 813/253-2424). The average fare from the airport to downtown Tampa is $10 to $12 and the ride takes about 15 minutes. In addition, the **Hillsborough Area Regional Transit Authority/HARTline** (☎ **813/254-HART**) operates service between the airport and downtown on its no. 31 bus. This is not an airport express bus, but a local route that makes stops at the airport between the hours of 6am and 8:15pm. Look for the HARTline bus sign outside each airline terminal; the fare is $1.

Amtrak trains arrive at the **Tampa Amtrak Station,** 601 Nebraska Ave. North, Tampa (☎ **813/221-7600,** or 800/USA-RAIL for reservations).

VISITOR INFORMATION   Contact the **Tampa/Hillsborough Convention and Visitors Association, Inc. (THCVA),** 111 Madison St., Tampa, FL 33602-4706 (☎ **813/223-2752,** or 800/44-TAMPA). The THCVA also maintains unstaffed information/brochure centers at the Convention Center and at the Shops on Harbour Island.

A good source of on-the-spot information north of downtown in the Busch Gardens area is the **Tampa Bay Visitor Information Center,** 3601 E. Busch Blvd., Tampa, FL 33612 (☎ **813/985-3601**). It offers free brochures about attractions in Tampa and other parts of Florida as well as a sightseeing tour-booking service.

CITY LAYOUT   Tampa's downtown district is laid out according to a grid system. **Kennedy Boulevard** (Fla. 60) cuts across the city in an east-west direction. The two major arteries bringing traffic into the downtown area are **I-275,** which skirts the northern edge of the city, and the **Crosstown Expressway,** which extends along the southern rim.

All the streets in the central core of the city are one-way, with the exception of pedestrians-only Franklin Street. From the southern tip of Franklin, you can also board the People Mover, an elevated tram to Harbour Island.

The core of Tampa, the compact **downtown** area is primarily a business and financial hub, where John F. Kennedy Boulevard (Fla. 60) and Florida Avenue intersect.

While downtown Tampa is virtually dead after 5pm, **Ybor City** comes alive after dark. This is Tampa's Latin Quarter, settled for more than 100 years by Cuban immigrants. Today it's home to dozens of hot new restaurants, clubs, and shops run by local artists and craftspeople.

South of downtown, small **Harbour Island** is linked by an elevated People Mover to the mainland. It has an elegant hotel and busy marina, but most of the struggling restaurants and shops have closed.

West of downtown, **Hyde Park** is the city's poshest residential neighborhood, complete with upscale shops and trendy restaurants. Many of its homes are part of a National Register Historic District.

West of Hyde Park, **West Shore** runs from Tampa International Airport southward, particularly along Westshore Boulevard. It's a commercial and financial hub, with office buildings, business-oriented hotels, and a popular shopping mall.

The **Courtney Campbell Causeway** runs west of the airport, as Kennedy Boulevard (Fla. 60) crosses Old Tampa Bay. It's a small beach strip with several hotels and restaurants. You don't want to be near here at rush hour when commuters turn this area into a parking lot of cars.

North of downtown, the **Busch Gardens** area surrounds the famous theme park of the same name. Busch Boulevard, which runs east-west, is a busy commercial tourist strip just south of the Busch Gardens entrance where you'll find dozens of restaurants and hotels.

GETTING AROUND   Although downtown Tampa's Franklin Street area was designed as a pedestrian mall with no cars, it's virtually impossible to see the major sights and enjoy the best restaurants without a car.

Nevertheless, the **Hillsborough Area Regional Transit/HARTline** (☎ 813/ 254-HART) provides regularly scheduled bus service between downtown Tampa and the suburbs. The service is geared mainly to commuters, although visitors staying at downtown hotels certainly can use a bus to get to the airport or major shopping centers. Fares are $1 for local services, $1.50 for express routes; correct change is required. Many buses start or finish their route downtown at the Marion Street Transit Parkway, between Tyler and Whiting streets. It provides well-lit open-air terminal facilities including 40-foot shelters with copper roofs, informational kiosks, benches, newspaper stands, landscaping, and 24-hour security.

The **People Mover,** a motorized tram on elevated tracks, connects downtown Tampa with Harbour Island. It operates from the third level of the Fort Brooke Parking Garage, on Whiting Street between Franklin Avenue and Florida Street. Travel time is 90 seconds, and service is continuous, Monday to Saturday from 7am to 2am and Sunday from 8am to 11pm. The fare is 25¢ each way.

The city of Tampa provides a **trolley service** from downtown. It makes frequent stops at the Florida Aquarium and Garrison Seaport Center. Trolleys operate daily from 7:30am to 5:30pm, with a fare of 25¢ per person. For more information contact the visitors bureau (☎ 813/223-2752).

The **Tampa Town Water Taxi** (☎ 813/253-3076) provides a scheduled shuttle service along the Hillsborough River via a 44-passenger air-conditioned ferry, connecting downtown locations including Harbour Island, the Tampa Convention Center, the Tampa Performing Arts Center, and the University of Tampa / Henry

B. Plant Museum. The shuttle operates at half-hour intervals, Monday to Thursday from 2pm to 11pm, on Friday from 2pm to 1am, on Saturday from noon to 1am, and on Sunday from noon to 11pm. Daytime round-trips cost $5 and evening round-trips (after 8pm) cost $6.

Taxis in Tampa don't normally cruise the streets for fares, but they do line up at public loading places, such as hotels, the performing arts center, and bus and train depots. If you need a taxi, call **Tampa Bay Cab** (☎ 813/251-5555), **Yellow Cab** (☎ 813/253-0121), or **United Cab** (☎ 813/253-2424).

BUSCH GARDENS

Yes, admission prices are high, but **Busch Gardens** remains Tampa Bay's most popular attraction. The 335-acre family entertainment park, at 3000 E. Busch Blvd. (☎ **813/987-5171**), features a unique combination of thrill rides, live entertainment, animal habitats in naturalistic environments, shops, restaurants, and games. Capturing the spirit of turn-of-the-century Africa, the park ranks among the top zoos in the country, with nearly 3,400 animals.

Busch Gardens was slated to open Montu in the summer of 1996. Named for the falconlike ancient Egyptian sun and war god, it was designed to be the tallest and longest inverted roller coaster in the world. This takes place during the introduction of **Egypt,** the park's ninth themed area. The area will mirror the country's culture and history and includes a replica of King Tutankhamen's tomb. A sand dig area for kids to discover their own treasures is also planned.

Timbuktu is an ancient desert trading center with African craftspeople at work, plus a sandstorm-style ride, a boat-swing ride, a roller coaster, and an electronic games arcade.

Morocco, a walled city with exotic architecture, has Moroccan craft demonstrations, a sultan's tent with snake charmers, and the Marrakesh Theaters.

The **Serengeti Plain** is an open area with more than 500 African animals roaming freely in herds. This 80-acre natural grassy veldt may be viewed from the monorail, Trans-Veldt Railway, or skyride.

Nairobi is home to "Myombe Reserve: The Great Ape Domain," a natural habitat for various types of gorillas and chimpanzees, and a baby animal nursery, as well as a petting zoo, reptile displays, and Nocturnal Mountain, a simulated environment that allows visitors to observe animals that are active in the dark.

Stanleyville, a prototype African village, has a shopping bazaar and live entertainment, as well as two water rides: the Tanganyika Tidal Wave and Stanley Falls.

The Congo features Kumba, the largest steel roller coaster in the southeastern United States, and Claw Island, a display of rare white Bengal tigers in a natural setting, plus white-water raft rides.

Bird Gardens, the original core of Busch Gardens, offers rich foliage, lagoons, and a free-flight aviary for hundreds of exotic birds, including golden and American bald eagles, hawks, owls, and falcons. This area also offers Land of the Dragons, a new children's adventure area that was added in mid-1995. Designed to entertain the younger set, it contains a variety of play elements in a fairytale setting as well as such just-for-kids rides as a small ferris wheel, dragon carousel, slides, and a mini-flume ride. The area is dominated by Dumphrey, a whimsical dragon who interacts with visitors and guides children around a three-story tree house with winding stairways, tall towers, stepping stones, illuminated water geysers, and an echo chamber.

Crown Colony is the home of a team of Clydesdale horses as well as the Anheuser-Busch hospitality center. Questor, a flight simulator adventure ride, is also located in this area.

To get the most from your visit, arrive early and wear comfortable shoes. Many visitors pack a bathing suit because some of the rides get you totally soaked. Don't forget to bring extra money for snacks.

A **1-day ticket** costs $34.60 for adults, $28.20 for children 3 to 9, free for children 2 and under. The park is open daily from 9:30am to 6pm, with extended hours in summer and holiday periods. To get there, take I-275 northeast of downtown to Busch Boulevard (Exit 33), and go east 2 miles to the entrance on 40th Street (McKinley Drive). Parking is $3.

YBOR CITY

A few short years ago this part of Tampa was known simply as the Latin Quarter, the historic district famous for cigars and the Columbia, the largest Spanish restaurant in the world (see "Where to Dine," below, for more information).

Today Ybor has suddenly become the happening part of Tampa. By day, you can stroll past the art galleries, boutiques, and trendy new restaurants and cafés that line 7th Avenue. At night, good food and great music dominate the scene. It's a cross between New Orleans's Bourbon Street, Key West, and New York's SoHo. Unique shops offer a wide assortment of goodies from silk boxer shorts to unique tatoos. Dozens of outstanding nightclubs and dance clubs have waiting lines out the door. There are lots of police around in the wee hours, but be as cautious here as you would exploring any big city at night.

✪ **Ybor City Walking Tours** are an ideal way to check out the the highlights of this historic district. Free 1¹/₂-hour tours are sponsored by the Ybor City State Museum (☎ 813/247-6323) and are led by enthusiastic local volunteers. Tours start at the information desk in Ybor Square, between 8th and 9th avenues, and cover over three dozen points of interest. January to April the tours depart on Tuesday, Thursday, and Saturday at 10:30am; May to December, only on Thursday and Saturday. Reservations are suggested.

Ybor City Brewing Company

2205 N. 20th St., Ybor City. ☎ **813/242-9222.** Admission $2 per person. Tues–Sat 11am–3pm or by appointment. Take I-4 to Exit 1 (Ybor City) and the brewery is just off the exit between 11th and 12th avenues.

Housed in a 100-year-old, three-story, red-brick building, formerly a cigar factory, this newly established microbrewery produces 15,000 barrels a year of Ybor Gold, Calusa Wheat, and Ybor Brown Ale. Visitors are welcome to tour the brewery and watch the process; tours end with a tasting of the product. Check out the gift shop for funky cigars. Half the tour/admission charge is donated to the restoration of other historic Ybor City buildings.

Ybor City State Museum

1818 9th Ave., Ybor City. ☎ **813/247-6323.** Admission (including a guided tour of the cigar worker's cottage) $2 adults and children 6 and up, free for children 5 and under. Tues–Sat 9am–noon and 1–5pm. Head northeast of downtown, between 18th and 19th streets.

The focal point of Ybor City, this museum is housed in the former Ferlita Bakery (1896–1973), a century-old yellow-brick building. Various exhibits in the museum depict the political, social, and cultural influences that shaped this section of Tampa, once known as "the cigar capital of the world." You can take a self-guided tour around the museum, which includes a collection of cigar labels, cigar memorabilia, and works by local artisans.

Adjacent to the museum is **La Casita,** the site of a renovated cigar worker's cottage, furnished as it was at the turn of the century.

Tampa Area Attractions

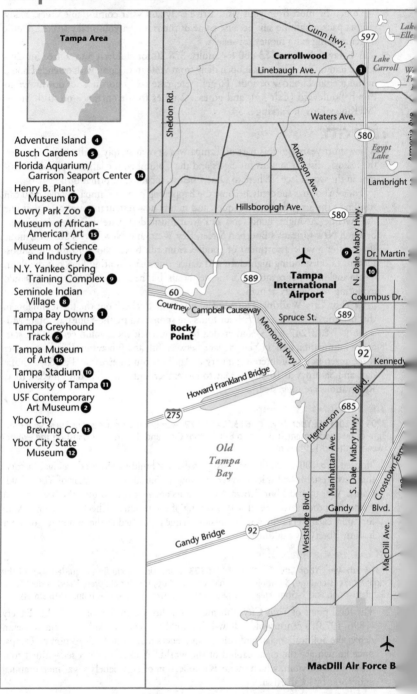

Tampa Area

Adventure Island ④
Busch Gardens ⑤
Florida Aquarium/
  Garrison Seaport Center ⑭
Henry B. Plant
  Museum ⑰
Lowry Park Zoo ⑦
Museum of African-
  American Art ⑮
Museum of Science
  and Industry ③
N.Y. Yankee Spring
  Training Complex ⑨
Seminole Indian
  Village ⑧
Tampa Bay Downs ①
Tampa Greyhound
  Track ⑥
Tampa Museum
  of Art ⑯
Tampa Stadium ⑩
University of Tampa ⑪
USF Contemporary
  Art Museum ②
Ybor City
  Brewing Co. ⑬
Ybor City State
  Museum ⑫

2541

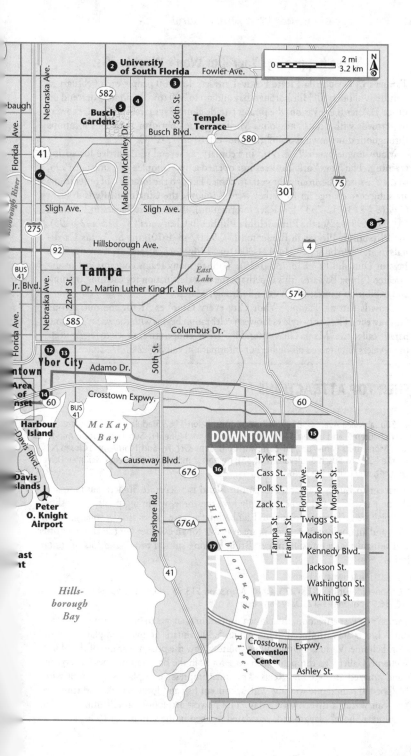

Tampa

Three Happenings Your Kids Won't Want to Miss

Tampa's ✪ **Gasparilla Pirate Festival** attracts 400,000 people each February as hundreds of boats fill Hillsborough Bay and up to 700 rowdy "pirates" descend on the city. After the invasion, the pirates parade along Bayshore Boulevard, showering crowds with beads and coins. Musical groups perform at various locations throughout downtown. For information, call 813/272-1939.

Major-league baseball heats up in February, as several teams arrive for **spring training.** The **New York Yankees** just opened a new complex in Tampa in 1996, so they're sure to be around for years to come. Though the locations of other teams are subject to change, in 1996 they were as follows: the **Cincinnati Reds** in Plant City (☎ 813/752-7337 for ticket information), the **Detroit Tigers** in Lakeland (☎ 941/499-8229); the **Philadelphia Phillies** in Clearwater (☎ 813/442-8496), the **Pittsburgh Pirates** in Bradenton (☎ 941/748-4610), the **St. Louis Cardinals** in St. Petersburg (☎ 314/421-3060 or 813/894-4773), and the **Toronto Blue Jays** in Dunedin (☎ 813/733-0429). With so many teams concentrated in the Greater Tampa Bay area, this is perhaps the best destination for catching training and exhibition games, which extend through March.

Crowds throng Tampa's Ybor City every October 31 for the outrageous **Guavaween.** The Latin-style Halloween celebration begins with the wacky costume parade called the "Mama Guava Stumble." Later, concerts from rock to reggae keep the revelers entertained all night. For information, call 813/248-3712.

OTHER TOP ATTRACTIONS

Adventure Island

4545 Bougainvillea Ave. ☎ **813/987-5600.** Admission $18.95 adults, $16.95 children 3–9, free for children 2 and under; $1 for lockers. Mar to mid-June, Fri–Sun 10am–5pm; mid-June to Aug, Mon–Thurs 9am–7pm, Fri–Sun 9am–8pm; Sept–Oct, Fri–Sun 10am–5pm. Closed Nov–Feb. Take I-275 to Busch Boulevard (Exit 33); go east 2 miles to 40th Street (McKinley Drive), make a left, and follow the signs.

Adjacent to Busch Gardens, Adventure Island is a separate 36-acre outdoor water theme park. Kids and teens especially love the three swimming pools, water slides, and play areas. There are picnic and sunbathing areas, a games arcade, volleyball complex, and an outdoor café. Lockers are available for an extra fee (a little annoying after you've paid that admission price). Bring bathing suits, a towel, and lots of suntan lotion.

✪ The Florida Aquarium

701 Channelside Dr. ☎ **813/273-4000.** Admission $13.95 adults, $12.55 seniors and teens 13–18, $6.95 children 3–12. Daily 9am–6pm.

Tampa's newest attraction, the Florida Aquarium manages to be both educational and fun. Visitors are introduced to more than 5,300 aquatic animals and plants that call Florida home. Various exhibits allow you to follow the pristine springs of the Florida Wetlands Gallery, go through a mangrove forest in the Bays and Beaches Gallery, and stand amazed at the Coral Reefs. The most impressive display is a 43-foot-wide, 14-foot-tall panoramic window with schools of fish and lots of sharks and stingrays. You can watch a diver twice a day. The newest attraction, a half-million-dollar "Explore a Shore" playground, was slated to open in the summer of 1996.

Lowry Park Zoo

7530 North Blvd. ☎ **813/932-0245**. Admission $6.50 adults, $5.50 seniors, $4.50 children 3–11, free for children 2 and under. Daily 9:30am–5pm. Take I-275 to Sligh Avenue (Exit 31) and follow the signs to Lowry Park Zoo.

Watching the 2,000-pound manatees (also known as sea cows) is the highlight here. With lots of greenery, bubbling brooks, and cascading waterfalls, this 24-acre zoo displays animals in settings similar to their natural habitats. Other major exhibits include the Florida wildlife display, the Asian Domain, Primate World, and children's petting zoo.

✪ Museum of African American Art

1308 N. Marion St. (between Scott and Laurel sts.), downtown. ☎ **813/272-2466**. Admission $2 adults, $1 seniors and children grades K–12. Daily Tues–Sat 10am–4:30pm. Take Exit 26 off I-275.

Recently renovated to the tune of $200,000, the museum is touted as the first of its kind in Florida and one of four in the United States. It's the home of the Barnett-Aden collection, considered the state's foremost collection of African-American art. More than 80 artists are represented in the display, which includes sculptures and paintings that depict the history, culture, and lifestyle of African-Americans from the 1800s to the present, with special emphasis on the works of artists active during the Harlem Renaissance.

Museum of Science and Industry (MOSI)

4801 E. Fowler Ave. ☎ **813/987-6300**. Admission $8 adults, $7 seniors, $5 children 2–12, free for children under 2. Daily 9am–5pm or later. Head north of downtown, 1 mile east of Busch Gardens.

MOSI is the largest science center in the Southeast and has more than 450 interactive exhibits. Guests can step into the Gulf Hurricane and experience gale-force winds, defy the laws of gravity in the unique *Challenger* space experience, or cruise the mysterious world of microbes in LifeLab. Three major exhibitions have been added in MOSI's new West Wing: The Amazing You allows visitors to explore the body, Our Florida focuses on environmental factors, and Our Place in the Universe introduces guests to space, flight, and beyond. The museum has also recently added MOSIMAX, Florida's first IMAX DOME theater.

Tampa Museum of Art

600 N. Ashley Dr. ☎ **813/274-8130**. Admission $5 adults, $4 seniors and college students, $3 children 6–18, free for children 5 and under, free for everyone Wed 5–9pm and Sun 1–5pm. Mon–Tues and Thurs–Sat 10am–5pm, Wed 10am–9pm, Sun 1–5pm. Take I-275 to Exit 25 (Ashley Street).

Located on the east bank of the Hillsborough River, just south of the Tampa Bay Performing Arts Center, this fine-arts complex offers eight galleries with changing exhibits ranging from classical antiquities to contemporary Florida art. There's also a new 7-acre riverfront park and sculpture garden. Museum tours are offered on Wednesday and Saturday at 1pm and on Sunday at 2pm.

Henry B. Plant Museum

401 W. Kennedy Blvd. ☎ **813/254-1891**. Free admission; suggested donation, $3 adults, $1 children 12 and under. Tues–Sat 10am–4pm, Sun noon–4pm. Take Fla. 60 west of downtown.

Modeled after the Alhambra in Spain, the 13 silver minarets and distinctive Moorish architecture make this National Historic Landmark the focal point of the Tampa skyline. Originally built in 1891 as the 511-room Tampa Bay Hotel by railroad tycoon Henry B. Plant, it's filled with art and furnishings from Europe and the Orient. Other exhibits focus on the history of the original railroad resort and Florida's early tourist industry.

ORGANIZED TOURS

Sea Wings Aviation, Inc., 2047 Los Lomas Dr., Clearwater (☎ 813/445-9464), offers sightseeing tours of the Tampa Bay area via a three-seat float plane. What a great way to see the area! Flights depart from various points, including Rocky Point Drive off the Courtney Campbell Causeway. The 15-minute trips start at $54 per person; longer trips can be arranged. They've even been known to fly couples over to nearby islands to become formally engaged. Flights are available throughout the day, but advance reservations are required.

Alternatively, you can soar above the Tampa skyline aboard **The Big Red Balloon,** 16302 E. Course Dr., Tampa (☎ 813/969-1518). The 1-hour trips are operated daily at sunrise only; the cost is $150 per person and includes a champagne brunch.

Located opposite Busch Gardens, **Swiss Chalet Tours,** 3601 E. Busch Blvd. (☎ 813/985-3601), operates guided bus tours of Tampa, Ybor City, and environs. The 4-hour half-day tours are given on Monday and Thursday; they cost $35 for adults and $20 for children. The 8-hour full-day tours are given on Tuesday and Friday, and cost $45 for adults and $35 for children. Reservations are required at least 24 hours in advance; passengers are picked up at major hotels and various other points in the Tampa/St. Petersburg area. Tours can also be booked to Sarasota, Bradenton, and other regional destinations.

PARKS & NATURE PRESERVES

Hillsborough River State Park, 15402 U.S. 301 North (☎ 813/986-1020), is a 2,994-acre state park offering 118 campsites year round. Located 6 miles southwest of Zephyrhills, the park is open daily from 8am to sunset. Picnic facilities, swimming, freshwater fishing, nature and hiking trails, plus a ramp for boats and canoes are available. Visitors may rent canoes and there's a fee for swimming in a half-acre pool. Admission is $3.25 per car.

Eureka Springs, Eureka Springs Road (☎ 813/626-7994), is the only botanical garden in the local park system. It features 31 acres with a greenhouse, trellised walks, trails, boardwalks, and a picnic area. Located north of I-4 near the junction of I-4 and U.S. 301, it's open daily from 8am to 6pm.

Lettuce Lake, 6920 E. Fletcher Ave. at the Hillsborough River, just west of I-75 (☎ 813/985-7845), is one of the area's newest parks. It encompasses 240 acres and includes an interpretive center featuring exhibits where visitors can observe a cypress swamp inhabited by birds and other wildlife. Other facilities include picnic areas and a playground. The park is open daily from 8am to 8pm. A $1 donation is requested.

McCay Bay Nature Park, Crosstown Expressway and 34th Street, is a 150-acre nature habitat. McKay Bay is a refuge for more than 180 species of birds, rabbits, snakes, turtles and other wildlife. Boardwalk plans are in the future.

Upper Tampa Bay, 8001 Double Branch Rd., off Fla. 580 on Old Tampa Bay (☎ 813/855-1765), is a 595-acre peninsula filled with freshwater ponds, pine flatwoods, salt marshes, oyster beds, salt barrens, and a mangrove forest. Open daily (except Christmas) from 8am to sunset. Picnic facilities are available.

OUTDOOR ACTIVITIES

Tampa Outdoor Adventures (☎ 813/223-2752, or 800/44-TAMPA, ext. 6), is a one-stop source of information and reservations for a variety of recreational activities in the Tampa area, from fishing to yachting and other sports. In addition, try these contacts directly:

BOAT RENTALS   Paddle downstream in a two- to four-person canoe along a 20-mile stretch of the Hillsborough River amid 16,000 acres of rural lands in **Wilderness Park,** the largest regional park in Hillsborough County. The trips take 2 to 4 hours, covering approximately 2 to 3 miles per hour. **Canoe Escape,** 9335 E. Fowler Ave. (☎ 813/986-2067), charges $26 for 2-hour trips, $30 for 4-hour trips, and is open Monday to Friday from 9am to 5pm and on Saturday and Sunday from 8am to 6pm.

FISHING   There's good freshwater fishing for trout in **Lake Thonotosassa,** east of the city, or for bass along the **Hillsborough River.** Pier fishing on Hillsborough Bay is also available from **Ballast Point Park,** 5300 Interbay Blvd. (☎ 813/ 831-9585).

  Light Tackle Fishing Expeditions (☎ 813/963-1930) offers sportfishing trips for tarpon, redfish, cobia, trout, and snook. Chartering the boat for a half-day trip costs $250, and a full-day trip is $350.

GOLF   The **Arnold Palmer Golf Academy World Headquarters** is located 12 miles north of Tampa at the renowned Saddlebrook Resort, 5700 Saddlebrook Way, Wesley Chapel (☎ 813/973-1111). Programs are available for adults and juniors of all skill levels. There are 2-, 3-, and 5-day programs available from $235 per person per night. You'll receive accommodations, breakfast, daily instruction, 18 holes of golf daily, cart and greens fees, and nightly club storage and cleaning. If you're not staying here, you can still call ahead and use the facilities for a fee.

  Situated north of Lowry Park, the **Babe Zaharias Municipal Golf Course,** 11412 Forest Hills Dr. (☎ 813/932-8932), is an 18-hole, par-70 course with a pro shop, putting greens, and a driving range. Golf-club rentals and lessons are available. Greens fees run $13.50 to $18.50, $20 to $25 with a cart. The course is open daily from 7am to dusk.

  Just south of the airport, play a round of golf at the 18-hole, par-72 course at the **Hall of Fame Golf Club,** 2222 N. Westshore Blvd. (☎ 813/876-4913). Facilities include a driving range and club rentals; lessons are also available. Greens fees, which include a cart, are $22 to $24. It's open daily from 7am to dusk.

  The **Rocky Point Golf Municipal Golf Course,** 4151 Dana Shores Dr. (☎ 813/ 884-5141), located between the airport and the bay, is an 18-hole, par-71 course, with a pro shop, practice range, and putting greens. Lessons and club rentals are available. Greens fees are $20 to $25, including a cart, and it's open daily from 7am to dusk.

  On the Hillsborough River in north Tampa, the **Rogers Park Municipal Golf Course,** 7910 N. 30th St. (☎ 813/234-1911), is an 18-hole, par-72 championship course with a lighted driving and practice range. Lessons and club rentals are available. Greens fees, including cart, are $20 to $25. It's open daily from 7am to dusk.

  The **University of South Florida Golf Course,** Fletcher Avenue and 46th Street (☎ 813/974-2071), is just north of the USF campus. This 18-hole, par-72 course is nicknamed "The Claw" because of its challenging layout. It offers lessons and club rentals. Greens fees are $18, $30 with a cart. It's open daily from 7am to dusk.

IN-LINE SKATING   Rent in-line skates at **Blades & Bikes,** the authority on blade skating in the area. Look for the pink-and-blue shop at 201-A W. Platt St. (☎ 813/ 251-1780) in Tampa, near Bayshore Boulevard. Ask about their free in-line skating classes every Saturday. Call for reservations.

JOGGING **Bayshore Boulevard,** a 7-mile stretch along Hillsborough Bay, is famous for its 6.3-mile sidewalk. Reputed to be the world's longest continuous sidewalk, it's a favorite for runners, joggers, walkers, and in-line skaters. The route goes from the western edge of downtown in a southward direction, passing stately old homes, condos, retirement communities, and houses of worship, ending at Gandy Boulevard.

For more information on other recommended running areas, contact the **Parks and Recreation Department,** 7225 North Blvd. (☎ 813/223-8230).

TENNIS The **City of Tampa Tennis Complex,** at the Hillsborough Community College, 4001 Tampa Bay Blvd. (☎ 813/870-2383), across from Tampa Stadium, is the largest public complex in Tampa, with 16 hard courts and 12 clay courts. It also has four racquetball courts, a pro shop, locker rooms, showers, and lessons. Reservations are recommended. Prices range from $1.75 (non–prime time) to $4.50 per person per hour. It's open Monday to Friday from 8am to 9pm and on Saturday and Sunday from 8am to 6pm.

On the water and overlooking Harbour Island, **Marjorie Park,** 59 Columbia Dr., Davis Islands (☎ 813/253-3997), has eight clay courts. Reservations are required. The price is $4.50 per person per hour and it's open Monday to Friday from 8am to 9pm and on Saturday and Sunday from 8am to 6pm.

The **Harry Hopman Tennis Academy,** 5700 Saddlebrook Way, Wesley Chapel (☎ 813/973-1111, or 800/729-8383), with its 45 tennis courts, is a well-equipped school that caters to beginners as well as skilled players of all ages. A basic 5-day/6-night package includes 25 hours (minimum) of tennis instruction, unlimited playing time, match play with instructors, audiovisual analysis, agility exercises, and accommodations at the Saddlebrook Resort. Prices range from $678 to $1,092 per person, double occupancy. You must be a member or a guest to play here.

SPECTATOR SPORTS

BASEBALL The **New York Yankees** moved to Tampa for spring training in 1996. Situated opposite Tampa Stadium, at the southwest corner of Dale Mabry Highway and Dr. Martin Luther King, Jr., Boulevard, the new Yankee complex, **Legends Field** (☎ 813/875-7753), is the largest spring-training facility in Florida, with a 10,000-seat capacity. You can catch the Bronx Bombers in action every February and March.

About a half-hour drive from downtown Tampa, the **Plant City Stadium,** Park Rd., Plant City (☎ 813/757-9221), is the spring-training turf of the **Cincinnati Reds.** The season runs from mid-February to April and admission is $4 to $7.

DOG RACING The **Tampa Greyhound Track,** 8300 N. Nebraska Ave. (☎ 813/932-4313), features 13 races daily. Live races are run July to December, Monday to Saturday at 7:30pm, and on Monday, Wednesday, and Saturday at 12:30pm. From January to June, there's simulcasting for horse and dog racing. Admission is $1 to the grandstand, $2 to $3 to the clubhouse. Self-parking is free; valet parking costs $3.

FOOTBALL Home field to the **Tampa Bay Buccaneers** is Tampa Stadium, 4201 N. Dale Mabry Hwy. (☎ 813/872-7977 or 813/879-BUCS). At press time, Tampa Bay residents were fighting to keep the Bucs in town and the coach had just been fired. What's happening next is anybody's guess. Stay tuned to the local sports pages for updates to see if Tampa still even has a football team.

HOCKEY Starting with the 1996 season, the NHL's **Tampa Bay Lightning** were scheduled to be based at the new $153-million, 20,000-seat "Ice Palace," located between the Tampa Convention Center and the new Florida Aquarium. For complete details at the time of your visit, contact the Tampa Bay Lightning, 501 Kennedy Blvd., Tampa (☎ 813/229-8800). Ticket prices range from $8 to $50.

HORSE RACING   The only oval thoroughbred race course on Florida's west coast, ✪ **Tampa Bay Downs,** 11225 Racetrack Rd., Oldsmar (☎ 813/855-4401), is the home of the Tampa Bay Derby. The program features 10 races a day. Admission is $1.50 to the grandstand, $3 to the clubhouse; there's free grandstand admission for seniors on Wednesday and for women on Friday. Parking costs $1. From December to May, post time is 12:30pm on Monday, Tuesday, Thursday, and Friday, and at 1pm on Saturday and Sunday. The track presents simulcasts June to November.

JAI-ALAI   This Spanish game, reminiscent of indoor lacrosse, is considered the world's fastest ball game: The ball can go over 180 m.p.h. At the **Tampa Jai-Alai Fronton,** 5125 S. Dale Mabry Hwy. (☎ 813/831-1411), professional players volley the lethal *pelota* with a long, curved glove called a *cesta*. Spectators, protected by a wall of glass, place bets on the players. Admission is $1 to $3 and parking is $1 or free. It's open year round, with games Monday to Saturday beginning at 7pm, and matinees on Monday, Wednesday, and Saturday beginning at noon.

POLO   Mallets swing at the **Tampa Bay Polo Club,** Walden Lake Polo and Country Club, 2001 Clubhouse Dr., Plant City (☎ 813/754-2234). Admission is $3; it's open mid-January to May, with play beginning at 2pm on Sunday.

SHOPPING

SHOPPING CENTERS & COMPLEXES

Brandon Town Center
2000 block of Brandon Blvd. (just south of I-4), in Brandon. ☎ 813/661-5100.

The major suburb of Brandon, just east of Tampa, is home to the first new mall to open in the area in years. No, it doesn't have a Saks Fifth Avenue or a Neiman Marcus, but dozens of specialty stores lend an upscale feel.

✪ Old Hyde Park Village
1509 W. Swann Ave., Hyde Park. ☎ 813/251-3500.

This is a terrific alternative to those cookie-cutter suburban malls. Walk around little shops outside in the sunshine and check out one of the city's oldest and most historic neighborhoods at the same time. A cluster of 50 upscale shops and boutiques is set in a village layout. The selection includes William Sonoma, Pottery Barn, Banana Republic, Brooks Brothers, Crabtree & Evelyn, Godiva Chocolatier, Laura Ashley, Polo Ralph Lauren, and Talbots, to name a few. Open Monday to Wednesday and Saturday from 10am to 6pm, on Thursday and Friday from 10am to 9pm, and on Sunday from noon to 5pm.

Ybor Square
1901 13th St., Ybor City. ☎ 813/247-4497.

Listed on the National Register of Historic Places, this complex consists of three brick buildings (dating from 1886) that once comprised the largest cigar factory in the world. Today it's a specialty mall, with over three dozen shops selling everything from clothing, crafts, and jewelry to (of course) cigars. Open Monday to Saturday from 10am to 6pm and on Sunday from noon to 5:30pm.

SPECIALTY STORES

Adam's City Hatters
1621 E. 7th Ave., Ybor City. ☎ 813/229-2850.

Established over 75 years ago and reputed to be Florida's largest hat store (with a mind-boggling inventory of more than 18,000 hats), this shop offers all types of head-gear, from Stetsons and Panamas to top hats, sombreros, and caps. Open Monday to Friday from 9:30am to 5:30pm.

Head's Flags
4109 Henderson. ☎ **813/248-5019.**

Here you'll find colorful flags from all nations and all states, as well as banners, ethnic items, T-shirts, and hats. Open Monday to Friday from 9:30am to 5:30pm and on Saturday from 9:30am to 3pm.

La France
1612 E. 7th Ave. ☎ **813/248-1381.**

Racks upon racks of vintage clothing and costumes fill this funky store. Open Sunday to Friday from 11am to 6pm and on Saturday from 11am to 10:30pm.

Tampa Rico Cigar Co.
1901 13th St. North. ☎ **813/247-6738.**

Check out these hand-rolled stogies, brought to you by the same family for the past 50 years. Open daily from 11am to 5pm.

✪ One World Gift Shop
412 Zack St. ☎ **813/229-0679.**

Tucked into a garden entrance of the First Presbyterian Church, this downtown shop sells handcrafted jewelry and gifts made by artisans from Central and South America, Asia, India, and Mexico. Open Monday to Friday from 11am to 2pm and on Sunday (October to December only) from 11:30am to 1:30pm.

St. Fiacre's Herb Shop
1709 N. 16th St., Ybor City. ☎ **813/248-1234.**

Named after the Irish monk who became the patron saint of gardeners, this unique shop stocks a wide array of fresh herbs, herbal products, fragrances, exotic teas, T-shirts, herbal gift baskets, and books. Open Monday to Thursday from 10am to 6pm, on Friday and Saturday from 10am to 8pm, and on Sunday from noon to 5pm.

Whaley's Markets
533 S. Howard Ave. ☎ **813/254-2904.**

This is a favorite source for Florida Indian River citrus fruit, marmalades, and other local foods, including gourmet picnic items. Open Monday to Saturday from 7am to 9pm and on Sunday from 7am to 8pm.

WHERE TO STAY

Business travelers will most likely stay downtown, near Tampa International Airport, along Westshore Boulevard and the Courtney Campbell Causeway. North of downtown, near the Busch Gardens area, are a number of family-oriented hotels. The Saddlebrook Resort is an international sports mecca located north of Busch Gardens. No matter where you stay, you'll most likely find a swimming pool on the premises. With the exception of a few downtown hotels, parking is free.

Price-wise, the high season in Tampa for rooms is generally January to April. Most hotels offer terrific discounted package rates in the summer, but don't forget that you'll have to deal with those tropical downpours that pop up out of the blue. The sun usually comes out 20 minutes later, so don't discount the discounts.

Many hotels offer great weekend specials as well, dropping their rates by as much as 50%. Hotels often combine tickets to major attractions like Busch Gardens in their package deals. Always ask about special deals when you're booking your room.

The local hotel-occupancy tax is 11%, added to your hotel room bill.

VERY EXPENSIVE

✪ Hyatt Regency Westshore

6200 Courtney Campbell Causeway, Tampa, FL 33607. ☎ **813/874-1234,** or 800/233-1234. Fax 813/870-9168. 445 rms. A/C TV TEL. $204 double Sun–Thurs, $165 double Fri–Sat. AE, CB, DC, DISC, MC, V.

Very elegant and civilized, this 14-story hostelry a mile west of Tampa International Airport is nestled on a 35-acre nature preserve overlooking Old Tampa Bay. Most guest rooms provide expansive views of the bay and evening sunsets. Since many of the guests are business folks, this is probably not the best bet if you're traveling with rowdy kids.

Dining/Entertainment: Armani's is an elegant, candlelit rooftop restaurant known for its northern Italian cuisine and views. The "create your own" antipasto bar is the best-kept secret in town. Behind the hotel is a 250-foot boardwalk leading to Oystercatchers, a Key West–style seafood eatery with indoor and outdoor seating overlooking the bay.

Services: Concierge, room service (18 hours), baby-sitting, valet laundry, airport courtesy shuttle.

Facilities: Two outdoor swimming pools, two lighted tennis courts, whirlpool, saunas, health club, nature walks, jogging trails.

✪ Saddlebrook Resort

5700 Saddlebrook Way, Wesley Chapel, FL 33543. ☎ **813/973-1111,** or 800/729-8383. Fax 813/973-4504. 500 rms and suites. A/C TV TEL. High season, $215–$360 double. Off-season, $180–$325 double. AE, DC, DISC, MC, V. Head 1 mile east of I-75 off Fla. 54 (Exit 58).

Set on 480 acres of natural countryside, this internationally renowned resort is off the beaten path (30 minutes north of Tampa International Airport) but worth the trip. Join pros such as Pete Sampras and Jim Courier at the Harry Hopman Tennis Academy, or perfect your swing at the World Headquarters of the Arnold Palmer Golf Academy.

Dining/Entertainment: The casual but elegant Cypress Restaurant consistently wins accolades. It's famous for grand holiday buffets and popular Friday-night seafood buffets throughout the year. Enjoy indoor or outdoor dining at Terrace on the Green, overlooking the Cypress Lagoon and the 18th green. The Little Club offers an American menu and the popular TD's sports bar/tavern. The Poolside Cafe is great for dining in your bathing suit alfresco.

Services: Concierge, room service, baby-sitting, airport courtesy shuttle.

Facilities: Two 18-hole championship golf courses, year-round programs at the Arnold Palmer Golf Academy, 45 tennis courts (Har-Tru, Laykold, grass, and clay), the Harry Hopman Tennis Academy for adults and juniors of all skill levels, 270-foot-long half-million-gallon superpool, whirlpool, fitness center, wellness program.

Sheraton Grand Hotel

4860 W. Kennedy Blvd., Tampa, FL 33609. ☎ **813/286-4400,** or 800/325-3535. Fax 813/286-4053. 324 rms. A/C TV TEL. Winter Sun–Thurs, $164 double. Summer and Fri–Sat year round, $105–$164 double. AE, CB, DC, MC, V.

This is a perfect place to stay if you have business in the busy Westshore district. In addition to a steady business clientele, it attracts vacationers who enjoy the panoramic

Tampa Area Accommodations & Dining

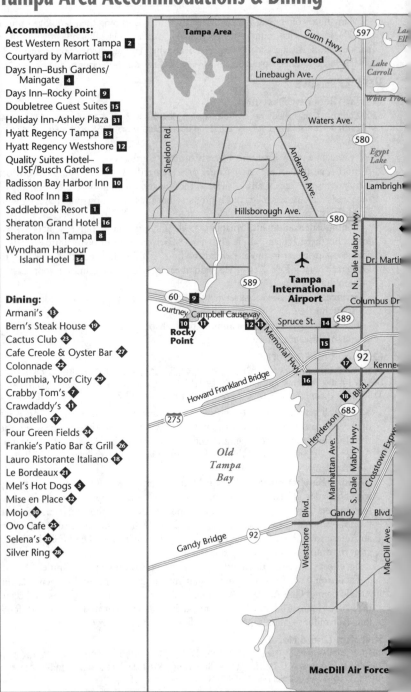

Accommodations:
Best Western Resort Tampa **2**
Courtyard by Marriott **14**
Days Inn–Bush Gardens/
  Maingate **4**
Days Inn–Rocky Point **9**
Doubletree Guest Suites **15**
Holiday Inn-Ashley Plaza **31**
Hyatt Regency Tampa **33**
Hyatt Regency Westshore **12**
Quality Suites Hotel–
  USF/Busch Gardens **6**
Radisson Bay Harbor Inn **10**
Red Roof Inn **3**
Saddlebrook Resort **1**
Sheraton Grand Hotel **16**
Sheraton Inn Tampa **8**
Wyndham Harbour
  Island Hotel **34**

Dining:
Armani's **13**
Bern's Steak House **19**
Cactus Club **23**
Cafe Creole & Oyster Bar **27**
Colonnade **22**
Columbia, Ybor City **29**
Crabby Tom's **7**
Crawdaddy's **11**
Donatello **17**
Four Green Fields **24**
Frankie's Patio Bar & Grill **26**
Lauro Ristorante Italiano **18**
Le Bordeaux **21**
Mel's Hot Dogs **5**
Mise en Place **32**
Mojo **30**
Ovo Cafe **25**
Selena's **20**
Silver Ring **28**

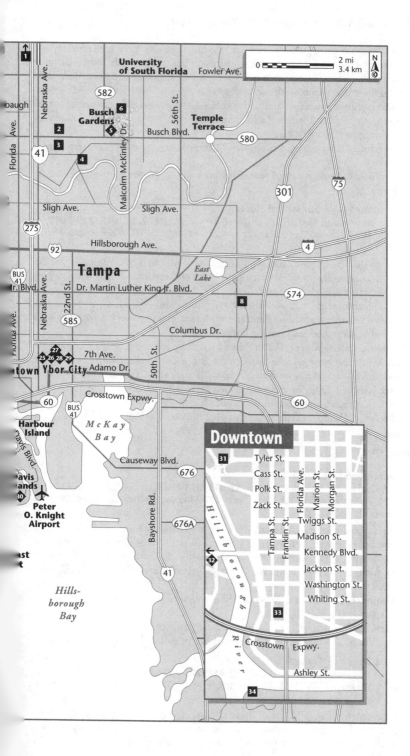

views from the three glass elevators, and the bright atriums filled with greenery and cascading fountains. They've added a fitness room on the ninth floor. The guest rooms have all been renovated in soft-toned color schemes with traditional dark-wood furnishings. The rooms on the upper floors have views of Old Tampa Bay.

Dining/Entertainment: Beef is king at Shula's Steak House. Locals rave about the custom-cut certified Angus beef selections. Eat a 48-ounce Porterhouse and have your name engraved on a gold plaque.

Services: Concierge, room service (24 hours), valet laundry, courtesy airport shuttle.

Facilities: Outdoor heated swimming pool, gift shop, florist, two banks, news/ tobacco shop.

✪ Wyndham Harbour Island Hotel
725 S. Harbour Island Blvd., Harbour Island, Tampa, FL 33602. ☎ **813/229-5000,** or 800/WYNDHAM. Fax 813/229-5322. 300 rms. A/C MINIBAR TV TEL. $209 double. AE, CB, DC, MC, V.

Though there's not much action on this little island, you'll enjoy quiet elegance at this 12-story luxury property. It has great views of the surrounding channels which link the Hillsborough River and the bay. The bedrooms, all with views of the water, are furnished in dark woods and floral fabrics, and each has a well-lit marble-trimmed bathroom, executive desk, and work area, plus in-room conveniences such as a coffeemaker, iron, and ironing board.

Dining/Entertainment: Watch the yachts drift by as you dine at the Harbourview Room, or enjoy your favorite drink in the Bar, a clubby room with equally good views. Snacks and drinks are available during the day at the Pool Bar.

Services: Concierge, room service, secretarial services, notary public, evening turn-down, valet laundry, courtesy airport shuttle.

Facilities: Outdoor heated swimming pool and deck, 50 boat slips, newsstand/gift shop, guest privileges at the Harbour Island Athletic Club.

EXPENSIVE

⑤ Doubletree Guest Suites
4400 W. Cypress St., Tampa, FL 33607. ☎ **813/873-8675,** or 800/222-TREE. Fax 813/ 879-7196. 260 suites. A/C TV TEL. High season, $99–$149 suite for two. Off-season, $89 suite for two. AE, CB, DC, MC, V.

With its Spanish-style architecture, this eight-story building adds an old-world charm to the busy corridor beside the airport and Westshore Boulevard. The interior includes a plant-filled atrium with cascading waterfalls and a tropical garden courtyard. All guest units are suites with separate bedrooms and living areas, perfect for families.

Dining/Entertainment: Regional dishes and local seafoods are the specialties at the St. James Bar & Grill.

Services: Room service, valet laundry, airport courtesy shuttle.

Facilities: Indoor swimming pool, sauna, steam room, gift shop.

✪ Hyatt Regency Tampa
2 Tampa City Center, Tampa, FL 33602. ☎ **813/225-1234,** or 800/233-1234. Fax 813/ 273-0234. 518 rms. A/C TV TEL. $139–$169 double. AE, CB, DC, DISC, MC, V. Ask about summer specials.

This award-winning AAA Four Diamond hotel is a convenient place to stay while conducting business downtown, since you can walk everywhere. Not surprisingly, it caters primarily to the corporate crowd. The eight-story atrium lobby has a cascading waterfall and lots of foliage, though some guest rooms are looking a little worn lately. Many units on the upper floors have bay or river views.

Dining/Entertainment: Creative American cuisine is featured at City Center Cafe. Light lunches are offered at Deli Express. For libations with piano music, try Saltwaters Lounge.

Services: Concierge, room service (24 hours), valet laundry, airport courtesy shuttle.

Facilities: Outdoor heated swimming pool, whirlpool, health club.

MODERATE

Best Western Resort Tampa at Busch Gardens

820 E. Busch Blvd., Tampa, FL 33612. ☎ **813/933-4011,** or 800/288-4011. Fax 813/932-1784. 255 rms. A/C TV TEL. $59–$99 double. AE, CB, DC, DISC, MC, V.

This place used to be called the Colony Hotel and sits off the Busch Boulevard exit, a few miles from Tampa's best-known attractions. It's great for families on a budget. The lobby leads to an enclosed skylit atrium-style courtyard with fountains, streetlights, benches, a pool, and tropical foliage. The guest rooms have outside doors and surround the courtyard. They have standard furnishings, enlivened by colorful, eye-catching fabrics.

Dining/Entertainment: Palm Grill Restuarant, off the lobby, features a variety of dishes. Charades Nite Club offers themed happy hours.

Services: Concierge desk, secretarial services, valet laundry, courtesy transport to Busch Gardens.

Facilities: Indoor and outdoor heated swimming pools, two Jacuzzis, sauna, four lighted tennis courts, exercise room, games room, coin-operated laundry, gift shop.

Holiday Inn–Ashley Plaza

111 W. Fortune St., Tampa, FL 33602. ☎ **813/223-1351,** or 800/ASK-VALUE. Fax 813/221-2000. 311 rms. A/C TV TEL. $99.50–$109.50 double. AE, CB, DC, DISC, MC, V.

Downtown Tampa is pretty dead, but this modern 14-story hotel is within walking distance of the Tampa Bay Performing Arts Center and the Tampa Museum of Art. The guest rooms are spacious, with dark-wood furnishings and full-length wall mirrors. Most rooms on the upper floors have views of the Hillsborough River.

Dining/Entertainment: The lobby level offers three choices: the Backstage Restaurant, for moderately priced meals in a theatrical setting; the Deli, for light fare; and the Encore Lounge, for drinks and occasional live music.

Services: Room service, valet laundry, airport courtesy shuttle.

Facilities: Outdoor heated swimming pool, whirlpool, fitness room, coin-operated laundry, gift shop.

⑤ Quality Suites Hotel–USF/Busch Gardens

3001 University Center Dr., Tampa, FL 33612. ☎ **813/971-8930,** or 800/228-5151. Fax 813/971-8935. 150 suites. A/C TV TEL. $72–$155 suite for one; $79–$162 suite for two. AE, DC, DISC, MC, V. Rates include full breakfast and evening cocktail reception.

This hacienda-style all-suite hotel sits directly behind Busch Gardens, although the entrance to the theme park is 4 blocks away. Each guest unit has a separate bedroom with built-in armoire and well-lit mirrored vanity area, a living/dining room with sofa bed, plus wet bar, coffeemaker, microwave, and stereo/VCR unit. The decor relies heavily on art deco–style furnishings.

Services: 24-hour gift shop / food store, VCR rentals, valet laundry.

Facilities: Outdoor heated swimming pool, Jacuzzi, meeting rooms, coin-operated laundry.

Radisson Bay Harbor Inn

7700 Courtney Campbell Causeway, Tampa, FL 33607. ☎ **813/281-8900,** or 800/333-3333. Fax 813/281-0189. 257 rms. A/C TV TEL. $59–$130 double. AE, CB, DC, MC, V.

This six-story hostelry is a good choice if you want to head about 20 minutes west to the beaches of Pinellas County or 15 minutes north to the tourist attractions of Tampa. Plus, it's only 2 miles west of the airport. The guest rooms all have a balcony or patio, and many have views of Old Tampa Bay. The decor reflects art deco influences.

Dining/Entertainment: Views of the water are the prime attraction at the lobby-level Damon's Restaurant and Lounge.

Services: Valet laundry, airport courtesy shuttle.

Facilities: Heated outdoor swimming pool, two lighted tennis courts, hair salons for men and women, gift shop.

Sheraton Inn Tampa

7401 E. Hillsborough Ave., Tampa, FL 33610. ☎ **813/626-0999,** or 800/325-3535. Fax 813/622-7893, ext. 246. 276 rms. A/C TV TEL. $109–$135 double. AE, CB, DC, MC, V.

Ten minutes from downtown and adjacent to the Seminole Gaming Palace, this hostelry recently added a six-story tower. It's conveniently situated off I-4 in a palm tree–shaded setting, close to the State Fairgrounds and an hour away from Orlando area attractions. The guest rooms, many of which surround a central courtyard and pool area, are contemporary in decor, with dark woods, brass fixtures, and restful tones. Most units have balconies or patios. They have great summer packages, including a Busch Gardens deal.

Dining/Entertainment: The lobby area has a lounge bar with an informal atmosphere; or follow a covered walkway to an adjacent building and the Cypress Landing Restaurant and Sky Box Sports Bar.

Services: Room service, valet laundry, secretarial services, airport courtesy shuttle.

Facilities: Outdoor heated swimming pool, health club, gift shop.

INEXPENSIVE

In addition to the listings below, there's the **Days Inn Busch Gardens/Maingate,** 2901 E. Busch Blvd. (☎ 813/933-6471, or 800/DAYS-INN), charging $59 double in high season. It's great for families on a budget; you can walk to Busch Gardens from here. There's also a **Red Roof Inn,** 2307 E. Busch Blvd. (☎ **813/932-0073,** or 800/THE-ROOF), less than a mile from Busch Gardens. Rates are $51 double in high season. Both motels have outdoor pools.

⑤ Courtyard by Marriott

3805 W. Cypress St., Tampa, FL 33607. ☎ **813/874-0555,** or 800/321-2211. Fax 813/870-0685. 145 rms. A/C TV TEL. $59–$109 double. AE, CB, DC, DISC, MC, V.

You wouldn't want to walk around this part of town at night, but this contemporary four-story hotel is a clean "find" if you have business around the Dale Mabry Highway, 3 miles from the airport. Like other properties of this chain, it follows the usual layout, with guest rooms surrounding a central courtyard. The rooms, which offer a choice of a king-size bed or two double beds, feature dark-wood furnishings and have in-room coffeemakers.

Facilities include a café/lounge, an outdoor swimming pool, an indoor whirlpool, an exercise room, and a guest laundry. The hotel offers complimentary airport transportation.

✪ Days Inn Rocky Point

7627 Courtney Campbell Causeway, Tampa, FL 33607. ☎ **813/281-0000,** or 800/DAYS-INN. Fax 813/281-1067. 152 rms. A/C TV TEL. $65–$75 double. AE, DC, DISC, MC, V.

No, it's not on the Gulf of Mexico, but it does have a small strip of beach near the Causeway overlooking Old Tampa Bay. Cars whiz by, but it's set back from the main road. Just 2 miles west of the airport, the motel-style property encompasses four two-story wings, surrounding an outdoor swimming pool with landscaped courtyard, so the bedrooms offer either bay views or poolside views. The units have a cheery decor with cherrywood furniture.

For dining or drinking, try the Waterfront Cafe and Sports Bar. Facilities include an outdoor swimming pool, two tennis courts, a shuffleboard court, horseshoe pit, badminton, two volleyball courts, a children's playground, rentals for jet and water skis, and a coin-operated guest laundry.

CAMPING

Hillsborough River State Park, 15402 U.S. 301 North, 6 miles southwest of Zephyrhills (☎ **813/986-1020**), offers 118 campsites year round, plus fishing, canoeing, and boating.

WHERE TO DINE
VERY EXPENSIVE

Bern's Steak House

1208 S. Howard Ave. ☎ **813/251-2421.** Reservations required. Main courses $18.50–$156.00 AE, CB, DC, DISC, MC, V. Daily 5–11pm. AMERICAN.

Don't forget to make reservations at this popular hot spot—you'll be out of luck if you don't. It's a local institution, famous for steak. You order a prime, well-aged steak according to the thickness and weight you prefer. Your steak is then cut and broiled over charcoal to your specifications. If beef is not your fancy, there are dozens of other menu options. Depending on the season, most vegetables served at Bern's are grown in the restaurant's own organic garden. All main dishes come with onion soup, salad, baked potato, garlic toast, and onion rings. The phone book–size wine list offers more than 7,000 selections.

Many guests skip the main meal and head straight upstairs to the dessert room at Bern's. The atmosphere is a little too dark for some, but plush booths are equipped with TVs and phones for placing music requests. Ports, special after-dinner drinks, and more than 40 desserts are served. It's possible to reserve a booth for dessert only, but preference is given to those who dine.

Donatello

232 N. Dale Mabry Hwy. ☎ **813/875-6660.** Reservations recommended. Main courses $15.95–$28. AE, CB, DC, MC, V. Mon–Fri noon–3pm and 6–11pm, Sat–Sun 6–11pm. NORTHERN ITALIAN.

Some patrons arrive dressed formally for black-tie events later in the evening. Others find it this place too pretentious, but still come for the delicious fresh ingredients. With stucco arches, Italian tilework, and peach-colored linens, Donatello has a Mediterranean flair, artfully enhanced by soft individual table lighting, and an attentive tuxedoed waiting staff. Specialties include a variety of veal dishes with delightful accents from truffled wine sauce to artichokes.

EXPENSIVE

Armani's

In the Hyatt Regency Westshore, 6200 Courtney Campbell Causeway. ☎ **813/281-9165.**
Reservations required. Jackets required for men. Main courses $14–$26.75. AE, CB, DC, DISC,
MC, V. Mon–Sat 6–11pm. NORTHERN ITALIAN.

This is the most elegant dining room in town; the ambience is romantic and subdued.
The candlelit lounge is perfect for intimate gatherings. Outstanding dishes are scaloppine Armani's and the lamb and marinated salmon filet stuffed with spinach and
fennel.

✪ Lauro Ristorante Italiano

3915 Henderson Blvd. ☎ **813/281-2100.** Reservations recommended. Main courses $10.95–
$19.95. AE, CB, DC, MC, V. Mon–Fri 11:30am–2pm and 6–11pm, Sat 6–11pm, Sun 5:30–
10pm. ITALIAN.

Known for extraordinary sauces and pastas, chef/owner Lauro Medeglia is a native
Italian who cooks with love. Though his restaurant is off the beaten track, Lauro's
classic decor, soft music, and smartly attired waiters make it worth the detour southwest of downtown, off the Dale Mabry Highway. Try the caprese, putanesca,
gnocchi, or agnoloeti.

Selena's

In the Old Hyde Park shopping complex, 1623 Snow Ave. ☎ **813/251-2116.** Reservations
recommended. Main courses $7.95–$17.95. AE, CB, DC, MC, V. Sun–Wed 11am–10pm, Thurs
11am–11pm, Fri–Sat 11am–midnight. CREOLE/SICILIAN.

Catering mostly to the "ladies who lunch" bunch, this charming restaurant seems
straight out of New Orleans. Sit in the plant-filled Patio Room, the eclectic Queen
Anne Room, or the watch the world go by at the outdoor café. Local seafoods, especially grouper and shrimp, top the menu at dinner, with many of the dishes served
Créole style or blackened, as well as broiled or fried. Choices also include pastas,
chicken, steaks, and veal. At night, jazz sounds enliven the proceedings, as musical
groups perform in the upstairs lounge.

MODERATE

✪ Cafe Creole and Oyster Bar

1330 9th Ave., Ybor City. ☎ **813/247-6283.** Reservations recommended. Main courses $8.95–
$14.95. AE, CB, DC, MC, V. Mon–Thurs 11:30am–10pm, Fri–Sat 11:30am–11pm, Sun noon–
4pm. CREOLE/CAJUN.

Enjoy Tampa's great weather at this indoor/outdoor restaurant in the heart of Ybor
City and breathe in the history. The building, dating back to 1896, was originally
known as El Pasaje, the home of the Cherokee Club, a gentlemen's hotel and
private club with a casino and a decor rich in stained-glass windows, wrought-iron
balconies, Spanish murals, and marble bathrooms. Specialties include Louisiana crab
cakes, oysters, blackened grouper, and jambalaya.

⑤ The Colonnade

3401 Bayshore Blvd. ☎ **813/839-7558.** Reservations accepted only for large parties.
Main courses $7.95–$16.95. AE, DC, MC, V. Sun–Thurs 11am–10pm, Fri–Sat 11am–11pm.
AMERICAN/SEAFOOD.

Locals love this place and have been coming here since the 1930s. You'll often see
big groups of families. Nestled in Hyde Park's palm-shaded residential neighborhood,
the Colonnade overlooks Hillsborough Bay. Fresh seafood is the specialty: grouper
in lemon butter, crab-stuffed flounder, even wild Florida alligator. Prime rib, steaks,
and chicken are also available.

✪ The Columbia

2117 7th Ave. East, Ybor City. ☎ **813/248-4961.** Reservations recommended. Main courses $10.95–$21.95. AE, CB, DC, DISC, MC, V. Daily 11am–11pm. SPANISH.

This is the restaurant everyone talks about, dating back to 1905 and occupying a full city block in the heart of Ybor City. Tourists flock here to soak up the ambience, and so do the locals because it's so much fun. You can't help coming back time after time for the famous Spanish bean soup and original "1905" salad. The paella a la valenciana is outstanding, with more than a dozen ingredients from gulf grouper and gulf pink shrimp to calamares, mussels, clams, chicken, and pork. The decor throughout is graced with hand-painted tiles, wrought-iron chandeliers, dark woods, rich red fabrics, and stained-glass windows. The Cigar Room is a new addition.

ⓢ Crabby Tom's Old Time Oyster Bar and Seafood Restaurant

3120 W. Hillsborough Ave. ☎ **813/870-1652.** Reservations accepted only for parties of 10 or more. Main courses $4.95–$16.95. AE, DISC, MC, V. Mon–Thurs 11am–10pm, Fri–Sat 11am–11pm, Sun 4–9pm. SEAFOOD.

Although this casual spot lacks waterside views and an impressive decor, nobody cares. Sit back, relax, and crack open a pile of stone crab claws or a huge lobster at a picnic table.

Crawdaddy's

2500 Rocky Point Dr. ☎ **813/281-0407.** Reservations recommended. Main courses $10.95–$17.95. AE, CB, DC, MC, V. Mon–Thurs 11am–2pm and 5–10pm, Fri 11am–2pm and 5–11pm, Sat 5–11pm, Sun 5–10pm. REGIONAL/SEAFOOD.

Overlooking Old Tampa Bay near the airport off the Courtney Campbell Causeway, this informal spot is named after Beauregard "Crawdaddy" Belvedere, a Roaring Twenties tycoon. He owned a fish camp on this site and the decor hasn't changed much since—the seven dining rooms are all bedecked with Victorian furnishings, books, pictures, and collectibles. The down-home menu ranges from beer-battered shrimp and fish camp fry (shrimp, scallops, and fresh fish, deep-fried in corn crisp and almond coating, with jalapeño hush puppies) to shrimp and chicken jambalaya, prime ribs, and steaks.

ⓢ Le Bordeaux

1502 S. Howard Ave. ☎ **813/254-4387.** Reservations accepted only for parties of six or more. Main courses $12–$18. AE, DC, MC, V. Mon–Thurs 5:30–10pm, Fri–Sat 5:30–11pm, Sun 5:30–9:30pm. FRENCH.

This bistro's authentic French food and affordable prices make it a real find. The domain of French-born chef/owner Gordon Davis, it offers seating in a living room–style main dining area or a plant-filled conservatory. The menu changes daily, but you can count on homemade pâtés and pastries, and the specials often include salmon en croûte, pot au feu, veal with wild mushrooms, and filet of beef au roquefort.

✪ Mise en Place

442 W. Kennedy Blvd. (directly opposite the University of Tampa). ☎ **813/254-5373.** Reservations accepted only for parties of six or more. Main courses $4.95–$7.95 at lunch, $9.95–$17.50 at dinner. AE, CB, DC, DISC, MC, V. Mon 11am–3pm, Tues–Thurs 11am–3pm and 5:30–10pm, Fri 11am–3pm and 5:30–11pm, Sat 5:30–11pm. NEW AMERICAN.

Look around at all those happy, stylish people soaking up the trendy ambience and you'll know why chef Marty Blitz and his wife, Marianne, are the culinary darlings of Tampa. They continue to present the freshest of ingredients, with a creative "Floribbean" menu that changes daily. Main courses often include such choices as roast duck with Jamaica wild-strawberry sauce or grilled swordfish with tri-melon mint salsa. A recent addition is "442," the upscale bar with live jazz and blues.

INEXPENSIVE

Cactus Club

1601 Snow Ave. ☎ **813/251-4089** or 813/251-6897. Reservations not required. Main courses $5.95–12.95. AE, MC, V. Mon–Thurs 11am–midnight, Fri–Sat 11am–1am, Sun 11am–11pm. AMERICAN SOUTHWEST.

Watch all the shoppers go by at Old Hyde Park from this fun and casual café with a southwestern accent. Dine on fajitas, tacos, enchiladas, chili, hickory-smoked baby back ribs, Texas-style pizzas, blackened chicken, or guacamole/green-chili burgers. It's always packed at lunchtime—get there early.

Four Green Fields

205 W. Platt St. ☎ **813/254-4444.** Reservations not required. Main courses $3.95–$8.95. AE, MC, V. Mon–Sat 11am–2am, Sun noon–2am. IRISH/AMERICAN.

Set in the style of a traditional Irish cottage complete with thatched roof, the pub offers authentic Irish cooking near the heart of downtown Tampa. It smells of beer, but attracts all the youngish people in town. Ideal for salads and sandwiches with Irish music on Tuesday to Saturday nights.

Frankie's Patio Bar & Grill

1905 E. 7th Ave., Ybor City. ☎ **813/249-3337.** Reservations accepted only for large parties. All items $3.95–$12.95. AE, MC, V. Mon 11am–3pm, Tues 11am–10pm, Wed–Thurs 11am–1am, Fri–Sat 11am–3am. INTERNATIONAL.

Known mostly as a venue for outstanding musical acts, this Ybor City attraction is also fun at lunch and dinner. With exposed industrial pipes, the large three-story restaurant stands out from the usual Spanish-themed, 19th-century architecture of Ybor City. There's seating indoors, on a large outdoor patio, or on an open-air balcony overlooking the action on the street. It's a fun atmosphere, and the food blends Cuban, American, Jamaican, Créole, and Italian influences. House specials include Frankie's fancy meatloaf of veal and mushrooms on a bed of mashed potatoes, peppers, and onions. Live jazz, blues, reggae, and rock add to the atmosphere Wednesday to Saturday.

✪ Mel's Hot Dogs

4136 E. Busch Blvd. ☎ **813/985-8000.** Main courses $3–$6. No credit cards. Mon–Sat 10am–10pm, Sun 11am–9pm. AMERICAN.

Catering primarily to area collge students and hungry families craving inexpensive all-beef hot dogs after a visit to Busch Gardens, this place has been here forever. It's the big daddy of hot-dog eateries. This informal place offers everything from "bagel-dogs" and corndogs to a bacon/Cheddar Reuben. All choices are served on a poppyseed bun and most come with french fries and a choice of cole slaw or baked beans. Even the decor is dedicated to weiners: The walls and windows are lined with hot-dog memorabilia. And just in case hot-dog mania hasn't won you over, there are a few alternative choices (sausages, chicken breast, and beef and veggie burgers).

MoJo

238 E. Davis Blvd., Davis Island. ☎ **813/259-9949.** Reservations not necessary. Main courses $9.95–$12.95. AE, DC, DISC, MC, V. Tues–Thurs 11am–11pm, Fri–Sat 11am–midnight. SOUTH AMERICAN.

The creators of Tampa's popular Mise en Place restaurant opened this hot new restaurant on sleepy Davis Island. The atmosphere is casual with bright-yellow colors shouting "have fun" and paper tablecloths saying "relax." The dishes are hot and spicy, so be prepared. Mojo's roast pork loin with plaintains is perfection.

Ovo Cafe

1901 E. 7th Ave., Ybor City. ☎ **813/248-6979.** Reservations not necessary. Main courses $8.95–$12.95. AE, MC, V. Mon–Tues 11am–4pm, Wed–Sat 11am–2am, Sun 11am–10pm. INTERNATIONAL.

This café, popular with the business set by day and the club crowd at night, is Tampa's answer to SoHo. You'll find a blend of good food, eclectic art, and pleasing surroundings. Locals love the "menage à trois" omelets at breakfast. The fresh Ovo's chicken feta salad is a great lunch choice. An eclectic menu includes pierogies, smoked tuna sandwiches, and shrimp bisque soup. The big surprise is finding Dom Perignon on the menu, as well as root-beer floats with made with Absolut vodka.

Silver Ring

1831 E. 7th Ave., Ybor City. ☎ **813/248-2549.** Reservations not required. Main courses $2.25–$4.95. No credit cards. Mon–Sat 6:30am–5pm. SPANISH/AMERICAN.

Operating since 1947, this place is an Ybor City tradition. The walls are lined with old pictures, vintage radios, a 1950s jukebox, fishing rods, and deer heads. Most of all, it's *the* place to get a genuine Cuban sandwich—smoked ham, roast pork, Genoa salami, Swiss cheese, pickles, salad dressing, mustard, lettuce, and tomato on Cuban bread. Other menu items include Spanish bean soup, deviled crab, and other types of sandwiches.

TAMPA AFTER DARK

Tampa never used to have much nightlife, but the rebirth of Ybor has changed all that. The new hot spot doesn't even get started until after midnight, with an ecclectic offering of nightlife activities that extend into the wee hours.

To assist visitors, the Tampa/Hillsborough Arts Council maintains an **Artsline** (☎ **813/229-ARTS**), a 24-hour information service providing the latest on current and upcoming cultural events.

THE PERFORMING ARTS

With a prime downtown location on 9 acres along the east bank of the Hillsborough River, the huge **Tampa Bay Performing Arts Center,** 1010 N. MacInnes Place (☎ **813/229-STAR,** or 800/955-1045), is a four-theater complex that's the focal point of Tampa's performing-arts scene. It presents a wide range of Broadway plays, classical and pop concerts, operas, cabarets, improv, and special events.

The 74,296-seat **Tampa Stadium,** 4201 N. Dale Mabry Hwy. (☎ **813/872-7977**), is frequently the site of headliner concerts. The **USF Sun Dome,** 4202 E. Fowler Ave. (☎ **813/974-3111**), on the University of South Florida campus, hosts major concerts by touring pop stars, rock bands, jazz groups, and other contemporary artists.

Theaters

Mystery Cafe

725 S. Harbour Island Blvd., Harbour Island. ☎ **813/935-0846.** Show and dinner $29.95.

Audience participation is encouraged at this weekend murder-mystery dinner show, performed in the elegant setting of the Wyndham Harbour Island Hotel. It's on Friday at 8pm and on Saturday at 7pm.

Off Center Theater

Tampa Bay Performing Arts Center, 1010 N. MacInnes Place. ☎ **813/221-1001** or 813/222-1021. Tickets $3–$12.

The Off Center Theater has recently been recognized for its excellence and innovation. It's dedicated to local artists who present dance, comedy, music, film, and poetry. Open every weekend. The resident theater company, The LOFT, presents a six-show season.

✪ Tampa Theatre

711 Franklin St. ☎ **813/223-8981.** Tickets $5.25 adults, $4 seniors, $2.25 children 2–12; $3.25 adults and seniors on Tues and at weekend matinees; $15–$20 or more for some special events.

On the National Register of Historic Places, this restored 1926 theater is the jewel of the Franklin Street Mall and presents a varied program of classic, foreign, and alternative films, as well as concerts and special events.

Warehouse Theater

112 S. 12th St., Ybor City. ☎ **813/223-3076.** Tickets $10.50–$12.50.

Located in the heart of the city's artsy Latin Quarter, this theater presents original scripts by contemporary writers, including mysteries and one-person shows.

THE CLUB & MUSIC SCENE

Blues Ship

1910 E. 7th Ave., Ybor City. ☎ **813/248-6097.** Cover $2–$5.

With a mural of a ship adorning the wall, this club presents live blues, jazz, and reggae in an informal meeting-house atmosphere. Most gigs start at 8:30pm, Tuesday to Sunday.

Brass Mug Pub

1441 E. Fletcher Ave. ☎ **813/972-8152.** Cover $3.

This pub near the University of South Florida features nightly music, from heavy metal to rock 'n' roll. There's a jam session on Monday, and pool, darts, and video games are always available.

Brothers Lounge

5401 W. Kennedy Blvd. ☎ **813/286-8882.** Cover $1–$3.

This place has been around for 20 years. It concentrates solely on jazz, Tuesday to Saturday to 2:30am.

Jazz Cellar

1916 N. 14th St., Ybor City. ☎ **813/248-1862.** Cover $2–$3.

Situated in the heart of the city's Latin Quarter, this place features the Jazz Cellar Underground Orchestra, drawing jazz fans from near and far. Performances are Thursday to Saturday from 9pm to 2am.

Skipper's Smokehouse Restaurant & Oyster Bar

910 Skipper Rd. ☎ **813/971-0666** or 813/977-6474. Cover $3–$8, $10 and up for special events.

Because it's great for dinner as well as concerts, music lovers from all over Tampa Bay keep this place in north Tampa constantly sold out. It's a prime spot for live reggae, blues, and zydeco. Open on Tuesday, Wednesday, Saturday, and Sunday from 6:30 to 11pm, and on Friday from 8 to 11pm.

Yucatan Liquor Stand

4811 W. Cypress St. ☎ **813/289-8454.** No cover.

This is as close as you can get to a beach bar without actually being on a beach—counters made of old surfboards, tiki-hut trim, mounted fish specimens, and tropically painted booths within. The music ranges from pop to reggae, country, or progressive. Open nightly to 3am. Drinks cost $1 and up.

Comedy Clubs

The Comedy Works
3447 W. Kennedy Blvd. ☎ **813/875-9129.** Cover $5–$10.

An ever-changing program of live comedy is on tap at this club 3 miles west of downtown. Shows are Sunday and Tuesday to Thursday at 8pm and on Friday and Saturday at 8 and 10:15pm.

Sidesplitters Comedy Club
12938 N. Dale Mabry Hwy. ☎ **813/960-1197.** Cover $6–$8.

Located northwest of downtown, Sidesplitters presents professional stand-up comedians on most nights. Shows begin at 8:30pm Tuesday to Thursday and at 8 and 10:30pm on Friday and Saturday.

5 St. Petersburg & Clearwater

20 miles SW of Tampa, 289 miles NW of Miami, 84 miles SW of Orlando   *by Cindy Dupre*

Almost four million visitors come to this part of the world each year in search of sun and surf. According to a study from the world's foremost beach experts, three of the area's beaches are among the absolute tops in the country: Caladesi Island State Park in Dunedin, Ft. DeSoto Park in St. Petersburg, and Sand Key Park in Clearwater attract sun worshippers year round.

The grandaddy of all beaches in the area is the $7^1/_2$-mile St. Pete Beach. Today, however, it's often overcrowded and is considerably overrun with fast-food eateries and souvenir shops. North of St. Pete Beach are a cluster of beaches stretching from Treasure Island northward to Clearwater Beach; these are better suited to families. Clearwater Beach is actually a barrier island connected to downtown Clearwater by the Memorial Causeway Bridge. Here you'll find Clearwater's best selection of hotels, especially for active families and couples. Another bridge connects Clearwater Beach to Sand Key, also a barrier island.

St. Petersburg is a city that blends sleek high-rise office and condominium towers with historic Spanish-style haciendas and palm-lined parks. The bayfront section of the city has become a hot spot for visitors since the pyramid-shaped pier offers a great water view plus shops, restaurants, and a mini-aquarium.

For the first time in more than a decade the city of Clearwater has a redevelopment plan to help create more activity in its sleepy downtown. City officials hope to attract more shops and restaurants with their plan, which calls for $150 million in public and private financial investments over a 20-year period. Four nightclubs, each themed by a different decade, were slated to open at press time.

ESSENTIALS

GETTING THERE   The St. Petersburg area is linked to the Interstate system and is accessible from I-75, I-275, I-4, U.S. 19, and Fla. 60.

Tampa International Airport, off Memorial Highway and Fla. 60 in Tampa, approximately 16 miles northeast of St. Petersburg, is the prime gateway for all scheduled domestic and international flights serving the area. See Section 1 of this chapter for a list of airlines and their phone numbers.

St. Petersburg–Clearwater International Airport, Roosevelt Boulevard / Fla. 686, Clearwater, is approximately 10 miles north of St. Petersburg. It's primarily a charter facility.

All major car-rental firms are represented at the airports and in the St. Pete/ Clearwater area, including **Avis** (☎ 813/867-6662), **Dollar** (☎ 813/367-3779), **Hertz** (☎ 813/360-1631), and **National** (☎ 813/530-5491). Local car-rental companies include **Pinellas** (☎ 813/535-9891) and **Suncoast** (☎ 813/393-3133).

The Limo, Inc. (☎ **813/572-1111,** or 800/282-6817), offers 24-hour door-to-door van service between Tampa International or St. Petersburg–Clearwater airport and any St. Petersburg area destination or hotel. No reservations are required on arrival; just proceed to any Limo desk outside each baggage-claim area. The flat-rate one-way fare is $13 from the Tampa airport and $10.50 from the St. Petersburg–Clearwater airport to any St. Pete or gulf beach destination. **Red Line Limo, Inc.** (☎ **813/535-3391**), also provides a daily 24-hour van service from Tampa International or St. Petersburg–Clearwater airport to St. Petersburg or any other destination in Pinellas County. The cost is $10.75 from the Tampa airport, $10 from St. Petersburg–Clearwater; reservations are required 24 hours in advance.

Yellow Cab Taxis (☎ **813/821-7777**) line up outside the baggage-claim areas. The average fare from the Tampa airport to St. Petersburg or any of the gulf beaches is approximately $25 to $35 per taxi (one or more passengers). The fare from the St. Petersburg–Clearwater airport is approximately $15 to $20.

Amtrak (☎ **800/USA-RAIL** for reservations) passengers heading for St. Petersburg arrive first at the **Tampa Amtrak Station** at 601 Nebraska Ave. North in Tampa (☎ **813/221-7600**) and are then transferred by bus to the St. Petersburg Amtrak Station, 33rd Street North and 37th Avenue North, St. Petersburg (☎ **813/ 522-9475**).

VISITOR INFORMATION   Contact the **St. Petersburg/Clearwater Area Convention & Visitors Bureau,** ThunderDome, 1 Stadium Dr., Suite A, St. Petersburg, FL 33705-1706 (☎ **813/582-7892,** or 800/354-6710 for advance hotel reservations).

Specific information about downtown St. Petersburg is also available from the **St. Petersburg Area Chamber of Commerce,** 100 2nd Ave. North, St. Petersburg, FL 33701 (☎ **813/821-4069**). There are also walk-in **visitor information centers** at the Pier in downtown St. Petersburg, and at St. Pete Beach, Treasure Island, Madeira Beach, Indian Rocks Beach, Clearwater, and Clearwater Beach.

ORIENTATION   St. Petersburg is laid out according to a grid system, with streets running north-south and avenues running east-west. **Central Avenue** is the dividing line for north and south addresses.

With the exception of Central Avenue, most streets and avenues downtown are one-way. Two-way traffic is permitted on boulevards, usually diagonal thoroughfares west or north of downtown, such as Tyrone Boulevard, Gandy Boulevard, and Roosevelt Boulevard.

St. Petersburg's **downtown** district sits between two bays—Tampa and Boca Ciega. The major focus is on the section lining Tampa Bay, known as the Bayfront. Here you'll find the Pier, major museums, and most downtown hotels. Fanning out from the Bayfront, the city is composed of various residential neighborhoods.

St. Pete Beach, west of downtown and between Boca Ciega Bay and the Gulf of Mexico is a 7^1/$_2$-mile stretch of beach. **Gulf Boulevard** is the main two-way north-south thoroughfare, and most avenues, which cross in an east-west direction, have two-way traffic.

Quiet **Pass-A-Grille,** at the southern tip of St. Pete Beach, is a mostly residential enclave, with ecclectic shops and tiny B&Bs to discover.

The **Clearwater** area is located north of St. Pete Beach and west of downtown. It encompasses Clearwater Beach, Denedin, and Treasure Island (only 3¹/₂ miles in length), plus Sand Key Island. The latter is a 12-mile island composed of Madeira Beach, Redington Beach, North Redington Beach, Redington Shores, Indian Shores, Indian Rocks Beach, and Belleair Beach.

GETTING AROUND   The **Pinellas Suncoast Transit Authority/PSTA** (☎ 813/530-9911) operates regular bus service. The fare is $1.

BATS City Transit (☎ 813/367-3086) offers bus service along the St. Pete Beach strip. The fare is $1.

Treasure Island Transit System (☎ 813/360-0811) runs buses along the Treasure Island strip. The fare is $1.

The **Jolley Trolley** (☎ 813/445-1200), operated in conjunction with the City of Clearwater, provides service in the Clearwater Beach area. The ride costs 25¢.

If you need a cab, call **Yellow Cab** (☎ **813/821-7777**) or **Independent Cab** (☎ **813/327-3444**). Along the beach, the major cab company is **BATS Taxi,** 5201 Gulf Blvd., St. Pete Beach (☎ **813/367-3702**).

HITTING THE BEACH

According to one of the world's foremost beach experts, Dr. Stephen Leatherman of the University of Maryland, three of the area's beaches are among the finest in the United States. I'll preview these in greater detail below, but they're only a sampling of what's available along this stretch of the coast.

St. Petersburg Municipal Beach lies on Treasure Island. **Clearwater Beach,** with its silky sands, is the place for beach volleyball. Water-sports rentals, lifeguards, rest rooms, showers, and concessions are available. The swimming is excellent and there's a pier for fishing. Parking is $7 a day in gated lots. And **Honeymoon Island** isn't great for swimming, but it has its own rugged beauty and a fascinating nature trail.

CALADESI ISLAND STATE PARK   This 3¹/₂-mile stretch of sand, at 3 Causeway Blvd. in Dunendin (☎ 813/469-5918 for information), was voted the second-finest beach in the country. Its no-cars policy means no noise and no pollution. The island is accessible only by a **ferry** (☎ **813/734-1501** for ferry information), charging $4 for adults and $2.50 for kids, that leaves from Honeymoon Island hourly every day year round. There's another ferry service (☎ **813/442-7433** for a recording with details) operating less frequently from downtown Clearwater.

The lovely, relatively secluded beach has fine soft sand, and is edged in sea grass and palmettos. Dolphins cavort in the calm waters offshore.

In the park itself, there's a nature trail. Rattlesnakes, black racers, raccoons, armadillos, and rabbits live on the island. A concession stand, ranger station, and bathhouses (with rest rooms and showers) are available at no charge.

FORT DESOTO PARK   This group of five connected barrier islands has been set aside as a bird, animal, and plant sanctuary. Besides a glorious white-sugar sand beach where you can watch the manatees and dolphins play, this 900-acre Pinellas County park has a Spanish-American War–era fort, fishing piers, and a campground that's almost always sold out. Not surprising—this was ranked the 10th-finest beach in the country. It has over 230 camping sites that go for $17.75 a night, which includes electric hookup and water. Reservations must be made in person and paid in cash within 30 days of your stay. The fishing is great, there's a large playground for kids, and 4 miles of trails wind through the park for in-line skaters, bicyclists, and joggers. The park is located off I-275 South, Exit 4, on the Pinellas Byway (☎ **813/866-2662**).

SAND KEY PARK This county park south of Clearwater Beach consistently ranks up there around the 15th finest in the country. It's nice because it's off the beaten path from the more commercial Clearwater Beach, and visitors love the wide beach and gentle surf. For information, call 813/464-3347.

OUTDOOR ACTIVITIES

With year-round sunshine and 28 miles of coastline along the Gulf of Mexico, the St. Petersburg area offers a wealth of recreational activities.

When visiting St. Petersburg, you can get up-to-the-minute recorded information about the city's sports and recreational activities by calling the **Leisure Line** (☎ 813/893-7500).

BICYCLING With miles of flat terrain, St. Petersburg is ideal for bikers. Among the prime biking routes are Straub Park and along the bayfront, Fort DeSoto Park, and Pass-a-Grille.

Beach Cyclist, 7517 Blind Pass Rd. (☎ 813/367-5001), on the northern tip of St. Pete Beach, offers several types of bikes, from beach cruisers (allowed on the beaches at Treasure Island and Madeira Beach) to standard 10-speeds. Prices start at $10 for 4 hours, $12 for 24 hours, and $39 per week. It's open Monday to Saturday from 10am to 6pm.

Transportation Station, 652 Bayway Blvd. (☎ 813/443-3188), on Clearwater Beach, rents all types of in-line skates, single- and multispeed bikes, tandems, mountain bikes, and one- and two-passenger scooters. Helmets and baby seats are also available. Bicycles are priced at $5 to $8 an hour, $14.95 to $21.95 for the overnight special, $44 to $66 per week; scooters run $13 to $18 an hour, $39.95 to $54.95 for the overnight special, $109 to $169 per week. It's open daily from 9am to 7pm.

BIRDING **Shell Key,** one of Florida's last completely undeveloped barrier islands, is located south of St. Petersburg, about a 15-minute boat ride from the sleepy town of Pass-a-Grille (see details on the Shell Key Shuttle in "Bay Cruises," under "Seeing the Sights," below). Birders will have the opportunity to view some of North America's rarest shorebirds. A remarkable 88 different species of birds have been recorded here.

BOAT RENTALS **Captain Dave's Watersports,** 9540 Blind Pass Rd., St. Pete Beach (☎ 813/367-4336), offers Wave Runner and powerboat rentals, parasail rides, snorkeling trips, sailing, and shelling trips. Prices for Wave Runner rentals begin at $35 per half hour, $60 per hour; powerboat rentals are $50 and up for 1 hour, $70 and up for 2 hours, $135 and up per day; parasail rides are $30 to $35; snorkeling trips are $35. It's open daily from 9am to 5pm or later.

Fun Rentals, Municipal Marina, Slip 300, 555 150th Ave., Madeira Beach (☎ 813/397-0276), rents Wave Runners for $35 to $55 per hour and pontoon boats for $100 to $200 a day to sightsee, fish, or play on the waters of the Intracoastal Waterway. It's open daily from 9:30am to 5:30pm.

A downtown facility, **Waterworks Rentals,** The Pier (☎ 813/363-0000), rents Wave Runners and jet boats. A second location is at 200D 150th Ave., Madeira Beach (☎ 813/399-8989). Prices for Wave Runners begin at $25 for a half hour; for jet boats, from $45 per hour. The place is open daily from 9am to 6pm or later.

FISHING One of the largest party-boat fishing fleets in the area, Capt. Dave Spaulding's **Queen Fleet,** Slip 52, Clearwater Beach Marina, 25 Causeway Blvd. (☎ 813/446-7666), offers trips of varying duration. Prices are $22 for a half day, $35 for three-quarters of a day. Bait is furnished, but rod rental is $5 extra.

Biking or Blading Along the Pinellas Trail to Dunedin

Founded in 1870, the Scottish town of Dunedin is located less than 10 miles north of Clearwater off Alt. U.S. 19 and is filled with kooky antiques shops and cafés. It's worth visiting this sibling city of Stirling, Scotland, for its picturesque waterfront, revitalized downtown, and villagelike atmosphere.

Anglers, swimmers, and boaters know this area well. Honeymoon State Park is a 5-minute drive from the mainland, and Caladesi State Park is here also, though accessible only by private boat or public ferry. The islands are refuges to many endangered species of birds and are a nesting site for the osprey.

The Pinellas Trail, a 15-foot-wide, paved 47-mile trail built along an abandoned railroad, passes right through the heart of downtown Dunedin. Cars are forbidden on the trail, making it popular with joggers, in-line skaters, bikers, and walkers exploring nature. It's packed on the weekends.

Forget your skates? You can rent them at **Skate 2000** (☎ 813/734-7849), located right off Main Street in a converted old boxcar. They have free lessons on Sunday from 10am to noon.

Downtown, you can skate right into the pink, European-style **Cafe Alfresco** at 344 Main St. (☎ 813/736-4299). It features a light lunch and dinner menu with salads and sandwiches, offers a famous weekend brunch, and is great for people-watching.

Also very casual and people-friendly is a coffee shop–type place called **Kelly's for Just About Anything,** at 319 Main St. (☎ 813/736-5284). It has great breakfast items like blueberry flapjacks.

Bon Appetit, at 148 Marina Plaza (☎ 813/733-2151), caters to the upscale crowd. Open daily, it serves up continental cuisine with a waterfront view. The tiny, chic, romantic **Sabel's** offes an eclectic menu at 315 Main St. (☎ 813/734-DINE).

Within walking distance of Main Street is the **Jamaica Inn,** at 150 Marine Plaza (☎ 813/733-4121), which overlooks St. Joseph's Sound. Every room faces the water and, though they're tiny, all have microwaves, minibars, and refrigerators. A touch of Scotland comes to Dunedin every spring with the **Highland Games and Festival.** Bands and dancers from around the world compete in games. For further information about Dunedin, contact the **Dunedin Chamber of Commerce,** 301 Main St., Dunedin, FL 34698 (☎ 813/733-3197).

Capt. Kidd, Dolphin Village Shopping Center, 4737 Gulf Blvd., St. Pete Beach (☎ 813/360-2263), now conveniently located in the heart of the downtown St. Pete beach strip, takes passengers on half- and full-day fishing trips in the gulf. Rates, including rod, reel, and bait, are $25 for adults and $22 for children and seniors on a half-day trip; $37.25 for adults and $34.25 for seniors on a full-day outing.

If you want a change from the usual fishing boat, try **Double Eagle's Deep Sea Fishing Boats,** Slip 50, Clearwater Beach Marina, 25 Causeway Blvd., Clearwater Beach (☎ 813/446-1653). It offers two catamarans, 88 feet and 65 feet in length. The vessels go 20 to 25 miles offshore into the gulf, on 4- or 8-hour trips, with bait provided. Prices are $22 to $35 for adults, $18 to $30 for children, and $4 to $5 for tackle. The 4-hour trip departs daily, 8am to noon and 1 to 5pm, and the 8-hour trip leaves daily at 9am, returning at 5pm.

Miss Pass-A-Grille, Dolphin Landings Charter Boat Center, 4737 Gulf Blvd., St. Pete Beach (☎ 813/367-4488 or 813/367-7411), is conveniently docked in the heart of the St. Pete Beach hotel strip. This fishing boat offers daily trips into Tampa Bay and the gulf. Prices are $24.95 for 4 hours and $37.95 for 7 hours. Children 11 and under are charged $5 less, and seniors $3 less, in both cases. Sailings are scheduled on Tuesday, Wednesday, and Friday at 8am and 1pm, and on Thursday, Saturday, and Sunday at 9am.

GOLF   Adjacent to the St. Petersburg–Clearwater airport, the **Airco Flite Golf Course,** 3650 Roosevelt Blvd., Clearwater (☎ 813/573-4653), is a championship 18-hole, par-72 course, with a driving range. Golf-club rentals are also available. Greens fees, including cart rental, are $28. It's open daily from 7am to 6pm.

The **Bardmoor Golf Club,** 7919 Bardmoor Blvd., Largo (☎ 813/397-0483), is often the venue for major tournaments. This club offers an 18-hole, par-72 course, plus a driving range. Lessons and rental clubs are also available. Greens fees are $58 Monday to Friday, and $60 on Saturday and Sunday, including carts. Rates are lower in summer. It's open daily from 7am to dusk.

One of the top 50 municipal golf courses in the United States, the **Mangrove Bay Golf Course,** 875 62nd Ave. NE (☎ 813/893-7797), hugs the inlets of Old Tampa Bay and offers 18-hole, par-72 play. Facilities include a driving range; lessons and golf-club rental are also available. Prices are $19, $29 including a cart. It's open daily from 6:30am to 6pm.

SAILING   The **Annapolis Sailing School,** 6800 34th St. South (☎ 813/867-8102, or 800/638-9192), can teach you to sail or perfect your sailing skills. Various courses are offered at this branch of the famous Maryland-based school, lasting 2, 5, or 8 days. Prices, depending on season and length of course, range from $225 to $1,920 per person.

If you prefer to be part of the crew or just want to relax for 2¹/₂ hours, enjoying the views of the gulf waters, sail aboard the 40-foot racing yacht **Southern Romance,** Slip 16, Clearwater Beach Marina, Clearwater Beach (☎ 813/446-5503). Reservations are required. Prices are $18 per person. The boat departs daily at 11am, 1:30pm, 4:30pm, and sunset.

TENNIS   **Hurley Park,** 1600 Pass-a-Grille Way, Pass-a-Grille, St. Pete Beach, sports just one court that's available on a first-come, first-served basis. It's free, but there's a 1-hour limit. It's open daily from 8am to 10pm.

On a larger scale, with 15 Har-Tru courts, the **St. Petersburg Tennis Center,** 650 18th Ave. South (☎ 813/893-7301), provides lessons, clinics, and open play. Prices are $6 per person per day or $4.50 per person after 1pm. It's open Monday to Friday from 8am to 9pm and on Saturday and Sunday from 8am to 6pm.

WATERSKIING   **Captain Dave's Watersports,** 9540 Blind Pass Rd., St. Pete Beach (☎ 813/367-4336), offers waterskiing lessons for $45 per half hour or $70 per hour.

SEEING THE SIGHTS
THE TOP ATTRACTIONS

✪ **The Pier**

800 2nd Ave. NE. ☎ **813/821-6164.** Free admission to all the public areas and decks; donations welcome at the aquarium; parking $1. Shops, Mon–Sat 10am–9pm, Sun 11am–7pm; restaurants, daily 11am–11pm; bars, daily 10am–midnight or 1am; aquarium, Mon and Wed–Sat 10am–9pm, Sun 11am–7pm.

Walk out on the Pier and enjoy this festive waterfront complex overlooking Tampa Bay. Dating back to 1889, it was originally built as a railroad pier, but over the years it was redesigned in various formats until taking its present inverted pyramid shape in 1988. It offers five levels of shops and restaurants, plus an aquarium, tourist information desk, observation deck, catwalks for fishing, boat docks, a small bayside beach, miniature golf, water-sports rentals, and sightseeing boats. A free trolley service operates between the Pier and nearby parking lots.

St. Petersburg Thunderdome

1 Stadium Dr. ☎ **813/825-3100.** Tours available when events are not scheduled.

This is a huge year-round venue for sporting events, concerts, and conventions. The skyline of St. Petersburg was dramatically changed with "the dome." The translucent roof is the first cable-supported dome of its kind in the United States and the largest of its type in the world.

✪ Salvador Dalí Museum

1000 3rd St. South. ☎ **813/823-3767.** Admission $6 adults, $5 seniors, $4 students, free for children 9 and under. Mon–Sat 9:30am–5:30pm, Sun noon–5pm. Closed Thanksgiving and Christmas Day.

Nestled on Tampa Bay south of the Pier, this starkly modern museum houses the world's largest collection of works by the renowned Spanish surrealist. The museum was created in 1982, thanks to a donation by Cleveland industrialist A. Reynolds Morse and his wife, Eleanor R. Morse, who were friends of Dalí and his wife, Gala.

Valued at over $150 million, the collection includes 94 oil paintings, over 100 watercolors and drawings, and 1,300 graphics, plus posters, photos, sculptures, objets d'art, and a 5,000-volume library on Dalí and surrealism.

Museum of Fine Arts

255 Beach Dr. NE. ☎ **813/896-2667.** Admission $5 adults, $3 seniors, $2 students. Tues–Sat 10am–5pm, Sun 1–5pm; third Thurs of each month 10am–9pm.

Resembling a Mediterranean villa on the waterfront, this museum houses a permanent collection of European, American, pre-Columbian, and Far Eastern art, with works by such artists as Fragonard, Monet, Renoir, Cézanne, and Gauguin. Other highlights include period rooms with antiques and historical furnishings, plus a gallery of Steuben crystal, a new decorative-arts gallery, and world-class rotating exhibits.

Florida International Museum

100 2nd St. North. ☎ **813/822-3693** or 800/777-9882. Admission $14.50 adults, $13.25 seniors, $5 children 5–16. Daily 9am–6pm. From I-275, take Exit 10 to I-375; then go east to 2nd Street North and make a right.

The Florida International Museum attracted 600,000 visitors from around the world in 1995 when it opened its first exhibition, called "Treasures of the Czars." At press time the museum was having trouble getting its second exhibit up and running because of complications with Egyptian officials. The 1997 exhibit is slated to be a Greek show to coincide with the Greek Epiphany celebration in nearby Tarpon Springs. The museum is housed in the former Maas Brothers Department Store, long an area landmark.

Call in advance of your visit to check what's going on. Tickets must be reserved and purchased in advance for a specific day and entry time. Each visitor is equipped with an audio guide as part of the admission price; allow at least 2 hours to tour a major exhibition.

✪ St. Petersburg Museum of History

335 2nd Ave. NE. ☎ **813/894-1052.** Admission $4.50 adults, $3.50 seniors, $1.50 children 7–17, free for children 6 and under. Mon–Sat 10am–5pm, Sun 1–5pm.

Located on the approach to the Pier, this museum features a permanent interactive exhibition chronicling St. Petersburg's history. The thousands of items on display range from prehistoric artifacts to documents, clothing, and photographs. There are also computer stations enabling visitors to "flip through the past." Walk-through exhibits include a prototype general store and post office (ca. 1880) and a replica of the Benoist airboat, suspended "in flight" from a 25-foot ceiling and commemorating the first scheduled commercial flight in the world, which took off from St. Petersburg in 1914.

✪ Suncoast Seabird Sanctuary

18328 Gulf Blvd., Indian Shores. ☎ **813/391-6211.** Free admission, but donations welcome. Daily 9am–dusk. Take I-275 north of downtown to Fla. 694 (Exit 15) west, cross over the Intracoastal Waterway to Gulf Boulevard, and turn left; the sanctuary is a quarter of a mile south.

At any one time there are usually more than 500 sea and land birds living at the sanctuary, from cormorants, white herons, and birds of prey to the ubiquitous brown pelican. The nation's largest wild-bird hospital, dedicated to the rescue, repair, recuperation, and release of sick and injured wild birds, is also here.

MORE ATTRACTIONS

Clearwater Marine Science Center Aquarium

249 Windward Passage, Clearwater. ☎ **813/447-0980.** Admission $5.25 adults, $3.50 children 3–11, free for children 2 and under. Mon–Fri 9am–5pm, Sat 9am–4pm, Sun 11am–4pm. From the mainland, turn right at Island Way; the center is 1 mile east of Clearwater Beach on Island Estates.

This little jewel of an aquarium on Clearwater Harbor is very low key and friendly; it's dedicated to the rescue and rehabilitation of marine mammals and sea turtles. Exhibits include dolphins, otters, sea turtles, sharks, stingrays, mangroves, and sea grass.

Great Explorations

1120 4th St. South. ☎ **813/821-8885.** Admission $5 adults, $4.50 seniors, $4 children 4–17, free for children 3 and under. Mon–Sat 10am–5pm, Sun noon–5pm.

With a variety of hands-on exhibits, this museum is great for kids who've overdosed on the sun and need to cool off inside. They can explore a long, dark tunnel; measure their strength, flexibility, and fitness; paint a work of art with sunlight; and play a melody with a sweep of the hand.

✪ John's Pass Village and Boardwalk

12901 Gulf Blvd., Madeira Beach. ☎ **813/391-7373.** Free admission. Shops and activities, daily 9am–6pm or later; most restaurants, daily 7am–11pm. From downtown, take Central Avenue west via the Treasure Island Causeway to Gulf Boulevard; turn right, go for 20 blocks, and cross over the bridge; the entrance is on the right.

Casual and charming, this rustic Florida fishing village lies on the southern edge of Madeira Beach. A string of simple wooden structures topped by tin roofs rests on pilings 12 feet above sea level, connected by a 1,000-foot boardwalk. Most of the buildings have been converted into shops, art galleries, and restaurants. The focal point is the large fishing pier and marina, where many water sports are available for visitors.

Sunken Gardens

1825 4th St. North. ☎ **813/896-3186.** Admission $14 adults, $8 children 3–11, free for children 2 and under. Daily 10am–5pm.

One of the city's oldest attractions, this 7-acre tropical garden park dates back to 1935. It contains a vast array of 5,000 plants, flowers, and trees. In addition, there are bird and alligator shows, a walk-through aviary, and a wax museum depicting biblical figures.

BAY CRUISES

The **Shell Key Shuttle,** Merry Pier, 801 Pass-a-Grille Way, St. Pete Beach (☎ **813/ 360-1348**), offers shuttle service to nearby Shell Island, south of St. Petersburg, via a 57-passenger catamaran. The ride takes 15 minutes, and you can return on any shuttle you wish. Boats leave daily at 10am, noon, 2pm, and (summer only) 4pm. Prices are $10 for adults, $5 for children 12 and under.

Cruises around Boca Ciega Bay are offered on the **Lady Anderson,** St. Pete Beach Causeway, 3400 Pasadena Ave. South (☎ **813/367-7804**). The three-deck boat offers luncheon, dinner-dance, and gospel music cruises from October to mid-May. The lunch cruises operate Tuesday to Friday and cost $19.50 for adults and $13.50 for children 9 and under. Dinner cruises are offered on Friday and Saturday from 6:30 to 10pm and cost $29.50 for adults, $19.50 for children; cocktails extra. Gospel music cruises operate on Tuesday and Thursday, boarding at 6:30pm, for $24.50 for adults and $17.50 for children. Reservations are required.

The **Caribbean Queen** (☎ **813/895-BOAT**) departs from the Pier and offers 1-hour sightseeing and dolphin-watching cruises around Tampa Bay. Sailings are daily at 11:30am and 1, 3, and 5pm; they cost $10 for adults, $8 for juniors 12 to 17, $5 for children 3 to 11, and free for children 2 and under.

Captain Memo's Pirate Cruise, Clearwater Beach Marina, Slip 3 (☎ **813/ 446-2587**), sails on the *Pirate's Ransom,* an authentic reproduction of a pirate ship. Swashbuckling 2-hour daytime "pirate cruises" and evening champagne cruises are offered under the direction of fearless Captain Memo and his crew. Cruises operate year round, daily at 10am and 2, 4:30, and 7pm. For adults, daytime cruises cost $25; evening cruises, $28; both daytime and evening cruises cost $18 for seniors and juniors 13 to 17, $15 for children 2 to 12, free for children under 2. This outfit is now offering sunset cruises, weddings, and birthday parties as well.

The **Sea Screamer,** Clearwater Beach Marina, Slip 10, Clearwater Beach (☎ **813/ 447-7200**), claims to be the world's largest speedboat. This 73-foot turbo-charged twin-engine vessel provides an exhilarating spin in Gulf of Mexico waters with opportunities to view birds and marine life along the way. Prices are $9.35 for adults, $6.55 for children 6 to 12. Sailings are September to May, daily at noon, 2pm, and 4pm; and June to September, daily at noon, 2pm, 4pm, and 6pm.

SPECTATOR SPORTS

BASEBALL   The **St. Petersburg ThunderDome,** 1 Stadium Dr. (☎ **813/ 825-3100**), is St. Petersburg's sporting centerpiece. This $110-million domed stadium has a seating capacity of 43,000. The locals are going wild getting ready for the major-league baseball team, the **Tampa Bay Devil Rays,** who will start playing here in April 1998. Exact details of schedule and prices were not available at press time.

The area is also the winter home of several other major-league teams; the **spring training** season for all major-league teams runs from mid-February to April. The **Baltimore Orioles** and the **St. Louis Cardinals** play at Al Lang Stadium, 180 2nd Ave. SE (☎ **813/822-3384**). The **St. Petersburg Cardinals,** a Class A minor-league team, play here from April to September. Admission is $3 to $7. The **Philadelphia Phillies** play their spring-training season at the Jack Russell Stadium, 800 Phillies Dr., Clearwater (☎ **813/442-8496**). Admission is $7 to $8. The **Clearwater Phillies,** a Class A minor-league team, play here from April to September. Admission is $2 to $4. The recently expanded Grant Field, 373 Douglas Ave., Dunedin (☎ **813/ 733-0429**), is the winter home of the **Toronto Blue Jays.** Admission is $7 to $9.

DOG RACING   Founded in 1925, **Derby Lane,** 10490 Gandy Blvd. (☎ **813/ 576-1361**), is the world's oldest continually operating greyhound track, with indoor and outdoor seating and standing areas. Admission is $1, $2.50 for the Derby Club. It's open January to June. Races are held Monday to Saturday at 7:30pm and Monday, Wednesday, and Saturday at 12:30pm as well.

SHOPPING
SHOPPING CLUSTERS

Gas Plant Antique Arcade
1246 Central Ave. ☎ 813/895-0368.

Housed in a former gas plant, this four-story complex is the largest antiques mall on Florida's west coast, with over 100 dealers displaying their wares. Open Monday to Saturday from 10am to 5pm and on Sunday from noon to 5pm.

John's Pass Village and Boardwalk
12901 Gulf Blvd., Madeira Beach. ☎ 813/391-7373.

Situated on the water, this converted fishermen's village houses more than 60 shops selling everything from antiques and arts and crafts to beachwear. There are also several art galleries, including the Bronze Lady, which is the largest single dealer in the world of works by Red Skelton, the comedian-artist. Open daily from 9am to 6pm or later.

✪ The Pier
800 2nd Ave. NE. ☎ 813/821-6164.

The hub of shopping for the downtown area, this five-story inverted pyramid–shaped complex houses more than a dozen boutiques and craft shops. The Pier also leads to Beach Drive, one of the most fashionable downtown strolling and shopping streets. Open Monday to Saturday from 10am to 9pm and on Sunday from 11am to 7pm.

SPECIALTY SHOPS

Evander Preston Contemporary Jewelry
106 8th Ave., St. Pete Beach. ☎ 813/367-7894.

If you're in the market for some one-of-a-kind hand-hammered jewelry, try this unique gallery/workshop, housed in a 75-year-old building on Pass-a-Grille. Open Monday to Saturday from 10am to 5:30pm.

Florida Craftsmen Gallery
237 2nd Ave. South. ☎ 813/821-7391.

This is a showcase for the works of more than 150 Florida artisans and craftspeople: jewelry, ceramics, woodwork, fiberworks, glassware, paper creations, and metal works. Open Tuesday to Saturday from 10am to 4pm.

Glass Canvas Gallery
233 4th Ave. NE, St. Petersburg. ☎ 813/821-6767.

Located just off Beach Drive, this modern gallery features a dazzling array of glass sculpture, tableware, art, and craft items, many of which have a sea, shell, or piscine theme. Open Monday to Friday from 10am to 6pm and on Saturday and Sunday from 10am to 5pm.

✪ Haslam's
2025 Central Ave. ☎ 813/822-8616.

Although the St. Pete area has lots of bookshops, this huge emporium, established in 1933, claims to be Florida's largest, with over 300,000 books—new and used, hardcover and paperback, and electronic. Open Monday to Thursday and Saturday from 9am to 5:30pm, on Friday from 9am to 9pm.

P. Buckley Moss
190 4th Ave. NE. ☎ 813/894-2899.

This gallery/studio features the works of one of Florida's most individualistic artists, best known for her portrayal of the Amish and the Mennonites. The works include paintings, graphics, figurines, and collector dolls. Open Monday to Saturday from 10am to 5pm, and from September to April also on Sunday from noon to 5pm.

✪ Red Cloud
208 Beach Dr. NE. ☎ 813/821-5824.

This is an oasis for Native American crafts, from jewelry and headdresses to sculpture and art. Open Tuesday to Saturday from 10am to 6pm and on Sunday from 10am to 4pm.

✪ Senior Citizen Craft Center Gift Shop
940 Court St., Clearwater. ☎ 813/442-4266.

Opened about 30 years ago, this is one of the area's most unique gift shops—an outlet for the work of about 400 local senior citizens/consignors. The items for sale include knitwear, crochetwork, woodwork, stained glass, clocks, scrimshaw, jewelry, pottery, tilework, ceramics, and hand-painted clothing. It's well worth a visit, even though it's a little off the usual tourist track. Open June to August, Monday to Friday from 10am to 4pm; and September to May, Monday to Saturday from 10am to 4pm.

The Shell Store
440 75th Ave., St. Pete Beach. ☎ 813/360-0586.

This shop specializes in corals and shells and an on-premises mini-museum illustrates how they both live and grow. In addition, you'll also find a good selection of shell home decorations, shell hobbyist supplies, shell art, planters, and jewelry. Open Monday to Saturday from 9:30am to 5pm.

WHERE TO STAY

Contact the **St. Petersburg/Clearwater Area Convention and Visitor Bureau** (☎ 813/582-7892) for the "Superior Small Lodgings" brochure, which covers Pinellas County.

Price-wise, the high season is from January to April. The best bargains are available in May and September to November. Ask about special hotel packages in the summer, when great discounts can be found for the asking. Any time of year, though, it's wise to make reservations early, especially at the more popular beach resorts.

The hotel tax rate is 10%.

DOWNTOWN ST. PETERSBURG
Very Expensive

✪ Renaissance Vinoy Resort
501 5th Ave. NE, St. Petersburg, FL 33701. ☎ 813/894-1000, or 800/HOTELS-1. Fax 813/822-2785. 360 rms. A/C MINIBAR TV TEL. High season, $189–$279 double. Off-season, $129–$169 double. AE, CB, DC, DISC, MC, V.

This place exudes elegance. With its Mediterranean-style facade, this sprawling seven-story resort has greatly enhanced the downtown area. Dating back to 1925 and originally known as the Vinoy Park after its builder, oil tycoon Aymer Vinoy Laughner, it counted some of the country's most influential people as guests in the early years: Calvin Coolidge, Herbert Hoover, Babe Ruth, and F. Scott Fitzgerald. The hotel reopened in 1992 after a total and meticulous $93-million restoration and refurbishment. It overlooks Tampa Bay and is within walking distance of the Pier, Central Avenue, museums, and other attractions.

All the guest rooms, many of which enjoy lovely views of the bayfront, are designed to offer the utmost in comfort and include three phones, an additional TV in the bathroom, hair dryer, and more; some units in the new wing have individual Jacuzzis and private patios/balconies.

Dining/Entertainment: Marchand's Grille, an elegant room overlooking the bay, specializes in steaks, seafood, and chops. The Terrace Room is the main dining room for breakfast, lunch, and dinner. Casual lunches and dinners are available at the indoor-outdoor Alfresco, near the pool deck, and at the Clubhouse, at the golf course on Snell Isle. There are also two bar/lounges.

Services: Concierge, room service (24 hours), laundry service, tour desk, child care, complimentary coffee and newspaper with wakeup call.

Facilities: Two swimming pools, 14-court tennis complex (9 lighted courts), 18-hole private championship golf course on nearby Snell Isle, private 74-slip marina, two croquet courts, fitness center (with sauna, steam room, spa, massage, and exercise equipment), access to two bayside beaches, shuttle service to gulf beaches, hair salon, gift shop.

MODERATE

Bay Gables Bed & Breakfast

136 4th Ave. NE, St. Petersburg, FL 33701. ☎ **813/822-8855** or 800/822-8803. Fax 813/822-8855. 9 rms. A/C. $85–$125 double. AE, MC, V. Rates include continental breakfast.

You can walk to the Pier from this charming B&B, which was built in the 1930s. It overlooks a flower-filled garden with a gazebo and faces a fanciful Victorian-style house that operates as a tea room/restaurant. The guest rooms have been furnished with ceiling fans and period-style pieces, including some canopy beds. All units have bathrooms outfitted with clawfoot tubs and modern showers; half the rooms have a porch, while the rest have a separate sitting room and kitchenette. Each morning a champagne continental breakfast is served in the common room, on the garden deck, or in the gazebo.

✪ Bayboro Bed and Breakfast

1719 Beach Dr. SE, St. Petersburg, FL 33701. ☎ **813/823-4955.** Fax 813/823-4955. 4 rms. A/C TV. $85–$120 double; $145 suite. MC, V. Rates include breakfast.

Situated in a residential area a few minutes south of Bayboro Harbor, this three-story Victorian historic landmark overlooks Tampa Bay opposite Lassing Park and a small beach. An Old South ambience prevails here; the wide veranda is bedecked with rockers. The cozy upstairs bedrooms are filled with antique beds and armoires, lace, and quilts; they all have VCRs, and you'll get the morning paper, too. Splurge on the romantic suite with roses and champagne.

✪ The Heritage/Holiday Inn

234 3rd Ave. North, St. Petersburg, FL 33701. ☎ **813/822-4814** or 800/283-7829. Fax 813/823-1644. 75 rms. A/C TV TEL. $60–$95 double. AE, CB, DC, MC, V. Rates include continental breakfast.

With a sweeping veranda, French doors, and tropical courtyard, the Heritage attracts an eclectic clientele, from older folks to families. It's the closest thing to a Southern mansion you'll find in the heart of downtown. Dating back to the early 1920s, the furnishings include period antiques in the public areas and in the guest rooms. The

Heritage Grille is one of the area's most popular restaurants with a creative menu of light regional cuisine. There's an outdoor heated swimming pool and a Jacuzzi.

○ St. Petersburg Bayfront Hilton

333 1st St. South, St. Petersburg, FL 33701. ☎ **813/894-5000** or 800/HILTONS. Fax 813/823-4797. 333 rms. A/C TV TEL. $109–$149 double. AE, CB, DC, MC, V. Ask about special discounts and packages.

This 15-story convention hotel has a spacious lobby with a rich decor of marble, crystal, tile, antiques, artwork, and potted trees and plants. The bedrooms are furnished with traditional dark woods, floral fabrics, a king-size bed or two double beds, and an executive desk; many have views of the bay. This place has had troubles in the past with slow service, but things have changed for the better. Facilities include an outdoor heated swimming pool, Jacuzzi, and health club with a sauna.

There are several dining and entertainment options: Charmene's is a full-service restaurant specializing in continental cuisine; for light fare, try the First Street Deli; and for a quiet drink with a piano background, settle into Brandi's Lobby Bar.

INEXPENSIVE

Days Inn Marina Beach Resort

6800 Sunshine Skyway Lane South, St. Petersburg, FL 33711. ☎ **813/867-1151** or 800/544-4111. Fax 813/867-1151. 157 rms, 11 lodges. A/C TV TEL. High season, $79–$139 double; $129 suite. Off-season, $49–$91 double; $99 lodge. AE, CB, DC, MC, V. Take Exit 3 off I-275 on the approach to the Skyway Bridge.

Come for the week and learn to sail at this resort's well-known Annapolis Sailing School. Located on the southern tip of the city, this is a sprawling two-story motel. Offering quick access to downtown, it has a tropical setting on 18 acres along the Tampa Bay shoreline. The guest rooms have an airy decor with dark woods, ceiling fans, plants, and private balconies or patios; the lodges also offer kitchenettes.

For dining there's a restaurant, a beach bar, a lounge, and a snack bar. Other facilities include a private bayside beach, two outdoor swimming pools (one heated), a Jacuzzi, seven tennis courts, a fishing pier, a marina, shuffleboard and volleyball courts, water-sports rentals, a games room, a children's playground, and a coin-operated laundry.

ST. PETE BEACH

Very Expensive

○ Don CeSar Beach Resort and Spa

3400 Gulf Blvd., St. Pete Beach, FL 33706. ☎ **813/360-1881** or 800/637-7200 or 800/282-1116. Fax 813/367-3609. 277 rms. A/C TV TEL. High season, $265–$300 double. Off-season, $165–$205 double. AE, CB, DC, MC, V.

This is the ultimate tropical getaway—it's so romantic you may bump into six or seven honeymooning couples in one weekend. Sitting majestically on $7^1/_2$ acres of beachfront, the landmark "Pink Palace" dates back to 1928 and has an interior of classic high windows and archways, crystal chandeliers, marble floors, and original artworks. It's listed on the National Register of Historic Places. Most rooms have high ceilings and offer views of the gulf or Boca Ciega Bay. Sometimes the front desk gets too busy and overwhelmed at check-in.

Dining/Entertainment: The King Charles Restaurant offers a sumptuous Sunday brunch. Craving cavier? The very pricy but very intimate Maritana Grille can't be beat for fresh gourmet seafood. Other outlets include Zelda's Seaside Café, the Lobby Bar, and the Beachcomber Bar and Grille for light snacks and drinks served outdoors.

St. Petersburg Area Accommodations & Attracti

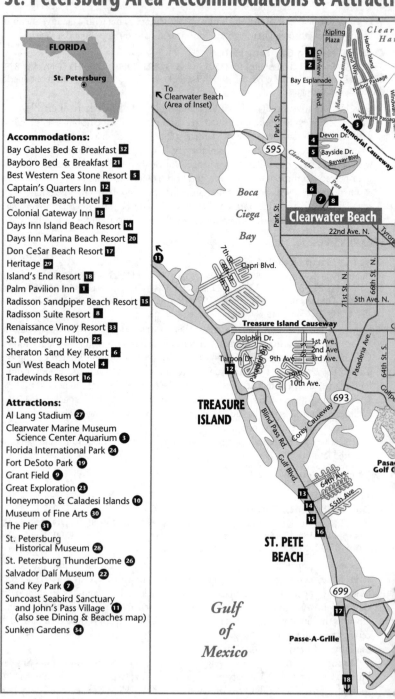

FLORIDA

St. Petersburg

Accommodations:
Bay Gables Bed & Breakfast **32**
Bayboro Bed & Breakfast **21**
Best Western Sea Stone Resort **5**
Captain's Quarters Inn **12**
Clearwater Beach Hotel **2**
Colonial Gateway Inn **13**
Days Inn Island Beach Resort **14**
Days Inn Marina Beach Resort **20**
Don CeSar Beach Resort **17**
Heritage **29**
Island's End Resort **18**
Palm Pavilion Inn **1**
Radisson Sandpiper Beach Resort **15**
Radisson Suite Resort **8**
Renaissance Vinoy Resort **33**
St. Petersburg Hilton **25**
Sheraton Sand Key Resort **6**
Sun West Beach Motel **4**
Tradewinds Resort **16**

Attractions:
Al Lang Stadium **27**
Clearwater Marine Museum
  Science Center Aquarium **3**
Florida International Park **24**
Fort DeSoto Park **19**
Grant Field **9**
Great Exploration **23**
Honeymoon & Caladesi Islands **10**
Museum of Fine Arts **30**
The Pier **31**
St. Petersburg
  Historical Museum **28**
St. Petersburg ThunderDome **26**
Salvador Dalí Museum **22**
Sand Key Park **7**
Suncoast Seabird Sanctuary
  and John's Pass Village **11**
  (also see Dining & Beaches map)
Sunken Gardens **34**

To Clearwater Beach
(Area of Inset)

Kipling Plaza

Clear Ha

Bay Esplanade

Island Way

Harbor Passage

Mandalay Channel

Windward Passag

Windward Passage

Devon Dr.

Memorial Causeway

Bayside Dr.

Bayway Blvd.

Clearwater Pass

Clearwater Beach

22nd Ave. N.

Tyron

Park St.

595

Clearwater

*Boca
Ciega
Bay*

Park St.

Capri Blvd.

7th St.

8th St.

9th St.

Z

Z

71st St.

66th St. N.

5th Ave. N.

Treasure Island Causeway

Dolphin Dr.

1st Ave.
2nd Ave
3rd Ave.

Tarpon Dr.

9th Ave.

Pasadena Ave.

64th St. S.

Paradise Blvd.

19th

10th Ave.

693

Colipe

**TREASURE
ISLAND**

Corey Causeway

Pasa
Golf C

Blind Pass Rd.

Gulf Blvd.

64th Ave.

Pasa
Golf C

13

64th Ave.

14

55th Ave.

15

16

**ST. PETE
BEACH**

699

*Gulf
of
Mexico*

17

Passe-A-Grille

18

2543

244

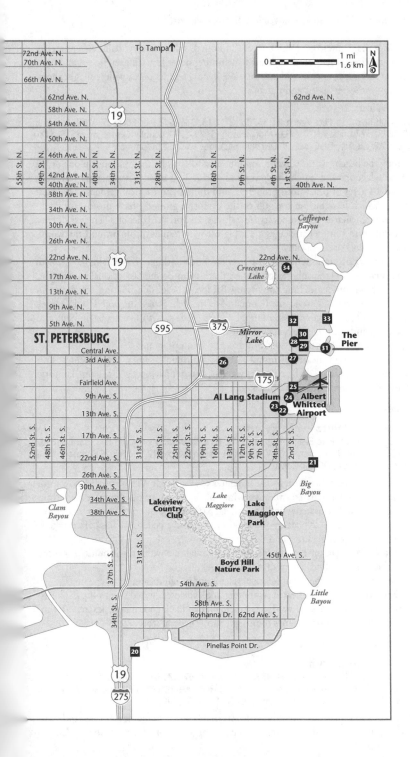

Services: Concierge, room service (24 hours), valet, laundry, children's program.

Facilities: Beach, outdoor heated swimming pool, Jacuzzi, exercise room, sauna, steam room, whirlpool, resident masseuse, lighted tennis courts, volleyball, gift shops, rentals for water-sports equipment.

TradeWinds Resort

5500 Gulf Blvd., St. Pete Beach, FL 33706. ☎ **813/367-6461** or 800/237-0707. Fax 813/ 360-3848. 377 units. A/C TV TEL. High season, $179–$221 double. Off-season, $119–$180 double. AE, CB, DC, DISC, MC, V. Discount packages available in summer.

Enjoy the beach, swim, play, or hop into a paddleboat with your kids on one of the private lagoons and watch the swans and ducks. This six- and seven-story resort sits amid 18 acres of beachfront property, sand dunes, and tropical gardens. The guest units, which look out on the gulf or the extensive grounds, have up-to-date kitchens or kitchenettes, contemporary furnishings, and private balconies. Their children's program and summer packages are a big hit with families from around the world, attracting lots of Europeans.

Dining/Entertainment: The top spot for lunch or dinner is the Palm Court, with an Italian-bistro atmosphere; for dinner, there's also Bermudas, a casual family spot. Other food outlets include the Flying Bridge, a beachside floating restaurant in Florida cracker-house style; the Fountain Square Deli; Pizza Hut; and Tropic Treats. Bars include Reflections piano lounge; B. R. Cuda's, with live entertainment and dancing; and the poolside Salty's Beach Bar.

Services: Room service, valet laundry, children's program.

Facilities: Four heated swimming pools, whirlpools, sauna, fitness center, four tennis courts, racquetball, croquet, water-sports rentals, gas grills, guest laundry, video-game room, gift shops, hair salon.

Expensive

Radisson Sandpiper Beach Resort

6000 Gulf Blvd., St. Pete Beach, FL 33706. ☎ **813/360-5551** or 800/333-3333. Fax 813/ 367-4567. 36 rms, 123 suites. A/C TV TEL. High season, $135–$177 double. Off-season, $89– $109 double. AE, CB, DC, DISC, MC, V.

Right on the beach, and run by the same folks as the TradeWinds, a well-landscaped, tropical courtyard separates the two wings of this six-story building, set back from the main road. Decorated with light woods, pastel tones, and touches of rattan, most units have two double beds or one king- or queen-size bed, as well as coffeemakers, toasters, small refrigerators, and wet bars.

Dining/Entertainment: Piper's Patio is a casual café with indoor/outdoor seating; and the Sandbar offers frozen drinks and snacks by the pool.

Services: Concierge, room service, valet laundry, child care.

Facilities: Beachfront heated swimming pool, enclosed heated swimming pool, two air-conditioned sports courts (for racquetball, handball, and squash), exercise room, volleyball, shuffleboard, games room, gift shop / general store.

Moderate

Colonial Gateway Inn

6300 Gulf Blvd., St. Pete Beach, FL 33706. ☎ **813/367-2711** or 800/237-8918. Fax 813/ 367-7068. 100 rms, 100 efficiencies. A/C TV TEL. High season, $93–$121 double. Off-season, $69–$101 double. Efficiencies $10 more. AE, CB, DC, DISC, MC, V.

Spread over a quarter mile of beachfront, this U-shaped complex of one- and two-story units is a favorite with families. The rooms, most of which face the pool and a central landscaped courtyard, are contemporary, with light woods and beach tones. About half the units are efficiencies with kitchenettes.

On the premises is a branch of Shells seafood restaurant, Bambooz Lounge, and the Swigwam beach bar offering light refreshments. Facilities include an outdoor heated swimming pool, a kiddie pool, shuffleboard, a games room, and parasailing and water-sports rentals.

Days Inn Island Beach Resort

6200 Gulf Blvd., St. Pete Beach, FL 33706. ☎ **813/367-1902** or 800/DAYS-INN. Fax 813/367-4422. 51 doubles, 51 efficiencies. A/C TV TEL. $78–$148 double. Efficiencies $10 more. AE, CB, DC, DISC, MC, V.

Located on the gulf beachfront, this two-story complex sits on 5 acres of tropical property. The guest rooms, furnished in dark woods and rich tones, have picture-window views of the beach or a central courtyard with the pool, lush greenery, and fountains. About half the units are efficiencies with kitchenettes. Jimmy B.'s beach bar provides outdoor refreshment and evening entertainment. Facilities include two outdoor heated swimming pools, volleyball, horseshoes, shuffleboard, and a games room.

Inexpensive

✪ Island's End Resort

1 Pass-a-Grille Way, St. Pete Beach, FL 33706. ☎ **813/360-5023.** Fax 813/367-7890. 6 cottages. A/C TV TEL. $68–$99 one-bedroom cottage; $160 three-bedroom cottage. MC, V.

Far from the madding crowd, this hideaway is nestled in the quiet southern tip of Pass-a-Grille, where the Gulf of Mexico meets Tampa Bay. This is a good choice for those who want to avoid the typical hotel atmosphere. Six contemporary cottages enjoy a shady setting on the water's edge. Each cottage has a dining area, a living room with a sofa bed, a VCR, a kitchen, a bathroom, a bedroom (one unit has three bedrooms), and a private pool. Facilities include a lighted fishing dock, patios, decks, barbecues, and hammocks. A public beach is less than a block away.

CLEARWATER & CLEARWATER BEACH AREA

Very Expensive

Belleview Mido Resort Hotel

25 Belleview Blvd. (P.O. Box 2317), Clearwater, FL 34617. ☎ **813/442-6171** or 800/237-8947. Fax 813/441-4173 or 813/443-6361. 292 rms. A/C MINIBAR TV TEL. High season, $190–$260 double. Off-season, $150–$190 double. AE, CB, DC, DISC, MC, V.

This Clearwater landmark hotel, located on 21 acres in a quiet neighborhood, is celebrating 100 years of operation in 1997. It's so huge you could get lost meandering around the hallways. Though it's located away from the beaches along the Gulf of Mexico, this massive white clapboard Victorian hotel attracts a clientele who appreciate staying in a charming building listed on the National Register of Historic Places. It's the largest occupied wooden structure in the world and has an attractive health spa. The lobby decor is a strange mixture of Victorian accents and modern marble and glass. The large, high-ceilinged guest rooms are decorated in Queen Anne style, with dark-wood period furniture. The new 3,400-square-foot Presidential Suite is incredible, and has a huge dining room.

Dining/Entertainment: The main restaurants are the informal indoor/outdoor Terrace Café for breakfast, lunch, or dinner; and elegant upscale Madame Ma's for gourmet Chinese cuisine. There's also a pub in the basement, a lounge, and a poolside bar.

Services: Room service, dry cleaning and valet laundry, nightly turndown, currency exchange, baby-sitting.

Facilities: 18-hole par-72 championship golf course, four red clay tennis courts, indoor and outdoor heated swimming pools (one with a waterfall), Jacuzzi, sauna, Swiss showers, workout gym, jogging and walking trails, bicycle rentals, yacht charters, gift shops, art gallery, newsstand; access to a private Cabana Club on the Gulf of Mexico.

Expensive

✪ Clearwater Beach Hotel

500 Mandalay Ave., Clearwater Beach, FL 34630. ☎ **813/441-2425** or 800/292-2295. Fax 813/449-2083. 157 rms. A/C TV TEL. High season, $105–$180 double. Off-season, $95–$105 double. AE, CB, DC, MC, V.

Besides the great beach location, you'll enjoy easy access to the many shops and restaurants around busy Mandaley Avenue from this pretty hotel. It's been owned and operated by the same family for 40 years and attracts an older clientele. The complex, which sits directly on the gulf, consists of a six-story main building and two- and three-story wings. Rooms and rates vary, according to location—bay-view or gulf-view, poolside or beachfront; some have balconies.

Dining/Entertainment: The Dining Room is romantic at sunset and offers great views of the gulf. The nautically themed Schooner Lounge has entertainment nightly. Outdoor service is provided at the Pool Bar.

Services: Room service, valet laundry.

Facilities: Heated outdoor swimming pool.

✪ North Redington Beach Hilton

17120 Gulf Blvd., N. Redington Beach, FL 33708. ☎ **813/391-4000** or 800/HILTONS or 800/447-SAND. Fax 813/391-4000, ext. 7777. 125 rms. A/C MINIBAR TV TEL. High season, $125–$190 double. Off-season, $100–$160 double. AE, CB, DC, DISC, MC, V.

At this outstanding beach resort, guests of all ages live in bathing suits at the pool and hang out at the outside bar enjoying music. The six-story hostelry edges 250 feet of beachfront and the guest rooms are decorated in pastel tones, with extra-large bathrooms and full-length-mirrored closets. Each unit has a balcony with a view of either the gulf or Boca Ciega Bay.

Dining/Entertainment: The Gulffront Steakhouse is popular with locals at the holidays and offers outdoor and indoor dining, and the poolside Tiki Bar is popular each evening for its sunset-watching festivities.

Services: Room service, valet laundry.

Facilities: Outdoor heated swimming pool, sundeck.

✪ Radisson Suite Resort

1201 Gulf Blvd., Clearwater Beach, FL 34630. ☎ **813/596-1100** or 800/333-3333. Fax 813/595-4292. 220 suites. A/C MINIBAR TV TEL. High season, $169–$259 suite for two. Off-season, $99–$199 suite for two. AE, CB, DC, DISC, MC, V.

Discover the beauty of Sand Key Island from this 10-story all-suite hotel overlooking Clearwater Bay, with the Gulf of Mexico just across the street. The whole family will enjoy exploring the nearby boardwalk with 25 shops and restaurants. Each suite has a bedroom with a balcony offering water views, as well as a complete living room with a sofa bed, wet bar, entertainment unit, coffeemaker, and microwave oven.

Dining/Entertainment: The Harbor Grille specializes in fresh seafood and steaks, and the Harbor Lounge has live entertainment, while Kokomo's offers light fare and tropical drinks.

Services: Room service, laundry, free trolley to the beach, year-round children's activities program at "Lisa's Klubhouse."

Facilities: Outdoor heated swimming pool, sundeck, sauna, exercise room, water-front boardwalk with a variety of shops and restaurants.

Safety Harbor Resort and Spa

105 N. Bayshore Dr., Safety Harbor, FL 34695. ☎ **813/726-1161** or 800/237-0155. Fax 813/726-4268. 172 rms. $177–$265 per person. AE, DISC, MC, V. Spa packages available for 2, 4, and 7 nights. Check for summer bargain packages as well.

If your spirit needs a lift and your body needs a little R&R, try this tranquil, water-front retreat on Old Tampa Bay. The rooms, each with two double beds, are all newly renovated. The new owners, the South Seas Resorts Company, have added a new management team and an Outward Bound program. An overall multi-million-dollar renovation is almost complete.

The full-service spa offers pampering from massages to hydrotherapy and a full menu of fitness classes from boxercise to yoga. The resort sits on 22 waterfront acres in the sleepy town of Safety Harbor. Guests have been enjoying the curative mineral waters for over 50 years and the water-fitness programs receive acclaim every year. Ask about special theme week packages like Mother/Daughter and Cooking for Your Health.

Dining/Entertainment: A new chef has created nutritious menus using lots of Florida ingredients in both the Spa Dining Room and the resort's Cafe, which is open to the public for lunch and dinner. The popular "Heart Saver Soup," with five different beans and seven vegetables, is a favorite.

Services: Room service, transportation to the airport,

Facilities: Clarins Skin Institute, spa salon, fitness center, Phil Green Tennis Academy, natural mineral springs.

Sheraton Sand Key Resort

1160 Gulf Blvd., Clearwater Beach, FL 34630. ☎ **813/595-1611** or 800/325-3535. Fax 813/596-8488. 390 rms. A/C TV TEL. High season, $140–$170 double. Off-season, $130–$160 double. AE, CB, DC, DISC, MC, V.

Away from the honky-tonk of Clearwater, this hotel is situated along 32 gulf-front acres on the island of Sand Key, overlooking a 10-acre private beach. It's a big favorite with water-sports enthusiasts. The guest rooms currently offer standard beach-toned decor with light-wood furniture. All units have a balcony or patio with views of the gulf or the harbor.

Dining/Entertainment: Rusty's Restaurant serves breakfast and dinner; for lighter fare, try the Island Café, the Sundeck, or Slo Joe's Poolside Bar.

Services: Valet laundry, baby-sitting.

Facilities: Outdoor heated swimming pool, fitness center, Jacuzzi, three lighted tennis courts, beach volleyball, newsstand, games room, children's pool, playground, water-sports rentals, 24-hour general store.

Moderate

✪ Best Western Sea Stone Resort

445 Hamden Dr., Clearwater Beach, FL 34630. ☎ **813/441-1722** or 800/444-1919 or 800/528-1234. Fax 813/449-1580. 65 rms, 43 suites. A/C TV TEL. High season, $103–$201 double. Off-season, $58–$108 double. AE, CB, DC, DISC, MC, V.

Located just across the street from the beach, the Sea Stone Suites is a six-story building of classic Key West–style architecture containing 43 one-bedroom suites, each with a kitchenette and a living room. A few steps away, the older five-story Gulfview Wing offers 65 bedrooms. The furnishings are bright and airy, with pastel tones, light

woods, and sea scenes on the walls. The on-site Marker 5 Restaurant serves breakfast only. Facilities include a heated outdoor swimming pool, Jacuzzi, boat dock, coin-
operated guest laundry, and meeting rooms.

Palm Pavilion Inn

18 Bay Esplanade, Clearwater Beach, FL 34630. ☎ **813/446-6777** or 800/433-PALM. 26 rms,
4 efficiencies. A/C TV TEL. $49–$110 double; $64–$95 efficiency. AE, MC, V.

A real find, this quiet spot is removed from the noise of Clearwater Beach tourists
yet within walking distance of all the action. This three-story art deco building is artfully trimmed in pink and blue. The lobby area and guest rooms, also art deco in
design, feature rounded light-wood and rattan furnishings, bright sea-toned fabrics,
photographs from the 1920s to 1950s era, and vertical blinds. Rooms in the front
of the house face the gulf and those in the back face the bay; four efficiencies have
kitchenettes. Facilities include a rooftop sundeck, beach access, heated swimming
pool, and complimentary coffee.

Inexpensive

Alpaugh's Gulf Beach Motel Apartments

68 Gulf Blvd., Indian Rocks Beach, FL 34635. ☎ **813/595-2589.** 16 apts. A/C TV TEL. $56–
$80 apt for two. MC, V.

A long-established tradition in the area, this family-oriented motel sits beside the
beach with a grassy central courtyard area. The rooms offer modern furnishings, and
each unit has a kitchenette and dining area. Facilities include coin-operated laundry,
lawn games, picnic tables, and shuffleboard at each location.

There's a second Alpaugh's motel at 1912 Gulf Blvd., Indian Rocks Beach, FL
34635 (☎ **813/595-9421**), with similar facilities and room rates, plus a one-
bedroom cottage for $68 to $91 and some two-bedroom suites for $74 to $103.

ⓈCaptain's Quarters Inn

10035 Gulf Blvd., Treasure Island, FL 33706. ☎ **813/360-1659** or 800/526-9547. 6 efficiencies, 3 suites. A/C TV TEL. $45–$70 efficiency for one or two; $65–$95 suite. MC, V.

This nautically themed property is a real find, offering well-kept accommodations on
the gulf at inland rates. Six units are efficiencies with new mini-kitchens (including
microwave oven, coffeemaker, and wet bar or sink), and three suites have a separate
bedroom and a full kitchen. The complex sits on 100 yards of beach, an ideal vantage point for sunset-watching. Facilities include an outdoor solar-heated freshwater
swimming pool, a sundeck, guest barbecues, and a library.

ⓈPelican–East & West

108 21st Ave., Indian Rocks Beach, FL 34635. ☎ **813/595-9741.** 4 suites, 4 apts. A/C TV. $35–
$55 suite for two at Pelican East; $55–$75 apt for two at Pelican West. MC, V.

"P.D.I.P." (Perfect Day in Paradise) is the motto at this well-kept motel complex,
which offers a choice of two settings, depending on your budget. The lowest rates
are at Pelican East, 500 feet from the beach, with four suites, each with a bedroom
and a separate kitchen. Pelican West sits on the beachfront, offering four apartments,
each with a living room, bedroom, kitchen, patio, and unbeatable views of the gulf.

✪ Sun West Beach Motel

409 Hamden Dr. South, Clearwater Beach, FL 34630. ☎ **813/442-5008.** 4 rms, 10 efficiencies. A/C TV TEL. $40–$61 double; $48–$79 efficiency. DISC, MC, V.

Overlooking the bay and yet only a 2-block walk from the beach, this well-
maintained one-story motel has a heated pool, fishing/boating dock, sundeck,

shuffleboard court, and guest laundry. All units, which face either the bay, the pool, or the sundeck, have contemporary resort-style furnishings. The four motel rooms have small refrigerators and the 10 efficiencies have kitchens.

WHERE TO DINE
DOWNTOWN ST. PETERSBURG
Moderate

Apropos
300 2nd Ave. NE. ☎ **813/823-8934.** Reservations accepted only for dinner. Main courses $8–$15. CB, DC, MC, V. Tues–Wed 7:30–10:30am and 11am–3pm; Thurs–Sat 7:30–10:30am, 11am–3pm, and 6pm–midnight; Sun 8:30am–2pm (brunch) and 6pm–midnight. AMERICAN.

The view is spectacular when you sit overlooking the marina and the Pier at this trendy art deco–style restaurant. In warm weather you can dine on the outdoor deck. The menu, which features small portions of light nouveau cuisine, specializes in fresh seafood.

Bay Gables Tea Room
136 4th Ave. NE. ☎ **813/822-0044.** Reservations recommended for lunch, required for afternoon tea. Main courses $6–$12 plus 18% service charge. MC, V. Tues–Sat 11am–2pm, plus afternoon tea at 3pm. AMERICAN.

Set in a beautifully restored 1910 Victorian house, replete with Old Florida antiques and frilly trimmings, this spot located on a residential street less than 2 blocks from the bayfront caters mostly to the "ladies who lunch" crowd. Meals are served on heirloom china and silver in the cozy atmosphere of three small rooms and a tiny porch upstairs or on a wraparound ground-floor veranda. The menu is simple but freshly prepared, featuring salads, quiches, soups, and finger sandwiches.

The Garden Bistro
217 Central Ave. ☎ **813/896-3800.** Reservations recommended for dinner. Main courses $5.95–$12.95. AE, MC, V. Daily noon–2pm and 5–10pm. MEDITERRANEAN.

A popular hot spot with those in the know, this lively restaurant in the heart of downtown has a European feel. The decor blends a 19th-century tiled floor with modern local art and lots of flowers and plants. The creative menu offers many fresh seafood selections such as salmon and shrimp. On Friday and Saturday nights live jazz adds to the ambience, starting at 8:30pm.

Heritage Grill
256 2nd St. North. ☎ **813/823-6382.** Reservations recommended. Main courses $14.25–$21.95. AE, CB, DC, MC, V. Mon–Fri 11:30am–2:30pm and 5:30–9:30pm, Sat 5:30–9:30pm. AMERICAN.

Folks from all over Tampa Bay drive to downtown St. Pete to enjoy the inviting ambience at this popular restaurant. Chef Angus Donaldson presents "casual American cuisine" in a dining room filled with modern art on the walls. Waiters in tuxedo shirts serve dishes like sautéed macadamia nut–crusted chicken breast stuffed with prosciutto and sun-dried tomatoes and the roasted walnut-Dijon rack of lamb.

Keystone Club
320 4th St. North. ☎ **813/822-6600.** Reservations recommended. Main courses $8.95–$17.95. MC, V. Mon–Thurs 11am–2:30pm and 5–10pm, Fri 11am–2:30pm and 5–11pm, Sat 5–11pm. AMERICAN.

This is the closest thing to a men's club in downtown St. Petersburg. Beef is king here and served in an atmosphere that's reminiscent of a Manhattan-style chophouse.

St. Petersburg Area Dining & Beaches

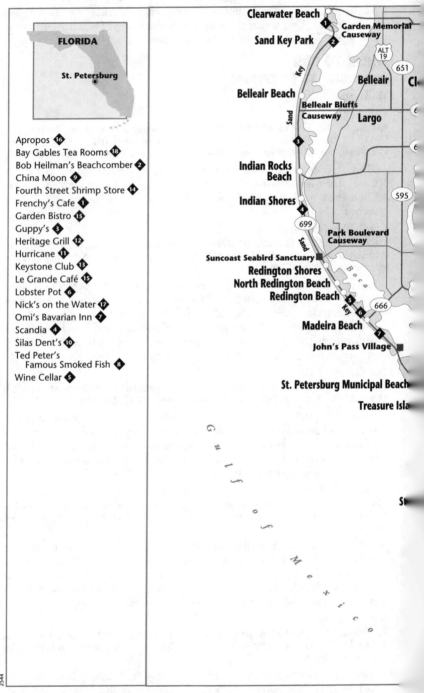

FLORIDA

St. Petersburg

Apropos ⑯
Bay Gables Tea Rooms ⑱
Bob Heilman's Beachcomber ❷
China Moon ❾
Fourth Street Shrimp Store ⑭
Frenchy's Cafe ❶
Garden Bistro ⑮
Guppy's ❸
Heritage Grill ⑫
Hurricane ⑪
Keystone Club ⑬
Le Grande Café ⑮
Lobster Pot ❻
Nick's on the Water ⑰
Omi's Bavarian Inn ❼
Scandia ❹
Silas Dent's ⑩
Ted Peter's
    Famous Smoked Fish ❽
Wine Cellar ❺

Clearwater Beach ❶
Garden Memorial Causeway
Sand Key Park ❷
ALT 19
651
Belleair
Cl
Belleair Beach
Belleair Bluffs Causeway
Largo
Sand Key
❸
Indian Rocks Beach
595
Indian Shores
❹
699
Park Boulevard Causeway
Suncoast Seabird Sanctuary
Redington Shores
North Redington Beach
Redington Beach
Boca Key
666
❺
❻
Madeira Beach
❼
John's Pass Village
St. Petersburg Municipal Beach
Treasure Isla
Gulf of Mexico
St

2544

252

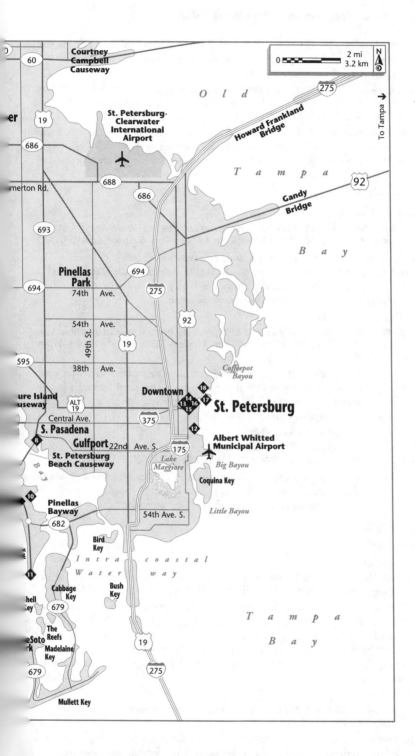

Specialties include roast prime rib of beef, New York strip steak, and filet mignon. Seafood also makes an appearance on the nightly special menu.

Le Grand Cafe

247 Central Ave. North. ☎ **813/821-6992.** Reservations recommended. Main courses $10.95–$18.95. AE, DC, MC, V. Mon–Thurs 11:30am–3pm and 6–10pm, Fri–Sat 11:30am–3pm and 6–10:30pm, Sun 1–9pm. CONTINENTAL.

It's a bit pricy and the service is slow at times, but this charming sidewalk café brings a little bit of Paris to the heart of downtown. Guests enjoy the art-filled bistro interior and French background music. The menu blends classic and creative cooking, offering dishes such as pot au feu and roast duck.

Inexpensive

Fourth Street Shrimp Store

1006 4th St. North. ☎ **813/822-0325.** Reservations not accepted. Main courses $4–$12. No credit cards. Mon–Thurs and Sat 11:30am–8:30pm, Fri 11am–9pm, Sun noon–8pm. SEAFOOD.

Here there's great down-and-dirty seafood on a busy street north of downtown. The tablecloths, utensils, and glasses are plastic and the plates are made of paper, but the seafood is the real thing—heaping servings of fresh grouper, smelts, or frogs' legs, shrimp of all sizes, oysters, and clams are on the menu.

Nick's on the Water

On the Pier, 800 2nd Ave. NE. ☎ **813/898-5800.** Reservations recommended for dinner. Main courses $4.95–$17.95. AE, DC, MC, V. Sun–Thurs 11:30am–10pm, Fri–Sat 11:30am–11pm. ITALIAN/SEAFOOD.

Located on the ground level of the Pier, this informal restaurant offers expansive views of downtown St. Petersburg and the bayfront marina. The menu features a variety of Italian specialties, including Nick's tortellini. All the veal dishes are a big hit, especially the veal française, with sautéed medallions.

Ted Peters' Famous Smoked Fish

1350 Pasadena Ave. South. ☎ **813/381-7931.** Reservations not accepted. Main courses $3.95–$13.95. No credit cards. Wed–Mon 11:30am–7:30pm. SMOKED SEAFOOD.

Seafood lovers looking for a very casual restaurant should head southwest of downtown toward the aroma of smoked fish. The menu is limited, focusing primarily on smoked salmon, mackerel, or mullet, served with German potato salad.

ST. PETE BEACH

Moderate

China Moon

4399 Gulf Blvd. ☎ **813/367-3008.** Reservations accepted. Main courses $6.50–$14.50. MC, V. Mon–Thurs 11am–9pm, Fri 11am–10pm, Sat 5–10:30pm, Sun 5–9pm. CHINESE.

Dining among the chic crowd at China Moon will change your perception of St. Pete Beach as a place for older folks. Chef Edward Chang, whose varied background has included stints in New York, Dallas, and Taiwan, creates outstanding dishes. Leave the kids behind. It's a romantic spot where the tables are black and the candles are glowing. Try grilled duck in ginger/port wine or citrus scallops with vegetables and raspberry vinegar.

Hurricane

807 Gulf Way. ☎ **813/360-9558.** Reservations not accepted. Main courses $6.95–$17.95. MC, V. Daily 8am–1am. SEAFOOD.

Join the locals and toast the sunset at this fun place, where grouper sandwiches are a big hit. Overlooking quiet Pass-a-Grille Beach, this informal, three-level indoor/

outdoor restaurant is extra-special at night when you can choose between dancing on one level and dining on another.

Silas Dent's

5501 Gulf Blvd. ☎ **813/360-6961.** Reservations recommended. Main courses $7.95–$18.95. AE, CB, DC, DISC, MC, V. Sun–Thurs 5–10pm, Fri–Sat 5–11pm. STEAK/SEAFOOD.

With a rustic facade of driftwood and an interior of palm fronds and cedar poles, this restaurant seeks to replicate the home of popular local folk hero Silas Dent, who inhabited a nearby island for many years early in this century. The menu aims to reflect Silas's diet of local fish, using such ingredients as alligator, amberjack, grouper, and squid, along with such modern favorites as mahi mahi, lobster tails, and scallops. Charcoal-broiled steaks, barbecued ribs, and chicken Silas (with red-bell-pepper sauce) are also offered.

CLEARWATER BEACH AREA

Very Expensive

✪ Lobster Pot

17814 Gulf Blvd., Redington Shores. ☎ **813/391-8592.** Reservations recommended. Main courses $12.95–$36.95. AE, CB, DC, MC, V. Mon–Sat 4:30–10pm, Sun 4–10pm. SEAFOOD.

Step into this weathered-looking restaurant near the beach and owner Eugen Fuhrmann will tell you to get ready to experience the finest seafood in the area. The prices are high but the variety of lobster dishes is amazing. The lobster américaine is flambéed in brandy with garlic and the bouillabaisse is as authentic as what you'd find in the south of France. In addition to lobster, there's a wide selection of grouper, snapper, salmon, swordfish, shrimp, scallops, crab, and Dover sole, prepared simply or in elaborate sauces.

✪ The Wine Cellar

17307 Gulf Blvd., North Redington Beach. ☎ **813/393-3491.** Reservations recommended. Main courses $11.75–$28.75. AE, CB, DC, MC, V. Tues–Sun 4:30–11pm. CONTINENTAL.

In the high season the cars pack the parking lot at this restaurant, which is highly popular with locals and visitors alike. You'll find an assortment of divided dining rooms, and the cuisine offers the best of Europe and the States. Start off with cavier, move on to a fresh North Carolina rainbow trout or chateaubriand, and top it all off with chocolate velvet torte. There's jazz in the lounge in the evening, and you'll often find noisy private parties going on.

Expensive

✪ Bob Heilman's Beachcomber

447 Mandalay Ave., Clearwater Beach. ☎ **813/442-4144.** Reservations recommended. Main courses $10.95–$25.95. AE, DC, MC, V. Mon–Sat 11:30am–11pm, Sun noon–10pm. AMERICAN.

This huge white restaurant across from the beach has been popular with generations of happy customers for more than 45 years. The menu presents a variety of fresh seafood, beef, veal, and lamb selections. The "back-to-the-farm" fried chicken—from an original 1910 Heilman family recipe—is incredible.

Moderate

Frenchy's Cafe

41 Baymont St., Clearwater Beach. ☎ **813/446-3607.** Reservations not accepted. Main courses $3.95–$15. AE, MC, V. Daily 11:30am–midnight. SEAFOOD.

Always popular with locals and visitors in the know, this casual café makes the best grouper sandwiches in the area and has all the awards to prove it. They're fresh, thick and juicy, and always delicious. The atmosphere is pure Florida casual style, and there's always a wait.

Owner Michael "Frenchy" Preston also has the more upscale **Frenchy's Mandalay Seafood Company** at 453 Mandalay Ave. in Clearwater (☎ 813/443-2100). For more casual fare directly on the beach, **Frenchy's Rockaway Grill,** at 7 Rockaway St. (☎ 813/446-4844), has wonderful outdoor dining.

Guppy's

1701 Gulf Blvd., Indian Rocks Beach. ☎ **813/593-2032.** Reservations not accepted. Main courses $5.25–$19.95. MC, V. Daily 11am–10:30pm. SEAFOOD.

Constantly voted "Best Seafood" in local publications by the folks who live nearby, this small bar and grill on the beach provides the real thing. Order amberjack, mahi mahi, swordfish, black grouper, tuna, snapper, or wahoo. They're all native to the waters and always fresh. The atmosphere is casual beach friendly. The bar is fun and you can dine outside as well. For dessert, Scotty's famous upside-down apple-walnut pie is terrific, especially when topped with ice cream.

Scandia

19829 Gulf Blvd., Indian Shores. ☎ **813/595-5525.** Reservations recommended. Main courses $6–$19.95. DISC, MC, V. Tues–Sat 11:30am–9pm, Sun noon–8pm. Closed Sept. SCANDINAVIAN.

Unique in decor and menu along the Gulf Coast, this chalet-style restaurant brings a touch of Hans Christian Andersen to the beach strip. The menu offers Scandinavian favorites, from smoked salmon and pickled herring to roast pork, sausages, schnitzels, and Danish lobster tails. There are also a few international dishes such as curried chicken, North Sea flounder, Canadian scallops, Boston scrod, and shrimp and grouper from gulf waters.

Inexpensive

Omi's Bavarian Inn

14701 Gulf Blvd., Madeira Beach. ☎ **813/393-9654.** Reservations recommended. Main courses $6.95–$14.95. AE, DISC, MC, V. Daily 3–9:30pm. GERMAN.

This little restaurant is a small patch of Germany on the gulf, featuring schnitzels, sauerbraten and schweinebraten (roast pork), chicken paprikash, beef goulash, Bavarian bratwurst, and stuffed peppers. A variety of seafoods and steaks are also on the menu.

THE ST. PETERSBURG AREA AFTER DARK
THE PERFORMING ARTS

The **St. Petersburg ThunderDome,** 1 Stadium Dr. (☎ 813/825-3100), has a capacity of 50,000 for major concerts, but also hosts a variety of smaller events.

The **Bayfront Center,** 400 1st St. South (☎ 813/892-5767, or 813/892-5700 for recorded information), houses the 8,100-seat Bayfront Arena and the 2,000-seat Mahaffey Theater. The schedule includes a variety of concerts, Broadway shows, big bands, ice shows, and circus performances.

The 2,200-seat **Ruth Eckerd Hall,** 1111 McMullen-Booth Rd., Clearwater (☎ 813/791-7400), hosts a varied program of Broadway shows, ballet, drama, symphonic works, popular music, jazz, and country music.

The **American Stage Company,** 211 3rd St. South (☎ 813/822-8814), is St. Petersburg's resident professional theater, presenting contemporary dramas and comedies.

THE CLUB & MUSIC SCENE

Beach Nutts
9600 W. Gulf Blvd., Treasure Island. ☎ 813/367-7427. No cover.

This is a quintessential beach bar, perched atop a stilt foundation like a wooden beach cottage on the Gulf of Mexico. The music ranges from Top 40 to reggae and rock. Open daily to 1am.

Big Catch
9 1st St. NE. ☎ 813/821-6444. Cover $3.

This casual downtown club features live and danceable rock and Top 40 hits, as well as darts, pool, and hoops. Open Thursday to Saturday to 2am.

Club Detroit
16 2nd St. North. ☎ 813/896-1244. Cover $2 and up indoors, $10–$18 for outdoor concerts.

Housed in the landmark Hotel Detroit, this lively spot includes a lounge, Channel Zero, and an outdoor courtyard, Jannus Landing. Look for blues, reggae, and progressive DJ dance music indoors and live rock concerts outdoors. Open daily to 2am.

Coconuts Comedy Club
5300 Gulf Blvd., St. Pete Beach. ☎ 813/360-5653. Cover $7–$10.

One of the oldest and best-known comedy spots on the beach strip, this club features an ever-changing program of live stand-up comedy acts. Shows are Wednesday to Sunday at 9:30pm.

Coliseum Ballroom
535 4th Ave. North. ☎ 813/892-5202. Cover $4–$15.

Dating back to 1924, this landmark Moorish-style building is the place to go in downtown St. Petersburg for an evening of dancing to big-band, country, ballroom, and other kinds of music.

Gators on the Pass
12754 Kingfish Dr., Treasure Island. ☎ 813/367-8951. $2 cover charge for most acts.

Located at Kingfish Wharf on the northern tip of Treasure Island, this place claims to have the world's longest waterfront bar, with a huge deck overlooking the waters of John's Pass. The complex also includes a no-smoking sports bar and a three-story tower with a top-level observation deck for panoramic views of the Gulf of Mexico. There's live music, from acoustic and blues to rock, most nights from 8 or 9pm to 1am.

The Hurricane Lounge
807 Gulf Way, St. Pete Beach. ☎ 813/260-4875. No cover.

Long recognized as one of the best local places for jazz, this beachside spot has a varied program of jazz on Sunday, Wednesday, and Thursday from 9pm to 1am and on Friday and Saturday from 9:30pm to 1:30am.

Jammin'z Dance Shack
470 Mandalay Ave., Clearwater Beach. ☎ 813/441-2005, or 813/442-5754 for recorded information. Cover $3–$5.

This nightclub offers a beachy atmosphere and a dance floor with state-of-the-art sound, light, video, and laser effects. A DJ spins Top 40 tunes till 2am daily.

Joyland

11225 U.S. 19, Clearwater. ☎ **813/573-1919.** Cover $3–$10.

This is the area's only country-western ballroom, featuring live bands and well-known performers Wednesday to Sunday.

Manhattans

11595 Gulf Blvd., Treasure Island. ☎ **813/363-1500.** No cover.

Nestled on the beach strip, this club offers a variety of live music, from country to contemporary and classic rock, 7 nights a week until 2am.

Ringside Cafe

2742 4th St. North, St. Petersburg. ☎ **813/894-8465.** Cover $2 or more.

Housed in a renovated boxing gymnasium, this informal neighborhood café has a decided sports motif, but the music focuses on jazz and blues (and sometimes reggae), on Friday and Saturday nights from 10pm to 2am.

Index

- **Available at participating properties.**
- **This coupon cannot be combined with any other special discount offer.**
- **Limit one coupon per room, per stay.**
- **Not valid during blackout periods or special events.**
- **Void where prohibited.**
- **No reproductions accepted.**
- **Expires December 31, 1997.**

1-800-DAYS INN

For Your Information:
Offer available at participating Hertz U.S. Corporate locations through 12/31/97. Leisure Weekly rentals require a 5 day minimum keep, including Saturday night. Minimum age is 25. Advanced reservations are required. Black out periods apply. This coupon must be surrendered at time of rental and may not be combined with any other discount, offer, coupon or promotion. Standard rental qualifications and return restrictions must be met. Car must be returned to renting location. Taxes and optional services, such as refueling, are extra and are not subject to discount.

Hertz rents Fords and other fine cars.

FOR RESERVATIONS CALL:

Sleep 1-800-62-SLEEP

Comfort 1-800-228-5150

Quality 1-800-228-5151

Clarion 1-800-CLARION

Econo Lodge 1-800-55-ECONO

Rodeway 1-800-228-2000

Advance reservations are required through 1-800-4-CHOICE. Discounts are based on availability at participating hotels and cannot be used in conjunction with other discounts or promotions.

MEARS MOTOR SHUTTLE
BOOTH LOCATIONS

2ND LEVEL

- **"A" TERMINAL: Exit through the doors in front of American baggage claim carousel #5**

- **"B" TERMINAL: Exit through the doors in front of United baggage claim carousel #8 or Delta baggage claim carousel #14**

*THANK YOU FOR USING
MEARS TRANSPORTATION*

Discount valid for up to 6 people
through 12/31/97. Coupon has no cash value
and is not valid with any other offers.
Offer subject to change without notice.
Parking fee not included.
©1996 Universal Studios Florida
All Rights Reserved.

6183958001991
FROMMERS AM ON WHEELS
$3.00 A1 C1

Gatorland
Orlando

Located on Hwy 441 in South Orlando. From I-4 take exit 26A to 417 north - take exit 11 to Hwy 441 south one mile and Gatorland is on the left.

Call: 800-393-JAWS or 407-855-5496

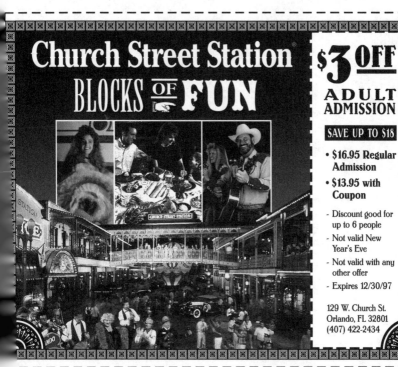

A World of Orchids
2501 Old Lake Wilson Road
Kissimmee, FL 34747

2 miles west on US 192 from exit 25B off 1-4 then 1 mile sout
on Old Lake Wilson Road (CR 545)

Green Meadows Farm, Ltd.
P.O. Box 420787
Kissimmee, FL 34742-0787

Call: 407/846-0770

FROMMER'S COMPLETE TRAVEL GUIDES

*(Comprehensive guides to destinations around the world, with
selections in all price ranges—from deluxe to budget)*

Acapulco/Ixtapa/Taxco
Alaska
Amsterdam
Arizona
Atlanta
Australia
Austria
Bahamas
Bangkok
Barcelona, Madrid & Seville
Belgium, Holland & Luxembourg
Berlin
Bermuda
Boston
Budapest & the Best of Hungary
California
Canada
Cancún, Cozumel & the Yucatán
Caribbean
Caribbean Cruises & Ports of Call
Caribbean Ports of Call
Carolinas & Georgia
Chicago
Colorado
Costa Rica
Denver, Boulder & Colorado Springs
Dublin
England
Florida
France
Germany
Greece
Hawaii
Hong Kong
Honolulu/Waikiki/Oahu
Ireland
Italy
Jamaica/Barbados
Japan
Las Vegas
London
Los Angeles
Maryland & Delaware
Maui

Mexico
Mexico City
Miami & the Keys
Montana & Wyoming
Montréal & Québec City
Munich & the Bavarian Alps
Nashville & Memphis
Nepal
New England
New Mexico
New Orleans
New York City
Northern New England
Nova Scotia, New Brunswick & Prince
    Edward Island
Paris
Philadelphia & the Amish Country
Portugal
Prague & the Best of the Czech Republic
Puerto Rico
Puerto Vallarta, Manzanillo & Guadalajara
Rome
San Antonio & Austin
San Diego
San Francisco
Santa Fe, Taos & Albuquerque
Scandinavia
Scotland
Seattle & Portland
South Pacific
Spain
Switzerland
Thailand
Tokyo
Toronto
U.S.A.
Utah
Vancouver & Victoria
Vienna
Virgin Islands
Virginia
Walt Disney World & Orlando
Washington, D.C.
Washington & Oregon

FROMMER'S FRUGAL TRAVELER'S GUIDES

(The grown-up guides to budget travel, offering dream vacations at down-to-earth prices)

Australia from $45 a Day

Berlin from $50 a Day

California from $60 a Day

Caribbean from $60 a Day

Costa Rica & Belize from $35 a Day

Eastern Europe from $30 a Day

England from $50 a Day

Europe from $50 a Day

Florida from $50 a Day

Greece from $45 a Day

Hawaii from $60 a Day

India from $40 a Day

Ireland from $45 a Day

Italy from $50 a Day

Israel from $45 a Day

London from $60 a Day

Mexico from $35 a Day

New York from $70 a Day

New Zealand from $45 a Day

Paris from $65 a Day

Washington, D.C. from $50 a Day

FROMMER'S PORTABLE GUIDES

(Pocket-size guides for travelers who want everything in a nutshell)

Charleston & Savannah

Las Vegas

New Orleans

San Francisco

FROMMER'S FAMILY GUIDES

(The complete guides for successful family vacations)

California with Kids

Los Angeles with Kids

New England with Kids

New York City with Kids

San Francisco with Kids

Washington, D.C. with Kids

FROMMER'S AMERICA ON WHEELS

(Everything you need for a successful road trip, including full-color road maps and ratings for every hotel)

California & Nevada

Florida

Mid-Atlantic

Midwest & the Great Lakes

New England & New York

Northwest & Great Plains

South Central & Texas

Southeast

Southwest

FROMMER'S WALKING TOURS

(Memorable neighborhood strolls through the world's great cities)

Berlin

Chicago

England's Favorite Cities

London

Montréal & Québec City

New York

Paris

San Francisco

Spain's Favorite Cities

Tokyo

Venice

Washington, D.C.

SPECIAL-INTEREST TITLES

Arthur Frommer's Branson!

Arthur Frommer's New World of Travel

The Civil War Trust's Official Guide to the
Civil War Discovery Trail

Frommer's America's 100 Best-Loved State
Parks

Frommer's Caribbean Hideaways

Frommer's Complete Hostel Vacation Guide
to England, Scotland & Wales

Frommer's Food Lover's Companion to
France

Frommer's Food Lover's Companion to Italy

Frommer's National Park Guide

Outside Magazine's Adventure Guide to
New England

Outside Magazine's Adventure Guide to
Northern California

Places Rated Almanac

Retirement Places Rated

USA Sports Traveler's and TV Viewer's
Golf Tournament Guide

USA Sports Minor League Baseball Book

USA Today Golf Atlas

Wonderful Weekends from NYC

FROMMER'S IRREVERENT GUIDES
(Wickedly honest guides for sophisticated travelers)

Amsterdam	Miami	Santa Fe
Chicago	New Orleans	U.S. Virgin Islands
London	Paris	Walt Disney World
Manhattan	San Francisco	Washington, D.C.

BAEDEKER
(With four-color photographs and a free pull-out map)

Amsterdam	Greece	San Francisco
Athens	Greek Islands	St. Petersburg
Austria	Hawaii	Scandinavia
Bali	Hong Kong	Scotland
Belgium	Israel	Singapore
Budapest	Italy	South Africa
California	Lisbon	Spain
Canada	London	Switzerland
Caribbean	Mexico	Venice
Copenhagen	New York	Vienna
Crete	Paris	Tokyo
Florence	Prague	Tuscany
Florida	Provence	
Germany	Rome	

FROMMER'S BY NIGHT GUIDES
(The series for those who know that life begins after dark)

Amsterdam	Los Angeles	New York
Chicago	Miami	Paris
Las Vegas	New Orleans	San Francisco
London		

FROMMER'S BEST BEACH VACATIONS
(The top places to sun, stroll, shop, stay, play, party, and swim, with ratings for each beach)

California	Mid-Atlantic (from New York to
Carolinas & Georgia	Washington, D.C.)
Florida	New England
Hawaii	

FROMMER'S BED & BREAKFAST GUIDES
(Selective guides with four-color photos and full descriptions of the best inns in each region)

California	Mid-Atlantic	Rockies
Caribbean	New England	Southeast
Great American Cities	Pacific Northwest	Southwest
Hawaii		

FROMMER'S DRIVING TOURS
(Four-color photos and detailed maps outlining spectacular scenic driving routes)

Australia	Germany	Scotland
Austria	Ireland	Spain
Britain	Italy	Switzerland
Florida	Scandinavia	U.S.A.
France		

FROMMER'S BORN TO SHOP
(The ultimate guides for travelers who love to shop)

France	Hong Kong	Mexico
Great Britain	London	New York

TRAVEL & LEISURE GUIDES
(Sophisticated pocket-size guides for discriminating travelers)

Amsterdam	London	San Francisco
Boston	New York	Washington, D.C.
Hong Kong	Paris	

UNOFFICIAL GUIDES
(Get the unbiased truth from these candid, value-conscious guides)

Atlanta	Euro Disneyland	Skiing in the West
Branson, Missouri	The Great Smoky & Blue	Walt Disney World
Chicago	Ridge Mountains	Washington, D.C.
Cruises	Las Vegas	
Disneyland	Miami & the Keys	